19th Edition

Every Landlord's Tax Deduction Guide

Stephen Fishman, J.D.

NOLO
LAW for ALL

NINETEENTH EDITION	JANUARY 2023
Editor	AMY LOFTSGORDON
Book Design	SUSAN PUTNEY
Proofreading	MARTHA C. BENCO
Index	RICHARD GENOVA
Printing	SHERIDAN

ISSN: 1945-8770 (print)
ISSN: 2325-2960 (online)

ISBN: 978-1-4133-3036-6 (pbk)
ISBN: 978-1-4133-3037-3 (ebook)

This book covers only United States law, unless it specifically states otherwise.

Please note

Accurate, plain-English legal information can help you solve many of your own legal problems. But this text is not a substitute for personalized advice from a knowledgeable lawyer. If you want the help of a trained professional—and we'll always point out situations in which we think that's a good idea—consult an attorney licensed to practice in your state.

Acknowledgments

Many thanks to:

Amy Loftsgordon, Diana Fitzpatrick, and Janet Portman
for their superb editing

Susan Putney for book design, and

Richard Genova for the useful index.

About the Author

Stephen Fishman is an attorney and tax expert who has been writing about the law for over 25 years. He is the author of many do-it-yourself law books published by Nolo, including *Every Airbnb Host's Tax Guide, Deduct It! Lower Your Small Business Taxes*, and *Working for Yourself: Law & Taxes for Independent Contractors, Freelancers & Gig Workers of All Types*.

He is often quoted on tax-related issues by news publications across the country, including the *Chicago Tribune*, the *San Francisco Chronicle*, and the *Wall Street Journal*.

Table of Contents

Introduction

This is a book about income tax deductions for landlords—that is, people who own residential rental property. If you're one of the millions of Americans who owns a small number of residential rental units (one to ten), this book is for you. And even landlords who own dozens of residential rental properties will find lots of useful information in this book that can help them save money.

As you probably know, being a landlord isn't easy. But one thing you have going for you is the tax law. Few profit-making activities provide more tax benefits than owning rental property.

No landlord would pay more than necessary for utilities or other operating expenses for a rental property. But, every year millions of landlords pay more taxes on their rental income than they have to. Why? Because they fail to take advantage of all the tax deductions available to owners of residential rental property. That's where this book comes in. It gives you all the information you need to maximize your deductions—and avoid common deduction mistakes. You can (and should) use this book all year long, to make April 15 as painless as possible.

When it comes to understanding your taxes, you need guidance more than ever. In 2017, Congress enacted the most sweeping changes to the tax code in over 30 years when it passed the Tax Cuts and Jobs Act (TCJA), which took effect in 2018. In an effort to stave off economic devastation in the wake of the coronavirus (COVID-19) pandemic, Congress revised the nation's tax laws yet again for 2020 and 2021, temporarily suspending many of the harshest provisions of the TCJA. In 2022, most of these temporary measures ended. For better or worse, U.S. tax law has entered the post-COVID era.

Even if you work with an accountant or another tax professional, you need the information in this book. It will help you provide your tax professional with better records, ask better questions, obtain better advice, and, just as importantly, evaluate the advice you get from tax professionals, websites, and other sources.

If you do your taxes yourself (as more and more landlords are doing, especially with the help of tax preparation software), your need for knowledge is even greater. Not even the most sophisticated tax software can decide which tax deductions you should take or tell you whether you've overlooked a valuable deduction. This book provides do-it-yourselfers with the practical advice and information they need to take full advantage of the many deductions available to landlords.

This book is written for traditional landlords who rent out their property full time to long-term tenants. If you rent your property to short-term guests through Airbnb, VRBO, or any other short-term rental platform and want tax guidance, see *Every Airbnb Host's Tax Guide* by Stephen Fishman.

Get Updates to This Book on Nolo.com

When important changes to the information in this book happen, we'll post updates online, on a page dedicated to this book:

www.nolo.com/back-of-book/DELL.html

Tax Deduction Basics for Landlords

T he tax code is full of deductions for landlords. Before you can start taking advantage of these deductions, however, you need a basic understanding of how landlords pay taxes and how tax deductions work. This chapter gives you all the information you need to get started, including:

- how the IRS taxes landlords
- how tax deductions work, and
- how forms of property ownership affect landlord taxes.

How Landlords Are Taxed

When you own residential rental property, you're required to pay the following taxes:

- income taxes on rental income and property sales
- Social Security and Medicare taxes (for some landlords)
- net investment income tax (for some landlords), and
- property taxes.

Let's look at each type of tax.

Income Taxes on Rental Income

You must pay federal income taxes on the net income (rent and other money minus expenses) you receive from your rental property each year. When you file your yearly tax return, you add your net rental income to your other income for the year, such as salary income from a job, interest on savings, and investment income. The seven different tax rates (called "tax brackets") range from 10% of taxable income to 37%. (See the chart below.)

This book covers rental property deductions for federal income taxes. However, 42 states also have income taxes. State income tax laws generally track federal tax law, subject to some exceptions. The states without income taxes are Alaska, Florida, Nevada, South Dakota, Tennessee, Texas, Washington, and Wyoming. New Hampshire taxes only dividends and interest. For details on your state's income tax law, visit your state tax agency's website, or contact your local state tax office. You can find links to all 50 state tax agency websites at the Federation of Tax Administrators website, at www.taxadmin.org.

2022 Federal Personal Income Tax Rates		
Rate	**Married Filing Jointly**	**Individual Return**
10%	0–$20,550	$0–$10,275
12%	$20,551–$83,550	$10,276–$41,775
22%	$83,551–$178,150	$41,776–$89,075
24%	$178,151–$340,100	$89,076–$170,050
32%	$340,101–$431,900	$170,051–$215,950
35%	$431,901–$647,850	$215,951–$539,900
37%	Over $647,850	Over $539,900

Income Taxes When You Sell Your Property

When you sell your property, any profit you earn is added to your income for the year and is subject to taxation. Profits from the sale of rental property owned for more than one year are taxed at capital gains rates. These rates are lower than income tax rates, except for taxpayers in the lowest tax brackets. (See Chapter 5 for an example of the tax effects of a rental property sale.)

But you might be able to defer tax on your profits—perhaps indefinitely—by selling your property through a like-kind exchange (also called a "Section 1031 exchange" or "tax-free exchange"). This kind of exchange involves swapping your property for similar property owned by someone else. These property swaps are subject to complex tax rules that are beyond the scope of this book because they have nothing to do with income tax deductions. For more information, see IRS Publication 544, *Sales and Other Dispositions of Assets*.

Social Security and Medicare Taxes

Everyone who works as an employee or who owns a business must pay Social Security and Medicare payroll taxes (known as "FICA," or "Federal Insurance Contributions Act," taxes). Employees pay half of these taxes themselves and their employers pay the other half. Self-employed people must pay them all themselves. These are two separate taxes.

Social Security tax. The Social Security tax is a flat 12.4% tax on net self-employment income or employee wages up to an annual ceiling, which is adjusted for inflation each year. In 2022, the ceiling was $147,000.

Medicare payroll tax. The two Medicare tax rates are: a 2.9% tax up to an annual ceiling—$200,000 for single taxpayers and $250,000 for married couples filing jointly. All income above the ceiling is taxed at a 3.8% rate.

For both the self-employed and employees, the combined Social Security and Medicare tax is 15.3%, up to the Social Security tax ceiling.

You might have to pay (and withhold) Social Security and Medicare taxes if you hire employees to work in your rental activity—for example, if you hire a resident manager. The employer's share of such taxes is a deductible expense. (See Chapter 13.)

The income you earn from your rental property isn't subject to Social Security and Medicare taxes even if your rental activities constitute a business for tax purposes. (I.R.C. § 1402(a)(1).) (See Chapter 2.) This is one of the great tax benefits of owning rental property. A person who owns a hot dog stand must pay the 15.3% self-employment tax on their annual profits, whereas a person who owns a rental house or other real estate pays no self-employment taxes on their rental income.

An important exception to the rule that landlords don't have to pay Social Security or Medicare taxes on their rental income is that landlords who provide "substantial services" to their tenants must pay this tax. "Substantial services" are services provided for tenants' convenience that hotels or bed-and-breakfasts typically provide, such as maid service, food, or concierge services. The services' value must be equal to at least 10% or 15% of the rent charged to be substantial. If you provide substantial services to your tenants, your activity is classified as a regular business, not a rental activity. If you're an individual owner, you report your income or losses on IRS Schedule C, *Profit or Loss From Business (Sole Proprietorship)*. Traditional landlords who rent to long-term tenants rarely provide substantial services.

Estimated Taxes for Landlords

If your rentals earn a profit and you expect to owe at least $1,000 in income tax on the profit, you might need to pay estimated taxes to the IRS to prepay your tax liability. However, if you work and have income tax withheld from your pay, you'll need to pay estimated tax only if your total withholding (and any tax credits) amounts to less than 90% of the total tax you expect to pay for the year. So, you can avoid paying any estimated tax at all by having your withholding increased. But you'll be able to hold on to your money a bit longer if you pay estimated tax instead of having the money taken out of your paychecks every pay period.

If you pay estimated tax, the payments are due four times per year: April 15, June 15, September 15, and January 15. To avoid having to pay an underpayment penalty, your total withholding and estimated tax payments must equal the lesser of either (1) 90% of your tax liability for the current year, or (2) 100% of what you paid the previous year (or 110% if you're a high-income taxpayer—those with adjusted gross incomes of more than $150,000, or $75,000 for married couples filing separate returns).

The easiest way to calculate your quarterly estimated tax payments is to subtract your total expected income tax withholding for the current year from the total income tax you paid last year. The balance is the total amount of estimated tax you must pay this year. But, if you're a high-income taxpayer, add 10% to the total. Note, however, that if your income is higher this year than last, you'll owe extra tax to the IRS on April 15. To account for this increase, you can increase your estimated tax payments or simply save the money you'll need to pay the taxes when you file your annual return.

You pay the money directly to the IRS in four equal installments, so divide the total by four. You can pay by mail, by electronic withdrawal from your bank account, or by credit or debit card. For details, see the IRS estimated tax webpage at www.irs.gov/Businesses/Small-Businesses-Self-Employed/Estimated-Taxes.

Net Investment Income Tax

The net investment income tax went into effect in 2013. This 3.8% tax affects many higher-income landlords. (For details, see Chapter 19.)

Property Taxes

Property owners in all states pay property taxes that cities, counties, and other local governments impose. These taxes are based on your rental property's value. Property taxes are not covered in this book.

What Is Rental Income?

You only pay tax on your net rental income each year—your total income minus your deductible expenses. Your rental income consists primarily of the rent your tenants pay you for the use of your property. However, rental income can include other types of payments as well. As a rule, neither tenants nor anyone else reports the rent and other payments landlords receive to the IRS.

Government-Paid Rent

During the COVID-19 pandemic, federal, state, and local government agencies made rental payments for many low-income tenants. These payments are taxable rental income for the landlord, even if a government agency paid them directly. However, for tenants, the payments are government grants and not taxable income.

Other Rental Income

Tenants typically make various kinds of payments to their landlords in addition to rent, or provide things of value other than money. Many of these payments must be included in landlord income.

Security deposits. When you receive a security deposit that you plan to use for the tenant's final rent payment, you should include that amount in your income for the year when you receive it. However, do not include security deposit money in your income when you receive it if you plan to return the money to your tenant at the end of the rental term. If you keep part or all of the security deposit at any time because your tenant doesn't live up to the terms of the rental agreement, include the amount you keep in your income for that year.

Interest earned on security deposits is also rental income that should be included in your income in the year it is earned, unless your state or local law requires landlords to credit that interest to tenants.

Property or services in lieu of rent. Property or services you receive from a tenant as rent (instead of money) must be included in your rental income. For example, if your tenant is a painter and offers to paint your rental property instead of paying rent for two months, you must include in your rental income the amount the tenant would have paid for two months' worth of rent.

Rental expenses paid for by tenant. Any rental expenses a tenant paid are rental income, including payments a tenant makes to you for repairs, utilities, or other rental costs. These costs are then deductible by you as rental expenses.

Lease cancellation payments. If a tenant pays you to agree to cancel a lease, the amount you receive is rent that must be included in your rental income in the year you receive it.

Leases with option to buy. A lease with an option to buy occurs if the rental agreement gives your tenant the right to buy your rental property. The payments you receive under such an agreement are generally rental income.

Advance rent payments. Advance rent is any amount you receive before the period that it covers. Include advance rent in your rental income in the year you receive it, regardless of the period covered. For example, to get you to agree to a one-year lease, a tenant with poor credit pays you six months' rent in advance in December. You must include the entire amount as rental income in the year it was received.

Fees. Fees or other charges tenants pay are also rental income. These fees include:

- fees you charge tenants for paying rent late
- garage or other parking fees
- fees you charge tenants for use of storage facilities, and
- laundry income from washers and dryers you provide for tenants' use.

How Income Tax Deductions Work

The tax law recognizes that you must spend money on your rental properties for such things as mortgage interest, repairs, maintenance, and many other expenses. The law allows you to subtract these expenses, plus an amount for the depreciation of your property, from your effective gross rental income (all the money actually earned from the property) to determine your taxable income. You pay income tax only on your taxable income, if any. Expenses you can deduct from your income are called "tax deductions" or "tax write-offs." These deductions are what this book is about.

Although some tax deduction calculations can get a bit complicated, the basic math is simple. The entire tax regimen for rental real estate can be reduced to the following simple equation:

	Effective gross rental income
minus	Operating expenses (including mortgage interest)
minus	Depreciation and amortization expenses
=	Taxable income

(People who analyze real estate investments don't include mortgage interest as a real estate operating expense, but it is an operating expense for tax purposes.)

> EXAMPLE: Karla owns a rental house. This year, her effective gross rental income (all the income she actually earned from the property) was $10,000. She doesn't pay tax on the entire $10,000 because she had the following expenses—$5,000 in mortgage interest, $1,000 for other operating expenses, and $2,000 for depreciation. She gets to deduct these as outlined in the above equation:

Effective gross rental income	$ 10,000
Operating expenses	– 6,000
Depreciation and amortization	– 2,000
Taxable income	$ 2,000

Karla only pays income tax on her $2,000 taxable income.

Many landlords have so many deductions that they end up with a net loss when they subtract all their deductions from their effective gross rental income. In that situation, they owe no tax at all on their rental income. This situation is especially common in the early years of owning rental property when you haven't had time to raise the rents much. Indeed, it is common for landlords to have a loss for tax purposes even if they take in more in rental income than they pay in expenses each month.

Tax Credits for Landlords

Tax credits are not the same as tax deductions—they are even better. A "tax credit" is subtracted from your tax liability after you calculate your taxes. For example, a $1,000 tax credit will reduce your taxes for the year by $1,000. Many different types of federal income tax credits exist, but the only credit widely available to owners of residential rentals is the low-income housing credit.

Congress enacted the low-income housing tax credit to encourage new construction and rehabilitation of existing rental housing for low-income households. The IRS and state tax credit allocation agencies jointly administer the low-income housing tax credit, which is used mostly by large real estate developers to build new low-income housing projects. For more information, contact your state tax credit allocation agency. You can find a list at www.novoco.com/resource-centers/affordable-housing-tax-credits/2022-federal-lihtc-information-state. Useful information can also be obtained from the National Housing & Rehabilitation Association website at www.housingonline.com.

No federal income tax credits are available for the cost of eliminating lead paint, asbestos, or mold contamination. However, your state might offer tax credits or other tax incentives for such environmental remediation.

Having a tax loss on your rental property is not necessarily a bad thing. You might be able to deduct it from other income you earn during the year, such as salary income from a job or income from other investments. However, significant restrictions limit a landlord's ability to deduct rental losses from nonrental income. Many small landlords can avoid them, but not all. These restrictions—known as the "passive loss rules" and "at-risk rules"—are covered in detail in Chapter 16.

What Can You Deduct?

All tax deductions are a matter of legislative grace, which means that you can take a deduction only if it is specifically allowed by one or more provisions of the tax law. You usually don't have to indicate on your tax return which tax law provision gives you the right to take a particular deduction. If you're audited by the IRS, though, you'll have to provide a legal basis for every deduction you take. If the IRS concludes that your deduction wasn't justified, it will deny the deduction and charge you back taxes and penalties.

Landlords can deduct the following broad categories of rental expenses:

- start-up expenses
- operating expenses
- capital expenses, and
- a pass-through tax deduction.

This section provides an introduction to each of these categories (they're covered in greater detail in later chapters).

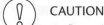 CAUTION
Keep track of your rental expenses. You can deduct only those expenses that you actually incur. You need to keep records of these expenses to know for sure how much you actually spent and prove to the IRS that you really spent the money you deducted on your tax return in case you are audited. Accounting and bookkeeping are discussed in detail in Chapter 17.

Start-Up Expenses

The first money you will have to shell out will be for your rental activity's start-up expenses. These expenses include most of the costs of getting your rental business up and running, like license fees, advertising costs, attorneys' and accounting fees, travel expenses, market research, and office supply expenses. Start-up expenses do not include the cost of buying rental property. If your rental activity qualifies as a business, up to $5,000 of start-up expenses may be deducted for the year in which they're incurred. The remainder, if any, must be deducted in equal installments over the first 180 months you're in business—a process called "amortization." (See Chapter 9 for a detailed discussion of deducting start-up expenses.)

Operating Expenses

Operating expenses are the ongoing, day-to-day costs a landlord incurs to operate a rental property. These expenses include mortgage interest, utilities, salaries, supplies, travel expenses, car expenses, and repairs and maintenance. These expenses (unlike start-up expenses) are currently deductible—that is, you can deduct them all in the same year when you pay them. (See Chapter 3.)

Capital Expenses

Capital assets are things you buy for your rental activity that have a useful life of more than one year. A landlord's main capital asset is the building or buildings the landlord rents out. However, capital assets also include, for example, equipment, vehicles, furniture, and appliances. These costs, called "capital expenses," are considered to be part of your investment in your rental activity, not day-to-day operating expenses.

The cost of your capital assets must be deducted a little at a time over several years—a process called "depreciation." Residential rental buildings (and building components) are depreciated over 27.5 years.

The cost of land isn't deductible—you must wait until land is sold to recover the cost. However, the cost of personal property used in your rental activity—computers, for example—can usually be deducted in a single year using 100% bonus depreciation or Section 179 of the tax code. (See Chapter 5 for more on this topic.) Personal property inside rental units can also be deducted in one year with bonus depreciation. (See Chapter 6.)

Expenses Paid With Paycheck Protection Program (PPP) Loans and Economic Injury Disaster Loan (EIDL) Advances

During the COVID-19 pandemic, two of the most popular government relief programs were the Paycheck Protection Program (PPP) and Economic Injury Disaster Loan (EIDL) program. The Small Business Administration (SBA) administered both programs.

A business with fewer than 500 full-time employees could obtain a PPP loan for up to 2.5 times its average monthly payroll costs for 2019 or 2020, up to $10 million. Landlords with employees, such as property managers, were eligible for PPP loans. However, these loans were often small because even large rental businesses usually have few employees. Landlords without employees were not eligible for PPP loans, which excluded the vast majority of small landlords.

All landlords were eligible for low-interest EIDLs from the SBA. These loans provided up to $2 million depending on financial need. EIDLs also came with emergency loan advances up to $10,000. Congress established a second round of EIDL emergency advances in 2020, targeted to businesses in low-income communities.

What made PPP loans so popular is that the SBA forgave them if the borrower spent at least 60% of the loan on employee payroll and maintained an employee head count for a specified period. EIDLs are not forgiven, but EIDL advances do not have to be paid back.

Forgiven PPP Loans and EIDL Advances Are Tax Free

Under normal tax rules, when a lender forgives a loan, the amount becomes taxable income, meaning it must be included in the borrower's income, and the borrower must pay income tax on it. But Congress enacted a special tax rule, making forgiven PPP loans and EIDL advances completely tax free for landlords and other businesses that received them. PPP and EIDL borrowers don't have to list the loans or advances in their tax returns. Lenders that process such loans don't have to file with the IRS, or furnish to borrowers, a Form 1099-C reporting the PPP loans or EIDL advances.

Deductions for Expenses Paid With Forgiven PPP Loans and EIDL Advances

Under ordinary tax rules, businesses that use tax-free government money to pay expenses can't also deduct those expenses from their taxes—a form of "double dipping." For example, if you used a $10,000 forgiven EIDL advance to pay for repairs or other rental expenses, you couldn't deduct $10,000 for those same expenses on your tax return. However, Congress enacted a special tax rule allowing businesses, including landlords, to fully deduct all expenses they paid with forgiven PPP loans and EIDL advances. (Rev. Rul. 2021-02.) You can safely deduct any rental business expenses you paid with EIDL advances or PPP loan proceeds.

Pass-Through Tax Deduction

From 2018 through 2025, landlords may qualify for a special pass-through tax deduction. This deduction enables them to deduct from their income taxes up to 20% of their net income from their rental activity. (See Chapter 7.)

How Your Tax Status Affects Your Deductions

Owning rental property can be a business for tax purposes, an investment, or, in some cases, a not-for-profit activity. Landlords whose rental activities qualify as a business are entitled to all the tax deductions discussed in this book. But those whose rentals are an investment lose certain useful deductions, such as the home office deduction. Tax deductions are extremely limited for landlords who, in the eyes of the IRS, are operating a not-for-profit activity.

Your tax status is determined by how much time and effort you put into your rental activity, and whether you earn profits each year or act like you want to. Most landlords who manage their property themselves qualify as for-profit businesses. (See Chapter 2 for more on determining your tax status.)

How Property Ownership Affects Taxes

How you own your residential rental property affects the tax returns you must file each year. The main ownership options for a small landlord are:

- sole proprietorship
- general partnership
- limited partnership
- limited liability company (LLC)
- corporation
- tenancy in common, or
- joint tenancy.

These options can be sorted into two broad categories: individual ownership and ownership through a business entity. If you don't know how you hold title to the rental property you already own, look at your property deed.

Individual Ownership

Most small landlords (owners of from one to ten residential rental units) own their property as individuals—either alone or with one or more co-owners.

One Property Owner

The simplest way to own rental property is for a single individual to own it in that person's own name. When you do this, you are a sole proprietor for tax purposes. Any rental income you earn is added to your other income, such as salary from a job, interest income, or investment income. Losses you incur can be deducted from your other income, subject to the restrictions discussed in Chapter 16. You report your rental income and losses on IRS Schedule E and attach it to your individual tax return. (See Chapter 18 for a detailed discussion of Schedule E.)

The situation is a bit more complex if you acquired the property while married and you live in one of the nine community property states: Arizona, California, Idaho, Louisiana, Nevada, New Mexico, Texas, Washington, and Wisconsin. Although the rental is held in your name alone, unless you and your spouse agree otherwise, it will be jointly owned community property under your state's marital property laws. However, for tax purposes, you may still treat the rental activity as a sole proprietorship with only one spouse listed as owner on Schedule E. (See "Spouses who live in community property states," below.)

Co-Owners Not Married to Each Other

It's not uncommon for two or more relatives, friends, or colleagues to own rental property together. If you acquire the property with one or more co-owners, you don't necessarily have to form a separate business entity like a partnership, limited liability company, or corporation to own and operate it. Instead, for tax purposes, each owner can in essence be treated like a sole proprietor, which can be accomplished where co-owners take title to the property together as tenants in common or, more rarely, joint tenants. (See "Co-Ownership by Spouses," below, for the difference between the two.) Each co-owner owns an undivided interest in the entire property. In the case of a tenancy in common, the interests can be equal or divided in unequal amounts, whatever the owners agree upon. The ownership interest of each owner should be listed on the property deed.

> **EXAMPLE:** AJ and Alina, brother and sister, buy a rental house together, taking title as tenants in common. They decide that because AJ put more money down on the property, he should own a 60% interest and Alina 40%. So, AJ is legally entitled to 60% of the income the property generates and is supposed to pay 60% of the expenses. Alina gets the remaining 40%.

Although they own rental property together, each cotenant is treated like a sole proprietor for tax purposes. Each cotenant reports their share of the income and deductions from the rental property on their own tax return, filing Schedule E. Each owner's share is based on their ownership interest—for example, Alina in the example above lists her 40% share of the income and deductions from the co-owned rental house on her Schedule E and pays tax on that amount. AJ lists the other 60% on his own Schedule E.

If one cotenant pays more than their proportionate share of the expenses, the overpayment is treated as a loan to the other cotenants and may not be deducted. The cotenant who overpays is legally entitled to be reimbursed by the other cotenants. (T.C. Memo 1995-562.)

> **EXAMPLE:** Alina from the example above pays 80% of the annual expenses for the rental house this year, instead of the 40% she should pay based on her ownership interest. She may not deduct her overpayment, which amounts to $10,000. Instead, it is treated as a loan to her cotenant, AJ. Alina is entitled to be repaid the $10,000 by AJ. If he doesn't pay, she can sue him to collect. If he does pay, he can deduct the amount as a rental expense.

Are cotenants partners? The type of cotenancy described above might seem like a partnership, but it's really not. Unlike in a partnership, a cotenant can't act or contract on behalf of the other cotenants without their authorization. Moreover, one cotenant isn't liable for any debts incurred by another cotenant without giving consent. Each tenant in common may lease, mortgage, sell, or otherwise transfer all or part of their interest without obtaining consent from the other cotenants, or even telling them about it. This power to transfer property also applies upon the death of a tenant in common. It's often desirable, but not required, that the co-owners enter into a written cotenancy agreement.

Not being in a partnership can save time and expense. Filing a partnership tax return and dealing with complex partnership tax laws is not easy. If you're a partnership, here's what you're supposed to do:

- Complete and file Form 1065, *U.S. Return of Partnership Income*, reporting all the partnership's income, deductions, gains, and losses.
- Complete a Schedule K-1 for each partner showing that partner's share of the partnership's income or loss.
- Transfer the Schedule K-1 information onto a Schedule E, *Supplemental Income and Loss*, for each partner.
- Complete a Schedule SE for each partner, listing that partner's share of partnership income as self-employment income.
- Transfer the data from the individual schedules onto the joint Form 1040.

Obviously, these tasks require a lot of time and money—tax pros can charge $1,000 or more to prepare partnership returns.

Co-owners who provide services to tenants. IRS regulations provide that tenants in common or joint tenants don't become partners in a partnership as long as all they do is own rental property together and merely maintain, repair, and rent it. (IRS Reg. § 1.761-1(a), IRS Reg. § 301.7701(a)(2).) (See also IRS Publication 541, *Partnerships*: "co-ownership of property maintained and rented or leased is not a partnership unless the co-owners provide services to the tenants.")

However, the tax situation changes if co-owners of a rental property provide significant services to their tenants. In this event, the IRS will consider them partners in a partnership for tax purposes.

Significant services don't include furnishing heat and light, cleaning of public areas, normal repairs, trash collection, or similar services. Instead, they are services that primarily benefit the tenants personally, such as maid service, linen changing, food service, or concierge services. (IRS Reg. § 301.7701-1(b); Rev. Rul. 75-374.) Providing occasional cleaning or concierge services would probably not constitute significant services. Would providing tenants with an internet connection or cable TV constitute significant services? It's unclear.

If co-owners are deemed to be partners in a partnership, the partnership must file a partnership tax return (unless they are married and elect qualified joint venture status—see "Co-Ownership by Spouses," below). Each individual or partnership members gets a Schedule K-1 from their partnership reporting their individual shares of annual income or loss from the rental activity. The individuals then list this amount in Part II of Schedule E, on page 2. This doesn't increase or decrease the owners' deductions but it does result in a more complex tax return.

Co-Ownership by Spouses

Spouses who own rental property together typically take title as joint tenants—rather than tenants in common. Joint tenants are treated exactly the same as tenants in common for tax purposes, but there are significant nontax differences. Joint tenants must own the property 50-50. In addition, joint tenancy always includes "the right of survivorship." When one joint tenant dies, that person's share automatically goes to the survivor, which isn't the case with tenants in common, who can leave their share of the co-owned property to anyone they want. Unmarried people can also be joint tenants, but this isn't commonly done.

If a married couple that jointly owes rental property files a joint income tax return, as most do, they are treated as a single taxpayer by the IRS. The spouses' shares of the income and deductions from the rental property are combined on their single joint tax return. The couple reports their income and deductions from the jointly owned property on a single Schedule E they file with their joint return.

Are co-owner spouses partners in a partnership? Like other co-owners of rental property, spouses who are landlords of property they own together are ordinarily not considered partners in a partnership as long as all they do is maintain, repair, and rent their property. However, spouses who provide significant services to their tenants will be viewed as partners in a partnership by the IRS. (See "Co-owners who provide services to tenants," above.) So, they would have to file a partnership tax return—unless they can elect joint venture status.

Electing qualified joint venture status to file Schedule C. To avoid having to file a partnership tax return, spouses who provide significant services to their tenants can elect to be taxed as a "qualified joint venture." When this election is done, both spouses are treated as sole proprietors of a Schedule C business for tax purposes. They each file an IRS Schedule C, *Profit or Loss From Business (Sole Proprietorship)*, with their joint return.

This election is available only where the spouses own the rental property as individuals in their own names. It may not be made when the activity is held in the name of a state law business entity such as a partnership or an LLC.

To qualify for qualified joint venture status, the spouses must share all their rental income, losses, deductions, and credits according to their ownership interest in the property. If, as is usually the case, each spouse owns 50% of the property, they equally split their rental income or loss on their Schedules C.

In addition, the spouses must:

- be the only owners of the activity
- file a joint return
- both elect not to be treated as a partnership, and
- both materially participate in the business.

Material participation is determined by the same rules as those used to determine whether real estate owners qualify as real estate professionals for purposes of the passive activity loss (PAL) rules. This means that each spouse must be involved with their business's day-to-day operations on a regular, continuous, and substantial basis. Working more than 500 hours in the business during the year meets this requirement. So does working over 100 hours if no one else worked more, or doing substantially all the work for the activity. (See "Material Participation Test" in Chapter 16 for a detailed discussion.)

In addition, the IRS says that married couples can't make a qualified joint venture election if the business is owned and operated through a state law entity, including a partnership, limited liability company, limited liability partnership, or corporation. So, you can't make this election if you've formed an LLC or a corporation to own and run the business.

If you qualify, you and your spouse elect this status simply by filing a joint IRS Form 1040 with the required Schedule C. Once you elect this status, it can't be revoked without IRS approval.

Electing qualified joint venture status to file Schedule E. The instructions for Schedule E provide that spouses whose rental activity constitutes a business for reasons other than providing their tenants with services may also elect qualified joint venture status. The same requirements discussed above must be satisfied. In this event, the co-owner spouses file one Schedule E to report their income and expenses from the rental property. However, each spouse must report that spouse's interest as separate properties on Schedule E. Check a special box on Schedule E to elect qualified joint venture status. (See Chapter 18 for a detailed discussion of Schedule E.)

It's not entirely clear when this election is necessary. The IRS regulations discussed above make clear that it isn't necessary if the spouses merely maintain, repair, and rent out their property—this activity is not a partnership for tax purposes. Something more must make the activity a partnership business—something other than providing services. What this is remains unclear. But, spouses who want to make absolutely sure that the IRS doesn't view their rental activity as a partnership might want to make this election if they meet the requirements. It costs nothing. The spouses will have to split their rental income and expenses between them for each rental property when they file their sole Schedule E.

Spouses who live in community property states. Some special rules apply for co-owner spouses who live in community property states: Arizona, California, Idaho, Louisiana, Nevada, New Mexico, Texas, Washington, and Wisconsin.

If you live in one of these states, you and your spouse will automatically be co-owners of any rental property you acquire while you're married, unless you agree otherwise. Like married people in non-community-property states, spouses in community property states ordinarily take title to their real property as joint tenants. However, they may take title as tenants in common instead, if they want; or just one spouse may be named on the deed as owner.

The IRS says that spouses in community property states may treat their rental activity either as a sole proprietorship (technically, a "disregarded entity") or as a partnership. Either one is fine. If sole proprietorship status is selected, they would file one Schedule E and would not have to allocate their rental income and expenses between themselves. All they need do to elect this status is file their one Schedule E. They don't need to elect qualified joint venture status to avoid having to file a partnership return. (Rev. Proc. 2002-69 (10/9/2002).)

Ownership Through a Business Entity

Instead of owning your rental property in your own name, you can form a business entity to own it, and own all or part of the entity.

> **EXAMPLE:** Venus and Vishonne, a married couple, own a small apartment building. Instead of taking title in their own names as joint tenants, they form a limited liability company (LLC). The LLC owns the building and they, in turn, own the LLC.

The tax deductions available from rental property are the same whether you own it in your own name or through any of the business entities discussed below, subject to one exception. Regular C corporations—which are rarely used to own rental real estate—do not qualify for the new pass-through tax deduction. (See Chapter 7.)

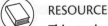 **RESOURCE**
This section provides only the briefest possible introduction to business entities. To learn more, refer to *LLC or Corporation? How to Choose the Right Form for Your Business,* by Anthony Mancuso (Nolo).

Types of Entities

Several different business entities can own rental property.

Partnerships. A "partnership" is a form of shared ownership and management of a business. The partners contribute money, property, or services to the partnership; in return, they receive a share of the profits it earns, if any. The partners jointly manage the partnership business. Although many partners enter into written partnership agreements, no agreement is required to form a partnership. A partnership can hold title to real estate and other property.

Limited partnerships. A "limited partnership" is a special type of partnership that can only be created by filing limited partnership documents with your state government. It consists of one or more general partners who manage the partnership and any number of limited partners who are passive investors—they contribute money and share in the partnership's income (or losses) but don't actively manage the partnership business. Limited partnerships are especially popular for real estate projects that are owned by multiple investors.

Corporations. A "corporation" can only be created by filing incorporation documents with your state government. A corporation is a legal entity distinct from its owners, who are called "shareholders." It can hold title to property, sue and be sued, have bank accounts, borrow money, hire employees, and perform other business functions. For tax purposes, the two types of corporations are S corporations (also called "small business corporations") and C corporations (also called "regular corporations"). The most important difference between the two types of corporations is how they're taxed. An S corporation pays no taxes itself—instead, its income or loss is passed on to its owners, who must pay personal income taxes on their share of the corporation's profits.

Limited liability companies. A "limited liability company" (LLC) is like a sole proprietorship or partnership in that its owners (called "members") jointly own and manage the business and share in the profits. However, an LLC is also like a corporation because its owners must file papers with the state to create the LLC and it exists as a separate legal entity. Today, the LLC is the most popular business entity used to own rental property.

Tax Treatment of Business Entities

Partnerships, limited partnerships, LLCs, and S corporations are all pass-through entities. A pass-through entity doesn't pay any taxes itself. Instead, the business's profits or losses are passed through to its owners, who include them on their own personal tax returns (IRS Form 1040). When a profit is passed through to the owner, the owner must add that money to any income from other sources and pay tax on the total amount. If a loss is passed through to the owner, that person can deduct it from other income, subject to the restrictions on deducting rental losses discussed in Chapter 16. Because pass-through taxation permits property owners to deduct losses from their personal taxes, it is considered the best form of taxation for real estate ownership.

Although pass-through entities don't pay taxes, their income and expenses must still be reported to the IRS as follows.

Partnerships and limited partnerships. Partnerships and limited partnerships must file an annual tax form with the IRS (Form 1065, *U.S. Return of Partnership Income*). Form 1065 is used to report partnership revenues, expenses, gains, and losses. The partnership must also provide each partner with an IRS Schedule K-1, *Partner's Share of Income, Deductions, Credits, etc.*, listing the partner's share of partnership income and expenses (copies of these schedules must also be attached to IRS Form 1065). The partners must then file IRS Schedule E, *Supplemental Income and Loss*, with their individual income tax returns, showing the income or losses from all the partnerships in which they own an interest. Partners complete the second page of Schedule E, not the first page, which individuals use to report their income and deductions from rental property. (See Chapter 18.)

S corporations. These entities must file information returns with the IRS on Form 1120-S, *U.S. Income Tax Return for an S Corporation*, showing how much the business earned or lost and each shareholder's portion of the corporate income or loss. (An information return is a return filed by an entity that doesn't pay any taxes itself. Its purpose is to show the IRS how much tax the entity's owners owe.) Like partners in a partnership, the shareholders must complete the second page of Schedule E, showing their shares of the corporation's income or losses, and file it with their individual tax returns.

LLCs. LLCs with only one member are ordinarily treated like a sole proprietorship for tax purposes. The member reports profits, losses, and deductions from rental activities on Schedule E. An LLC with two or more members is treated like a partnership for tax purposes, except in the unusual situation where the owners choose to have it treated like a C or an S corporation. However, an LLC owned by just one person is treated as a "disregarded entity" for tax purposes. So, the single LLC owner is treated the same as a sole proprietor.

Landlords who own their properties through business entities don't use individual Schedule Es to report their rental income or losses. Instead, the partnership, limited partnership, LLC, or S corporation files IRS Form 8825, *Rental Real Estate Income and Expenses of a Partnership or an S Corporation*, to report the income and deductions from the property owned by the entity. This form is very similar to Schedule E.

Why Form a Business Entity?

The primary reason small landlords form business entities to own their property has nothing to with taxes. Rather, they use business entities to attempt to avoid personal liability for debts and lawsuits arising from rental property ownership.

> TIP
> **Forming a business entity might help show your rental activity is a business.** Another reason to form a business entity that might be more important now than it was in the past is to help establish that the rental activity is a business for tax purposes, not an investment activity. Qualifying as a business provides a landlord with many benefits. (See "Business Owner Versus Investor" in Chapter 2.) Moreover, real estate professionals whose rental activities qualify as a business can completely avoid the 3.8% net investment income tax. (See Chapter 19.)

When you own rental property in your own name, alone or with co-owners, you're personally liable for all the debts arising from the property. So, a creditor—a person or company to whom you owe money for items you use in your rental activity—can go after all your assets, both business and personal. These assets might include, for example, your personal bank accounts, your car, and even your house. Similarly, a personal creditor—a person or company to whom you owe money for personal items—can go after your rental property. The main creditor that rental property owners worry about is the bank or some other financial institution from which they have borrowed money to purchase their property. If they default on their loan, they could be personally liable for the debt. (However, it depends on the nature of your loan and how your state law deals with real estate foreclosures.)

In theory, limited partnerships, LLCs, and corporations provide their owners with limited liability from debts and lawsuits. (Only the limited partners in a limited partnership have limited liability. General partners are personally liable for partnership debts and lawsuits.) Limited liability means that you aren't personally liable for the debts incurred by your business entity, or for lawsuits arising from its ownership of rental property. So, your personal assets aren't at risk; at most, you'll lose your investment in the business entity (which, of course, is often substantial).

In real life, however, limited liability is often hard to come by, even when you form a business entity. Lenders may require small landlords who form business entities to personally guarantee any loans their entities obtain to purchase property. This means the landlord will be personally liable if there is a default on the loan. In addition, you'll always be personally liable if someone is injured on your property due to your personal negligence. For example, if someone slips and falls on your property, they can sue you personally by claiming your own negligence caused or contributed to the accident. This is so even though your property is owned by a business entity, not you personally. You can far more effectively protect yourself from such lawsuits by obtaining liability insurance for your rental property. The cost is a deductible rental expense. (See Chapter 15.)

However, if you're dead set on owning your rental property through a business entity, the entity of choice is the LLC. It provides the same degree of limited liability as a corporation, while also giving its owners pass-through taxation—the most advantageous tax treatment for real property. As a result, LLCs have become very popular among real property owners in recent years.

Out of an abundance of caution (or paranoia), some landlords set up a separate LLC for each rental property they own. However, this process can be expensive, especially in states that make LLCs pay minimum annual taxes or fees, no matter how much money they earn. For example, LLCs in California must pay $800 per year. So, if you set up five California LLCs to own five buildings, you'd have to pay $4,000 in fees every year—even if your rental activates incurred losses. Again, you'd probably be better off spending the money on rental property insurance.

RESOURCE

For detailed guidance about LLCs, refer to *Form Your Own Limited Liability Company: Create an LLC in Any State,* by Anthony Mancuso (Nolo).

Landlord Tax Classifications

This chapter explains how to determine your tax status—that is, how to classify your rental activities for tax purposes. This topic is not one that most residential landlords give much thought to. But your tax status is extremely important because it will determine whether (and to what extent) you can deduct your rental expenses. Your tax status also significantly affects your taxes when you sell your property.

The Landlord Tax Categories

A landlord can fall into any one of the following tax categories:
- a business owner
- a real estate investor, or
- a person who owns rental property as a not-for-profit activity.

The vast majority of residential landlords are either business owners or investors—although this doesn't necessarily mean that you'll fall into one of these two categories. Ultimately, your behavior and motive for owning rental property will determine your tax status.

Initially, it's up to you to decide which category your rental activities fall into for tax purposes. However, if the IRS audits you, it can review your tax classification. If the IRS decides that you misclassified your rental activities, you could have to pay back taxes, interest, and penalties.

You can determine your status by answering the following questions:
- Do you work regularly and continuously at your rental activity?
- Is earning a profit the primary reason you own rental property?
- Do you make your money primarily by buying and selling real estate?

Let's take a look at each of these questions—this review will help you figure out which category you fall into. The tax consequences of the different classifications are also explained.

Business Owner Versus Investor

The crucial tax question for most landlords is whether they qualify as business owners or investors. This distinction has important tax consequences. If, like most landlords, you are a business owner, you get certain valuable tax deductions that investors can't use (including the home office and start-up expenses deductions, and Section 179 expensing). Most notably, landlords who are in business may qualify for the pass-through income tax deduction of up to 20% of their net rental income. (See Chapter 7.) So, it's important to understand the difference between these two categories and know where you belong.

> **CAUTION**
>
> **Do you continually lose money on your rentals?** If you do, the IRS might claim you're engaged in a not-for-profit activity, with disastrous tax consequences. (See "Are You Profit Motivated?" below, for detailed guidance on how to show the IRS that you want to earn a profit from your rental property.)

Are You a Business Owner or an Investor?

What's the difference between an investor and a business owner? It's not their motivation—they both want to earn a profit. The difference is that business owners earn their profits by actively running a business, either themselves or with the help of others they hire, such as managers. Investors are passive—they put their money in someone else's business and hope their investment will increase in value due to the other person's efforts. Or, they buy an item like land or gold, and then sit and wait for it to increase in value.

Whether owning rental property qualifies as a business is determined under Internal Revenue Code Section 162 and the legal decisions that have applied it. Section 162 is the tax code provision that allows businesses to deduct their expenses. It simply says that tax deductions are allowed "in carrying on any trade or business." It is left up to the courts to decide what landlords (and others) must do to be engaged in a "trade or business" for these purposes.

The general rule is that any activity, including a rental activity, qualifies as a business if you engage in it to earn a profit and work at it regularly and continuously. (*Comm'r. v. Groetzinger*, 480 U.S. 23 (1987); *Alvary v. United States*, 302 F.2d 790 (2d Cir. 1962).)

Applying this rather vague test is a highly factual determination. The IRS says that relevant factors that can be considered include, but are not limited to:

- the type of rented property (commercial versus residential property)
- the number of properties rented
- the owner's or the owner's agent's day-to-day involvement
- the types and significance of any ancillary services provided under the lease
- the terms of the lease (for example, a short-term versus long-term lease), and
- whether the landlord has filed all required information returns (Form 1099-NEC; see Chapter 13). (Preamble to IRS Reg. 1.199A-1.)

Both the courts and the IRS have consistently found that landlords don't need to own very much property or do very much work to qualify as a business under this test.

EXAMPLE: Edwin Curphey, a dermatologist, owned six rental properties in Hawaii. He converted a bedroom in his home into an office for his real estate activities. Curphey personally managed his rentals, which included seeking new tenants, supplying furnishings, and cleaning and otherwise preparing the units for new tenants. The court held that these activities were sufficiently regular and continuous to place him in the business of real estate rental. (*Curphey v. Comm'r*, 73 T.C. 766 (1980).)

You don't even have to do all the work yourself: You can hire a manager or others to help you and still qualify as a business as long as the manager or other person you hire works regularly and continuously.

EXAMPLE: Ms. Gilford, her two sisters, and other relatives jointly owned eight apartment buildings in Manhattan. They hired a real estate agent to manage the properties and pay each family member their share of the net income. Gilford was found to be in business even though she spent little or no time managing the buildings. The court reasoned that the ownership and management of the buildings was a business because it required considerable time and effort by the real estate agent over several years. Because the agent acted for Gilford and was ultimately under her control, Gilford was in business through her agent. (*Gilford v. Comm'r*, 201 F.2d 735 (2d Cir. 1953).)

Moreover, it's not necessary that your property actually be rented out for you to be in business. It's sufficient that you offer it for rent to the public at a fair market rental. The fact that you have had trouble finding a renter doesn't mean you're not in business.

> **EXAMPLE:** Mr. Jephson purchased a 26-room brownstone on Riverside Drive in Manhattan. He offered it for rent through a real estate agency, improved the heating system, and had a caretaker who was in charge of keeping it clean, making general repairs, and showing it to prospective renters. The owner, Mr. Jephson, received rental offers, but deemed none to be satisfactory. As a result, the house remained unoccupied for nine years. Nevertheless, his real estate activity qualified as a business for tax purposes. (*Jephson v. Comm'r.*, 37 B.T.A. 1117 (1938).)

How Many Units Must You Own to Be in Business?

No specific number applies to how many rental properties or rental units you must own for your rental activity to qualify as a business. In one case, a married couple was found to be engaged in business even though all they owned was a 25% timeshare interest in two condominium units. And, the actual work of renting out the units and keeping them in repair was performed by a management company that acted as their agent. (*Murtaugh v. Comm'r.*, T.C. Memo 1997-319.) Indeed, the tax court ruled back in 1946 that rental of one single-family residential unit constituted a business even though the only work the owner seemed to have done was listing the property for rent or sale with agents. (*Hazard v. Comm'r.*, 7 T.C. 372.) The IRS agreed to follow this case (GCM 38779 (7/27/81)) and the tax court continues to follow it throughout the country except the Northeast.

Moreover, the IRS has recently stated that "rental of a single property may require regular and continuous involvement such that the rental activity is a trade or business." (Preamble to IRS Reg. § 1.1411, TD 9644, https://federalregister.gov/a/2013-28410.)

However, the IRS and courts have also said that renting of a single unit (or more) doesn't always constitute a business—it all depends on the facts and circumstances, including the number of properties rented, the day-to-day involvement of the owner or its agent, and the type of rental—for example, a short-term versus long-term lease.

How Many Hours Must You Work to Be in Business?

Neither the IRS nor the courts have established a minimum number of hours you (or your agents) must work in your rental activity for it to qualify as a business. However, IRS regulations and safe harbor rules establish a minimum number of hours that a landlord must work to be considered a business for certain specific tax purposes. But these hourly requirements are optional safe harbor rules that landlords may choose to rely on. They don't establish a minimum number of hours all landlords must work to be in business.

500 hours for the net investment income tax. IRS regulations that went into effect in 2014 establish a safe harbor rule for when a rental activity conducted by a real estate professional is a business solely for purposes of the net investment income tax (NIIT): So long as a real estate professional devotes a minimum of 501 hours per year to the rental activity, it will automatically qualify as a business and the rental income will not be subject to the NIIT. (IRS Reg. § 1.1411-4(g)(7).) (See Chapter 19 for a detailed discussion of the NIIT.)

This regulation applies only to real estate professionals who own rental properties—people who work over half the time in the real estate field. (In Chapter 16, see "The Real Estate Professional Exemption.") Most small landlords do not qualify as real estate professionals; thus, the regulation doesn't directly apply to them.

250 hours for the pass-through deduction. In 2019, the IRS established a safe harbor rule that may be used to determine whether a landlord qualifies for the pass-through deduction. Under this rule, the IRS assumes that a rental activity is a business for purposes of the pass-through deduction if the landlord spends at least 250 hours per year working in the activity. (IRS Notice 2019-07; see Chapter 7.) Again, this is a safe harbor rule, and it is possible that a landlord could work less than 250 hours per year and still qualify for the pass-through deduction.

This safe harbor rule only applies to the pass-through deduction. It isn't supposed to be used for any other purposes, such as determining if a landlord may use Section 179 expensing or take the home office deduction. However, a landlord under audit could argue that if 250 hours is enough to be in business for the pass-through deduction, it should be enough for other purposes.

When Rentals Are Not a Business

If you own only one or a few units and spend minimal time dealing with them, you could have trouble showing that your management activities (or those of an agent) are sufficiently continuous, systematic, and regular to be a business. Ironically, this issue is more likely where you have good stable tenants who cause few problems and make little demand on your time.

> EXAMPLE: Edgar Grier inherited a house from his mother that she had rented out for many years to the same tenant. This same tenant continued to occupy the property until Grier sold it 14 years later. Over the years, Grier managed the property himself or with the help of an agent. Little management work was required, but Grier did take care of such details as replacing the furnace. The IRS and court found that the house was an investment, not a business, for Grier. The court noted that this was the only rental property Grier had ever owned and concluded that his landlord activities were too minimal to rise to the level of a business. (*Grier v. United States*, 120 F.Supp. 395 (D. Conn. 1954).)

Other cases where landlords have been found to be investors are those involving triple net leases of commercial properties where the tenant is required to manage the property and pay all taxes, insurance, and other expenses. The landlord does nothing but deposit the rent checks. (*Neill v. Comm'r.*, 46 B.T.A. 197.) Triple net leases are not usually used for residential rental properties. But if you have an arrangement with a tenant that requires the tenant, not you, to take care of the property, the IRS could conclude you're not in business. Courts have also held that landlords were not in business where they rented out their property only to their children or friends. (*Vandeyacht v. Comm'r.*, T.C. Memo 1994-148; *Rivera v. Comm'r.*, T.C. Summ. Op. 2004-81.)

Also, if your rental property is vacant all or most of the time, the IRS could decide that you are an investor, because you wouldn't need to spend much time dealing with the property. The IRS might also take the position that vacant properties involve a not-for-profit activity.

Finally, people who purchase interests in business entities that own real estate, but aren't actively involved in management of the entities, are also investors for tax purposes. These include the limited partners in limited partnerships that own real estate, and people who own shares in corporations and REITs (real estate investment trusts).

If none of these exceptions apply, your rental activity will likely qualify as a business for tax purposes if you actively offer your property for rent to the general public at a fair market rent.

The Importance of Good Records

If you want to make sure you qualify as a business owner, it's important that you keep track of the landlord tasks you perform and the time you spend performing these tasks. Your records don't have to be fancy—notes on a calendar will do. (See Chapter 17.) But keep track of the dates and time you spend on tasks such as taking care of repairs, dealing with tenant complaints, showing the property, negotiating leases, and so forth. This record will show that you were actively engaged in the business of being a landlord. Good record keeping will not only help establish you are in business, but can also help you avoid restrictive rules on deducting losses from real estate. (See Chapter 16.) In addition, whenever you pay $600 or more to an independent contractor during the year to perform services for your rental business, be sure to file all required IRS Form 1099-NECs. (See Chapter 13.)

Tax Consequences

At first glance, you might not see much difference, taxwise, between landlords who are business owners and those who are investors. They both file the same tax form to report their income and expenses—Schedule E. And, they don't need to indicate on their tax returns whether their rental activities are businesses or investments. In addition, neither one has to pay self-employment taxes on any rental income. (See Chapter 13.)

Investors and business owners are also entitled to many of the same deductions. People who own businesses are entitled to deduct their ordinary and necessary expenses. (I.R.C. § 162.) Investors are entitled to deduct any ordinary and necessary expenses they incur in connection with producing or collecting income, or managing, conserving, or maintaining property they hold to produce income—for example, a real estate rental. (I.R.C. § 212.)

So, both business owners and investors may deduct:

- repair costs (see Chapter 4)
- depreciation (see Chapter 5)
- bonus depreciation (see Chapter 5)
- interest (see Chapter 8)
- taxes (see Chapter 15)
- car and local travel expenses (see Chapter 11)
- long-distance travel expenses (see Chapter 12)
- meal expenses (see Chapter 15)
- the costs of hiring workers (see Chapter 13)
- casualty losses (see Chapter 14)
- payments for professional services (see Chapter 3), and
- other operating expenses, such as advertising and insurance (see Chapter 3).

And the requirements to qualify for these deductions are the same for business owners and investors.

The similarities end there, however. Taxwise, business owners are much better off than investors because they're entitled to take certain valuable deductions that investors can't take. These business-only deductions include:

- **Net investment income tax.** Rental income earned by a taxpayer who qualifies as a real estate professional for tax purposes will not be subject to the 3.8% net investment income tax if the rental activity qualifies as a business. If the activity is an investment, the rental income will be subject to the tax even though the landlord is a real estate professional.

- **Pass-through income tax deduction.** Investors can't take advantage of the pass-through tax deduction that enables business owners to deduct up to 20% of their net business income from their income taxes during 2018 through 2025. (See Chapter 7.)

- **Home office deduction.** Investors can't take a home office deduction. This important deduction is available only for businesses conducted from home. (See Chapter 10.)

- **Section 179 expensing.** Investors can't take advantage of Section 179, the tax code provision that allows businesspeople to deduct a substantial amount in purchases of long-term personal property in a single year. (See Chapter 5.)
- **Seminar or convention deductions.** Investors can't deduct their expenses for attending conventions, seminars, or similar events. So, for example, the cost of attending a real estate investment seminar isn't deductible for investors. Businesspeople can qualify for such deductions. (See Chapter 12.)
- **Start-up expense deduction.** Up to $5,000 of the costs you incur to start your rental business may be deducted in the first year your business is in operation. Any amount over the limit must be deducted in equal installments over the first 180 months you're in business. (See Chapter 9 for more on deducting start-up costs.) You get no deduction at all for expenses incurred in starting up an investment activity.
- **Real estate losses.** If an investor loses money when selling real estate, the loss is a capital loss. Investors can deduct only $3,000 in capital losses each year from their ordinary income—that is, income not derived from capital assets like real estate, stocks, bonds, and other investments. Business owners get much better tax treatment when it comes to losses. Any gains they earn when they sell real estate used in their business and held for more than one year are taxed at capital gains rates—usually lower than the normal income tax rates. But, if a business owner sells business real property at a loss, the loss is deductible in full from all of the owner's income, not just income from capital assets. (I.R.C. § 1231.) So, when it comes to buying and selling real estate, business owners have the best of both worlds—their gains are taxed as capital gains, but their losses are treated as ordinary losses. (See Chapter 16 for more on real estate losses.)

Because of these valuable deductions, it is better to qualify as a business owner than an investor. Be careful, however, when you decide which deductions you are entitled to take. If you decide you are a business and take some business-only deductions, the IRS could audit your return and conclude that you are an investor instead. Not only would you be denied the business-only deductions in the future, you would also have to pay back taxes and interest on any business-only deductions you took.

> EXAMPLE: Byron Anderson, a nurse-anesthetist, owned an 80-acre farm that he rented to a tenant farmer. He used a room in his home as a home office from which he conducted his landlord activities. He claimed a home office deduction for the room. The IRS audited Anderson and denied the deduction because it claimed his rental activities were an investment, not a business. The tax court agreed with the IRS, and Anderson lost the deduction. (*Anderson v. Comm'r.*, T.C. Memo 1982-576.)

Are You Profit Motivated?

It goes without saying that the primary reason most people own residential rental property is to earn a profit—that is, to make more money than they spend on the activity. But this isn't always the case. If your primary motivation for owning a rental is something other than earning a profit, your rental activity must be classified as a not-for-profit activity. This classification should be avoided whenever possible—it is a tax disaster.

SKIP AHEAD
If you earn a profit from your rental activities every year (or at least most years), you can skip this section. If you're earning a profit, you'll have no trouble showing the IRS that you're profit motivated. Indeed, under those circumstances, it's highly unlikely that the profit issue would even be brought up in an audit.

What Is a Not-for-Profit Activity?

A not-for-profit activity is something you do primarily for a reason other than earning money—for example, for recreational or charitable purposes. Activities like artwork, coin and stamp collecting, and writing typically qualify as not-for-profit activities for tax purposes. Horse and dog breeding are also frequently found to be not-for-profit activities by the IRS.

Owning rental real estate, on the other hand, is not usually a not-for-profit activity. However, three common situations exist where owning rental property could be a not-for-profit activity:

- you rent out a vacation home you or your family also use
- you rent property to others at below-market rates, or
- you allow your rental property to sit vacant for a substantial time.

Vacation Homes

If you consistently lose money on a vacation home or second home that you rent out part of the year and also live in part of the time, there's a good chance the IRS will question whether your rental activity is profit motivated, or you own the home primarily for the not-for-profit purpose of having a place to take vacations. To overcome this, you would have to be able to show that you made real efforts to find tenants to earn a profit.

> EXAMPLE: Mr. and Mrs. Hilliard, both full-time physicians, purchased a rental condominium for $106,000 in beautiful Lake Tahoe. Unfortunately, their investment didn't turn out to be so beautiful—they consistently spent more on mortgage payments, maintenance, interest, taxes, and depreciation than they took in in rental income. They averaged only $711 in rental income per year over a five-year period, while their expenses averaged over $19,000. They made almost no efforts to find tenants—for example, they did not place the property with a real estate agent. The only advertising they did was to post rental flyers at the hospitals where they practiced medicine. Meanwhile, they used the property for personal trips and recreational purposes. Both the IRS and tax court found that the Hilliards' vacation rental was a not-for-profit activity. (*Hilliard v. Comm'r.*, T.C. Memo 1995-473.)

Renting to Relatives

Renting out property at below-market rates (or for nothing) to relatives, friends, or others can be a red flag for the IRS and courts, indicating that you lack a profit motive.

EXAMPLE: Eugene Walet, a successful businessman, purchased a house in New Orleans and allowed his ex-wife and their son to live in it rent-free for seven years. Walet's ex-wife had health problems and didn't work, so Walet never expected to be able to collect rent from her. Both the IRS and tax court found that Walet had purchased and maintained the house for the personal motive of helping his ex-wife and son and not to earn a profit, either from rent or from appreciation. So, the activity had to be classified as a not-for-profit activity for tax purposes. As a result, Walet couldn't deduct depreciation and repair expenses for the house. (*Walet v. Comm'r.*, 31 T.C. 461.)

Vacant Rental Property

Allowing your rental property to stand vacant for a substantial time can also lead the IRS to conclude you lack a profit motive unless you have a good reason you've been unable to find a tenant.

Tax Consequences of Not-for-Profit Rentals

Operating an activity which is classified as a hobby for tax purposes has always been a tax disaster. However, as a result of the Tax Cuts and Jobs Act (TCJA), it is now a tax apocalypse. Under prior law, expenses from a hobby could be deducted as a personal itemized deduction on IRS Schedule A to the extent the expenses exceeded 2% of the taxpayer's adjusted gross income. But these deductible hobby expenses couldn't exceed hobby income. The TCJA completely removes the personal deduction for hobby expenses starting in 2018 through 2025. So, while the income from a rental activity classified as a hobby must be reported and tax paid on it, no expenses may be deducted.

EXAMPLE: Flora owns a rental home she rents to her son at 25% of the market rate. The IRS determines this rental is a not-for-profit activity. As a result, Flora must report and pay tax on the rental income she receives but can deduct none of her rental expenses during 2018 through 2025. Her son paid her $4,000 in rent during 2018. She must report and pay tax on the full amount, with no deductions for depreciation, repairs, property tax, or anything else.

How to Show Your Profit Motive

It's usually not difficult to show that your primary motive for owning real estate is to earn a profit. You can do this by actually earning a profit from your rental activities or acting like you want to earn a profit.

Three-of-Five Test

If you earn a profit from your rentals in three out of five consecutive years, the IRS must presume that you have a profit motive. Any legitimate profit no matter how small qualifies; you don't have to earn a particular amount or percentage. If you meet the three-of-five test, the IRS can still claim that your activity is a not-for-profit activity, but it will have to prove that you don't have a profit motive. In practice, the IRS usually doesn't attack ventures that pass the profit test unless the numbers have clearly been manipulated to meet the standard.

The presumption that you are engaged in a for-profit activity applies to your third profitable year and extends to all later years within the five-year period beginning with your first profitable year.

> EXAMPLE: Tom purchased a fixer-upper duplex in 2017 and rented out both units. Because Tom had to make extensive repairs to the property, the rent he collected was less than his expenses for the first two years. However, he managed to earn a profit in the next three years so he passed the three-of-five profit test.
>
> | Year | Losses | Profits |
> |------|--------|---------|
> | 2018 | $5,000 | |
> | 2019 | $2,000 | |
> | 2020 | | $2,000 |
> | 2021 | | $4,000 |
> | 2022 | | $5,000 |
>
> If the IRS audits Tom's taxes for 2022, it must presume that he was engaged in a for-profit activity during that year. Tom earned a profit during three out of the five consecutive years ending with 2022, so the presumption that Tom is not engaged in a not-for-profit activity extends to 2024, five years after his first profitable year.

The IRS doesn't have to wait for five years after you become a landlord to decide whether it is a for-profit or not-for-profit activity. It can audit you and classify your venture as a business or not-for-profit activity at any time. However, you can give yourself some breathing room by filing IRS Form 5213, which requires the IRS to postpone its determination until you've been engaged in the activity for at least five years. Although this might sound like a good idea, filing the election only alerts the IRS to the fact that you might be a good candidate to audit on the not-for-profit activity issue after five years. It also adds two years to the statute of limitations—the period in which the IRS can audit you and assess a tax deficiency. For this reason, almost no one ever files Form 5213.

Behavior Test

It is not necessary that you actually earn a profit for your rental activities to be viewed as profit motivated. Even if you consistently lose money, your rental activity is profit motivated if you entered into the activity primarily to earn profits—not to get tax deductions, help your relatives, have a place to vacation, or for some other reason not involving profit. Many people who want to earn profits from real estate rentals have negative cash flows—that is, they spend more on their rental property than they get back in rent. Indeed, IRS statistics show that of the 8.6 million tax returns filed by landlords in one recent year, more than 4.5 million showed a loss. However, these landlords expect to eventually earn a profit from an appreciation in the value of the real estate, an increase in rent, a decrease in expenses, or some combination of these.

How does the IRS figure out whether you really want to earn a profit? IRS auditors can't read your mind to establish your motives, and they certainly aren't going to take your word for it. Instead, the IRS looks at the following "objective" factors to determine whether you are behaving like a person who wants to earn a profit. You don't have to satisfy all of these factors to pass the test. The first three listed below (acting like a business, expertise, and time and effort expended) are the most important. Studies show that taxpayers who meet these three factors are always found to be profit motivated, regardless of how they do on the rest of the criteria listed below:

- **How the activity is carried on.** Among other things, acting like a business means you keep good books and other records and carry on your rental activities in a professional manner.

- **Your expertise.** People who are trying to make money usually have some knowledge and skill in the field of their endeavor.

- **The time and effort you spend.** People who want to make profits work regularly and continuously. You don't have to work full time, but you must work regularly.

- **Your track record.** Having a track record of success in other businesses —whether or not they are related to your landlord activities—helps show that you are trying to make money in your most recent venture.

- **Your history of income and losses.** Even if you can't satisfy the profit test described above, earning a profit in at least some years helps show that you have a profit motive.

- **Your profits.** Earning a substantial profit, even after years of losses, can help show that you are trying to make a go of it. On the other hand, earning only small or occasional yearly profits when you have years of large losses and/or a large investment in the activity tends to show that you aren't in it for the money.

- **Appreciation.** Your profit includes money you make through the appreciation (increase in value) of your business assets. For a landlord, this primarily includes the increase in value of the rental properties that are owned. Even if you don't make any profit from your day-to-day rental operations, you can still show a profit motive if you stand to earn substantial profits when you sell your real estate.

- **Your personal wealth.** The IRS figures that you probably have a profit motive if you don't have substantial income from other sources. After all, you'll need to earn money from your venture to survive. On the other hand, the IRS may be suspicious if you have substantial income from other sources (particularly if the losses from your real estate venture generate substantial tax deductions).

- **Elements of fun or recreation.** You'll have a harder time convincing the IRS that you're profit motivated if your rental activity involves fun or recreation. For example, a person who owns a rental unit at a resort and spends substantial time vacationing there will have a hard time claiming a profit motive (assuming no profits are earned on the rental).

How to Pass the Behavior Test

If you continually lose money on your rentals, particularly if you rent them out at below-market rates or keep them vacant, you should take steps to ensure that the IRS will not claim that you lack a profit motive in the event you're audited. Take these steps:

- **Keep good business records.** Keeping good records of your expenses and income from your activity is the single most important thing you can do to show that you want to earn a profit. Lack of records shows that you don't really care whether you make money or not. You don't need an elaborate set of books; a simple record of your expenses and income will usually suffice. (See Chapter 17 for a detailed discussion of record keeping.)
- **Keep a separate checking account.** Open up a separate checking account for your rental activity. This will help you keep your personal and rental expenses separate—another factor that shows you want to make money.
- **Keep track of the time you spend.** It is not necessary that you work full time at being a landlord to have a profit motive. However, the more time you spend at being a landlord, the more it will look like you want to earn a profit. Keep track of your time. This will also be necessary if you want to avoid application of the restrictive rules on deducting real estate losses (see Chapter 16).
- **Make efforts to rent your property.** Letting a property stand vacant without making any efforts to find a renter tends to show you don't care about earning a profit. If your property is vacant, try to find renters by advertising and listing it with rental services. Keep records of your efforts.
- **Establish your expertise.** If you lack a solid background in owning and managing rental property, make up for it by attending educational seminars and other programs—for example, educational events sponsored by your local apartment owners' association.

- **Show you expect your property to appreciate in value.** Real estate appreciation is often the pot of gold at the end of the landlord rainbow. The fact that you expect your property to substantially increase in value in the future is strong evidence you want to earn a profit, even if you are incurring losses right now. You can show the IRS that you expect your property to appreciate in value because (1) you've owned similar properties that have gone up in value, (2) similar properties in the area have appreciated, and (3) the property has, in fact, gone up in value since you bought it.
- **Prepare a business plan showing how much money you expect to earn or lose over the next several years.** This is a projection of how much money your rental activity will bring in, your expenses, and how much profit you expect to make (or losses you'll incur). The forecast should cover at least the next five or ten years. It should show you earning a profit sometime in the future (although it doesn't have to be within five years). This profit can result from anticipated increases in your rents, decreases in expenses, appreciation in the value of your property, or some combination of all three. You can prepare such projections yourself (special software is available for this purpose), or you can have an accountant or real estate professional create one for you.

What If You Make a Bad Investment?

What if you went into rental property ownership to make money, but your investment turned out badly? Fortunately, the IRS recognizes that owning rental property can end up being a bad investment, but still be profit motivated. IRS regulations provide that a taxpayer may be deemed to be profit motivated, even if the property isn't currently productive and "there is no likelihood that the property will be sold at a profit or will otherwise be productive of income; and even though the property is held merely to minimize a loss." (IRS Reg. § 1.212-1(b).) So, you can be profit motivated even if your rental property doesn't produce any current income. For example, an owner of a vacant rental might want to earn a profit, but be prevented from doing so by a bad rental market or other circumstances beyond the owner's control.

Deducting Your Operating Expenses

This chapter covers the basic rules for deducting operating expenses you incur from your residential rental activities. These expenses are the bread-and-butter expenses virtually every landlord has for things like repairs, management fees, and advertising.

Requirements for Deducting Operating Expenses

Because so many different kinds of operating expenses exist, the tax code couldn't possibly list them all. Instead, the code gives you the definition of an operating expense, and it's up to you to make sure the expenditures you deduct meet the requirements. If they do, they'll qualify as deductible operating expenses. To qualify, the expense must be:

- ordinary and necessary
- current
- directly related to your rental activity, and
- reasonable in amount. (I.R.C. § 162.)

Ordinary and Necessary

The first requirement is that the expense must be ordinary and necessary, which means that the expense is common and "helpful and appropriate" for your activity. (*Welch v. Helvering*, 290 U.S. 111 (1933).) The expense doesn't have to be indispensable to be necessary; it only has to help your rental activity in some way—even if it's minor. A one-time expenditure can be ordinary and necessary.

It's usually fairly easy to figure out whether an expense passes the ordinary and necessary test. Many of the most common types of landlord operating expenses are listed on IRS Schedule E, including:

- advertising your rental units
- auto and travel expenses you or your staff incur
- cleaning and maintenance
- commissions you pay to rental brokers, if you use them
- insurance, such as property and commercial general liability insurance, and part of your automobile insurance if you use your car for rental activities

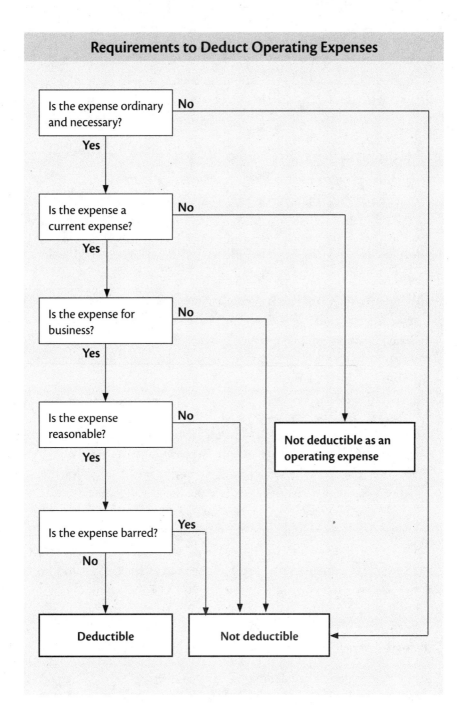

- legal and other professional fees, such as accounting fees
- management fees, should you decide to hire a management company to handle day-to-day operations
- mortgage interest paid to banks or other financial institutions
- other interest expenses, such as interest on a credit card you use to buy items for your rental activity
- repairs
- supplies to clean and refurbish your rental property
- taxes, and
- utilities.

This list the IRS created is by no means exhaustive. In addition to the items listed, you might also have deductible operating expenses for such things as office rent, equipment rental, publications and subscriptions (including the cost of this book!), education expenses, postage, software, payments to independent contractors, membership fees for landlord associations, and so on.

Generally, the IRS won't second-guess your claim that an expense is ordinary and necessary, unless the item or service clearly has no legitimate business purpose. You will not be allowed to deduct off-the-wall or clearly ridiculous expenses.

> **EXAMPLE:** Rayford Strickland owned two parcels of real estate about 500 miles from his Texas home. During a two-year period, he made 80 trips to the property at a claimed cost of $11,000. The properties generated a total of $1,653 in income during this time. The IRS and tax court disallowed Strickland's travel expense deductions. The court found that the 80 trips were not an ordinary and necessary expense because Strickland was unable to provide any explanation of why it was necessary to make so many trips to these two properties. (*Strickland v. Comm'r.*, 43 T.C. Memo 1061.)

Current Expense

Only current expenses are deductible as operating expenses. Current expenses are for items that will benefit your rental activity for less than one year. These expenses are the costs of keeping your rental venture going on a day-to-day basis, including money you spend on items or services that get used up, wear out, or become obsolete in less than one year. A good example of a current expense is the monthly fee a landlord pays to a gardener to perform landscaping work on a rental property. Each monthly fee benefits the landlord's rental activity for less than one year, so it is a current expense.

You deduct operating expenses in the year in which they're incurred —this helps your bottom line. Not everything you buy for your rental activity qualifies as a current expense. Anything you purchase that will benefit your rental activity for more than one year is a capital, not a current, expense. For example, if a landlord purchases a lawn mower to use for his rental properties, the purchase would be a capital expense (not a current expense) because the lawn mower will benefit the rental activity for more than one year. In some cases, capital expenses may only be deducted a little at a time over many years through a process known as "depreciation," which is the case for rental buildings and other real property. However, long-term personal property like a lawn mower can usually be deducted in one year using 100% bonus depreciation, Section 179 expensing, or the de minimis safe harbor.

Repairs to real property are current expenses that may be deducted in a single year. For example, replacing a few shingles on the roof of a rental house is a repair that can be currently deducted. However, improvements to real property that extend the property's useful life or make it more valuable must be depreciated. So, the cost of purchasing and installing a whole new roof for a rental home would be a capital expense that would have to be depreciated over several years. It is sometimes difficult to tell the difference between a deductible repair and depreciable improvement. This important issue is covered in detail in Chapter 5.

Business-Related

An expenditure must be *directly related to your rental activity* to be deductible as an operating expense. So, you can't deduct personal expenses. For example, the cost of a personal computer is a deductible operating expense only if you use the computer for your rental activities; it isn't deductible if you use it to pay personal bills or play computer games.

Allocating Business and Personal Use

If you buy something for both personal and landlord use, you can deduct only the business portion of the expense. You must figure out how much of the time you used the item for landlord purposes and how much for personal purposes. You then allocate the total cost between the two purposes, and deduct only the landlord portion of the cost.

> **EXAMPLE:** Sam rents a small outside office for $100 per month. He uses it five hours a week for his rental activities and 15 hours for personal use. So, he uses it 25% of the time for landlord purposes and 75% for personal reasons. He may deduct only 25% of the cost of the office, or $25 per month, as an operating expense.

The same allocation rule applies when you rent out part of a house that you live in.

> **EXAMPLE:** Sheila owns a three-bedroom house that she uses as her residence. She rents out one of the bedrooms, which represents 15% of the total house. Sheila may deduct 15% of the cost of utilities and maintenance for the whole house as a landlord operating expense. She could deduct 100% of the cost of any expense incurred just for the rented bedroom— for example, the cost of repainting the bedroom.

Stricter Rules for Certain Expenses

Many expenses have both a personal and a business component, which can make it difficult to tell if an expense is business related. For example, what if a landlord drives to the hardware store and buys one item for his rental property and another for his personal residence? Should he be allowed to deduct all, part, or none of the cost of driving to the hardware store?

The IRS has created rules and regulations for some operating expenses that commonly involve a crossover of personal and business use. Some of these rules lay out guidelines to help you figure out when an expense is and isn't deductible. Others impose record-keeping and other requirements to prevent abuses by dishonest taxpayers. Much of the complexity in determining whether an expense is deductible as a business operating expense involves understanding and applying these special rules and regulations.

The expenses that present the most common problems (and are, therefore, subject to the most comprehensive IRS rules and regulations) include:

- home office expenses (see Chapter 10)
- meals (see Chapter 15)
- travel (see Chapter 12)
- car and truck expenses (see Chapter 11)
- business gifts (see Chapter 15)
- bad debts (see Chapter 15)
- employee benefits (see Chapter 13)
- interest payments (see Chapter 8)
- casualty losses (see Chapter 14)
- taxes (see Chapter 15), and
- education expenses (see Chapter 15).

Landlord's Personal Labor Not Deductible

A landlord may never deduct the value of their own time and personal labor working on rental activities. For example, a landlord who spends 50 hours repainting an apartment building gets no deduction for the value of his time. He may only deduct the cost of the paint, brushes, and other materials he uses. This rule prevents the kind of abuse the IRS fears would happen if personal labor were deductible.

Landlords may deduct labor costs only when they hire other people to do the work and pay them for it. The labor can be performed by an employee or independent contractor (nonemployee), or even a member of the landlord's family. (See Chapter 13.)

However, this doesn't mean landlords should never do any work on their rental properties themselves. Although your personal labor is not deductible, you'll still save money by doing the work yourself because only a part of the money you deduct for labor costs ends up as a tax savings. (See Chapter 13.)

Reasonable in Amount

Subject to some important exceptions, no limit applies to how much you can deduct, as long as the amount is reasonable and you don't deduct more than you spend. As a rule of thumb, an expense is reasonable unless there are more economical and practical ways to achieve the same result. If the IRS finds that your deductions are unreasonably large, it will disallow them or at least disallow the portion it finds unreasonable.

Certain areas are hot buttons for the IRS—especially travel and meal expenses. The IRS won't allow any lavish expenses here, and you will have to follow strict rules requiring you to fully document these deductions (see Chapters 12 and 15). The reasonableness issue also comes up when a business pays excessive salaries to employees to obtain a large tax deduction. For example, a landlord might hire his 14-year-old son to do yard work for his rental units and pay him $50 an hour—clearly an excessive wage for this type of work.

For a few types of operating expenses, the IRS limits how much you can deduct. These include:

- the home office deduction, which is limited to the profit from your business (although you can carry over and deduct any excess amount in future years) (see Chapter 10)
- business meals, which are ordinarily only 50% deductible, but are 100% deductible if purchased from restaurants during 2021–2022 (see Chapter 15)
- travel expenses, which are limited depending on the length of your trip and the time you spend on business while away (see Chapter 12), and
- business gifts, which are subject to a $25 maximum deduction per individual per year (see Chapter 15).

Operating Expenses That Are Not Deductible

Even though they might be ordinary and necessary, some types of operating expenses aren't deductible under any circumstances. In some cases, Congress has declared that it would be morally wrong or otherwise contrary to sound public policy to allow people to deduct these costs. In other cases, Congress simply doesn't want to allow the deduction. These nondeductible expenses include:

- business-related entertainment expenses, including country club or ski outings, theater or sporting event tickets, entertainment at nightclubs, or hunting, fishing, or vacation trips; however, business-related meals are deductible (see Chapter 15)
- fines and penalties paid to the government for violation of any law—for example, tax penalties, parking tickets, or fines for violating city housing codes (I.R.C. § 162(f))
- illegal bribes or kickbacks to private parties or government officials (I.R.C. § 162(c))
- lobbying expenses or political contributions
- real estate examination or licensing fees, or other professional examination fees (see Chapter 9)
- charitable donations by any business other than a C corporation (these donations are deductible only as personal expenses; see Chapter 15)
- country club, social club, or athletic club dues
- federal income taxes you pay on your rental income (see Chapter 15), and
- certain interest payments (see Chapter 8).

Repairs

R epair expenses are among the most valuable deductions landlords have. However, many landlords are surprised to discover that some of the changes they make to their property aren't repairs at all; instead, they're improvements that must be deducted much more slowly than repairs. This chapter shows you how to tell the difference between a repair and an improvement, and how to deduct as quickly as possible the expenses you incur to maintain your property.

IRS Rules: Repairs Versus Improvements

Provided they are ordinary, necessary, and reasonable in amount, repairs to your rental property are operating expenses that are fully deductible in the year in which they are incurred. However, not all upkeep constitutes a repair for tax purposes. Some changes landlords make to their rental property are capital improvements. Unlike repairs, improvements to real property (rental buildings and building components) can't be deducted in a single year. Instead, their cost must be depreciated over several years. Improvements to residential rental real property must be depreciated over an especially long period—27.5 years.

In contrast, land improvements can usually be deducted in one year using bonus depreciation during 2018 through 2022. Improvements to personal property used in your rental activity—for example, new appliances or carpeting in rental units—can also usually be deducted in one year using bonus depreciation, Section 179 expensing, or the de minimis safe harbor. However, repairs still remain superior to improvements for tax purposes. (See "Why Repairs Are Better Than Depreciation Deductions," below.)

Unfortunately, telling the difference between a repair and an improvement isn't always easy. In an effort to clarify matters, the IRS issued a 222-page set of repair regulations that took effect in 2014. Moreover, larger landlords had to apply them to expenses for repairs and improvements to rental property owned before 2014 as well.

The repair regulations are contained in Internal Revenue Bulletin 2013-43 (available at www.irs.gov/irb/2013-43_IRB/ar05.html; the IRS has created a detailed set of FAQs about them at www.irs.gov/businesses/small-businesses-self-employed/tangible-property-final-regulations).

The repair regulations are a mixed bag for landlords. On the good side, they include three safe harbors that permit many landlords—particularly those with small holdings—to currently deduct all or most of their expenses, whether they are classified as repairs or improvements.

But, in cases where the safe harbors can't be used, the regulations make it more difficult to classify fix-ups and other building expenses as currently deductible repairs.

Why Repairs Are Better Than Depreciation Deductions

It's always better to deduct an expense as a repair (or using one of the safe harbors discussed below) than to depreciate the cost as an improvement. This is true even if 100% of the cost can be deducted in one year using bonus depreciation or Section 179 expensing (which is something you can only do with personal property and land improvements, not building improvements; see Chapter 5). The reason repairs are better is that they are treated as a business operating expense. You get to deduct the full amount in the year the repair expense is incurred and there will be no tax impact when you later sell the property.

In contrast, when you deduct an expense through regular depreciation, bonus depreciation, or Section 179 expensing, the expense can result in extra tax when you sell the property. If you sell real property at a profit, you must pay tax at a rate up to 25% on your total depreciation deductions. If separately deducted personal property is involved, you pay tax on your regular or bonus depreciation or Section 179 deductions at your ordinary income tax rates (as much as 37%). This is called "recapture" because deductions you previously took are recaptured into your income and taxed.

On the other hand, the regulations give landlords a new deduction: Landlords can elect to take an immediate deductible loss when building components are replaced instead of having to continue to depreciate the old components over many years. This greatly speeds up the process of deducting old building components that are replaced when they wear out, become obsolete, or are damaged.

Three Safe Harbors

The IRS repair regulations contain three safe harbors that enable landlords to currently deduct as a business operating expense certain building-related costs:

- a safe harbor for small taxpayers
- the routine maintenance safe harbor, and
- the de minimis safe harbor.

If an expense comes within any safe harbor, and it is an ordinary and necessary expense, you may automatically treat the item as a currently deductible operating expense. You don't have to worry about whether the asset involved constitutes real property or personal property, or whether the expense is for an improvement or repair—it's fully deductible either way. And, because you're not taking a depreciation deduction, the deduction is not later subject to recapture when you sell your property.

You always have the option of using the regular repair regulations if you wish. But the safe harbors are designed to make your life easier and simpler, and often enable you to deduct expenses that otherwise would have to be depreciated under the more complicated regular rules. So, you usually will want to take advantage of them if you can. It's possible for an expense to fall within more than one safe harbor although you only need to come within one of the three.

To determine whether an expense qualifies for a current deduction under the IRS's repair regulations, you can use a three-step approach:

1. Determine whether the expense qualifies as a current deduction under one of three new safe harbor tests.

2. If none of the safe harbors apply, determine whether the expense is a deductible repair or improvement under the regular repair versus improvement rules laid out in the IRS repair regulations.

3. If you determine the expense is for an improvement, determine if the asset is real property (building or building component) or personal property. If it's personal property, determine if you can deduct the expense in one year using the de minimis safe harbor, bonus depreciation, or Section 179 expensing. (See Chapter 5.)

When you are figuring out if an expense falls within a safe harbor, you should analyze it under the safe harbors in the order presented below.

Safe Harbor for Small Taxpayers (SHST)

The safe harbor for small taxpayers (SHST) is the single most important safe harbor for smaller landlords. (IRS Reg. § 1.263(a)-3h.) If you qualify to use it, you may currently deduct as an operating expense on Schedule E all your annual expenses for repairs, maintenance, improvements, and other costs for a rental building. If so, you won't need to worry about any of the other safe harbors or the regular repair versus improvement regulations. However, there are significant restrictions on which landlords may use this safe harbor. In addition, to take advantage of this safe harbor, landlords need to keep careful track of all their annual expenses for repairs, maintenance, improvements, and similar items—something they should be doing anyway.

Rental Business Size Limitations

As the name implies, the SHST is intended to be used by landlords with relatively small rental businesses. So, strict limits apply to the value of buildings that may qualify under the safe harbor and to the annual amounts landlords can spend and earn. You can't use this safe harbor in any year any of these limits are exceeded. But, so long as you come within these limits, you may use the SHST for any number of rental buildings or units—you aren't limited to just one.

$1 million building value limit. The SHST may be used only for buildings—including condos and co-ops—with an unadjusted basis of $1 million or less. So, it can't be used for many larger apartment buildings or other more expensive rental buildings. "Unadjusted basis" usually means a building's original cost (also called its "cost basis"), not including the cost of the land. (See Chapter 5 for a detailed discussion of how to determine a building's basis.) To determine a building's unadjusted basis, you don't subtract the annual amounts you deduct for depreciation. But you add the value of any improvements you make to the building while you own it and that you are depreciating along with the rest of the building.

> **EXAMPLE:** Shaeeda owns an apartment building with an unadjusted basis of $900,000. This year, she installs a new roof at a cost of $110,000. Her building's basis is now over $1 million and does not qualify for the SHST.

If you own more than one rental unit or building, the $1 million limit is applied to each separately. So, for example, a landlord with ten rental buildings each with an unadjusted basis of less than $1 million can use the SHST for each of them. If the taxpayer is leasing the building, the unadjusted basis of the leasehold interest is equal to the total amount of (undiscounted) rent paid or expected to be paid over the entire lease term, including expected renewals.

Annual expense limit. A landlord may use the SHST only if the total amount paid during the year for repairs, maintenance, improvements, and similar expenses for a building does not exceed the lesser of $10,000 or 2% of the unadjusted basis of the building.

> **EXAMPLE:** Sam owns a rental home with a $100,000 unadjusted basis (that is, it cost $100,000). He may use the SHST only in those years where the total amount he spends on the building is $2,000 or less (2% × 100,000 = $2,000).

The 2% of the adjusted basis rule means that a building with basis greater than $500,000, but not more than $1,000,000, will still have the $10,000 annual limit.

Cost Segregation Can Help You Qualify for SHST

To come within the $1 million SHST limit, you can reduce a rental building's unadjusted basis by using cost segregation segmented depreciation. As discussed in Chapter 6, building owners ordinarily include the value of land improvements and personal property inside their buildings in the building's basis. However, by using cost segregation you can separately depreciate land improvements (like driveways and landscaping) and personal property in rental units such as appliances. This will reduce the basis of the building and can make the difference in a building qualifying for the SHST.

EXAMPLE 1: Sonia owns a five-unit apartment building that cost $1.2 million. This is $200,000 over the SHST limit. However, she determines that the land improvements cost $100,000 and the personal property in the units cost another $100,000. She depreciates the land improvements and personal property separately, over 15 and five years, respectively. This leaves the apartment building itself with an unadjusted basis of $1 million, allowing her to use the SHST.

Additionally, the money you spend on repairs, maintenance, and improvements for such separate land improvements and personal property is not counted toward the $10,000 annual SHST limit discussed below.

EXAMPLE 2: Assume that one year Sonia spends $5,000 to repave the parking lot of her apartment building and another $10,000 on maintenance and improvements for the building itself. She need not include the $5,000 when determining whether her building qualifies for the SHST because the parking lot is a land improvement she is depreciating separately from the building. As a result, her total expenses for the year are $10,000—within the SHST annual limit.

The limit is applied on a per-building basis—for example, if you own three rental homes, you apply the limit to each home separately. So, you might be able to use the SHST for some, but not others.

> **EXAMPLE:** Riley owns two rental homes, both with an unadjusted basis of $200,000. He may spend a maximum of $4,000 on each and qualify for the SHST. During the year he spends $3,000 on House A and $6,000 on House B. He may use the SHST for House A, but not House B.

When computing the amount you spend for purposes of the SHST annual limit, you count everything you spent during the year, including amounts that may come within the routine maintenance and de minimis safe harbors discussed below. If you can't use the SHST because the limit is exceeded, you may still use these other safe harbors.

> **EXAMPLE:** Stu owns a rental building with an unadjusted basis of $500,000. His annual SHST limit is $10,000. This year, Stu spends the following amounts on his rental building: $2,000 for new appliances that come within the de minimis safe harbor, $6,000 for a new furnace, and $4,000 on various maintenance items that come within the routine maintenance safe harbor. Stu doesn't qualify for the SHST because he spent $12,000 on his building. But he may still deduct $6,000 by using the de minimis and routine maintenance safe harbors.

Annual income limit. Finally, to qualify for the SHST a landlord must have average annual gross receipts of no more than $10 million during the three preceding tax years. Gross receipts include income from sales (unreduced by cost of goods), services, and investments. This poses no problem for smaller landlords.

Claiming the SHST

The SHST must be claimed anew each year by filing an election with your timely filed tax return, which must be filed no later than October 15 (if you obtain an extension; September 15 for returns filed by most multimember LLCs, corporations, and partnerships).

> **EXAMPLE:** Sam owns a single-family home that he rents out. It has a $100,000 unadjusted basis (that is, it cost $100,000). This year, he paid $200 to a plumber to fix a leak, repaired a window for $400, and replaced the home's water heater for $1,200. Sam qualifies for the SHST because

the $1,800 he spent on repairs, improvements, and maintenance during the year is less than 2% of his building's unadjusted basis (2% × $100,000 = $2,000). By filing an election to use the SHST, Sam may currently deduct the entire $1,800 on his IRS Schedule E. This is so whether or not any of these expenses, such as the water heater replacement, might constitute an improvement under the regular repair rules discussed below—those complex rules don't have to be applied where the SHST is used.

You can claim the SHST for some years and refrain from doing so for other years—it's entirely up to you. The SHST is also claimed on a building-by-building basis. So, if you own more than one rental building, you can claim the SHST for some rental buildings and not use it for others.

The IRS doesn't have a form for this election. However, it is a very simple document you can easily create yourself and attach to your return. You can use the following format:

Section 1.263(a)-3(h) Safe Harbor Election for Small Taxpayers

Taxpayer's name:
Taxpayer's address:
Taxpayer's identification number:

The taxpayer is hereby making the safe harbor election for small taxpayers under Section 1.263(a)-3(h) for the following building property:

_____[describe]_____.

If the rental property covered by the SHST is owned by a partnership, LLC, or S corporation, the election must be made by the business entity, not by the individual partners, LLC members, or corporate shareholders.

Once this annual election is made, it may not be revoked for the year it covers.

Routine Maintenance Safe Harbor

The second potentially useful safe harbor for landlords is the routine maintenance safe harbor. (IRS Reg. § 1.263(a)-3(i).) Expenses that qualify as routine maintenance under this provision are deductible in a single year. Unlike with the safe harbor for small taxpayers, there are no annual dollar limits with this safe harbor. Any landlord can use it, no matter the cost of the building involved, the amount of the landlord's income, or the amount spent on the maintenance. But some significant limits apply to when rental building owners may use this safe harbor.

What Is "Routine Maintenance"?

Routine maintenance consists of recurring work a building owner does to keep an entire building, or each system in a building, in ordinarily efficient operating condition. Under the IRS's regulations, a building includes the building structure as a whole and nine separate systems (see "Defining the 'Unit of Property' (UOP)," below).

Routine maintenance includes two activities:

- inspection, cleaning, and testing of the building structure and/or each building system, and
- replacement of damaged or worn parts with comparable and commercially available replacement parts.

The first activity—inspection, cleaning, and testing of buildings and building systems—is typically currently deductible in any event as an ordinary and necessary business expense. The ability to currently deduct replacement parts for the building structure and each of the nine separate building systems is the particularly helpful part of this safe harbor.

EXAMPLE: Hasan buys an apartment building that contains a heating, ventilation, and air conditioning (HVAC) system that requires maintenance by an outside contractor every four years. This maintenance includes disassembly, cleaning, inspection, repair, replacement, reassembly, and testing of the HVAC system and many of its component parts. If inspection or testing discloses a problem with any component, the part is repaired or, if necessary, replaced with a comparable and commercially available replacement part. This expense—no matter how much—qualifies for the routine maintenance safe harbor and is currently deductible by Hasan. No muss, no fuss; just deduct the entire amount.

However, two big limitations apply to routine maintenance: the ten-year rule and the no betterments rule.

Ten-Year Rule

Routine maintenance can be performed and deducted under the safe harbor at any time during the property's useful life, including after it has been fully depreciated. However, building maintenance qualifies for the routine maintenance safe harbor only if, when you placed the building or building system into service, you reasonably expected to perform such maintenance more than once every ten years.

> EXAMPLE: Sue owns a duplex she rents out. She reasonably expects to have to touch up the exterior paint on the building at least once every five years. Because Sue expects to perform this maintenance at least twice within ten years, she may deduct the cost of touching up the exterior paint under the routine maintenance safe harbor. Note that Sue could also deduct this expense under safe harbor for small taxpayers (SHST) if she qualified to use it. The advantage of the SHST is that there is no twice-every-ten-years requirement.

In determining whether you can reasonably expect to have to perform the maintenance more than once every ten years, you are supposed to take into consideration factors such as the recurring nature of the activity, industry practice, manufacturers' recommendations, and your own experience with similar or identical property.

A nonexclusive list of examples of maintenance for rental properties routinely performed more than once every ten years likely includes such items as:

- inspecting, cleaning, and repairing HVAC units
- clearing and replacing rain gutters
- inspecting and replacing sprinklers

- smoke detector inspection and replacement
- lighting inspection and replacement
- paint touch-up
- chimney inspection and cleaning
- furnace inspection, cleaning, and repair, and
- inspection and replacement of washing machine hoses.

The more-than-once-every-ten-years requirement would seem to eliminate use of the routine maintenance safe harbor for building components that typically don't need such frequent maintenance—for example, roofs, windows, and wooden or tile flooring. However, repairs to such components may be currently deductible under the regular IRS repair regulations discussed below. For example, the regulations provide that installation of a new waterproof membrane (top layer) on a building's roof to eliminate leaks through an original (worn) membrane is a deductible repair.

Although not strictly required by the IRS, you might want to create a written long-term maintenance plan for your rental property, showing when major maintenance needs to be performed on each building system. You don't need to file the plan with your return. Just keep it in your tax files in the event of an IRS audit (or to show your tax pro who prepares your return).

What if you reasonably expected you'd have to do certain maintenance more than once every ten years, but it turns out it was not required? This situation isn't necessarily a problem. The IRS says that you'll still qualify for the safe harbor if you can show that, when you placed the property in service, you reasonably expected you'd have to perform the maintenance more than once in ten years. But your actual maintenance experience with similar property will be considered in determining whether your expectation was reasonable.

The IRS provides an example of an owner of an office building who reasonably expected that they would have to do detailed testing, monitoring, and preventive maintenance on their HVAC system every four years. The owner does in fact have such maintenance performed four years after the system was placed in service, but doesn't have such maintenance done again until seven years later—11 years after the placed-in-service date. Even so, the owner may use the routine maintenance safe harbor.

No Betterments or Restorations

The routine maintenance safe harbor is intended for expenses property owners incur to keep their property in ordinarily efficient operating condition. Moreover, the maintenance must be attributable to the taxpayer's use of the property, not that of a previous owner. So, the safe harbor doesn't apply to scheduled maintenance performed shortly after purchasing a building.

In addition, this safe harbor isn't supposed to be used to currently deduct major remodeling or restoration projects. It specifically doesn't apply to expenses for betterments or restorations of buildings or other business property in a state of disrepair. So, for example, you can't use the routine maintenance safe harbor to currently deduct the cost of a building remodel or replacing an entire roof. You also can't use the routine maintenance safe harbor for property on which you've taken a casualty loss or made a partial disposition election (see "Deducting Costs for Replaced Building Components" in Chapter 5 for a detailed discussion).

One example the IRS provides in its regulations is that of a cattle rancher who allows his irrigation system canals to fall into such a state of disrepair that they no longer function. The expenses the rancher incurs to drain the canals and do extensive cleaning, repairing, reconditioning, and replacement of parts do not fall within the safe harbor.

Counts Against STSH Limit

Any expense you deduct under the routine maintenance safe harbor is counted toward your annual limit under the SHST. For example, if your annual SHST limit is $5,000 and you deduct $4,000 for maintenance under the routine maintenance safe harbor, you'll only be able to deduct an additional $1,000 under the SHST.

No amount is deductible under the small taxpayer safe harbor if the annual limit is exceeded. So, for example, if your annual SHST limit is $5,000 and you deduct $6,000 under the routine maintenance safe harbor, you won't be entitled to any deduction under the small taxpayer safe harbor. But you can still use the routine maintenance safe harbor.

Applies to Personal Property

The routine maintenance safe harbor may be used for maintenance for personal property—that is, property other than buildings and building components. In this event, the safe harbor applies only if, when you placed the property into service, you reasonably expected to have to perform the maintenance more than once during the property's class life—that is, during the recovery period prescribed by the IRS under the Modified Accelerated Cost Recovery System (MACRS) Alternative Depreciation System (ADS). The ADS class lives for most types of property used by landlords are shown in the following chart.

Asset	ADS Class Life
Office furniture, fixtures, and equipment (includes furniture and fixtures that are not a structural component of a building—for example, refrigerators, stoves, countertops, carpets, kitchen cabinets)	10 years
Computers and peripherals	5 years
Automobiles	5 years
Construction equipment	6 years

So, for example, maintenance for a computer would come within the routine maintenance safe harbor only if the taxpayer reasonably expected to have to perform such maintenance at least twice during the first five years after the asset was placed into service.

Expenses for improvements to (or replacements of) personal property can usually be deducted in full in one year with bonus depreciation or Section 179 expensing. (See Chapter 5.)

Adopting the Routine Maintenance Safe Harbor

Unlike the safe harbor for small taxpayers discussed above, the routine maintenance safe harbor is not elective—that is, it is not claimed each year by filing an optional election with your tax return. Rather, the routine maintenance safe harbor is a method of accounting you adopt. Moreover, after you adopt it, you must use it every year. You adopt the routine maintenance safe harbor by currently deducting expenses that come within it on your books and on your tax return. If you don't want to use this safe harbor, don't adopt it. Its use is completely voluntary.

De Minimis Safe Harbor

The third safe harbor is the de minimis safe harbor (IRS Reg. § 1.263(a)-1(f).) Landlords may use this safe harbor to currently deduct any low-cost items used in their rental business, regardless of whether or not the item would constitute a repair or an improvement under the regular repair regulations. The safe harbor can be used for personal property and for building components that come within the deduction ceiling. For most landlords, the maximum amount that can be deducted under this safe harbor is $2,500 per item. Like the SHST, this safe harbor is claimed by filing an election with your annual tax return. You must also adopt an accounting policy requiring such treatment.

> **EXAMPLE:** Landlord Liam owns a five-unit apartment building. During the year, he purchases new electric stoves for each unit at a cost of $1,000 apiece. He may deduct the entire $5,000 cost using the de minimis safe harbor by filing an election with his tax return.

As with the routine maintenance safe harbor, all expenses you deduct using the de minimis safe harbor must be counted toward the annual limit for using the safe harbor for small taxpayers (the lesser of 2% of the rental's cost or $10,000). For example, if your annual SHST limit is $2,000, and you deduct $2,500 using the de minimis safe harbor, you may not use the SHST that year. But if you deducted only $1,000 using the de minimis safe harbor, you could deduct an additional $1,000 using the SHST.

Personal property items you can deduct with the de minimis safe harbor can usually also be deducted in full in one year with bonus depreciation or Section 179 expensing. But such deductions are subject to recapture when the property is sold. (See Chapter 5 for a detailed analysis of all these deductions.)

Repair Versus Improvement Analysis Under the Regulations

If you're unable to take advantage of any of the safe harbors described above, you must determine whether the expense involved is for an improvement or a repair. The cost of improvements must be depreciated over several years, while repair costs may be currently deducted in a single year. You must apply the complex IRS repair regulations to make this determination. To do so, you must:

- determine the unit of property involved, and
- decide whether the expense involved resulted in an improvement or repair to such property.

Defining the "Unit of Property" (UOP)

You will need to determine what property is involved to decide if you have an improvement or repair. The IRS calls this the "unit of property" (UOP). How the UOP is defined is crucial. The larger the UOP, the more likely work done on a component will be considered a repair as opposed to an improvement. For example, if the UOP for an apartment building is defined as the entire building structure, you could claim that replacing the fire escapes in the building is a repair because it isn't that significant in scope or cost when compared to the whole building. On the other hand, if the UOP consists of the fire protection system alone, replacing fire escapes would likely be considered an improvement.

Under the regulations, buildings must be divided up into as many as nine different UOPs, which makes it much harder to classify work as repair work.

UOP #1: The Building Structure

Under the IRS regulations, the building structure is a single UOP. A building structure consists of a building and its structural components (other than those components designated as building systems listed below). (IRS Reg. § 1.263(a)-3(e)(2)(ii).) The structural components include a building's walls, partitions, floors, and ceilings, as well as any permanent coverings for them such as paneling or tiling; windows and doors; the roof; and other components relating to the operation or maintenance of the building.

So, if a landlord improves a rental building's structural component—for example, by replacing the entire roof—the expense is treated as an improvement to the single UOP consisting of the building. On the other hand, a repair to a structural component—such as replacing a few roof shingles—may be currently deducted.

If you own an apartment complex consisting of more than one separate building, each building must be its own UOP. (See "What Is an Improvement?" below for more on the difference between a repair and an improvement.)

UOPs #2–#9: Building Systems

The following eight building systems are also considered separate UOPs under the IRS rules. The rules must be separately applied to each such system.

1. **Heating, ventilation, and air-conditioning ("HVAC") system.** This includes motors, compressors, boilers, furnaces, chillers, pipes, ducts, and radiators.
2. **Plumbing system.** This includes pipes, drains, valves, sinks, bathtubs, toilets, water and sanitary sewer collection equipment, and site utility equipment used to distribute water and waste.

3. **Electrical system.** This includes wiring, outlets, junction boxes, lighting fixtures and connectors, and site utility equipment used to distribute electricity.

4. **Escalators.**

5. **Elevators.**

6. **Fire-protection and alarm system.** This includes sensing devices, computer controls, sprinkler heads, sprinkler mains, associated piping or plumbing, pumps, visual and audible alarms, alarm control panels, heat and smoke detectors, fire escapes, fire doors, emergency exit lighting and signage, and firefighting equipment, such as extinguishers and hoses.

7. **Security system.** This includes window and door locks, security cameras, recorders, monitors, motion detectors, security lighting, alarm systems, entry and access systems, related junction boxes, associated wiring, and conduits.

8. **Gas distribution system.** This includes pipes and equipment used to distribute gas to and from the property line and between buildings.

Any work to any of the above building systems that improves that system must be depreciated under the IRS rules.

Condominiums

If you own a condominium, the individual unit you own and the structural components are the UOP. Therefore, any improvements you make in your unit to any portion of the eight building systems defined above must be depreciated.

Improvements to UOP

An improvement to a UOP is not ordinarily considered a separate UOP. Instead, it becomes part of the UOP that is improved. For example, an addition to a building is not a separate UOP. The UOP remains the entire building, including the addition, even though the improvement is separately depreciated starting in the year it is made. (IRS Reg. § 1.263(a)-3(e)(4).) However, as explained below, if the addition or improvement is not depreciated using the same depreciation period and method as the building, it is considered a separate UOP.

UOP for Separately Depreciated Property Components

As covered in detail in Chapter 6, it is possible to separately depreciate building components that are not part of the building structure itself. These include personal property items such as appliances in rental buildings and land improvements such as parking lots and landscaping. This property is depreciated over a much shorter period than a building structure. When you do this, either at the time you put the property in service or later, each separately depreciated property component is treated as a separate unit of property for depreciation purposes. (IRS Reg. § 1.263(a)-3(e)(5)(ii).)

> EXAMPLE: In Year One, the ABC LLC bought and placed in service an apartment building that included a paved parking lot. It depreciates the entire property as residential real property over 27.5 years. In Year Three, ABC completes a cost segregation study under which it properly determines that the parking lot qualifies as a land improvement that may be depreciated over 15 years. ABC changes its method of accounting to use a 15-year depreciation period and accelerated depreciation (the 150% declining balance method) for the parking lot. Beginning in Year Three, ABC must treat the parking lot as a UOP separate from the apartment building.

UOP for Personal Property

In the case of personal property—that is, property other than buildings—the unit of property consists of all components that are functionally interdependent. Personal property components are functionally interdependent if the placing in service of one component is dependent on the placing in service of the other component. (IRS Reg. § 1.263(a)-3(e)(3)(i).)

> EXAMPLE 1: Landlord Ben purchases a new refrigerator, stove, and dishwasher for his single-family residence rental. Each appliance is its own UOP because placing one into service doesn't depend on the other. For example, the stove can be placed into service regardless of whether the refrigerator and dishwasher are available for use in the home.

EXAMPLE 2: The refrigerator Ben purchased includes a cooling mechanism, light, and ice-cube maker. All of these components are functionally interdependent and thus make up the single UOP consisting of the refrigerator.

What Is an Improvement?

Under the regulations, a UOP is improved whenever it undergoes a betterment, adaptation, or restoration (or, B-A-R). The regulations provide few concrete "bright-line" tests for determining if something is an improvement. Rather, all the facts and circumstances must be considered, including the purpose and nature of the work performed and its effect on the UOP. Repairs usually cost less than improvements, but under the IRS regulations quite large expenditures can qualify as repairs. It all depends on the extent and nature of the change to the UOP involved.

Repair Versus Improvement Checklist

To determine whether an expense is a currently deductible repair or an improvement that must be depreciated over many years, you must ask the following three questions. If the answer to all three is "no," the expense is a repair. If the answer to any question is "yes," the expense is an improvement.

1. Does the expense add to the value of the UOP (betterment)? Yes _____ No _____

2. Does the expense adapt the UOP to a new or different use (adaptation)? Yes _____ No _____

3. Does the expense substantially prolong the useful life of the UOP (restoration)? Yes _____ No _____

If the need for the expense was caused by a particular event—for example, a storm—you must compare the UOP's condition immediately before the event to after the work is done to make your determination. On the other hand, if you're doing normal wear and tear work to a UOP, you must compare the item's condition after the last time normal wear and tear work was done (whether maintenance or an improvement) to its condition after the new work is done. If you've never had any wear and tear work done on the UOP, use its condition when placed in service as your point of comparison.

 CAUTION
Repairs made before property is placed in service are not deductible. You are allowed to deduct the cost of repairs to a rental building only if they are made after it is placed in service in your rental activity—that is, after you have offered it for rent to the public. The cost of repairs you make before a building is in service must be added to its tax basis (cost) and depreciated along with the rest of the building. (IRS Reg. § 1.263(a)-2(d)(1).)

For example, if you purchase a building and, before offering it for rent, you pay to repaint the interior or exterior, patch holes in the walls, or refinish the wood floors, you must add the cost to the basis of the building and depreciate it. However, if you incur these same expenses after the building is placed in service, you can currently deduct them.

The only exception to this rule is where the repairs qualify as start-up expenses for a brand-new rental business. This is a limited deduction of up to $5,000 you may take for getting a new rental business up and going. It normally doesn't apply if you already have an ongoing rental business and purchase a new building. (See Chapter 9 for a detailed discussion of business start-up expenses.)

Maintenance Versus Repairs

Maintenance isn't the same thing as repairs. Maintenance is undertaken to prevent something from breaking down. A repair is done after a breakdown has occurred. For example, the cost of oiling the circulator pump in a hot water heater is maintenance; the cost of fixing an unlubricated pump that has failed is a repair. Maintenance and repairs have no practical tax difference—they're both currently deductible operating expenses. However, because IRS Schedule E requires that you separately list what you spent for each category, you must keep track of these expenditures separately.

Betterments

An expenditure is for a betterment if it:

- ameliorates a "material condition or defect" in the UOP that existed before it was acquired
- is for a "material addition" to the UOP—for example, physically enlarges, expands, or extends it, or adds a new component
- is for a material increase in the capacity of the UOP, such as additional cubic or linear space, or
- is reasonably expected to materially increase the productivity, efficiency, strength, or quality of the UOP or its output (the productivity and output factors don't usually apply to buildings). (IRS Reg. § 1.263(a)-3(j)(1).)

It's important to understand that only "material" changes to the UOP are betterments that must be depreciated. A material change is one that is significant or important. For example, adding a new bathroom to a rental home would be a material change to the UOP (the building structure). However, punching a hole in a kitchen wall to open up the space between the kitchen and dining room would likely not be viewed as material.

Moreover, no betterment happens if you replace part of a UOP with an improved, but comparable, part because the old part wasn't available. For example, the IRS says no betterment happens if a building owner replaced the entire wood shingle roof of a building with comparable asphalt shingles because wood shingles were unavailable.

Fixing preexisting material conditions. Fixing a material defect or condition that existed before you acquired the UOP is a betterment. It makes no difference whether or not you were aware of the material defect before you purchased the property. Fixing conditions that occur after you acquire a UOP is not a betterment, but might be a restoration.

Betterment	Repair
Remediation of contaminated soil caused by leakage from underground gas storage tanks that were in place before landowner purchased the property (IRS Reg. § 1.263(a)-3(j)(3), Ex. 1.)	Replacing asbestos insulation in an old building that was constructed when dangers of asbestos were unknown and that began to deteriorate after building was purchased (IRS Reg. § 1.263(a)-3(j)(3), Ex. 2.)

Building refreshes. Work you periodically do to refresh a rental is not a betterment and need not be depreciated if the refresh consists of cosmetic and layout changes and general repairs and maintenance to keep the unit in ordinarily efficient condition. For example, the cost of painting an apartment or refinishing the floors after a tenant moves out need not be depreciated. However, any substantial remodeling you perform during a refresh must be depreciated. Also, any refresh you pay for before a building you purchase is available to rent must be depreciated (unless it constitutes a start-up expense incurred before your rental business began; see Chapter 9).

Betterment	Repair
Extensive building remodel including replacing large parts of exterior walls with windows, rebuilding interior and exterior facades, replacing vinyl floors with ceramic flooring, replacing ceiling tiles with acoustical tiles, and removing and rebuilding walls to move rooms (IRS Reg. § 1.263(a)-3(j)(3), Ex. 8.)	Cosmetic and layout changes to retail store building, including flooring repairs, moving one wall, patching holes in walls, repainting, replacing damaged ceiling tiles, cleaning and repairing wood flooring, and power washing building exterior (IRS Reg. § 1.263(a)-3(j)(3), Ex. 6.)

Material increases in capacity, efficiency, quality of UOP. The regulations provide no percentages as to what constitutes a material increase in capacity, efficiency, or quality of a UOP. However, various examples included in the regulations indicate that a 25% or less increase would likely be viewed as not material and therefore not a betterment.

Betterment	Repair
Reinforcing the columns and girders supporting a building's second floor to permit storage of supplies with a gross weight 50% greater than the previous load-carrying capacity of the storage area (IRS Reg. § 1.263(a)-3(j)(3), Ex. 14.)	Replacement of worn rubber roof membrane (top layer) with comparable new membrane after water seepage and leaks began— change merely restored roof to its condition when placed in service (IRS Reg. § 1.263(a)-3(j)(3), Ex. 13.)
Paying an insulation contractor to apply new insulation throughout a building, including the attic, walls, and crawl spaces, resulting in a 50% reduction in the building's annual energy and power costs (IRS Reg. § 1.263(a)-3(j)(3), Ex. 21.)	Replacing two of ten roof-mounted HVAC units that are many years old with new units that are 10% more efficient (IRS Reg. § 1.263(a)-3(j)(3), Ex. 20.)
Adding a stairway and mezzanine to a building to increase the structure's usable square footage (IRS Reg. § 1.263(a)-3(j)(3), Ex. 19.)	Removing a building interior's drop ceiling to fully expose windows on building's first floor and repainting the original ceiling (IRS Reg. § 1.263(a)-3(j)(3), Ex. 18.)

Restorations

An expenditure is for a restoration if you:

- replace a major component or a substantial structural part of a UOP
- rebuild the UOP to like-new condition after it has fallen into disrepair

- replace a component of a UOP and deduct a loss for that component (other than a casualty loss)
- replace a component of a UOP and realize gain or loss by selling or exchanging the component
- restore damage to a UOP caused by a casualty event and make a basis adjustment to the UOP (see Chapter 14), or
- rebuild a UOP to like-new condition after the end of its IRS class life. (IRS Reg. § 1.263(a)-3(k).)

Replacing a major component or structural part. Replacing a major component or a substantial structural part of a UOP is a restoration that must be depreciated. A major component is a part or combination of parts that perform a discrete and critical function in the UOP—for example, the furnaces contained in a building's HVAC system, the sprinklers in a building's fire protection system, or the wiring in a building's electrical system. A substantial structural part of a UOP is a combination of parts that constitute a large portion of the UOP's physical structure—for example, a building's roof, floors, windows, or walls.

The replacement of a *significant portion* of a major component of the building structure as a whole, or any of the eight building systems, is also a restoration. (IRS Reg. § 1.263(a)-3(k)(6)(ii)(A).) The IRS repair regulations provide no precise numerical guidelines as to how much is a "significant portion." However, numerous examples in the regulations indicate that replacing no more than 30% or so of a major component of a UOP is a deductible repair, while replacing more than this amount is usually a restoration.

Fixing UOPs in disrepair. Once you allow a unit of property to fall into disrepair—that is, it no longer performs its intended function—amounts you spend to get it working again are improvements.

> EXAMPLE: A taxpayer allows a building he uses for storage to fall into disrepair—that is, it could no longer be used because it was structurally unsound. He pays a contractor to shore up the walls and replace the siding. This expense constitutes a restoration that must be depreciated. (IRS Reg. § 1.263(a)-3(k)(7), Ex. 6.)

A disrepair restoration must be depreciated even if the expense would have qualified for the routine maintenance safe harbor if the UOP was not in a state of disrepair. The routine maintenance safe harbor cannot be used for UOPs in a state of disrepair.

Restoration	Repair
Replacing 200 of 300 exterior building windows (IRS Reg. § 1.263(a)-3(k)(7), Ex. 26.)	Replacing 100 of 300 windows (IRS Reg. § 1.263(a)-3(k)(7), Ex. 25.)
Replacing entire leaking roof that caused structural damage to building (IRS Reg. § 1.263(a)-3(k)(7), Ex. 14.)	Replacing only the waterproof membrane portion of roof to solve leakage problem—membrane not a significant portion of the roof (IRS Reg. § 1.263(a)-3(k)(7), Ex. 15.)
Replacing the sole chiller unit in a building's HVAC system (IRS Reg. § 1.263(a)-3(k)(7), Ex. 17.)	Replacing one of three furnaces in a building's HVAC system (IRS Reg. § 1.263(a)-3(k)(7), Ex. 16.)
Replacing old wood flooring with new wood flooring in all of a building's public areas, amounting to 40% of building's square footage (IRS Reg. § 1.263(a)-3(k)(7), Ex. 29.)	Replacing wood flooring only in building lobby, amounting to less than 10% of building's square footage (IRS Reg. § 1.263(a)-3(k)(7), Ex. 28.)
Replacing all wiring in building's electrical system (IRS Reg. § 1.263(a)-3(k)(7), Ex. 20.)	Replacing 30% of wiring in building's electrical system (IRS Reg. § 1.263(a)-3(k)(7), Ex. 21.)
Replacing plumbing fixtures in all of building's restrooms, including all the toilets and sinks (IRS Reg. § 1.263(a)-3(k)(7), Ex. 22.)	Replacing eight of a total of 20 sinks located in a building's restrooms (IRS Reg. § 1.263(a)-3(k)(7), Ex. 23.)

Rebuild to like-new condition after class life ends. The IRS has established class lives for all types of business assets. For example, the class life for residential rental property is 40 years, while the class life for furniture and fixtures that aren't a structural component of a building—such as refrigerators, stoves, countertops, carpets, kitchen cabinets—is ten years. If you rebuild an asset to like-new condition after its class life ends, you must treat the cost as a restoration and depreciate it. You can find a list of the class lives for all kinds of assets in IRS Publication 946, *How to Depreciate Property* (look for the ADS depreciation chart in Appendix B).

Replace component for which a loss is taken. The IRS has issued proposed regulations that permit a building owner to elect to recognize a loss when a building structural component such as a roof is replaced, or not make the election and continue to depreciate the replaced component (see Chapter 5). If you elect to take a loss on a replaced component, you must treat the cost of the new component as a restoration and depreciate it.

> EXAMPLE: The owner of a building containing four elevators replaces one of the elevators. If the owner doesn't elect to recognize a loss on the retirement of the old elevator, he may treat the cost of the new elevator as a repair. But, if he does recognize a loss on the old elevator, he must depreciate the new one. (IRS Reg. § 1.263(a)-3(k)(7), Exs. 30, 31.)

Adaptations

You must also depreciate amounts you spend to adapt a UOP to a new or different use. A use is "new or different" if it is not consistent with your "intended ordinary use" of the UOP when you originally placed it into service. (IRS Reg. § 1.263(a)-3(l).) Adaptations aren't terribly common in the context of residential rentals. Examples would include converting an office or factory building to an apartment building, or converting a regular rental building to a bed-and-breakfast.

Other Issues Under the Repair Regulations

Additional significant issues arising under the regulations include the following.

Repairs Combined With Improvements

Repairs and maintenance are often conducted at the same time as improvements. The IRS repair regulations provide that a taxpayer must depreciate all the direct costs of an improvement, and all the indirect costs that directly benefit from, or are incurred due to, an improvement. Repairs and maintenance are never included within the direct costs of an improvement. But they will constitute indirect costs that must be depreciated if they directly benefit from, or were incurred because of, an improvement. To put it another way, expenses for repairs made at the same time as an improvement to a UOP don't have to be depreciated if they don't directly benefit from the improvement, and (2) they were not incurred because of it. (IRS Reg. § 1.263(a)-3(g)(1)(i).)

> EXAMPLE: The owner of a hotel building pays to replace all the bathtubs, toilets, and sinks in the guest rooms. This expense constituted an improvement—the restoration of a major component of the building's plumbing system. Installation of these new plumbing system components also made it necessary to repair, repaint, and retile the bathroom walls and floors in the guest rooms. The building owner must treat these costs as improvements because they directly benefited from, and were incurred by reason of, the improvement to the building. (IRS Reg. § 1.263(a)-3(k)(7), Ex. 24.)

To be on the safe side, if you hire a contractor or repairperson to perform both improvements and repairs on a building, ask to be billed separately for each category of work. That is, have the contractor submit one (or more) invoices for the improvements and another for the repairs. If both kinds of work are covered in a single bill, you must separate the charges for repairs from those for improvements and deduct them accordingly.

Plan of Rehabilitation Doctrine Eliminated

The IRS repair regulations eliminate the plan of rehabilitation doctrine, a judge-created rule that often trapped building owners into treating repairs as improvements. Under this rule, repairs that were part of an overall plan of rehabilitation or modernization to property had to be depreciated as improvements—even though the work, standing alone, would be currently deductible. As a result, you had to depreciate any routine repair work that was performed at the same time as other major improvements. Under the new regulations, it makes no difference if repairs are made as part of an overall plan of improvement.

EXAMPLE: Jessica owns a two-unit rental. She hires a plumber to install a new bathtub and toilet in one unit and to fix a leak in the plumbing of another unit. The cost of the tub and toilet replacement is an improvement, whereas fixing the leak is a repair. She should have the contractor submit separate invoices for each.

Removal Costs

The basic rule is that the cost of removing a unit of property or a component of a UOP must be depreciated if done as part of an improvement, but may be currently deducted if done as part of a repair.

EXAMPLE 1: The owner of a building with a leaky roof pays to have the roof shingles replaced with comparable new shingles. The expense is a repair, not an improvement. So, the cost of removing the old shingles may be currently deducted as part of the repair. (IRS Reg. § 1.263(a)-3(g)(2)(ii), Ex 3.)

EXAMPLE 2: A building owner pays to have the original columns and girders on the building's first floor removed and replaced with new substantially stronger girders and columns. The expense is a building improvement. So, the cost of removing the girders and columns must be depreciated. (IRS Reg. § 1.263(a)-3(g)(2)(ii), Ex 1.)

However, the IRS regulations give property owners the option of deducting the adjusted basis of building components that are replaced and disposed of. In this event, the removal costs need not be depreciated, even if they were removed as part of an improvement. But the cost of the new components must be depreciated. (See Chapter 5 for a detailed discussion.)

> EXAMPLE: A building owner replaces and disposes of the building's old roof shingles. The owner elects to treat the disposal of these components as a partial disposition of the building and deducts their adjusted basis as a loss. The removal costs don't have to be depreciated. But, because a loss was taken on the old shingles, the cost of the new shingles must be depreciated as an improvement. (IRS Reg. § 1.263(a)-3(g)(2)(ii), Ex 4.)

Note that the cost of demolishing a building must always be depreciated. (I.R.C. § 280B.) For a building other than a certified historic structure, a modification of a building is not a demolition if: (1) 75% or more of the existing external walls of the building are retained in place as internal or external walls, and (2) 75% or more of the existing internal structural framework of the building is retained in place. (Rev. Rul. 95-27, 1995-1 CB 704.)

Work Done to Comply With Government Regulations

As far as the IRS is concerned, the fact that you made changes to a rental property to comply with government regulations, such as bringing the building up to building health codes, is irrelevant. The normal repair rules apply.

> EXAMPLE: To comply with new building code earthquake standards, a building owner pays for the installation of new expansion bolts to anchor the building's wooden frame to its cement foundation. This expense was an improvement because it materially increased the building's strength. The fact the change was made to comply with the building code is irrelevant. (IRS Reg. § 1.263(a)-3(j)(3), Ex. 11.)

Tax Break Unaffected by New Regulations

A special tax break permits building owners to take a deduction for changes to make a building more accessible to the disabled. This is not affected by the IRS regulations. (For a detailed discussion, see "Tax Break for Accessibility Changes" in Chapter 15.)

How IRS Repair Regulations Affect Prior Years

The IRS repair regulations took effect on January 1, 2014. Starting on that date, you had to apply the regulations to all improvements and repairs you made to long-term property used in your rental activity. If your rental activity began during 2014 or later, that's the end of the story and you don't need to read the rest of this section.

For others who owned rental real estate before 2014, it was more complicated. Initially, the IRS required all landlords to apply the repair regulations retroactively—that is, to years before 2014. This involved reviewing depreciation, repair, and improvements records for 2013 and earlier years to see whether depreciation practices followed in prior years were in accord with the new regulations. If not, landlords had to depreciate amounts previously deducted and recognize taxable income based on the difference in treatment. On the other hand, they might have also been able to currently deduct some amounts previously depreciated and take an immediate deduction for the difference. All landlords were supposed to file IRS Form 3115, *Application for Change in Accounting Method*, along with schedules supporting any adjustments no later than the due date for their 2014 tax return (plus extensions).

However, in response to widespread complaints about the expense and difficulties involved in filing IRS Form 3115 and applying the IRS repair regulations to years before 2014, the IRS issued new regulations in mid-February 2015 (Revenue Procedure 2015-20). These new regulations provided smaller landlords with optional relief from the requirement that they apply the IRS repair regulations retroactively to years before 2014. This relief was available for all landlords with (1) assets under $10 million (as of the first day of the tax year) or (2) less than $10 million in annual gross receipts for each distinct business they own. Obviously, the vast majority of landlords qualified to use Revenue Procedure 2015-20.

To choose this option, landlords simply had to file their 2014 returns as normal and begin applying the repair regulations as of January 1, 2014. They didn't need to go back to years before 2014 and make any changes in how they classified expenses as repairs or improvements or make any changes in their depreciation deductions. And they did not have to file the complex Form 3115, *Application for Change in Accounting Method*. There was no requirement that landlords include any statement in their returns that they were adopting Revenue Procedure 2015-20. So, if you filed your 2014 return without Form 3115, you might have adopted this option without even being aware of it.

Large landlords with assets or receipts over $10 million who were not eligible for the relief provided by Revenue Procedure 2015-20 had to apply the repair regulations retroactively and file IRS Form 3115, *Application for Change in Accounting Method*, with their 2014 tax returns. For calendar year taxpayers, these were due by October 15, 2015 for individuals and single-member LLCs, and September 15, 2015 for multimember LLCs, partnerships, and corporations. If you were required to file this form with your 2014 tax return and failed to so, you should consult a tax professional.

For more details on this complex topic, visit the IRS Tangible Property Regulations—Frequently Asked Questions webpage at www.irs.gov/businesses/small-businesses-self-employed/tangible-property-final-regulations.

How to Deduct Repairs and Maintenance

Repairs and maintenance expenses are operating expenses that you deduct on IRS Schedule E (see Chapter 18). They are both currently deductible so whether an expense is classified as a repair or maintenance makes no practical difference to your bottom line. But you're required to list each type of expense separately in Schedule E. As a result, you must track them separately throughout the year. The cost includes what you spend on materials, parts, and labor. If you do the work yourself, you don't get a deduction for the value of your own labor.

> **EXAMPLE:** One of Kim's tenants complains that the fan in his bathroom is making a funny noise. Kim hires Andy, a handyman, to repair the fan. Andy finds that the fan just needs to be cleaned. He does so, and charges Kim $50, which she pays. Kim may add the $50 to the expenses she lists in her Schedule E for the year.
>
> If instead of hiring Andy, Kim cleans the fan herself, the value of her labor does not count as a deductible maintenance. Kim spent nothing for materials or parts, so she gets no deduction for repairing the fan herself.

Making Tenants Pay for Repairs

It's common for landlords to require their tenants to pay for repairs when they cause damage. Typically, this is done after the tenant moves out, and the landlord deducts the cost of the repair from the tenant's security deposit. Landlords may charge tenants for any repairs necessary to restore a rental unit to its condition at the beginning of the tenancy, including the cost of repairing damage to rental property that tenants caused and restoring property subjected to unreasonable wear and tear. Landlords may not, however, use the tenant's security deposit to cover the costs of ordinary wear and tear.

Moreover, you may not use a tenant's deposit to repair damage the tenant did not cause—for example, you can't deduct the cost of repairing a broken window that a windstorm caused. Nor may you use a deposit to pay for improvements to a rental unit—for example, replacing a wooden kitchen countertop with a granite countertop.

A security deposit doesn't constitute taxable income for a landlord. But, where a landlord keeps all or part of a security deposit because the tenant has caused damage to the rental unit, that amount is taxable income. When the landlord fixes the damage, the amount spent on the repair is a deductible expense that will offset the landlord's additional income.

EXAMPLE: Ed owns a three-unit apartment building. After one of his tenants moves out, he discovers a broken window in the unit. He hires a repairman to fix the window at a cost of $100 and deducts the amount from the tenant's $1,000 security deposit. He refunds the remaining $900 to the tenant. The $100 Ed kept is rental income he must report on his Schedule E for the year. But the $100 he spent to fix the window is an expense he can deduct that year. This offsets the $100 he kept, so he ends up paying no tax on the amount.

If you deduct money from a tenant's deposit for damage and don't fix it, you'll have no expense deduction to offset the increased rental income. Of course, no decent landlord would do this. This is one case where the tax law encourages landlords to act honestly.

Ordinary Wear and Tear: Landlord's Responsibility	Damage or Excessive Filth: Tenant's Responsibility
Curtains faded by the sun	Cigarette burns in curtains or carpets
Water-stained linoleum by shower	Broken tiles in bathroom
Dents in the wall where a door handle bumped it	Door off its hinges
A few small tack or nail holes in wall	Lots of picture holes or gouges in walls that require patching as well as repainting
Worn gaskets on refrigerator doors	Broken refrigerator shelf
Faded paint on bedroom wall	Water damage on wall from hanging plants
Toilet flushes inadequately because mineral deposits have clogged the jets	Toilet won't flush properly because it's stopped up with a diaper

Repairs That Tenants Paid For or Performed

What happens if a tenant pays for a repair? For example, your tenant hires a handyman to fix a broken bathroom fan and pays him $50. If you reimburse the tenant or allow the tenant to deduct the amount from the next month's rent, the repair is treated like any other repair for tax purposes: You get to currently deduct the full amount.

However, if a tenant pays for a repair without your prior knowledge and consent, you have no legal obligation to reimburse the tenant. The same goes for improvements the tenant pays for without your approval. If you don't reimburse the tenant, you'll get no tax deduction, but you'll get a free repair or improvement. You'll also own the repaired item or improvement because of an age-old doctrine of property law called "the law of fixtures": Whatever a tenant attaches to a landlord's property, as an alteration or an improvement, becomes the landlord's property unless there is an agreement to the contrary. You don't have to pay any tax on the value of a repair or improvement the tenant makes without your approval.

The rules are exactly the same if a tenant performs a repair, instead of hiring someone else to do it. You can deduct the amount of any reimbursement you give the tenant, whether in cash or a rent reduction. But you have no legal obligation to pay for any repairs a tenant performs without your prior approval.

Properly Document Repairs

Good documentation is the key to winning any argument with the IRS. Here are some tips for properly documenting your repairs:

- Repairs to rental property usually happen after a tenant complains. Document the complaint by writing a note—this can be on your calendar, appointment book, or on an invoice a repairperson gives you. This record will help show that something was broken and you had it fixed—which is what a repair is. (For a sample written request for repair form, see *Every Landlord's Legal Guide*, by Marcia Stewart, Janet Portman, and Ann O'Connell (Nolo).)

- Get an invoice for every repair. Make sure it describes the work in a way that is consistent with a repair, not an improvement. Good words to use include repair, fix, patch, mend, redo, recondition, and restore. An invoice should not include any words that indicate an improvement—for example: improvement, replacement, remodel, renovation, addition, construction, rehab, upgrade, or new. Of course, your invoice will not, by itself, establish whether something is a repair or an improvement—the facts must be consistent with what the invoice says.
- Make sure your repairs are classified as such in all your books and accounting records. This problem can easily crop up if you have a bookkeeper or an accountant do your books—they might list a repair as a capital improvement. If an IRS auditor sees this, it will be curtains for your repair deduction.
- If you're doing an extensive repair, take before-and-after photographs to show the extent of the work and that the property has not been made substantially more valuable.

Do Preventive Maintenance

Maintenance means taking steps to prevent your property from breaking down or deteriorating. Preventive maintenance costs are always currently deductible operating expenses. A great way to avoid the repair versus improvement hassle—and to keep your tenants happy—is to keep your rental property well maintained. This proactive step will prevent it from breaking or wearing out quickly, thereby avoiding the need for replacements. Examples of preventive maintenance include periodically changing the filters on your heating and air conditioning system, and installing zinc control strips on a wood shake or shingle roof to keep fungus and algae away. Such maintenance may qualify for the routine maintenance safe harbor discussed above. But, even if it doesn't, it will usually be currently deductible.

Delay Big Repair Expenses

Under the IRS regulations, expenses that would normally be considered currently deductible repairs must be depreciated along with the rest of the building if they are incurred before the building is placed in service—that is, before it is offered for rent to the public (except in cases where the repairs qualify as start-up expenses for a new rental business; see Chapter 9).

For this reason, you'll get larger repair deductions if you spend as little money as possible refreshing a building immediately after you buy it. Instead, do as much of this work as possible after the building is offered for rent. Of course, you should do whatever work is necessary to make the property rentable and habitable.

Depreciation Basics

O f all the chapters in this book, this one should give you the most pleasure to read. Admittedly, depreciation is a rather dry, technical subject. But depreciation means money in a landlord's pocket. So, whenever you hear the word "depreciation," think "money."

This chapter covers the basics of depreciation. It shows you why depreciation is such a great deal for landlords, and how to calculate and take the deduction. It also explains Section 179 expensing, an alternative to depreciation that landlords can use for certain personal property.

Depreciation: The Landlord's Best Tax Break

The largest expense landlords have is the purchase price for the rental property they own. However, unlike the interest you pay on a loan to buy the property or other operating expenses related to the property, you can't deduct the cost of the rental property in the year in which you pay for it. Because real estate lasts for more than one year, you must deduct its cost over a much longer time period through a process called "depreciation."

The basic idea behind depreciation is simple: Real estate and other long-term property may last longer than a year, but not forever. Little by little, year by year, buildings and other types of long-term property wear out, decay, become unusable or obsolete, or get used up. The annual decline in the value of such property is a cost of doing business or engaging in an investment activity. Depreciation is an annual tax deduction that business owners and investors take to reflect this annual cost.

The reason depreciation is such a valuable deduction for landlords is that you get it year after year (27.5 years for residential real property) without having to pay anything beyond your original investment in the property. Moreover, rental real property owners are entitled to depreciation even if their property goes up in value over time (as it usually does).

> **EXAMPLE:** George buys a rental condominium with a depreciable value of $400,000. He is entitled to an annual depreciation deduction of $14,545 for the next 27.5 years (excluding the first and last years, which will be somewhat less). All George has to do to get these annual deductions is

continue to own the condo as a rental property, file a tax return every year, and do some simple bookkeeping. He doesn't have to spend an additional penny on his property. And he is entitled to depreciation even though his condominium increases in value every year. What a deal!

It's true that if you sell your property you'll likely have to pay a tax of up to 25% on the total amount of depreciation deductions you took over the years. (See "Effect of Adjusted Basis When You Sell," below.) However, in the meantime, these annual deductions have lowered your annual taxes. In effect, depreciation allows you to defer payment of tax on your rental income from the years in which it was earned to the year it is sold. And, you'll get an additional tax savings if your regular income tax rate when you sell is more than the 25% rate you'll have to pay on your depreciation deductions. Moreover, if you never sell the property you'll never have to pay the 25% tax, which is one reason why many veteran landlords hold onto their property for years and years.

Depreciation is a complicated subject. The IRS publication describing it is over 100 pages long (IRS Publication 946, *How to Depreciate Property*). Many landlords simply have their accountants handle their depreciation and never bother to learn much about it. However, it's worth your time and trouble to understand it in some detail. This will enable you to:

- make sure your accountant determines your depreciation deductions properly—depreciation is not as cut and dried as you might think, and the way your accountant figures your depreciation might not be the best way
- figure your depreciation deduction yourself if you choose to prepare your own tax returns, and
- make better-informed decisions on whether to invest in a particular rental property because you fully understand the tax benefits.

Depreciation is one of the largest deductions a landlord has. It can be the difference between a profit and a loss each year on a rental property. That's why it's so important that you understand it.

CAUTION

Depreciation is not optional. Unlike all the other tax deductions discussed in this book, depreciation is not optional. You *must* take a depreciation deduction if you qualify for it. If you fail to take it, the IRS will treat you as if you had taken it. So, when you sell your property, its basis (value for tax purposes) will be reduced by the amount of depreciation you failed to claim. As a result, you'll have a larger profit from the sale that you'll have to pay taxes on.

If you have unclaimed depreciation, you should act to claim it this year. To claim such depreciation, you must make what is known as an "I.R.C. Section 481(a) adjustment." You can deduct the entire amount in a single year by filing IRS Form 3115 to request a change in accounting method. This type of change ordinarily is granted automatically by the IRS (Rev. Proc. 2004-11) and you don't need to file any amended tax returns. Unfortunately, IRS Form 3115 is an extremely complex form. You'll likely need help from a tax professional to complete it properly.

Tax Reform Speeds Up Deductions for Personal Property and Land Improvements

The Tax Cuts and Jobs Act didn't change the depreciation rules for residential real property (residential buildings and building components). However, one of the major changes of the tax reform law was an increase in the first-year bonus depreciation amount from 50% to 100% starting in 2018 through 2022. This enables landlords to deduct in a single year the full cost of personal property used in a rental activity, as well as certain land improvements. Personal property, including property in rental units, may also be fully deducted using Section 179 expensing. For details, see "Depreciating Land Improvements" and "Deducting Personal Property," below.

Understanding the Basics

The fundamentals of depreciation aren't difficult to grasp. Gaining familiarity with these basic concepts will help you understand the later sections in this chapter that describe in detail how to depreciate real and personal property.

What Property Can Be Depreciated?

You may depreciate property that:

- lasts for more than one year
- wears out or gets used up over time
- you own for more than one year, and
- you use in your rental activity (or some other business or income-producing activity). (I.R.C. § 167.)

Let's look at these requirements in some detail.

Long-Term Property

You can depreciate only property that lasts longer than one year—for example, buildings, tangible personal property like stoves and refrigerators, office or construction equipment, cars, and other vehicles. In tax parlance, such long-term property is called a "capital asset" because it is part of your capital investment in your rental business or investment activity.

Items you buy that are for, or related to, your rental activity that are not long-term property (such as the food you eat when traveling for your rental activity, fertilizer you use for your rental property landscaping, and chlorine you buy to clean an apartment complex swimming pool) can usually be fully deducted in the year in which you purchase them as operating expenses. (See Chapter 3.)

Property That Wears Out or Gets Used Up

You can depreciate only property that wears out, decays, gets used up, or becomes obsolete over time. So, for example, you can't depreciate stocks, bonds, or other securities. These assets never wear out. And you can't depreciate collectibles that appreciate in value over time—for example, antiques, coins, or artwork.

Land—that is, the ground a building rests on and the surrounding area—can't be depreciated because, for all practical purposes, it lasts forever. (If the land you own permanently disappears due to flooding, earthquake, or some other catastrophe, you'll have a deductible casualty loss; see Chapter 14.) When you determine your depreciation deduction for a rental building or other structure, you can't include the value of the land it rests on in its value for tax purposes. Only the cost of the building itself can be depreciated.

Unlike land, buildings and structures on land don't last forever and, therefore, can be depreciated. Indeed, all or most of your depreciation deduction will come from the value of your rental buildings. You can depreciate any type of structure you use for your rental activity— apartment buildings, houses, duplexes, condominiums, mobile homes, swimming pools, parking lots, parking garages, tennis courts, clubhouses, and other facilities for your tenants. You can also depreciate structures that you own and use for your rental activity even though they are not used by your tenants—for example, a building you use as your rental office, or a storage shed where you keep maintenance equipment. The cost of landscaping for rental property can also be depreciated.

You can also depreciate tangible *personal* property that lasts for more than one year. This includes property inside a rental unit, such as stoves, refrigerators, furniture, and carpets. Other personal property that you use in connection with your rental activity can also be depreciated, even if it is not located on your rental property—for example, a computer, cell phone, lawn mower, or automobile you use to conduct your rental activity.

You get no annual tax deductions for capital assets that can't be depreciated. This is one reason why depreciable assets like rental properties are better investments, taxwise, than nondepreciable assets like stocks, antiques, or art.

Property You Own for More Than One Year

You can only depreciate property that you own. You can't depreciate property that you lease for your rental activity (such as office space). In addition, you must own the property for at least one year to depreciate it. You get no depreciation for property you buy and sell, or otherwise dispose of, in the same year.

It makes no difference if you own the property free and clear or if you borrow money to buy it. If you hold title to the property, you get the depreciation—even if you have little or no equity in the property. The amount of your depreciation is determined by the cost of the property; how much you borrowed to purchase it is irrelevant.

Property You Use in Your Rental Activity

You may only depreciate property that you use in your rental business or investment activity (or some other business or investment activity you conduct). You may not depreciate property you use solely for personal purposes. So, you get no depreciation for your personal residence. If you convert a rental property to personal use, you must stop taking the depreciation for the property.

If you use property for both rental and personal uses, you may depreciate only a part of its value, based on the percentage of the property used for rental purposes.

> EXAMPLE: Jennifer owns a duplex. She lives in one unit and rents the other. Because she uses 50% of the duplex for rental purposes, she may depreciate only 50% of its value.

How Depreciation Works

At its core, depreciation is simple: You figure out how much the property is worth for tax purposes (the property's basis) and how long the IRS says you must depreciate it for (its recovery period), and then you deduct a certain percentage of its basis each year during its recovery period. The devil is in the details:

- When does depreciation begin (and end)? The answer to this question depends on when rental property is placed in service.
- How do you determine how much your property is worth for depreciation purposes? You'll have to understand the concept of basis and how to calculate it.
- How long do you have to depreciate your property? The answer lies in knowing which recovery period applies.

- How much of your property's value do you get to deduct each year? The answer to this question depends on which depreciation method you use and which depreciation convention applies.

All of these topics are explained below.

When Depreciation Begins and Ends

You don't necessarily begin to depreciate property when you buy it. Rather, depreciation begins when property is "placed in service." Property is considered placed in service in a rental activity when it is ready and available to rent, which can occur at the same time you buy the property, or later. (See "How to Depreciate Buildings," below.)

You stop depreciating property either when you have fully recovered its value or when you retire it from service, whichever occurs first. Property is retired from service when you stop using it for your rental activity, sell it, destroy it, or otherwise dispose of it.

> **EXAMPLE:** Willa purchased a rental house that she placed in service by advertising it as available for rent in January of 2005. She rented the property to various tenants over the next 16 years. She sold it on April 15, 2022. She gets no more depreciation as of the date of the sale—April 15, 2022. Had she not sold the property, she would have continued to depreciate the property over its 27.5-year depreciation period.

Determining Your Property's Basis

Depreciation allows you to deduct your total investment in a long-term asset that you buy for your rental activity. You take this deduction over the property's depreciation period, which the IRS determines. In tax lingo, your investment is called your "basis" or "tax basis." Basis is a word you'll hear over and over again when the subject of depreciation comes up. Don't let it confuse you; it just means the amount of your total investment in the property for tax purposes.

Usually, your basis is the cost of the property, plus expenses of the sale such as real estate transfer taxes and other fees. Land can't be depreciated, so it must be deducted from the cost of real property to determine its basis for depreciation.

EXAMPLE: Jenna buys a rental house that cost $500,000, not including the land's value. The $500,000 cost is her basis in the property. She uses this amount to determine her annual depreciation deduction.

Your Recovery Period

The depreciation period (also called the "recovery period") is the time over which you must take your depreciation deductions for an asset. The tax code has assigned depreciation periods to all types of business assets. These periods are somewhat arbitrary. However, property that can be expected to last a long time generally has a longer recovery period than property that has a short life. So, software has a three-year period, while the period for commercial real property is 39 years.

Real property placed into service after 1986 is depreciated under the Modified Accelerated Cost Recovery System (MACRS). Under this system, the depreciation period for residential real property placed in service after 1986 is 27.5 years. Prior to 1987, different depreciation methods with different depreciation periods were in effect. The depreciation period for commercial property is 39 years. Some dwellings rented on a short-term basis to multiple tenants may qualify as commercial property instead of residential. (See "The Depreciation Period," below.)

The periods are the same whether the property being depreciated is old or new. When you buy property, you start a new depreciation period beginning with year one, even if the prior owner previously depreciated the property for several years or fully depreciated it. If you buy an old building that has changed hands many times over the years, it might have been fully depreciated several times. This depreciation makes no difference to you— your depreciation period starts when you place the property in service in your rental activity.

Calculating Your Deduction Amount

Your depreciation deduction is a set percentage of the basis of your property each year. The amount of the percentage depends on the depreciation method you use. All real property must be depreciated using the straight-line method. Under this method, you deduct an equal amount each year over the depreciation period. (See "How to

Depreciate Buildings," below, for more on how to calculate your depreciation deduction.) The amount of your first year deduction is prorated depending upon which month you place your property into service. Special depreciation rules called "conventions" govern how much you can depreciate the first year.

Personal property can be deducted over its full recovery period using accelerated depreciation, which provides larger depreciation deductions in the early years than the straight-line method. (See "Deducting Personal Property," below, for more on depreciating personal property.) Alternatively, the full cost of personal property may usually be deducted in one year using 100% bonus depreciation (in effect 2018 through 2022), Section 179 expensing, or the de minimis safe harbor. See "Deducting Personal Property," below. Land improvements may also be deducted in one year with bonus depreciation. (See "Depreciating Land Improvements," below.)

Taking Separate Deductions

Typically, landlords don't have a single depreciation deduction. Instead, they have many separate depreciation deductions over time.

Rental Property Placed in Service

When a rental property is first placed in service, the landlord gets to depreciate its value. This includes the value of:

- the building and building components
- land improvements, such as landscaping and fences, and
- personal property items that are inside the building, but that are not physically part of it—for example, refrigerators, stoves, dishwashers, and carpeting.

These items can all be depreciated together over 27.5 years. However, you have the option of separately depreciating personal property inside a rental property and certain land improvements. This option is more complicated but can yield a larger total deduction during the first year or first few years that you own the property. Indeed, 100% of the cost of personal property and land improvements can now be deducted in the first year using bonus depreciation or Section 179 expensing.

This process is called "cost segregation" and is described in detail in Chapter 6.

Later Additions and Improvements

Landlords typically make additions and improvements to their rental property after it has been placed into service—that is, after it has been made available for rent. These improvements might consist of:

- improvements to the building itself, or building components— for example, replacing iron pipes with copper
- land improvements, such as planting new trees or shrubbery, and
- adding new personal property to the rental building—for example, placing a new refrigerator in a rental unit.

You depreciate these additions and improvements separately from the original rental property. Building improvements are depreciated over 27.5 years (starting the year they are placed in service). Land improvements and personal property are depreciated over a shorter term (15 years for land improvements, five or seven years for most personal property). But you now have the option of deducting 100% of the cost of personal property in the first year using bonus depreciation and/ or Section 179 expensing. (See "Deducting Personal Property," below.) Bonus depreciation can also be used to deduct land improvements. (See "Depreciating Land Improvements," below.)

Personal Property Used by the Landlord

Landlords usually have some personal property that they use in connection with their rental activity—computers and office furniture, for example. This property is for the landlord's use, not the tenant's. The landlord separately depreciates this property as it is placed into service each year.

How to Depreciate Buildings

By far, the largest portion of your depreciation deductions will consist of the building or buildings you use in your rental activities. The good news is that the rules for depreciating buildings are relatively simple. The bad news is that they require that buildings be depreciated over a long time using the slowest method possible, which reduces your annual deductions.

What Is a Building?

Buildings are made up of various structural components that are assembled together, including walls, floors, ceilings, windows, doors, plumbing fixtures (such as sinks and bathtubs), pipes, ducts, bathroom fixtures, stairs, fire escapes, electrical wiring, lighting fixtures, chimneys, air conditioning and heating systems, and other parts that form the structure. These structural components are all part of the building for depreciation purposes.

The land on which a building sits is not depreciable—it's not part of the building for depreciation purposes.

Buildings that are rented out for people to live in are called "residential real property." Buildings that people do not live in are called "nonresidential real property."

When a Building Is Placed in Service

Depreciation begins when property is placed in service, that is, when it's ready and available for use in your rental activity. A building doesn't have to be occupied by tenants to be depreciated. Rather, a building is considered placed in service in a rental activity when it is ready and available to rent. This can occur at the same time that you buy the property, or later.

EXAMPLE 1: On April 6, Jess purchased a house to use as residential rental property. She made extensive repairs to the house during May and June. By July 5, she had it ready to rent and placed an ad on Craigslist. She rented it in August with the rental date beginning September 1. The house is considered placed in service in July because it was ready and available for rent on that date. Jess can begin to depreciate the house in July.

EXAMPLE 2: On February 1, Jess buys a house that is already being used as a rental and is currently occupied by a tenant. She continues renting out the unit to the tenant. She can begin to depreciate the house on February 1 because she placed it in service on that date.

EXAMPLE 3: Jess moved from her home in July. During August and September, she made several repairs to the house. On October 1, she listed the property for rent with a real estate company and rented it on December 1. The property is considered placed in service on October 1.

 TIP
Keep documentation showing the date your property was placed in service. For example, keep copies of any rental ads or other rental listings you place to rent a newly acquired vacant property.

Determining a Building's Basis

How much you can depreciate each year depends, first and foremost, on how much your property is worth for tax purposes—its basis. The larger your basis, the larger your depreciation deductions will be.

Cost Basis

If, like most landlords, you've purchased your rental property, your starting point for determining the property's basis is what you paid for it. Logically enough, this is called its "cost basis." Your cost basis is the purchase price, plus certain other expenses, less the cost of your land.

Purchase price. You use the full purchase price as your starting point, regardless of how you pay for the property—with cash or a loan. If you buy property and take over an existing mortgage, you use the amount you pay for the property, plus the amount that still must be paid on the mortgage.

EXAMPLE: Jess buys a building for $60,000 cash and assumes a mortgage of $240,000 on it. The starting point for determining her basis is $300,000.

Facilitative costs. Facilitative costs are amounts you spend in the process of investigating or otherwise pursuing the purchase of a rental property. These costs include most of the transaction costs involved in purchasing real property. These costs must be added to the building's basis and depreciated. (IRS Reg. § 1.263(a)-2(f).)

The following costs are "inherently facilitative" and must always be included in the building's depreciable basis:

- bidding costs, application fees, and similar expenses
- costs to appraise or otherwise determine the property's value
- architectural, engineering, environmental, geological, or inspection services for the property—for example, termite inspection fees
- expenses for preparing or reviewing the property's acquisition documents, such as bids, offers, sales agreements, or purchase contracts
- costs to negotiate the purchase terms or structure, including tax advice
- expenses for evaluating and examining the property's title— for example, abstract fees and attorneys' fees
- costs to obtain regulatory approval or secure permits
- property conveyance costs, including sales and transfer taxes and title registration costs—for example, recording fees and title insurance fees
- finders' fees and brokers' commissions, including amounts contingent on successful closing of the purchase (broker's commissions are ordinarily paid by the seller, but include any in your basis if paid by you, the buyer), and
- the cost of services provided by a qualified intermediary in a like-kind exchange.

Many of these costs will be listed on the closing statement you receive after escrow closes. However, they might not all be listed there, so be sure to check your records to see if you've made any other payments that should be added to your property's basis.

Costs incurred before putting building into service. Expenses incurred before the building is placed in service—that is, before it is offered for rent to the public—must also be added to the building's basis and depreciated. These expenses include costs for installing utility services and any building refresh you perform.

The cost of any repairs or improvements you make to the building before it's offered for rent must be added to its basis. For example, if you purchase a building and, before offering it for rent, pay to repaint the walls or refinish the floors, you must add that cost to the basis of the building and depreciate it. However, if you incur this expense after the building is placed in service, you can currently deduct it. The only exception to this rule is where repairs qualify as start-up expenses for a brand-new rental business. This is a limited deduction of up to $5,000 you may take for getting a new rental business up and going. It normally doesn't apply if you already have an ongoing rental business and purchase a new building. It applies only to repairs, not improvements. (See Chapter 9 for a detailed discussion of business start-up expenses.)

Real estate taxes. If you buy a building and agree to pay real estate taxes on it that the seller owed and the seller didn't reimburse you, the taxes you pay are treated as part of your basis in the property. You can't deduct them as taxes paid.

If you reimburse the seller for real estate taxes the seller paid for you, you can usually deduct that amount. Do not include that amount in your basis in the property.

Other costs. You must also add to your property's basis any amounts the seller owes that you agree to pay, such as back taxes or interest, recording or mortgage fees, charges for improvements or repairs, and sales commissions.

The cost of your land. Ordinarily, when you purchase a building with a structure on it, you pay a single lump sum to the seller that includes the cost of the building and its contents, and the land. Because you can't depreciate land, you must deduct the value of the land from the purchase price to figure the basis for depreciation of the building.

> **EXAMPLE:** Lola buys a rental house for $400,000. She determines that the land is worth $80,000. She must deduct the value of the land ($80,000) from the purchase price ($400,000) to determine her basis ($320,000).

Several ways are available for determining how much your land is worth. Obviously, the less it's worth, the more depreciation you'll have to deduct. Land valuation is the single most important factor within your control affecting the amount of your depreciation deductions. This topic is covered in detail in Chapter 6.

Costs Not Included in Your Property's Basis

The following costs don't have to be added to your property's basis:

- **Investigatory expenses.** Investigatory expenses generally are those you incur to determine whether to buy real property or which property to buy. These costs, often called "whether or which" expenses, may be currently deducted if they are not one of the "inherently facilitative" expenses listed above. For example, if you hire a consultant to help you find the best location to buy an apartment building, the cost is a "whether or which" investigatory expense that is currently deductible. But you would have to add to the basis the cost of hiring an appraiser to value the properties the consultant recommends (appraisal fees are on the "inherently facilitative" list").

- **Fire insurance.** Fire insurance premiums are operating expenses deducted as paid (see Chapter 3).

- **Loan expenses.** Not included in your rental property's basis are charges connected with getting or refinancing a loan, such as points (discount points, loan origination fees), mortgage insurance premiums, loan assumption fees, credit report costs, and fees for an appraisal required by a lender. (See Chapter 8 for how to deduct these costs.)

- **Amounts left in escrow for future payments.** Do not include in your basis amounts placed in escrow for the future payment of items, such as taxes and insurance.

- **De minimis safe harbor.** You don't have to include expenses that are currently deductible under the de minimis safe harbor or as materials and supplies. For most landlords, these are personal property items that cost $2,500 or less. (See "De Minimis Safe Harbor" and "Materials and Supplies Deduction," below.)

Condos Have Land Too

Some people think that condominium owners own only the airspace inside their condo unit, and don't own any land. This belief isn't correct. When you buy a condo, you receive title to the airspace inside your unit, and you also get an undivided part interest in the land the condominium building occupies and other common areas. For example, if a condominium building contains ten units, each unit owner could own an undivided one-tenth interest in all the land. However, the interests don't have to be equal. The size of your undivided interest in the land should be listed on your deed. You need to calculate the land value to determine a rental condo's basis.

EXAMPLE: Ondine purchases a rental house for $200,000. She figures her starting basis in the property as follows:

Purchase price		$ 200,000
Other expenses		
Real estate taxes	1,200	
Transfer taxes	2,000	
Title insurance	250	
Recording fees	50	
Total other		3,500
Cost of land		(40,000)
Basis ($200,000 + $3,500) – $40,000		$ 163,500

When Cost Is Not the Basis

You can't use cost as a basis for property that you received:

- in an exchange for other property
- as a gift, or
- as an inheritance.

The basis of property you inherit is usually the property's fair market value at the time the owner died. So, if you hold on to your rental property until death, your heirs will be able to resell it and pay little or no tax—the ultimate tax loophole.

EXAMPLE: Victoria inherits an apartment building from her late Uncle Ralph. Ralph bought the building for $100,000 in 1990. But, the property's fair market value (excluding the land) is $500,000 at the time of Ralph's death. Victoria's basis is its $500,000 current value. She sells the property for $510,000. Her total taxable profit on the sale is only $10,000 (her profit is the sales price minus the property's tax basis). Had Ralph sold the property for $510,000 when he was alive, his taxable profit would have been $410,000 ($510,000 − $100,000).

The basis of rental property you receive as a gift is its adjusted basis in the hands of the gift giver when the gift was made. (The adjusted basis is generally the property's original basis, minus depreciation deductions, plus the cost of improvements.)

EXAMPLE: Victoria's Uncle Ralph gave her his apartment building before he died. Ralph purchased the building in 1990 and his adjusted basis in the property at the time he gave it to her was $150,000. This amount is Victoria's basis.

(For more information about determining basis other than cost basis, see IRS Publication 551, *Basis of Assets*.)

Property Converted to Rental Use

When you change property you held for personal use to rental use (for example, you rent your former home), your basis is the *lesser* of the following values on the date of the change:
- the property's fair market value, or
- your adjusted basis.

Your adjusted basis is calculated as described in "Cost Basis," above. Fair market value is the price at which the property would change hands between a buyer and a seller, neither under undue pressure to buy or sell, and both having reasonable knowledge of all the relevant facts. Sales of similar property in the area are helpful in figuring out the fair market value of the property. You may also elect to have the property's value appraised as of the date of its conversion to rental property.

Ordinarily, your adjusted basis will be lower than the fair market value because residential real estate usually appreciates in value each year.

> **EXAMPLE:** Several years ago, John built his home for $140,000 on a lot that cost $14,000. Before changing the property to rental use last year, he added $28,000 of permanent improvements. Because land is not depreciable, John only includes the cost of the house and improvements when figuring his adjusted basis for depreciation—$168,000 ($140,000 + $28,000). The house has a fair market value of $450,000. John must use his adjusted basis of $168,000 as the basis for depreciation on the house because it is less than the fair market value on the date of the conversion to rental use.

Because of this rule, if your personal residence has lost value since you bought it, turning it into a rental home won't allow you to deduct the loss when you eventually sell it. Only the drop in value *after* the conversion is deductible.

> **EXAMPLE:** Jessica purchased a home in Chicago for $250,000; $50,000 of the total cost was for the land. She lived in the home for seven years and then moved to Houston. Because of the poor real estate market, Jessica decided to rent her house instead of sell it. The home's adjusted basis when she moved out was $200,000. However, due to the decline in real estate values, its fair market value was only $175,000—a loss of $25,000. Jessica must use the $175,000 fair market value as the basis for depreciation on the house because it is less than its adjusted basis on the date of conversion to rental use. If she sells the house instead for $175,000, she has no deductible loss.

Mixed-Use Property

If you use a building for both rental and personal purposes, you must reduce your depreciable basis by the proportion of the property you use personally.

> **EXAMPLE:** Moriah owns a triplex whose cost, excluding the cost of the land, was $300,000. She rents two of the units and lives in the other one. All of the units are the same size. She must reduce her depreciable basis by one-third—that is, her basis is $200,000. If the units were different sizes, she would determine their value by counting the number of rooms or by comparing their square footage (see Chapter 10).

Buildings You Construct Yourself

If you construct a rental building yourself, your basis is the cost of construction. The cost includes the cost of materials, equipment, and labor. However, you may not add the cost of your own labor to the property's basis. Add the interest you pay during the construction period, but deduct interest you pay before and after construction as an operating expense. (See Chapter 3.)

Property Acquired in an Exchange

A like-kind exchange is where you swap your property for similar property owned by someone else. If the two properties have the same value, the basis of your old property becomes the basis of the new property received in the exchange. The new property's basis is called a "substitute basis" because the basis of the old property is substituted for the basis of the new property. This is one of the most complex areas of real estate taxation and is beyond the scope of this book. (For more information, see IRS Publication 544, *Sales and Other Dispositions of Assets*, and IRS Inst. 8824, *Instructions for Form 8824, Like-Kind Exchanges*.)

The Depreciation Period

The depreciation period for residential real property is 27.5 years. The period for nonresidential real property is 39 years. Either way, it takes a long time to collect all of your depreciation deductions. Indeed, the great majority of landlords sell their rental property before they fully depreciate it. The recovery periods for personal property—office furniture and computers, for example—are much shorter, usually five or seven years.

Mixed-Use Property

If a building is used for both commercial and residential purposes, the 27.5-year period applies only if 80% or more of the gross rental income for the tax year is from the dwelling units. How much space the dwelling units take up in the building is irrelevant; all that counts is how much money you earn from them. So, you could have to use the 39-year period for nonresidential property even if a majority of the space in the building is used for dwelling units.

EXAMPLE 1: Will owns a two-story building that consists of a storefront on the first floor and four apartments on the second floor. He receives $1,000 rent per month from the store and $4,000 per month from the four apartments. He may use the 27.5-year depreciation period because 80% of his total rental income from the property comes from the apartments ($4,000 is 80% of $5,000).

EXAMPLE 2: Will raises the rent on the store to $1,500 per month, while leaving the rents on the apartments the same. Now, less than 80% of his total rental income comes from the apartments ($4,000 of $5,500 is only 73%). So, he must use the 39-year depreciation period, which gives him a much smaller depreciation deduction each year.

If you live in any part of the building, the gross rental income includes the fair rental value of the part you occupy.

How Much You Depreciate Each Year

To depreciate buildings, use the straight-line method, which is the simplest—though the slowest—depreciation method. Deduct an equal amount of the property's basis each year, except for the first and last years. If your property qualifies as residential property, you deduct 1/27 of its depreciable basis each year. If your property is classified as commercial property, you deduct 1/39 of its basis each year.

You can continue to claim a deduction for depreciation on property used in your rental activity even if it is temporarily idle (not in use). For example, if you must make repairs after a tenant moves out, you still depreciate the rental property during the time it is not available for rent.

You don't get a full year's worth of depreciation for the first year your property is placed in service. Instead, your first-year deduction depends on what month of the year you placed the property into service—the later in the year, the less depreciation you get. No matter what day of the month you place your residential real property into service, you treat it as being placed in service at the midpoint of that month. You then get an extra one-half month of depreciation the year you sell your property. This rule is called the "mid-month convention."

The IRS has a table in Publication 946, *How to Depreciate Property*, showing how much depreciation you are entitled to for each year you own residential real property (expressed as a percentage of the property's starting basis). The table takes into account the mid-month convention. Except for the first and last years, you depreciate 3.636% of the residential property's basis each year (give or take 0.001%). The percentage is 2.564% for commercial property. If you use the IRS tables to figure your depreciation for the first year, you must continue to use them for the remainder of the asset's recovery period unless you deduct a casualty loss, in which case you must stop using them.

Using the IRS tables is not mandatory. If you use tax preparation software, it will calculate your depreciation deduction for you.

Depreciating Additions and Improvements

Additions and improvements to a building must also be depreciated. However, you'll do this separately from the original building itself.

What Is a Building Improvement?

A building addition or improvement is a change you make to the structures on your land, or to structural components of the building, that makes it much better than it was before (a "betterment"), restores it to operating condition after it has fallen into disrepair (a "restoration"), or adapts it to a new use (an "adaptation"). For example, you:

- add a new bathroom or bedroom
- replace the roof
- put up a fence
- repave the parking lot, or
- install a new plumbing or wiring system.

Changes that are not a betterment, restoration, or adaptation are repairs, not improvements—for example, painting a bedroom or patching a roof. Unlike improvements to a building, the cost of repairs is a landlord operating expense that can be fully deducted in one year. Obviously, you're much better off taxwise if you can characterize a change as a repair, rather than an improvement. The differences between repairs and improvements are discussed in detail in Chapter 4.

Note that additions or improvements to personal property contained in a rental building can usually be deducted in one year with bonus depreciation, Section 179 expensing, or the de minimis safe harbor. (See "Deducting Personal Property," below.)

Special Assessments for Improvements

If your rental is in a condominium complex that is governed by a home-owners' association, you might be required to pay special assessments to cover building improvements. Such assessments are depreciated in the same way as any building improvement described above. Special assessments are not the same as the monthly homeowners' association fees condo owners must pay to cover the condo's operating expenses. These monthly fees are currently deductible each year as an operating expense.

> EXAMPLE: Isabella owns a one-bedroom condominium in a 20-story high-rise that she rents out. The condominium homeowners' association requires every owner to pay a special $2,000 assessment for a major upgrade of the building's aging plumbing system. This is a building improvement that Isabella must depreciate over 27.5 years. Isabella also pays $2,400 each year in homeowners' association fees. She may deduct that entire amount as an operating expense.

Depreciating Building Improvements

Treat depreciable additions or improvements that you make to a building or building component as separate property items for depreciation purposes.

When depreciation begins. Depreciation of an addition or improvement to a building begins when the improvement is placed in service—that is, when it is ready for use in your rental property.

Basis for depreciation. Depreciate the amount that an addition or improvement actually costs you, including any amount you borrowed to make the addition or improvement. This includes all direct costs, such as material and labor, but not your own labor. It also includes all expenses related to the addition or improvement. For example, if you had an architect draw up plans for remodeling your property, the architect's fee is a part of the cost; or, if you had your lot surveyed to put up a fence, the cost of the survey is a part of the cost of the fence.

Depreciation method and recovery period. If the improvement is to the building structure or structural components, depreciate it over 27.5 years, using the same method used for the original building as described above.

> **EXAMPLE:** Mona buys a rental house in 2019. In 2022, her old tenant moves out and she hires a contractor to remodel the house, adding a new kitchen and bathroom and installing new floors. The cost of this building improvement was $50,000. The work was completed on June 1, 2022, and she immediately placed the house into service as a rental unit by offering it for rent. She depreciates the $50,000 over 27.5 years. The beginning date for her first year of depreciation is June 2022. She gets $985 in depreciation for this improvement the first year and $1,835 each year thereafter. She claims this amount in addition to the depreciation she has already been receiving on the house since she placed it in service in 2019. She adds the $50,000 improvement expense to the home's basis and reduces her basis by the depreciation deductions she takes each year.

You must keep separate accounts for depreciable additions or improvements made after you place your rental property in service.

You add the cost of depreciable additions and improvements to the adjusted basis of your property, which will reduce your tax liability when you sell the property. However, you must reduce your basis by the amount of your depreciation deductions each year, which increases your tax liability when you sell the property. (See "When You Sell Your Property," below.)

Deducting Costs for Replaced Building Components

If you replace the old roof on your rental building with a new roof, you separately depreciate the cost of the new roof. But what about the old roof? Do you get to deduct its cost? Until recently, the answer was no. You had to go on depreciating building components you replaced along with the rest of the original structure. This meant that, in effect, you could end up depreciating two or more roofs at the same time! However, IRS regulations that went into effect in 2014 changed this rule. (IRS Reg. § 1.168(i)-8.)

The regulations apply when a building owner disposes of a structural component (or a portion of a component, no matter how small)—for example, roofs, HVAC units, and windows. The building owner has two options: (1) continuing to depreciate the cost of the replaced component, or (2) deducting the unrecovered cost of such component. (IRS Reg. § 1.168(i)-8.)

The building owner doesn't have to do anything to select Option 1. The component continues to be depreciated along with the rest of the building.

Option 2 is chosen by making a "partial disposition election" on the owner's tax return. In this event, the adjusted basis (original basis minus depreciation taken) of the retired component is deducted that tax year. In addition, the building owner must separately depreciate the cost of the replacement component, even if it might have otherwise been currently deductible as a repair under the IRS's repair regulations. This election must be made on a timely filed return including extensions in the taxable year in which the disposition occurs. No formal election statement is required. The taxpayer simply reports the loss on the disposed portion of the asset on their return.

> EXAMPLE: Alyssa has owned an apartment building for ten years. She replaces the roof, which is a structural component. Alyssa may not recognize a loss and must continue to depreciate the retired old roof unless she elects to treat the roof retirement as a partial disposition of the building. If she decides not to make this election, she separately depreciates the cost of the new roof and continues to include the cost of the old roof in the amount she depreciates for the building as a whole. If she does make the election, depreciation on the old roof ceases at the time of its retirement. Alyssa recognizes a loss upon the retirement equal to the remaining undepreciated basis of the roof.

When such an election is made, it is necessary to allocate a portion of the original cost (depreciable basis) of the whole building to the replaced component. For example, the cost of the replaced roof in Alyssa's building would have to be determined since depreciation was not separately claimed on the original roof. Any reasonable method may be used to determine the adjusted basis of the old replaced component at the time of its replacement, including:

- recreate the actual cost with invoices or other cost records
- if the replaced asset is a restoration, discounting the cost of the replacement asset to its placed-in-service year cost using the Producer Price Index for Finished Goods, and its successor, the Producer Price Index for Final Demand (may not be used for betterments or adaptations because they involve replacing an existing asset with a newer, more expensive, and/or dissimilar asset and the Producer Price Index would offer an unfair comparison)
- a pro rata allocation based on the replacement cost of the disposed-of component
- a study (that is, a cost segregation study) allocating the cost of the building's individual components, or
- any other reasonable method.

Online partial disposition calculators are available to help you make these calculations. (See www.kbkg.com/partial-disposition-calculator, or https://engineeredtaxservices.com/services/cost-segregation/disposition-calculator.)

> **EXAMPLE:** Alyssa elects to use the Producer Price Index for Final Demand (PPIFD) method to determine the basis of the old roof, which was placed in service ten years ago. She spent $10,000 to replace the roof this year. The PPIFD has risen by 24.7% over the last ten years, so the old roof's placed-in-service-year cost is valued at $7,530. Over ten years, Alyssa took a total of $2,790 in depreciation deductions for the roof, leaving her with a $4,740 adjusted basis she may deduct in full.

There are some exceptions to the rule that a building owner is not required to recognize a loss (or gain) on a disposition of a building component. The regulations make such recognition mandatory if the disposition is the result of casualty event, sale of a portion of an asset, like-kind exchange, or involuntary conversion.

Late Partial Asset Dispositions

If you decide not to do a partial asset disposition, you treat the new work as a repair and currently deduct the cost (if it qualifies under the IRS regulations). If you do a partial asset disposition, you must depreciate the new work, even if it would otherwise qualify as a repair. What happens if you elect not to do a partial asset disposition, deduct the new work as a repair, and the IRS later decides such work should have been treated as an improvement and depreciated? In this event, the IRS takes some pity on you. You have the option of doing a late partial asset disposition and deducting the adjusted basis of the replaced component.

Building Components That Cost $2,500 or Less

Building components that cost $2,500 or less may be deducted in a single year with the de minimis safe harbor deduction. For example, a bathroom sink is a building component. If a landlord spends $2,000 to replace a bathroom sink, the full amount can be deducted that year with the de minimis safe harbor deduction. To take this deduction, an election must be filed with your tax return. The cost of buildings and building components may not be deducted in one year with bonus depreciation or Section 179 expensing—these deduction methods are limited to personal property (except bonus depreciation can be used for some land improvements). So, the de minimis safe harbor is the only means available to currently deduct a building component that would otherwise have to be depreciated over several years.

Because this deduction is limited to $2,500 per item, it is usually taken for personal property. See "De Minimis Safe Harbor," below.

Depreciating Land Improvements

Land can't be depreciated because it lasts virtually forever. But certain improvements you make to your land can be depreciated. The two types of land improvements are:
- changes to the land itself, and
- changes or additions to permanent structures on the land other than buildings and building components.

Changes to Land

Changes to the land include grading, clearing, excavations, and land-scaping. The IRS says that such changes are depreciable only if they are "directly associated" with a building, rather than "inextricably associated" with the land itself. (Rev. Rul. 65-265.) Translated into English, this means that these land improvements are depreciable if they are intended for use with a specific building. Changes that permanently improve the land itself are not depreciable.

The rationale is that work directly associated with a building will cease to be useful when the building is demolished; thus, it has a determinable useful life. But work inextricably associated with land is not depreciable because we don't know whether it will cease to be useful. The cost of such work is added to the basis of the land. Thus, landscaping is depreciable if it will have to be replaced when the building is replaced.

> EXAMPLE 1: Michael plants some new bushes and trees right next to his rental triplex. If he replaced the building, he'd have to destroy these bushes and trees. They have a determinable useful life so he may depreciate them.

> EXAMPLE 2: Michael also plants trees and bushes around the outer boundary of his lot. These trees and bushes would not have to be replaced if the building was demolished. So, they can't be depreciated and Michael must instead add their cost to the basis of his land.

Similarly, preliminary land clearing and grading to get land ready for construction are not depreciable. However, excavating, grading, and dirt removal costs necessary for the proper setting of a specific building can be depreciated because this work will have to be redone when the building is replaced.

Structures Other Than Buildings

Permanent structures other than buildings include fences, outdoor lighting, swimming pools, driveways, paved parking areas and other pavements, sidewalks and walkways, sprinkler systems, and drainage facilities.

In contrast to changes to land, depreciation of permanent structures other than buildings is straightforward—they are depreciated over 15 years as described below or using bonus depreciation. You don't have to worry about the "directly associated" or "inextricably associated" test because human-made structures, unlike changes to land itself, have a determinable useful life—that is, none of them can last forever.

Depreciation Methods

You may deduct the cost of land improvement using regular or bonus depreciation and, in some cases, the de minimis safe harbor.

Bonus Depreciation

Bonus depreciation may be used to deduct land improvements that have a 15-year recovery period. During 2018 through 2022, 100% of the cost of these land improvements can be deducted in one year using bonus depreciation. Bonus depreciation for land improvements operates the same as for personal property discussed below. (See "Bonus Depreciation," below.)

Regular Depreciation

Land improvements can always be depreciated using regular depreciation. Regular depreciation for land improvements is done over 15 years, using the 150% declining balance method. This way, you get your depreciation deductions more quickly than you would for a building or building improvement, which you must depreciate over 27.5 years. Other than the fact that the 150% declining balance method and 15-year depreciation period must be used, regular depreciation for land improvements works the same as for personal property. See the discussion of regular depreciation for personal property below.

De Minimis Safe Harbor

The de minimis safe harbor can be used to deduct in a single year tangible property items that cost $2,500 or less. This can include personal and real property, but not the cost of land. For example, plants that cost $2,500 or less could be deducted with the safe harbor. You must file an election with your return to take this deduction. See "De Minimis Safe Harbor," below.

Determining Cost of Land Improvements

The depreciable basis of a land improvement is its cost, including labor and installation charges. If you depreciate a new improvement, you'll have no problem determining the cost—just look at your bills and use the total you paid for it.

If you wish to depreciate an existing improvement—for example, a driveway in a rental property you have purchased—you can determine the cost by using construction cost guides such as the *National Repair & Remodeling Estimator* (Craftsman Book Company, available as a download at www.craftsman-book.com). You can also obtain cost estimates from experts such as garden supply companies, landscape architects, and local builders and contractors. You don't need to obtain a precise formal written cost estimate prepared by the expert—which the expert will probably charge you for. You can simply obtain a ballpark estimate from the expert over the phone—be sure to write it down, date it, and keep it in your records. (See Chapter 6 for a detailed discussion of how to determine the tax basis of land improvements.)

Deducting Personal Property

Obviously, all landlords own real property—that is, land and buildings and other permanent structures on the land. But they own personal property as well—for example, computers, maintenance equipment, and appliances in rental units. So, you need to understand how to deduct personal property. Thanks to the Tax Cuts and Jobs Act and other tax changes over the past few years, landlords can usually deduct the full cost of personal property they use in their rental activity in a single year by using:

- bonus depreciation
- the de minimis safe harbor deduction
- Section 179 expensing, or
- the materials and supplies deduction.

Where required, or if desired, personal property can also be deducted over several years (typically five or seven) with regular depreciation.

What Is Personal Property?

For tax purposes, personal property is any tangible property other than:

- land and land improvements
- buildings and other inherently permanent structures, such as swimming pools and parking lots, and
- structural components of buildings and other permanent structures. (IRS Reg. § 1.48-1(e)(2); *Whiteco Industries, Inc. v. Comm'r*, 65 T.C. 664.)

Often, you'll be able to deduct all or most of the cost of personal property used in your rental business in a single year by using the de minimis safe harbor, materials and supplies deduction, bonus depreciation, or Section 179 deduction. However, if you can't use any of these methods, you must depreciate the cost of personal property. Fortunately, personal property is depreciated over a much shorter time period than real property—usually five or seven years. This means you'll get your full depreciation deduction much more quickly. It is to a landlord's advantage to be able to classify as much rental property as possible as personal property, rather than real property.

A landlord's personal property falls into one of two broad categories:

- personal property contained in a rental building or individual apartment, or
- other personal property used in a rental activity.

Personal Property Inside Rental Buildings

Anything inside your rental building that is not a structural component of the building is personal property. Often it is easy to tell whether or not an item is a structural component of a rental building—for example, refrigerators and other kitchen appliances are not structural components, while load-bearing walls obviously are. Other examples of items inside rental buildings that are not structural components include:

- carpeting that is tacked down (but not glued down)
- drapes and blinds
- furniture (only depreciable if you own it)
- personal signs
- movable and removable partitions
- laundry equipment in a laundry room
- weights and other exercise equipment in an exercise room
- pool tables, ping-pong tables, televisions, and other recreational equipment in a recreation room, and
- office furniture and equipment located in a manager's office.

In many cases, however, it can be very difficult to determine whether property is a structural component—for example, is tile flooring a structural component? The IRS says that it is if it is cemented, mudded, or otherwise permanently affixed to the floor. Many people have had disputes with the IRS on what constitutes a structural component, resulting in many court decisions, often disagreeing with each other. Refer to Chapter 6 for a detailed discussion of the tests used to determine if property is a structural component of a rental building.

Personal Property Not Inside Rental Buildings

Landlords typically own various items of long-term property that they use in connection with their rental activities, but the items are not actually inside their rental buildings—for example, lawn mowers and other landscaping and maintenance equipment, computers, cell phones, office furniture, and automobiles.

As long as this property isn't a structural component of a building or other permanent structure, it is personal property for depreciation purposes. For example, a lawn mower is personal property even if it is kept inside a building or other permanent structure such as a storage shed—a lawn mower is obviously not a building component. On the other hand, carpeting in your rental office will not be personal property if it is glued to the floor—such carpeting is a building component, and is considered part of the building for depreciation purposes. (See Chapter 6 for detailed guidance on when property is a building component.)

How to Deduct or Depreciate Personal Property

There can be differences in how you deduct personal property, depending on how and when you acquire it.

Personal Property Included in Purchase

When you buy a rental property, you pay one lump sum that covers both the structure and the personal property it contains. When you initially place the property into service, you can simply depreciate the entire property as a whole (as outlined in "How to Depreciate Buildings," above). The IRS requires no separate allocation for, or depreciation of, the personal property in the building, which saves you the time and trouble of having to figure out the basis of each item of personal property the building contains, and keeping separate depreciation records for them.

But you have the option of depreciating personal property within a rental building separately from the building itself—a process called "cost segregation." This process is often advantageous taxwise, because it will give you larger deductions in the first year or years you own the property. Indeed, using 100% bonus depreciation, it is now possible to deduct in a single year the full cost of personal property in rental buildings. Cost segregation is discussed in detail in Chapter 6.

Personal Property Improvements

You must separately depreciate or deduct personal property that you add to a building after you place it into service—for example, if you install a new stove or refrigerator in a rental property you've already made available for rent, you'll depreciate it separately from the other appliances already in the unit. Your depreciation begins the year you place the item in service.

Other Personal Property

Depreciate or deduct personal property not contained in your rental property, such as computers and office furniture, as you buy it. Depreciate or deduct each item separately.

Bonus Depreciation

Bonus depreciation enables a landlord to deduct a substantial percentage of a long-term asset's cost in a single year, instead of depreciating the full cost over many years. Bonus depreciation has been around for years, with the bonus percentage set at 50% most of the time. However, the Tax Cuts and Jobs Act vastly expanded its scope. The bonus amount has been increased from 50% to a whopping 100% for five years—in other words, the entire cost of an asset can be deducted in one year with bonus depreciation during 2018 through 2022.

Bonus depreciation may not be used for real property—thus, it may not be used for buildings and building improvements (see above). So, landlords may not use it for their greatest expense—the cost of their rental property. But it may be used by landlords when they purchase new or used personal property and place it in service in their rental activity—for example:

- appliances
- furniture purchased for rental units
- office furniture and equipment used in landlord offices
- removable flooring and carpeting
- cabinets and counters
- wall paneling, and
- decorative and track lighting.

Bonus depreciation may also be used to deduct depreciable land improvements such as swimming pools, sidewalks, fences, landscaping, hot tubs, and driveways.

Bonus depreciation is optional—you don't have to take it if you don't want to. If you don't want to take it, you must inform the IRS as described below. But if you want to get the largest depreciation deduction you can, you'll want to take advantage of the bonus.

> **EXAMPLE:** Bryson owns a large rental home. He spends $5,000 to purchase new carpeting for the entire home. He may deduct the entire $5,000 in one year with bonus depreciation.

Property That Qualifies for Bonus Depreciation

You can use bonus depreciation to deduct any property you acquire by purchase that has a depreciation period of 20 years or less—this includes all types of tangible personal property and off-the-shelf software, but not custom software. (See the chart of depreciation period below.) The property may be used or new, but you must not have used it before acquiring it. So, you can't convert property you previously used for personal use to rental use and deduct the cost with bonus depreciation—for example, you can't place your former living room couch in a rental unit and claim bonus depreciation for it. (Property acquired and placed in service before September 28, 2017 had to be new to qualify for bonus depreciation.)

You can use bonus depreciation only for property that you purchase —not for leased property or property you inherit or receive as a gift. You also can't use it for property that you buy from a relative or a corporation or an organization that you control. Special rules apply to cars. (See Chapter 11 for more about deducting car expenses.)

Bonus depreciation can't be used at all for:

- land
- buildings or building structural components
- intangible property such as patents, copyrights, and trademarks, or
- property outside the United States.

Because bonus depreciation is now available for both new and used property, you may use it to currently deduct personal property items and/or land improvements when you purchase an existing (that is, used) rental building and its contents during that year. You can separately deduct the building, personal property, and land improvements employing cost segregation, which can give you a substantial deduction the first year you own the property. (See Chapter 6.)

Bonus Depreciation Applies Class-Wide

If you use bonus depreciation, you must use it for all assets that fall within the same class. You may not pick and choose the assets you want to apply it to within a class. For example, if you buy a new refrigerator for your rental property and take bonus depreciation, you must take bonus depreciation for any other property you buy that year within the same class. Refrigerators are five-year property, so you must take bonus depreciation that year for any other five-year property—for example, computers and office equipment. (See below for a list of the various classes of property.) If you want to pick and choose which personal property items to deduct in one year, and which to depreciate, you should use Section 179 instead of bonus depreciation (see below).

Calculating the Bonus Amount

You figure your bonus depreciation deduction by multiplying the depreciable basis of the asset by the applicable bonus percentage. An asset's basis is its initial cost plus sales tax, delivery, and installation charges. It doesn't matter if you pay cash or finance the purchase with a credit card or bank loan. However, if you pay for property with both cash and a trade-in, bonus depreciation may only be applied to the cash paid in addition to the trade-in.

As shown in the following chart, the percentages vary depending on when the property was placed in service in your rental activity. The bonus percentage is 100% for property purchased and placed in service during September 27, 2017 through December 31, 2022. So, the full cost of qualifying property can be deducted for five years.

Year Property Placed In Service	Bonus Depreciation Percentage
1/1/2015 through 9/27/2017 (new property only)	50%
9/27/2017 through 2022	100%
2023	80%
2024	60%
2025	40%
2026	20%
2027 and later	0%

Property acquired before September 28, 2017 is subject to a 50% bonus depreciation rate if it was placed in service in 2017, 40% if placed in service in 2018, 30% if placed in service in 2019, and 0 if placed in service after 2019.

You can apply bonus depreciation even for an asset you use only part of the time in your rental activity, but you must adjust your depreciable basis accordingly. For example, if you use your computer 25% for your rental business, you may deduct 25% of the cost the first year with bonus depreciation. However, you must use listed property (primarily cars and light trucks) over 50% of the time to qualify for bonus depreciation.

No dollar limits apply to the total bonus depreciation deduction you may take each year. You may take your full deduction even if it exceeds your income for the year, resulting in a net operating loss.

Bonus Depreciation Recapture

It's important to understand that when you sell an asset you've deducted with bonus depreciation, you must "recapture" the bonus amount in your income for that year (up to the amount of sales proceeds) and pay tax on it at your ordinary income tax rates. In other words, you have to give back the bonus depreciation deductions you took and pay tax on them. However, because personal property usually declines rapidly in value, amounts earned when it is resold are typically small, limiting the amount of income to be recaptured. Additionally, because of the time value of money, taking a large deduction this year is worthwhile even if you'll have to pay some of it back in later years.

EXAMPLE: Nelson paid $5,000 to install a new hot tub for his rental home and deducted the full amount in one year with bonus depreciation. Five years later, he sold the used unit for $1,000. He earned a $1,000 profit on the sale ($1,000 sales price – 0 basis = $1,000). The $1,000 is recaptured into his income for the year and he must pay income tax on it at his ordinary rates (not the lower capital gains rates). His top rate was 37%, so he paid $370 in recapture tax. However, he benefited from an immediate $5,000 tax deduction that saved him $1,850 in tax five years earlier—he got the use of that money for all those years.

Opting Out of the Bonus

Bonus depreciation is applied automatically to all taxpayers who qualify for it. But the deduction is always optional. You don't have to take it if you don't want to. You can elect not to take the deduction by attaching a note to your tax return. It might be advantageous to do this if you expect your income to go up substantially in future years, placing you in a higher tax bracket, or if bonus depreciation will result in losses you're unable to deduct because of the passive loss rules (see Chapter 16).

CAUTION

When you opt out, you do so for the entire class of assets. It's very important to understand that if you opt out of the bonus, you must do so for the entire class of assets, not just one asset within a class. This is the same rule that applies when you decide to take the bonus.

De Minimis Safe Harbor

The IRS repair regulations that went into effect in 2014 created a new de minimis safe harbor deduction ("de minimis" is Latin for minor or inconsequential). (IRS Reg. § 1.263(a)-1(f).) Most landlords may use the de minimis safe harbor to currently deduct the cost of property items that cost up to $2,500 apiece. Because no limit applies to how many items costing up to $2,500 apiece can be deducted each year, the de minimis safe harbor can result in a substantial total deduction.

De Minimis Safe Harbor Versus Bonus Depreciation

The great virtue of the de minimis safe harbor is its simplicity. All expenses deducted with the safe harbor are currently deducted as business operating expenses. You may deduct them as "other" expenses on your Schedule E. You can list the total amount as "de minimis safe harbor expenses." Unlike with bonus depreciation, there is no need to list safe harbor expenses on IRS Form 4562, *Depreciation and Amortization*. You need not create or maintain depreciation schedules for such property items or include them in your accounting records as assets.

As a result of the Tax Cuts and Jobs Act, you can fully deduct most of the same expenses in a single year using 100% bonus depreciation through 2022. But starting in 2023, the bonus depreciation percentage is scheduled to go down by 20% each year through 2027. So, it will be 80% in 2023 and 60% in 2024, and so on. But 100% bonus depreciation could be extended beyond 2022.

Bonus depreciation has some advantages over the de minimis safe harbor: There is no $2,500 per item ceiling on bonus depreciation. More-over, property deducted with the safe harbor won't count for purposes of taking the pass-through deduction in effect from 2018 through 2025. At higher income levels ($170,050 for singles and $340,100 for marrieds) this deduction can be limited to 2.5% of the cost of a landlord's depreciable property. This would not include property you've deducted using the safe harbor but can include property deducted with bonus depreciation (or Section 179). (See Chapter 7 for a full discussion of the pass-through tax deduction.) For this reason, if you want to maximize your pass-through deduction, you may wish to avoid using the de minimis safe harbor and use bonus depreciation instead. You elect to use the safe harbor each year and you can use it some years and not use it others. Alternatively, you could reduce the dollar amount of your de minimis safe harbor election; $2,500 per item is the maximum amount allowed under the safe harbor (unless you have a financial statement; see below). But you can elect to deduct a smaller amount—for example, $1,000 or $500 per item, and use bonus depreciation to deduct more expensive items.

What Can Be Deducted

If you elect to use the de minimis safe harbor, you must use it to deduct all expenses for the following types of property whose cost is within your de minimis limit ($2,500 for most landlords as described below). The de minimis safe harbor can't be used to deduct the cost of land or inventory (items held for sale to customers).

Tangible personal property. The de minimis safe harbor is most often used to deduct the cost of tangible personal property items (units of property) you use in your rental business. Such property can be in a rental building or elsewhere, such as your office.

> EXAMPLE: John owns five rental homes. He purchases new refrigerators for each at a cost of $1,000 apiece. By using the de minimis safe harbor, he can deduct the entire $5,000 expense in a single year provided that the requirements to use the safe harbor are satisfied.

Components of property. Components acquired to repair or improve a unit of tangible property may also be deducted under the de minimis safe harbor if within the de minimis limit ($2,500 for most landlords). This deduction can include building components.

> EXAMPLE: Landlord Larson pays $2,000 for a new bathroom sink in an apartment building he owns. The new sink is an improvement to a unit of property—the building's plumbing system. Ordinarily, it would have to be depreciated (it may not be deducted with bonus depreciation or Section 179 because it's a building component, not personal property). However, because its cost is within the $2,500 de minimis limit, Larson may deduct it in one year using the de minimis safe harbor.

Production of unit of property. You may also deduct amounts paid to produce a unit of property, so long as they fall within the $2,500 limit.

> EXAMPLE: Landlord Larson spends $2,000 to build a small storage shed for his apartment building. The entire amount may be currently deducted as a de minimis expense.

Property with an economic useful life of 12 months or less. Any item with an economic useful life of 12 months or less must be deducted under the de minimis safe harbor if the cost is within the de minimis limit ($2,500 for most landlords). The economic useful life of a UOP is the period it may reasonably be expected to be useful to the taxpayer—which may be shorter than its depreciation period.

> **EXAMPLE:** Landlord Jill spends $1,000 for cut flowers to place in the lobby of her rental buildings during the holiday season. The flowers have a useful life of less than 12 months and may be deducted under the de minimis safe harbor.

Maximum De Minimis Amount

If you're like the vast majority of smaller landlords, you may use the de minimis safe harbor only for property whose cost doesn't exceed $2,500 per invoice, or $2,500 per item as substantiated by the invoice. If the cost exceeds $2,500 per invoice (or item), no part of the cost may be deducted by using the de minimis safe harbor: $2,500 is the maximum amount allowed under the safe harbor, but you can elect to use a smaller amount if you wish.

However, if you have an applicable financial statement, then you may increase the per item or per invoice amount up to $5,000. An applicable financial statement includes a certified financial statement prepared by a CPA, or SEC-type financial filings. Few smaller landlords have these. The $2,500/$5,000 are maximum limits; you can use a smaller limit if you wish, or even have different limits for different types of property. Be sure to save all your receipts and invoices for property you deduct using the de minimis safe harbor.

> **EXAMPLE:** Landlord Abe has no applicable financial statement. Abe purchases ten refrigerators for his rental units at $1,000 each for a total cost of $10,000 as indicated by the invoice. Abe has accounting procedures in place at the beginning of the year to expense amounts paid for property

costing less than $2,500, and Abe treats the amounts paid for the refrigerators as an expense on his books and records. The amounts paid for the refrigerators meet the requirements for the de minimis safe harbor. Abe may currently deduct the entire amount as an ordinary and necessary business expense.

Because the $2,500 de minimis limit is based on the cost of an item as shown on the invoice, you might be tempted to artificially break an item down into separate costs on the invoice, each of which is less than the limit. However, the IRS does not allow this. You can't break into separate components property that you would normally buy as a single unit.

EXAMPLE: Landlord Jill purchases a desk for her rental office for $3,000. She instructs the office supply store to separately bill her $250 for each of four desk drawers and $2,000 for the remainder of the desk. Because an office desk is normally purchased along with its drawers as a single unit, the IRS adds the cost of each component to determine that the actual cost is $3,000. So, the desk doesn't qualify for the de minimis safe harbor.

In determining whether the cost of an item exceeds the $2,500 (or $5,000) threshold, you must include all additional costs included on the same invoice with the property—for example, delivery and installation fees. If the additional costs on a single invoice apply to several items, you must divide the costs among them in a reasonable way. IRS regulations give you three options: (1) equal division for each item, (2) specific identification (for example, if the installation costs apply only to one item), or (3) weighted average based on the property's relative cost.

EXAMPLE: Alexander purchases three HVAC units for his rental building for $6,600. They cost $2,200 each. He also paid a single $600 fee for installation. He can treat the installation cost as $200 per unit ($600 ÷ 3 = $200), resulting in a total price of $2,400 for each HVAC unit. Because this amount is less than the $2,500 de minimis limit, he can currently deduct the entire $7,200 cost using the de minimis safe harbor.

Qualifying for the Safe Harbor

To qualify for the de minimis expensing safe harbor, a taxpayer must:

- establish before the first day of the tax year (January 1 for calendar year taxpayers) an accounting procedure requiring it to expense amounts paid for property (1) costing less than a certain dollar amount, and/or (2) with an economic useful life of 12 months or less, and
- actually treat such amounts as currently deductible expenses on its books and records.

If you have an "applicable financial statement" and wish to qualify to use the $5,000 de minimis limit, your accounting procedure must be in writing and signed before January 1 of the tax year. If you don't have such a statement and qualify only for the $2,500 limit, you don't need to put your procedure in writing (although you may do so). But—whether or not in writing—it should still be in place before January 1 of the tax year. Below is an example of such a written procedure for a taxpayer without an applicable financial statement.

De Minimis Safe Harbor Procedure

Effective January 1, 20xx, ABC hereby adopts the following policy regarding certain expenditures: Amounts paid to acquire or produce tangible personal property will be expensed, and not capitalized, in the year of purchase if: (1) The property costs less than $2,500, or (2) the property has a useful life of 12 months or less.

You don't have to attach your de minimis policy to your tax return. Just keep it in your accounting files. During the year you must follow your policy and actually treat all expenses that fall under the de minimis safe harbor as currently deductible expenses in your books and records.

Claiming the De Minimis Safe Harbor

To take advantage of the de minimis safe harbor, you must file an election with your tax return each year, using the following format:

Section 1.263(a)-1(f) De Minimis Safe Harbor Election

Taxpayer's name:
Taxpayer's address:
Taxpayer's identification number:

The taxpayer is hereby making the de minimis safe harbor election under Section 1.263(a)-1(f).

Materials and Supplies Deduction

IRS regulations that went into effect in 2014 established a new deduction for materials and supplies. "Materials and supplies" are tangible property used or consumed in your rental business operations that fall within any of the following categories:

- any item of tangible personal property (unit of property) that cost $200 or less
- any item of personal property with an economic useful life of 12 months or less, and
- components acquired to maintain or repair a unit of tangible property—that is, spare parts.

The cost of such items may be deducted in the year the item is used or consumed in your rental business—which may be later than the year purchased. To use this deduction, you are supposed to keep records of when such items are used or consumed in your business—something few small landlords do in practice. For this reason, this deduction will be useless for most landlords. Fortunately, they can use the de minimis safe harbor discussed above instead to deduct materials and supplies.

Incidental Materials and Supplies

"Incidental" materials and supplies are personal property items that are carried on hand and for which no record of consumption is kept or for which beginning and ending inventories are not taken. (IRS Reg. § 1.162-3(a)(2).) They must be small in both an operational and financial sense. In other words, these are inexpensive items not worth keeping track of. Costs of incidental materials and supplies are deductible in the year they are paid for, not when the items are used or consumed in your rental business.

> **EXAMPLE:** Landlord John purchases one dozen lightbulbs he plans to use as replacements for the bulbs in his rental units. The cost was minimal and he does not keep an inventory of each bulb. These are incidental compared to his business and deductible in the year he paid for them.

Interaction With De Minimis Safe Harbor

If you elect to use the de minimis safe harbor discussed above, you must apply it to amounts paid for all materials and supplies that meet the requirements for deduction under the safe harbor. (IRS Reg. § 1.263(a)-1(f)(3)(ii).) So, if you use the de minimis safe harbor, you can largely ignore the materials and supplies deduction. This is to your advantage because the de minimis safe harbor has a $2,500 limit for most landlords, as opposed to the $200 materials and supplies limit. Moreover, the de minimis safe harbor permits you to deduct the cost of items the year they are purchased, instead of when they are actually used or consumed in your rental business.

One exception where the materials and supplies deduction could prove useful, even where a de minimis safe harbor election is made, is for components used to repair property. If the components cost more than $2,500, the de minimis safe harbor can't be used. But the materials and supplies deduction can be used, no matter how much the components cost. The deduction may be taken in the year when the components are actually used in the course of a repair or maintenance.

> **EXAMPLE:** Landlord Parker purchases $3,000 worth of roofing shingles he keeps on hand to repair the roof of his apartment building as it deteriorates over time. He can't deduct the cost using the de minimis safe harbor because his deduction limit under the safe harbor is $2,500. However, he can deduct them as materials and supplies the year or years he uses them to repair the roof. The cost of installing the shingles is deductible as a repair.

Section 179 Expensing

Section 179 of the tax code is similar to bonus depreciation in that it allows you to deduct in one year the entire cost of personal property you use in your business. This is called "first-year expensing" or "Section 179 expensing." ("Expensing" is an accounting term that means currently deducting a long-term asset.) Section 179 may be used to deduct much the same property as bonus depreciation. However, during 2018 through 2022, Section 179 will likely not be used much by landlords because they can deduct 100% of the cost of the same property with bonus depreciation. Bonus depreciation is usually a better choice than the Section 179 deduction because Section 179 is subject to several severe restrictions explained below that don't apply to bonus depreciation.

After 2022, when the bonus amount is scheduled to be less than 100%, Section 179 will again become useful. Indeed, it will be far more useful to landlords than ever before because the Tax Cuts and Jobs Act eliminated the long-standing rule that Section 179 could not be used to deduct personal property used in residential rental units.

What Property Can Be Deducted

A business can use Section 179 to deduct tangible, long-term personal property. As with bonus depreciation, this must be used for new property you purchase for cash (including amounts you borrow) from an unrelated person or entity. You can't use Section 179 to deduct the cost of:

- land
- land improvements, including swimming pools, paved parking areas, and fences (these may be deducted with bonus depreciation)

- permanent structures attached to land, including buildings and their structural components, fences, swimming pools, or paved parking areas
- inventory, or
- property used outside the United States.

Before 2018, Section 179 couldn't be used to deduct personal property used in residential rental units—for example, kitchen appliances, carpets, drapes, or blinds. The Tax Cuts and Jobs Act eliminated this prohibition starting in 2018.

Restrictions on Using Section 179

Section 179 is subject to several restrictions that make it less desirable than 100% bonus depreciation (which is scheduled to end after 2022):

- First, you can't use Section 179 to deduct more in one year than your net taxable business income for the year (not counting the Section 179 deduction but including your spouse's salary and business income). Undeductible amounts are carried forward to be deducted in future years. Thus, Section 179 may never result in a loss. There is no such limitation on bonus depreciation.
- In addition, you may only use Section 179 for property you use over 50% of the time for business (this isn't the case with bonus depreciation, except for listed property—primarily cars and light trucks); if your use of the property falls below 50% you have to give back your Section 179 deduction through recapture (see below). There is no such recapture with bonus depreciation except for listed property.
- Section 179 can only be used if your rental activities qualify as a business for tax purposes. You can't use it if your rental activity is an investment, not a business. Bonus depreciation may be used for either business or investment activities.
- Finally, an annual limit applies to the amount of property that can be deducted with Section 179. For 2022, the limit is $1,080,000. The dollar limit is phased out if the amount of qualifying property you place into service during the year exceeds $2,700,000.

- The annual deduction limit applies to all of your businesses combined (rental and nonrental businesses), not to each business you own and run. If you're a partner in a partnership, member of a limited liability company (LLC), or shareholder in an S corporation, the limit applies both to the business entity and to each owner personally.

Unlike bonus depreciation, Section 179 expensing is not automatic. If you want to use it, you must elect to use it by completing IRS Form 4562, and checking a specific box. Also, unlike bonus depreciation, Section 179 does not apply class-wide. You may pick and choose which personal property you wish to deduct with this method.

Regular Depreciation

With bonus depreciation, Section 179, and the de minimis safe harbor and materials and supplies deductions, you might not need to use regular depreciation for personal property for the foreseeable future. However, you might need to use regular depreciation to write off the cost of long-term personal property assets that don't qualify for these methods. For example, you can't use any of these methods for:

- personal property items that you convert to business use
- items purchased from a relative, or
- property inherited or received as a gift or inheritance.

In all these cases, you must deduct the personal property involved with regular depreciation.

Also, under some circumstances, it might be better to use depreciation and draw out your deduction over several years instead of getting your deductions all at once with the other methods. This might be the case where you expect to have much more income in future years. In such years you would be in a higher tax bracket and your depreciation deductions would save more tax.

The passive activity loss rules may prevent you from benefiting from substantial depreciation deductions in the year they are taken if they result in a rental loss. However, these losses are not lost. Rather, they are "suspended losses" that you may deduct in future years when you have more rental income or you sell the property. (See Chapter 16.)

To depreciate personal property, you must have the following information:

- when the property was placed in service
- its depreciable basis
- the depreciation period
- which first-year convention applies
- the depreciation method, and
- whether the property is listed property.

When Is Personal Property Placed in Service?

Depreciation begins when property is placed in service. Personal property inside or attached to a building is placed in service when it's installed in the building and is available and ready for rental use. Keep copies of sales receipts showing when personal property was delivered.

Determining the Basis of Personal Property

Usually, your basis in personal property is whatever you paid for it. Its cost includes not only the purchase price, but also sales tax, delivery charges, installation, and testing fees, if any. You may depreciate the entire cost, no matter how you paid for the property—in cash, on a credit card, or with a bank loan. In certain situations, however, you can't use the cost basis method for personal property.

Property Converted to Rental Use

If you convert property you have been using personally to use in your rental activity, your starting basis is equal to the property's fair market value when you start using it for rental purposes.

> EXAMPLE: Jeff wants to add some furniture to a vacant apartment he's trying to rent. Rather than buying new furniture, he moves in some old furniture from his personal residence, including a sofa, dinette set, and bed. The fair market value of these items when Jeff places them in his rental is $400. This amount is his starting basis when he begins to depreciate the property.

You determine your property's fair market value by figuring out how much someone would be willing to pay for it. If the property is new, or fairly new, you can use the cost to replace it. If the property is older, you'll need to figure out the value based on the new price minus an amount for the wear and tear the property has undergone. Look at classified ads and listings for similar property online, or call people who buy and sell the type of property involved. If you think the property is extremely valuable, get an appraisal from an expert. Keep records of how you calculated the property's value.

Most personal property that you convert to rental use probably won't be worth much. You can't claim inflated values for old property just to maximize your depreciation deductions.

Property Bought With a Trade-In

Before 2018, if you traded in an old item of personal property for a new one, you could elect to do a tax-free exchange in which the tax basis of the old item was subtracted from the cost of the new item. With such an exchange, there would be no tax due on the sale of the trade-in. However, the Tax Cuts and Jobs Act eliminated such treatment for all personal property. Today, if you trade in old personal property for new, you must treat the trade-in transaction as a taxable sale. You subtract the old item's tax basis (original cost minus depreciation deductions) from what the dealer or other seller pays you for it and pay tax on any gain (or deduct any loss).

> EXAMPLE: Parker owns a pickup truck he uses exclusively for his rental business. He trades in the truck for a new model that cost $20,000. He paid the dealer $15,000 cash and received $5,000 from the dealer for trading in the old pickup. His old truck's adjusted basis was $4,000, so he earned a $1,000 profit on the trade-in on which he must pay tax at ordinary income rates. His starting basis in the new truck is $20,000.

Inherited and Gifted Personal Property

The starting basis of inherited personal property is its fair market value on the day the owner died. Your starting basis in gifted property is its fair market value at the time of the gift.

Mixed-Use Property

You may take a depreciation deduction for personal property you use both for your rental activity and for personal purposes. Reduce your depreciable basis in the property by the percentage of your personal use. This will, of course, reduce the amount you can depreciate.

> EXAMPLE: Miranda converts her personal lawn mower to rental use. Its basis is $400. She uses the lawn mower 75% of the time for her rental business and 25% of the time to mow her own lawn. Her depreciable basis in the mower is reduced by 25%, so her basis is $300 instead of $400 (75% × $400 = $300). Miranda can depreciate $300 over the asset's depreciation period.

You can take a depreciation deduction even if you use an asset only 1% of the time for business. (But special rules apply if you use cars and other types of listed property less than 50% of the time for business—see "Listed Property," below.)

If you use property for both business and personal purposes, you must keep a diary or log listing the dates, times, and reasons the property was used in order to distinguish business from personal use. (See Chapter 17.)

Depreciation Period

Virtually all of the personal property you use in your rental activity will have a five- or seven-year depreciation period. The depreciation periods for most types of personal property used by landlords are listed below. These periods are also called "recovery classes." All property that comes within a period is said to belong to that class. For example, computers have a five-year depreciation period and thus fall within the five-year class, along with automobiles and office equipment.

First-Year Depreciation

The IRS has established certain rules (called "conventions") that govern how many months of depreciation you can take for the first year that you own an asset. The conventions for personal property are different from those for real property.

Type of Property	Depreciation Period
Computer software (Software included in the price of a computer is depreciated as part of the computer, unless you're billed separately for the software; other software is separately depreciated.)	3 years
Computers and their peripheral equipment Office machinery Automobiles Light trucks (actual weight less than 13,000 pounds) Appliances, such as stoves, refrigerators, dishwashers, washing machines, clothes dryers, and window air conditioners Carpets Furniture used in rental property Drapes and blinds	5 years
Office furniture and equipment, such as desks and files Cell phones, riding lawn mowers, snow blasters Any property that does not have a class life and that has not been designated by law as being in any other class	7 years
Shrubbery Permanent fences Sidewalks Driveways Paved parking areas Landscaping Sewer and drainage facilities Swimming pools	15 years

The basic rule is that, no matter when you buy personal property, you treat it as being placed in service on July 1—the midpoint of the year. So, you can take half a year of depreciation for the first year that you own personal property you use for your rental activity.

You are not allowed to use the half-year convention if more than 40% of the long-term personal property you buy during the year is placed in service during the last three months of the year. The 40% figure is determined by adding together the basis of all the depreciable property you bought during the year and comparing that to the basis of all of the property you bought during the fourth quarter.

If you exceed the 40% ceiling, you must use the mid-quarter convention. Group all of the property that you purchased during the year by calendar quarter (depending on when you bought it) and treat it as if you had placed it in service at the midpoint of that quarter.

It's usually best to avoid having to use the mid-quarter convention, which means you'll want to buy more than 60% of your total depreciable personal property for your rental activity before September 30 of the year.

Depreciation Methods

Personal property is usually depreciated using the Modified Accelerated Cost Recovery System, or MACRS. (A slightly different system, called the Alternative Depreciation System or ADS, applies to certain property—see "Depreciating Listed Property," below.) You can ordinarily use three different methods to calculate personal property depreciation under MACRS: straight-line depreciation or one of two accelerated depreciation methods. Once you choose your method, you're stuck with it for the entire life of the asset.

In addition, you must use the same method for all property of the same class that you purchase during the year. For example, if you use the straight-line method to depreciate a computer, you must use that method to depreciate any other property in the same class as computers. Computers fall within the five-year class, so you must use the straight-line method for all other five-year property you buy during the year, such as office equipment.

Most people use accelerated depreciation to depreciate personal property. As the name implies, this method provides faster depreciation than the straight-line method. It does not increase your total depreciation deduction, but it permits you to take larger deductions in the first few years after you buy an asset. You make up for this by taking smaller deductions in later years.

Using accelerated depreciation isn't necessarily a good idea if you expect your income to go up in future years. Some restrictions also apply to when you can use accelerated depreciation. For example, you can't use it for cars, computers, and certain other property that you use for your rental activity less than 50% of the time (see "Listed Property," below).

You can figure out the amount of your yearly depreciation deduction using depreciation tables prepared by the IRS. These tables factor in the depreciation convention and method. They are all available in IRS Publication 946, *How to Depreciate Property*. There are also many online depreciation calculators you may use.

Listed Property

Fearing that taxpayers might claim depreciation for listed property but actually use it for personal reasons, the IRS imposes special rules on certain personal property that can easily be used for personal as well as business or investment purposes. These items, called "listed property," include:

- cars, light trucks, and certain other vehicles
- motorcycles, boats, and airplanes, and
- any other property generally used for entertainment, recreation, or amusement—for example, televisions, cameras, and camcorders.

To prevent this kind of behavior, the IRS requires you to document your use of listed property. You can satisfy this requirement by keeping a logbook showing when and how the property is used. (See Chapter 17 for more on record keeping.)

These rules apply only to listed property that you use yourself in your rental activity. They don't apply to personal property contained in a rental unit—for example, a television you place in a rental unit for a tenant's use.

Depreciating Listed Property

If you use listed property for your rental activity more than 50% of the time, you may deduct its cost just like any other long-term personal property under the normal depreciation rules. However, if you use listed property 50% or less of the time for your rental activity, you must use the straight-line method—the slowest method of depreciation. And, the property doesn't qualify for the 50% bonus depreciation. You also can't use the normal depreciation periods allowed under the MACRS depreciation system. Instead, you must use the depreciation periods the Alternative Depreciation System (ADS) provides. These periods are generally longer than the ordinary MACRS periods. However, you may still depreciate cars and trucks over five years.

If you start out using accelerated depreciation and in a later year your business use drops to 50% or less, you have to switch to the straight-line method and ADS period for that year and subsequent years. In addition, you are subject to depreciation recapture for the prior years—that is, you must calculate how much more depreciation you got in the prior years by using accelerated depreciation and count that amount as ordinary taxable income for the current year. This will, of course, increase your tax bill for the year.

When You Sell Your Property

When you sell your property, you'll have to pay tax on any gain (profit) you earn ("realize," in tax lingo), unless you do a like-kind exchange. If you lose money, you'll be able to deduct the loss, subject to important limitations covered in Chapter 16. Whether you have a gain or loss depends on your adjusted basis in the property.

Adjusted Basis

Your basis in property isn't fixed. It changes over time to reflect the true amount of your investment. This new basis is called the "adjusted basis" because it reflects adjustments from your starting basis. Increases in basis are good because they'll reduce any taxable profit when you sell your property. Decreases in basis are bad because they have the opposite effect.

Reductions in Basis

Each year, you must subtract from the property's basis the amount of depreciation allowed for the property—this is true regardless of whether you actually claimed any depreciation on your tax return. If you hold on to your property for the full recovery period—27.5 years for residential rental property—your adjusted basis will be reduced to zero, and there will be nothing left to depreciate.

Your starting basis in property must also be reduced by any items that represent a return of your cost. These include:

- the amount of any insurance or other payment you receive as the result of a casualty or theft loss
- any deductible casualty loss not covered by insurance (see Chapter 14), and
- any amount you receive for granting an easement.

Your basis is also reduced if you took the wrong amount of depreciation on your tax return. If you claimed too little depreciation, you must decrease the basis by the amount you should have taken. If you took too much depreciation, you must decrease your basis by the amount you should have deducted, plus the part of the excess you deducted that actually lowered your tax liability for any year.

Increases in Basis

You must increase the basis of any property by:

- the cost of any additions or improvements
- amounts spent to restore property after it is damaged or lost due to theft, fire, flood, storm, or other casualty (see Chapter 14)
- the cost of extending utility service lines to the property, and
- legal fees relating to the property, such as the cost of defending and perfecting title.

In addition, assessments for items that tend to increase the value of your property, such as streets and sidewalks, must be added to its basis. For example, if your city installs curbing on the street in front of your rental house, and assesses you for the cost, you must add the assessment to the basis of your property.

Effect of Adjusted Basis When You Sell

When you sell your rental property, your gain or loss for tax purposes is determined by subtracting its adjusted basis on the date of sale from the sales price (plus sales expenses, such as real estate commissions). So, reductions in basis can increase your tax liability when you sell your property because they will increase your gain. Increases in basis will reduce your gain and therefore your tax liability.

EXAMPLE: Viola bought a small apartment building in January 2017 for $200,000 and sold it for $300,000 in December 2022. Her starting basis was $200,000. The following chart shows her adjusted basis for each year.

Year	Depreciation Deduction	Increases in Basis	Adjusted Basis (increases − reductions)
Original Basis			$ 200,000
2017	$ 6,970	None	193,030
2018	7,272	None	185,758
2019	7,272	None	178,486
2020	7,272	None	171,214
2021	7,272	None	163,942
2022	6,969	$13,027 for new roof	170,000
Total Depreciation	$ 43,027		

Viola calculates her taxable gain on the property by subtracting her adjusted basis from the sales price: $300,000 − $170,000 = $130,000.

As you can see, when you sell your property, you effectively give back the depreciation deductions you took on it. Because they reduce your adjusted basis, they increase your taxable gain. So, Viola's taxable gain was increased by the $43,027 in depreciation deductions she took. The amount of your gain attributable to the depreciation deductions you took in prior years is taxed at a single 25% rate (however, if your top tax rate is below 25%, the lower rate applies). Viola, for example, would have to pay a 25% tax on the $43,027 in depreciation deductions she received. The remaining gain on the sale is taxed at capital gains rates for 2022. The gain must also be added to Viola's net investment income and her adjusted gross income. This could make her subject to the 3.8% net investment income tax (see Chapter 19).

		Tax Rate	Tax
Sales price	$300,000		
Adjusted basis	170,000		
Total gain (sales price – adjusted basis)	$130,000		
	$130,000		
Gain due to prior depreciation	– 43,027	× 25% =	$10,757
Remaining capital gain (total gain – depreciation)	$86,973	× 15% =	13,046
Total Tax			$23,803

You can't avoid this result by failing to take depreciation deductions each year. The IRS will treat you as if you had taken the depreciation and reduce your adjusted basis accordingly. So, you'll end up paying tax on depreciation deductions you never claimed. A true tax disaster!

Like-Kind Exchanges: Deferring Taxes on Rental Property

In a like-kind exchange (also called a "Section 1031 exchange"), you can defer paying taxes upon the sale of property by swapping your property for similar property owned by someone else. The Tax Cuts and Jobs Act eliminated like-kind exchanges for personal property after 2017. But they remain available for real property.

The great tax advantage of a like-kind exchange is that the property you receive in the exchange is treated as if it were a continuation of the property you gave up. The result is that you postpone the recognition (taxation) of gain by shifting the basis of the old property to the new property. So you defer paying taxes on any profit you would have received and own new property instead. Such deferral applies not only to regular capital gains taxes, but to the 3.8% net investment income tax as well.

Capital Gains Rates

2022 Income If Married Filing Jointly	Long-Term Capital Gains Tax Rates
$83,350 or less	0
$83,351 to $517,200	15%
All over $517,200	20%

2022 Income If Single	Long-Term Capital Gains Tax Rates
$41,675 or less	0
$41,676 to $459,750	15%
All over $459,750	20%

In addition, taxpayers subject to the net investment income tax have to pay an additional 3.8% tax on some or all of their gains. This tax applies to single taxpayers with an adjusted gross income (AGI) over $200,000, and married couples filing jointly who have an AGI over $250,000. Depending on their income, such taxpayers will pay an 18.8% or 23.8% tax on their gains. (See Chapter 19.)

CAUTION

Like-kind exchanges are one of the most complex areas of taxation. The IRS strictly enforces many rules. These exchanges should be done only with professional assistance.

EXAMPLE: Eve exchanges a rental house with an adjusted basis of $250,000 for other real estate held for investment. The fair market value of both properties is $500,000. The basis of Eve's new property is the same as the basis of the old ($250,000). No gain is recognized on the transaction.

You may only exchange property for other similar property, called "like-kind" property by the IRS. Like-kind properties have the same nature or character, even if they differ in grade or quality. All real estate owned for investment or business use in the United States is considered to be like-kind with all other such real estate in the United States, no matter the type or location. For example, an apartment building in New York is like-kind to an office building in California.

If you keep exchanging your property for property worth at least as much as yours, you'll never recognize any gain on which you must pay tax. However, sooner or later you'll probably want to sell the replacement property for cash, not exchange it for another property. When this occurs, the original deferred gain, plus any additional gain realized since the purchase of the replacement property, is subject to tax. For this reason, a like-kind exchange is tax deferred, not tax free.

> **EXAMPLE:** Assume that five years after the exchange described in the above example, Eve sells her rental house for $800,000 cash. Now she has to pay tax—and quite a lot at that—because she has a $550,000 long-term capital gain. Her gain is $550,000 because her basis in the property is only $250,000 (the basis of the property she exchanged for the building five years earlier). The $800,000 sales price minus the $250,000 basis = $550,000 gain.

However, if you convert the last property you exchange into your personal residence, you can permanently exclude up to $500,000 of your gain from its sale. You must own the property for at least five years and live in it for at least two years to qualify for this exclusion.

> **EXAMPLE:** Assume that Eve rents out her house for all of 2016, 2017, and 2018. On April 15, 2019, she moves into the house and uses it as her personal residence. She can sell the property any time after April 14, 2021 (after five years of ownership and living there for two years), and pay no tax at all on up to $500,000 of her gain because she is a married taxpayer filing jointly (the exclusion is only $250,000 for single taxpayers).

In practice, it's rarely the case that two people want to swap their properties with each other. Instead, one of the property owners usually wants cash for their property, not a swap. This transaction can still be structured as a like-kind exchange. This is often done with the help of a third party called a "qualified intermediary" or QI, in the business of facilitating like-kind exchanges.

> **EXAMPLE:** Abe owns a rental triplex he bought for $400,000 that is now worth $500,000. He wants to exchange it for other property instead of selling it and having to pay tax on his $100,000 profit. He puts his property up for sale and in the meantime contacts Carl, a qualified intermediary. Carl locates a small apartment building worth $500,000 that Abe likes. Bob, the owner of the building, however, has no interest in exchanging it for other property. Carl and Abe enter into an exchange agreement. Carl purchases Bob's building for $500,000 cash that he borrows and then exchanges it for Abe's triplex. Carl receives a fee for facilitating the exchange and sells Abe's triplex to repay the funds he borrowed to buy Bob's property. With Carl's help, Abe has exchanged his triplex for Bob's building, even though Bob didn't want to do an exchange.

Strict time limits apply to such delayed exchanges, which can be more complicated than the above example, involving as many as four parties. You must identify the replacement property for your property within 45 days of its sale. And your replacement property purchase must be completed within 180 days of the initial sale. Because of these time limits, it's a good idea to have a replacement property lined up before you sell your property. Professional exchange companies (also called "accommodators" or "facilitators") can help you find replacement property and handle the transaction for you. You can find listings for such companies through the website of the Federation of Exchange Accommodators at www.1031.org.

For more information on real property exchanges, see IRS Publication 544, *Sales and Other Dispositions of Assets*, and IRS Inst. 8824, *Instructions for Form 8824, Like-Kind Exchanges*.

The Home Sale Exclusion—
Avoiding Taxes When You Sell Your Rental

You might be familiar with the home sale exclusion, which allows individuals who sell their principal home to exclude from their taxable income up to $250,000 of the gain from the sale, or up to $500,000 if the sellers are a married couple who file a joint return. (The exclusion applies not only to regular income tax, but to the 3.8% net investment income tax as well; see Chapter 19.) What you might not know, however, is that this valuable exclusion can be used for rental property too. To qualify for the $250,000/$500,000 home sale exclusion, you (or your spouse or former spouse) must own and occupy a home as your principal residence for at least two of the five years before you sell it. This means that the home may not be a rental property during those two years.

However, you don't have to be living in the house at the time you sell it. Your two years of ownership and use may occur anytime during the five years before the date of the sale. So, for example, you can move out of the house for up to three years and still qualify for the exclusion. (I.R.C. § 121(a).) This rule has a very practical application: It means you may rent out your home for up to three years prior to the sale and still qualify for the exclusion. Be sure to keep track of this time period and sell the house before it runs out.

> **EXAMPLE:** Callie purchases a one-bedroom condo on January 1, 2016 and lives in it for two full years. She then moves to another state to take a new job. Rather than sell the condo, she elects to rent it out. If she sells the condo by January 1, 2022, she'll qualify for the $250,000 home sale exclusion because she owned and used the condo as her principal home for two years during the five-year period before the sale. If she waits even one more day to sell, she will get no exclusion at all.

There is an important limit on the $250,000/$500,000 exclusion: It doesn't apply to any depreciation deductions taken on the property after May 6, 1997. You must reduce your applicable exclusion by the total amount of depreciation you were entitled to take during these years—that is, you must include the amount as ordinary income on your tax return.

However, starting in 2009, the tax law limits the $250,000/$500,000 exclusion for taxpayers who initially use their home as a rental, as a vacation home, or for any other use than as a principal residence (a "nonqualifying use" in IRS-speak). The amount of gain eligible for the applicable exclusion is reduced pro rata based on how many years after 2008 the home was used other than as the taxpayer's principal residence. The effect is to reduce the exclusion for landlords who convert a rental home into their personal residence.

> **EXAMPLE:** Timmy, a single taxpayer, buys a home on March 1, 2016 for $500,000 and rents it out for the next two years. During this time, he takes $10,000 in depreciation deductions. He evicts his tenants and moves into the home on March 1, 2018, making it his personal residence. Timmy sells the property for $650,000 on March 1, 2021. Timmy owned the house for five years and had a $150,000 gain from the sale. However, because he used the home as a rental for two years before he converted it into his residence, 40% of his total use of the property during the five years he owned was a nonqualifying use. His $250,000 tax exclusion must be reduced by 40%, or $100,000. So, he qualifies for a $150,000 tax exclusion. But his exclusion of gain from the sale is limited to $140,000 because he must recapture his $10,000 in depreciation deductions.

This reduction in the $250,000/$500,000 exclusion can only occur if the home was used as a rental or other nonqualifying use before it became the taxpayer's principal residence. Rental or other uses of the home after it was used as the principal residence do not constitute a nonqualified use and thus do not reduce the exclusion. This is why Callie's rental of her condo in the first example above, after she lived in it, doesn't reduce her $250,000 exclusion.

This rule applies only to nonqualifying uses occurring during 2009 and later. Uses before 2009 are not counted and do not reduce the amount of gain eligible for the applicable exclusion.

RESOURCE
For more information on the home sale exclusion, refer to IRS Publication 523, *Selling Your Home.*

Tax Reporting and Record Keeping for Depreciation

You must report depreciation on IRS Form 4562, *Depreciation and Amortization (Including Information on Listed Property).* Carry over the amount of your depreciation to your Schedule E and subtract it from your gross rental income along with your other rental expenses.

> ( ) **TIP**
> **Use a tax software program for Form 4562.** Form 4562 is one of the most complex and confusing IRS forms. If you want to complete it yourself, do yourself a favor and use a tax preparation program.

You need to keep accurate records for each asset you depreciate showing:
- a description of the asset
- when and how you purchased the property
- the date it was placed in service
- its original cost
- the percentage of time you use it for business
- the amount of depreciation you took for the asset in prior years, if any
- the asset's depreciable basis
- the depreciation method used
- the length of the depreciation period, and
- the amount of depreciation you deducted for the year.

If you use tax preparation software, it should create a worksheet containing this information. Be sure to check these carefully and save them. You can also use an accounting program such as *QuickBooks* to keep track of your depreciating assets. (Simple checkbook programs like *Quicken* are not designed to track depreciation.) You may also use a spreadsheet program to create your own depreciation worksheet. Spreadsheet templates are available for this purpose. Of course, you can also do the job by hand.

The instructions to IRS Form 4562 contain a blank worksheet you can use.

An example of a filled-out worksheet is shown below.

Depreciation Worksheet

Description of Property	House 666 First St.	New roof 123 Main St.
Date Placed in Service	2/10/2021	4/10/2020
Cost or Other Basis	$200,000	$10,000
Business/Investment Use Percentage	100%	100%
Section 179 Deduction and Special Allowance	0	0
Depreciation in Prior Years	0	$258
Basis for Depreciation	$200,000	$10,000
Method/Convention	SL/MM	SL/MM
Recovery Period	27.5	27.5
Rate or Table Percentage	3.182%	3.636%
Depreciation Deduction	$6,364	$364

Be sure to keep all the documents you have showing the cost of your depreciable assets. These include:
- your real property purchase agreement
- the settlement statement and closing statement you receive from the escrow company when your property purchase is completed
- canceled checks, bank records of payment, and receipts for all the expenses you paid for the purchase
- receipts and canceled checks for all improvements you make to the property
- property tax bills, and
- evidence for the improvement ratio (see Chapter 6).

If you use cost segregation (see Chapter 6), you need evidence of the personal property that was included with your purchase and its age—this includes carpeting, stove, refrigerator, dishwasher, drapes and other window coverings, washers, and dryers. You can include this information in your purchase agreement or a separate statement signed by the seller.

Maximizing Your Depreciation Deductions

This chapter shows you two important ways to maximize your depreciation deductions. First, you'll learn how to best determine the value of your rental buildings and nondepreciable land. Next, you'll see how you can use cost segregation to greatly increase the depreciation deductions you get each year during the first few years you own rental property.

Beware the Passive Loss Rules

Using the methods described in this chapter to increase your depreciation deductions won't necessarily result in an immediate tax reduction, and might never do so. This will be the case if more deductions will only increase your real estate losses and the passive activity loss rules prevent you from currently deducting any more losses than you already are deducting (or deducting any losses at all). However, such losses are not lost: They are deductible in future years if you have sufficient rental or other passive income. See Chapter 16 for a detailed discussion of the passive loss rules.

Determining the Value of Your Land and Buildings

As discussed in Chapter 5, you can't depreciate land because it lasts forever. But when you buy a rental property, you usually pay one lump sum that covers the cost of both the land and buildings it contains. To determine the depreciable value of the buildings (their basis), you must allocate the purchase price between the land and buildings and other depreciable property.

How you do this allocation is the single most important factor that will determine how much depreciation you may deduct each year and in total. The more your land is worth, the less your basis in the property and the less depreciation you will receive.

EXAMPLE: Miranda owns a rental duplex that cost $200,000. If the land is worth $50,000, she'll have a $150,000 depreciable basis for the building. If the land is worth $20,000, her basis in the building will be $180,000. The chart below illustrates the difference in the depreciation deductions she'll receive assuming the property was placed in service in January. She receives over $1,000 more in depreciation each year with the lower land valuation.

Year	Depreciation: $150,000 basis ($50,000 land value)	Depreciation: $180,000 basis ($20,000 land value)
1	$5,228	$6,264
2–27	$5,454	$6,555
28	$2,955	$3,546

In addition, at higher income levels (for 2022, $170,050 for singles, $340,100 for marrieds filing jointly), the pass-through tax deduction is based wholly or partly on 2.5% of the value of your rental property, not counting the land. So, the less your land is worth, the greater your pass-through deduction will be. (See Chapter 7.)

Tax Penalties for Unreasonable Valuations

The IRS may impose tax penalties if it determines that you overstated the value of your buildings and other depreciable property—and correspondingly understated the value of your land. The penalty is equal to 20% of the amount of tax you underpaid. However, the penalty may be imposed only if you overstated the value of your depreciable property by at least 200% over the correct amount and the overstatement resulted in an underpayment of tax of at least $5,000. Few small landlords ever overstate the value of their property by this much. Moreover, even if you do overstate your values by this amount, the IRS must waive the penalty if you had a "reasonable basis" for your valuation and acted in good faith. (I.R.C. § 6662.) The fact that your property valuations must be wildly inflated before you'll be subject to tax penalties gives you an idea of how much leeway you have in deciding what depreciable rental property is worth.

It's up to you (or your accountant or tax preparer) to decide how much your land and buildings are worth in the first year you depreciate your property. You don't need to provide your allocation or explain how you arrived at it on the forms you file with the IRS to claim depreciation— you simply list your property's depreciable basis. However, the IRS can review your determination if you're audited. In that event, you'll need to explain how you arrived at your basis.

If the IRS determines that your valuation is too low, you'll have to pay back some of the depreciation you received, along with interest and, in some cases, tax penalties. (See "Tax Penalties for Unreasonable Valuations," above.)

Most people don't give their land valuation much thought; they simply use a standard formula or their property tax bill to determine its value. But, as explained below, there are other ways to value your land and buildings that may yield much better results.

No One Way to Determine Land and Building Values

The IRS gives landlords virtually no guidance on how to go about calculating the value of their land and buildings for depreciation purposes. Its regulations simply provide that: "In the case of the acquisition ... of a combination of depreciable and nondepreciable property for a lump sum, as for example, buildings and land, the basis for depreciation cannot exceed an amount which bears the same proportion to the lump sum as the value of the depreciable property at the time of acquisition bears to the value of the entire property at that time." (IRS Reg. § 1.167(a)-5.)

In other words, the basis of the nondepreciable land and the depreciable buildings and other improvements must be allocated in proportion to their relative values. But how do you arrive at these relative values? There is no single method to determine how much any property is worth, and the IRS does not require you to use any particular method. Different methods can yield very different results. The methods you may employ include using:

- your property tax bill
- the replacement cost of your building and improvements
- buyer–seller valuations, or
- comparable land sales.

You can try all these methods and use the best result, or average the various results you obtain. Remember, your valuation doesn't have to be precise; it just has to be a reasonable ballpark figure.

Figuring Your Improvement Ratio

The easy way to determine how much of the value of the property you can depreciate is to figure your property's improvement ratio (also called the "land-to-building ratio" or "land-to-improvement ratio"). This ratio is the amount the improvements (buildings) are worth compared to the value of the total property, expressed as a percentage. This ratio is a mathematical way to show the relative values of the land and improvements, as the IRS regulation requires.

For example, if you determine that the correct improvement ratio for your property is 80%, you multiply the total cost of the property by this amount to determine your depreciable basis. If your total cost (purchase price + certain depreciable expenses of the sale) is $100,000, the amount you can depreciate is $80,000 ($100,000 × 80% = $80,000). The other $20,000 is the value of the land, which may not be depreciated.

Improvement ratios vary from 85% to 40% or less depending on the location of the property. Obviously, land values vary widely—for example, land in Manhattan or San Francisco is worth much more than the same amount of land in Kansas City or Portland. So, an apartment building in San Francisco might have a 40% improvement ratio, while the same structure in Portland could have an 80% ratio.

It's important to understand that a precise improvement ratio for a property doesn't exist because land value is not a fact, like the size of a lot; rather, it's based on someone's opinion or calculations based on certain assumptions. Different opinions or assumptions can lead to different ratios. You want your improvement ratio to be as high as possible, but not so high that the IRS will likely conclude it's unreasonable if you're audited.

Don't Use a Standard Improvement Ratio

Many accountants and tax preparers use a standard ratio for every property—for example, 75% or 80%. They don't bother to look at any evidence of the property's value, such as the county tax assessor's valuation or lender's appraisal. Don't use this method—it leaves much to be desired. If the IRS audits you and questions the ratio, you'll have no evidence to back it up.

Property Tax Bill

Most landlords determine their improvement ratios by using their property tax bill. The bill usually provides a valuation of the land and buildings together, and a value for each alone, or for just the buildings alone. The ratio is determined by dividing the assessed improvement value by the total assessed value of the property (assessed improvement value ÷ total assessed value = improvement ratio).

If you don't have a copy of your tax bill handy, you might be able to find the assessor's valuation at its website. The following website provides links to local tax assessor websites in the various states: www.pulawski.net.

Often, the values listed on your property tax bill do not reflect the true market value of your property. This is not important, however, for purposes of determining your improvement ratio.

> EXAMPLE: Sara buys a rental duplex with a total basis of $200,000 (purchase price + depreciable sale expenses). The property tax bill lists the property's total value at $160,000, and provides that the improvements are worth $110,000 and the land $50,000. According to the county tax assessor, therefore, the property has a 69% improvement ratio ($110,000 ÷ $160,000 = 69%). Using this percentage, her depreciable basis is $138,000 (69% × $200,000 = $138,000). She may use this amount to determine her depreciation each year.

This is a very easy and simple way to calculate the value of your land and buildings. It is what most people do, and the IRS will almost never object if you use this method. Using this method has been approved by the tax court. (*Nielsen v. Comm'r.*, T.C. Summ. Op. 2017-31.) But improvement ratios determined from a property tax assessment often don't reflect reality. County tax assessors aren't greatly concerned about arriving at an accurate breakdown of the relative values of your land and improvements because it has no effect on your property tax bill—your tax is based on the total assessed value of your property. Often, county assessors apply a standard percentage to all property in the area—for example, 70%. Or, they might use sales data from previous years that is out of date.

As a general rule, tax assessor improvement ratios are on the low side. You can usually do better using a different means to determine your basis.

You Don't Have to Use the Assessor's Valuation

Many people believe they have to use their county tax assessor's valuations to calculate their basis. But nothing in the tax law or IRS regulations requires you to use a county tax assessor valuation or hire an appraiser to do a valuation. Indeed, in at least one case, the tax court found that the improvement ratio derived from the county assessor's valuation should not be used, declaring that there was no evidence that "the assessor's allocations of value between land and building comport with reality." (*Meiers v. Comm'r.*, T.C. Memo 1982-5.) This case is a good one to point out to any IRS auditor who says you have to use your county tax assessor's valuation.

Replacement Cost

Another way to determine your improvement ratio is to use the replacement cost of your building and other improvements. The replacement cost is the cost to build a brand-new structure that is identical to the structure currently on your land. If the building you're depreciating is not brand-new, you must reduce the replacement cost according to its age and useful life. The reference guides listed below can help you do this.

> **EXAMPLE:** Steven Meiers purchased two condominiums in 1977. His property tax bill gave an improvement ratio of 55%—that is, the land was worth 45% of the purchase price and the building 55%. Meiers didn't think this was good enough. He investigated the replacement costs for his buildings, and determined that a fair improvement ratio was 80%. This, of course, gave him a much higher depreciable basis. The IRS audited Meiers and insisted that he should use the tax assessor's ratio. Meiers appealed to the tax court and won. The court found that Meiers's 80% ratio was reasonable and should be used. How did Meiers calculate his ratio? He used the replacement cost of the buildings. (*Meiers v. Comm'r.*, T.C. Memo 1982-5.)

Several ways to determine replacement cost include:
- getting an appraisal
- doing your own calculations
- getting an expert opinion, or
- using construction records.

Appraisal

If you borrowed money from a bank or another lender to acquire the property, the lender almost certainly required an appraisal before approving your loan. You should make sure to obtain and keep a copy of the appraisal. It should contain the appraiser's estimate of how much it would cost to replace the structure and how much the land is worth. This estimate might be in the section of the appraisal report called "cost approach." The appraiser provides an estimate of how much it would cost to replace the structure with an identical new structure, and then reduces this amount with an allowance for depreciation, depending on the age of the building. The appraiser also gives an estimate of the cost of replacing improvements other than the building—for example, walkways. These costs are added together to come up with the total replacement cost—often called the "indicated value by cost approach." The IRS will probably accept the appraiser's valuation, unless it's clearly unreasonable.

You calculate your improvement ratio by dividing the amount of the appraiser's replacement cost by the appraised value of the entire property (structures and land). In other words, appraiser's replacement cost of building and land improvements ÷ appraised value of entire property = improvement ratio.

EXAMPLE: Recall Miranda from the first example, who bought a rental duplex for $200,000. Her lender's appraisal provides that the value of the entire property is $210,000. The cost method section says that the replacement cost of the duplex and other property improvements is $150,000, giving Miranda an improvement ratio of 71% ($150,000 ÷ $210,000 = 71%). This ratio is better than the 69% improvement ratio the county assessor's valuation provided.

Calculating Replacement Value Yourself

Appraisers aren't infallible. An appraisal is just one person's opinion as to how much a property is worth. Appraisals of the same property by different appraisers can and do differ. Your lender's appraisal of the replacement cost might have been poorly done or been too conservative. Like county tax assessors, lenders' appraisers are more concerned with the total value of the property than the relative values of the land and structures, so they might not have given the replacement cost calculation all the time and attention you would like.

If you think this is the case, you can hire an appraiser to do a new valuation of your property. An appraisal for a single-family residence typically costs $300 to $400. Appraising an income property of two or more units costs at least $800 to $1,000. Your appraisal will carry the most weight with the IRS if it's done by a well-qualified appraiser. Well-qualified real estate appraisers ordinarily belong to the Appraisal Institute and use the initials MAI (Member of the Appraisal Institute). You can find a directory of MAI appraisers at www.appraisalinstitute.org.

If you want to pay for an appraisal, go ahead. However, you don't have to hire an expensive appraiser to determine your property's replacement cost. You can do it yourself, which is what Steven Meiers in the above example did. This will require that you spend a little time and effort, but will enable you to cheaply double-check the replacement cost determined by the lender's appraiser.

Figuring out the replacement cost for a building might sound hard, but it really isn't. The Craftsman Book Company's *National Building Cost Estimator* software will calculate the replacement cost of a building for you (www.craftsman-book.com). All you have to do is plug in detailed information about the structure—its size, building materials, age, location, and so forth.

If you don't want to use software, you can calculate your building's replacement cost by using one of the many readily available publications that provide estimates of how much it costs to build any type of structure. These include:

- The *National Building Cost Manual* (Craftsman Book Company; www.craftsman-book.com)
- The *National Construction Estimator* (Craftsman Book Company), and
- *Walker's Building Estimator's Reference Book* (Frank R. Walker Company; www.frankrwalker.com).

You should be able to find one or more of these in your public library. Make sure to use the current edition. These books are updated each year.

> **EXAMPLE:** Miranda wants to figure the replacement value of her duplex herself. She refers to the *National Building Cost Manual* in her local library. It tells her that the cost to build a four-unit building like hers of average quality is $60 per square foot. Her building contains 3,000 square feet, resulting in a $180,000 replacement cost. However, the $180,000 amount represents the cost to build a brand-new building. Miranda's building is five years old. The *National Building Cost Manual* tells Miranda that a building like hers has approximately a 55-year useful life and will be worth 88% of its original cost after five years. 88% of $180,000 equals $158,400. This is the true approximate value of Miranda's building. This amount gives her an improvement ratio of 79% ($158,400 ÷ $200,000 = 79%). This ratio is better than the 75% improvement ratio she obtained using the appraiser's valuation. She decides to use this improvement ratio to calculate her depreciation. She takes care to keep all the documentation showing how she calculated her duplex's replacement value, including making copies of the relevant pages from the *National Building Cost Manual*.

Construction Records

Alternatively, if you built the building yourself, or bought it from a seller who built it, you might have ready access to construction documentation showing exactly how much it cost to build the structure. This information will make it easy to figure the replacement value—use the original cost less a reduction for depreciation that you can calculate using the references listed above.

Buyer–Seller Valuation

When you buy real estate, you usually pay one lump sum for everything on the property. But you and the seller could agree on how much the land and buildings are worth and list the values in your purchase agreement. IRS regulations provide that when buildings and land are sold together, an allocation of their relative values by the buyer and seller in an arm's-length agreement will be respected if the buyer and seller have adverse interests. (IRS Reg. 1.1250-1(a)(6)(i).) Residential real estate buyers and sellers typically do have adverse interests when it comes to the land–building allocation. The seller should want the land to be valued as highly as possible because any gain on the sale of land is taxed at low capital gains rates, while gain on personal property is taxed at much higher ordinary income rates (as high as 37%). Meanwhile, buyers want to value the building as highly as possible to increase their depreciation deductions. Because they have adverse interests, the IRS should follow a buyer–seller allocation of land versus property values. Nevertheless, as the following example shows, the IRS and tax court haven't always done so.

> EXAMPLE: Charles Nicholson had the following language added to the escrow instructions for commercial property he purchased in Northern California: "80% of the real estate value is attributed to the building and 20% to land." Unfortunately for Nicholson, the IRS didn't agree with this allocation and neither did the tax court. The court found that there wasn't a shred of evidence that the building was worth 80% of the property's purchase price. Instead, it concluded that a 10% improvement ratio was proper. (*Nicholson v. Comm'r.*, T.C. Memo 1993-183.)

Comparable Land Sales

An entirely different way to determine your depreciable basis is to estimate the value of your land alone by seeing what comparable unimproved real estate in the area sells for. To do this, you look at the selling prices of a number of vacant lots, calculate their average per-square-foot cost, and apply it to your land. Be warned, however, that this approach often leads to inflated land values.

> **EXAMPLE:** Miranda's rental duplex has a 10,000-square-foot lot. She looks at three similar vacant lots in the area that sold in the past two years. Their total square footage was 25,000, and the total sales price for the lots was $150,000. This results in an average per-square-foot cost of $6. By applying this average cost to her property, Miranda determines that her land is worth $60,000 ($6 × 10,000 square feet = $60,000). This is, by far, the worst result Miranda achieved with any of the methods she used. Even using the assessed valuation, her land was worth only $50,000.

You can look for comparable lots offered for sale in the area in the multiple listing service, or check the county recorder's office. However, it might be hard to find any comparable unimproved land if your property is in a highly urban area. Also, you need to make sure to compare the prices only of unimproved lots—that is, lots that don't have underground utilities, sidewalks, or grading. Improvements such as these increase land values, so you'll get an inflated result.

Cost Segregation

When you purchase a rental property—whether a house, duplex, apartment building, or condominium—you pay a single lump sum to the owner, but you are actually purchasing more than one asset. Rental property consists of:

- the land the building sits on, as well as any other surrounding land included with the purchase
- improvements that have been made to the land, such as landscaping
- the building itself, and
- personal property inside the building that is not building components—for example, refrigerators, stoves, dishwashers, and carpeting.

Most landlords depreciate all these items together (excluding the land, which is not depreciable), using the 27.5-year recovery period for buildings and the straight-line depreciation method—which is how buildings must be depreciated (see Chapter 5).

However, you have the option of depreciating each asset separately. The technical name for this type of depreciation is cost segregation.

Personal property and land improvements have much shorter depreciation periods than residential real property, so you can depreciate them much more quickly than a rental building. Your total depreciation deduction won't be any different, but you'll get it much more quickly.

In the past, cost segregation merely enabled you to deduct personal property over five years instead of 27.5 years, and land improvements over 15 years. However, the Tax Cuts and Jobs Act has supercharged cost segregation. Instead of merely speeding up your depreciation deductions, cost segregation now sends them into warp drive. Starting September 28, 2017 and lasting through December 31, 2022, 100% of the cost of personal property and land improvements in rental property can be deducted in a single year with bonus depreciation. Moreover, bonus depreciation may now be used for both new and used property. This means a landlord may purchase a used rental property and deduct the full cost of the personal property and land improvements—but not the building itself—in one year. All that is required is a cost segregation study as described below.

Typically, 20% to 30% of the value of rental property (not counting the land) consists of personal property and land improvements. So, with supercharged 100% bonus depreciation, your first-year depreciation deduction could be enormous (see the comprehensive example at the end of this section). However, 100% bonus depreciation is scheduled to end after 2022. Unless Congress extends the 100% bonus, the bonus depreciation percentage will be 80% for 2023, 60% for 2024, 40% for 2025, and 20% for 2026.

You don't have to use 100% bonus deprecation if you don't want to. You may opt out of bonus depreciation and separately depreciate your personal property and land improvements using regular depreciation. This way, most personal property would be depreciated over five years and land improvements over 15, instead of 27.5 years if they are depreciated along with the building.

The IRS has created a highly detailed guide to cost segregation for its auditors. It's designed primarily for high-value real property, but still contains a valuable overview of the topic. You can access the guide, *Cost Segregation Audit Techniques Guide*, for free on the IRS website at www.irs.gov (search under "cost segregation").

Problems With Cost Segregation

Before you go ahead with your cost segregation study, you should
be aware that this process has some potentially serious drawbacks—
for example:

- Your enhanced depreciation may not result in any extra tax savings
  because of the passive loss rules.
- You'll have to pay back your enhanced deductions when you sell
  your property—a process called "recapture."
- You won't be able to use a like-kind exchange to defer tax on the
  personal property you deducted using cost segregation.

Passive loss rules. The enormous first-year depreciation deductions
landlords may now take using cost segregation can easily result in a
rental loss for the year—that is, the deductions from the rental property
exceed the rental income it earns. You'll get no immediate benefit from
such a real estate loss if you can't deduct it because of the passive loss
rules. These rules prevent landlords from deducting losses over $25,000
unless they are real estate professionals. And even the $25,000 loss is
disallowed if a landlord's income exceeds $150,000.

But this doesn't necessarily mean you shouldn't do a cost segregation
study anyway. Rental losses you're unable to deduct are not "lost."
Instead, they become suspended passive losses that you may use in any
future year you have sufficient rental income (or other passive income)
to offset them. If not, you'll be able to deduct them when you sell
the property—but at this point there will be no benefit from a cost
segregation study. If you expect to have sufficient rental or other passive
income to offset these losses in the near future, a cost segregation study
may still be worthwhile. But if you doubt you'll have sufficient passive
income to soak up your losses for some time, if ever, a study may be a
waste of time and money. (See Chapter 16 for a detailed discussion of the
passive loss rules.)

Depreciation recapture. The benefits gained from cost segregation may
be minimal or nonexistent if you don't plan to keep the rental building
very long before selling—at least three to five years. This is because of
depreciation recapture. When you sell your rental building, you'll have
to recapture the depreciation you've previously taken on the personal
property it contains and pay tax on it.

To the extent of gain on the sale, the depreciation separately claimed on personal property (also called "Section 1245 property") is recaptured as ordinary income at tax rates up to 37%. In contrast, the gain attributable to depreciation of real property (also called "Section 1250 property") is taxed at a maximum rate of 25%. You must report the sale and recapture amount on IRS Form 4797, *Sales of Business Property*.

The longer you wait before you sell, the less impact the depreciation recapture taxes will have because you've had many years to make use of the additional tax savings that accrued from using cost segregation. Moreover, you might be in a lower bracket at the time you make the sale.

It's also possible to reduce the impact of recapture by separately allocating a portion of the purchase price to your personal property based on its fair market value at the time of the sale. This should be done in your purchase and sale agreement with the aid of an appraisal. Much of the personal property in a rental building—carpets, for example—has little or no value after a few years. The less of the purchase allocated to the personal property, the less recapture at ordinary income rates there will be.

Like-kind exchanges. One way to avoid the recapture problem is to do a tax-free like-kind exchange instead of a taxable sale. With a like-kind exchange, the basis of the old property is shifted to the new, with no depreciation recapture. However, as a result of the Tax Cuts and Jobs Act, starting in 2018 like-kind exchanges are allowed only for real property, not personal property. So, you could still have depreciation recapture (at ordinary income rates) on the gain of the personal property you've separately depreciated.

The IRS has issued detailed regulations on what constitutes real property for purposes of Section 1031 like-kind exchanges. (IRS Reg. 1.1031(a)-3.) The IRS adopts a broad definition of real property that includes most items identified in a cost segregation study that are affixed to a building. Such items are all eligible for a like-kind exchange.

Also, the fact that you classify property as real property for purposes of a Section 1031 exchange does not prevent you from classifying it as personal property for purposes of depreciation—the definitions of real and personal property for Section 1031 and depreciation are not the same. (IRS Reg. 1.1031(a)-3(a)(7).) For example, a kitchen sink and plumbing could be classified as real property for a 1031 exchange and personal property for depreciation purposes.

However, movable items, such as furniture, are personal property for Section 1031 purposes. Such property can't be exchanged under Section 1031. But the presence of such personal property will not prevent a Section 1031 exchange provided that:

- in standard commercial transactions, the personal property is typically transferred together with the real property, and
- the aggregate fair market value of the incidental personal property transferred with the real property does not exceed 15% of the aggregate fair market value of the replacement real property. (IRS Reg. 1.1031(k)-1(g)(7)(iii).)

Where the personal property contained in the replacement property does not exceed 15% of the total value of the combined real and personal property, no separate identification of the personal property is required.

But because it's personal property, incidental personal property is non-like-kind property that generally results in gain in a Section 1031 exchange. So, you must recognize gain to the extent of the fair market value of the personal property received in the exchange. (I.R.C. § 1031(b). Preamble to Treasury Decision 9935 (12/02/2020).)

> **EXAMPLE:** You sell a rental duplex for $1 million and exchange it into an apartment building worth $1 million. The apartment building includes furniture, laundry machines, and other personal property with a fair market value of $100,000. Because $100,000 is less than 15% of $1 million, the exchange qualifies for Section 1031 tax-free treatment. The apartment building, furniture, laundry machines, and other personal property are treated as one property for Section 1031. You must recognize gain of $100,000— the fair market value of the personal property acquired in the exchange.

Time for Cost Segregation

You can always perform a cost segregation study the first year you own or construct rental property, but you don't have to do it that year. You can wait until a future year—perhaps when you have enough rental or other passive income to make use of the speeded-up depreciation deductions. The year you do the study you may currently deduct the increased depreciation deductions that you could have taken if you had used cost segregation from the time you acquired the property.

The difference between what was deducted and what could have been deducted is known as an I.R.C. Section 481(a) adjustment. You can deduct the entire difference in a single year by filing IRS Form 3115 to request a change in accounting method. This type of change is ordinarily granted automatically by the IRS (Rev. Proc. 2004-11) and you don't need to file any amended tax returns. Unfortunately, IRS Form 3115 is an extremely complex form. You'll likely need help from a tax professional to complete it properly. An online fee-based calculator to help calculate such a 481(a) adjustment is available at www.kbkg.com/481a-calculator.

If you acquired and placed the property into service before September 28, 2017, you won't be able to use 100% bonus depreciation (or Section 179) to deduct in one year the full cost of the personal property; you must use regular depreciation instead. However, you may deduct personal property much more quickly than the building itself using regular depreciation (five or seven years for personal property), which would have given you larger depreciation deductions the first several years you owned the property. You may also be able to deduct 50% of the cost of new land improvements in one year using bonus depreciation. So, this type of catch-up depreciation can still amount to a large cash windfall.

No limit applies to how far back you can go to claim missed depreciation deductions on the personal property and land improvements in your rental property. But the benefits might be minimal for older buildings that have been mostly depreciated already. Cost segregation experts say that a rental property acquired less than 15 years ago is a good candidate for a cost segregation study.

Cost Segregation Studies

The key to cost segregation is preparing a good cost segregation study that identifies and values your rental building and structural components, personal property, and land improvements. Various ways are available to do this.

Study Prepared by an Engineer

Although not absolutely required by the IRS, you might want to hire an engineer to conduct a cost segregation study to determine how to classify and value your property's various components. A study by a qualified construction engineer is usually viewed as more reliable by the IRS. Indeed, the IRS's cost segregation audit guide provides that "a preparer's credentials and level of expertise may have a bearing on the overall accuracy and quality of a study. In general, a study by a construction engineer is more reliable than one conducted by someone with no engineering or construction background." A directory of cost segregation specialists can be found at the website of the American Society of Cost Segregation Professionals (https://ascsp.org).

IRS regulations that went into effect in 2014 make these studies more valuable than ever. (See Chapter 4 for a detailed discussion of these regulations.) The regulations divide buildings into up to nine separate units of property that a building owner may have to separately identify and value when building components are retired or replaced. A cost segregation study that values these units and components will prove useful for the life of the building.

The engineer should inspect the property and, wherever possible, use construction-based documents such as blueprints and specifications to determine the value of the building components. When estimates are required, they should be based on costing data from contractors or reliable published sources. The engineer should prepare a detailed written report that you can show to the IRS if you are audited and it questions your valuations. Such a study can be expensive—typically $5,000 to $10,000 or more—but the cost is a tax-deductible business expense. Whether paying for such a study makes sense for you depends on how much your rental property is worth. The speedier depreciation you'll obtain may justify the expense if your property is worth $750,000 or more (not counting the value of the land). You can use online cost segregation savings calculators to get an idea of how much you can save with a study; see, for example, the calculator at www.kbkg.com/costsegregation/calculator.

Cost Segregation Study Software

If a cost segregation study created by an engineer is too expensive, online applications and software are available to help you create a study yourself for a few hundred dollars. These are designed to be used for smaller properties where a full-blown study by an engineer is not economically feasible. They include:

- The online *Residential Cost Segregator*, which creates segregation studies for rental properties up to six units with a depreciable tax basis of $500,000 or less (purchase price not counting the land). For details, see www.kbkg.com/residential-costsegregator.
- The *Titan Echo Solution*, available for any cost property, with a low-cost version available for those with basis of $500,000 or less. For details, see https://titanecho.com/echo-solution.
- *DIY Cost Segregation*, available for any cost property, with a low-cost version for single-family homes up to fourplexes. See https://diycostseg.com.

These software applications use data provided by the building owner, construction cost data, and proprietary algorithms to assign costs to a building's components. However, the reports they generate don't meet all the requirements in the IRS *Cost Segregation Audit Techniques Guide*. The IRS hasn't indicated whether it will accept cost segregation studies prepared with such software. The creators of these software applications claim that the valuations they provide can easily withstand IRS scrutiny. But, if you're audited in the future, you might need to do a full-blown cost segregation study by an engineer to verify the results from the software. Make sure any software provider you choose will provide support in the event of an audit. Most will provide a free engineer cost segregation study if you're audited.

Preparing a Cost Segregation Study Yourself

It is also possible to prepare a cost segregation study yourself, perhaps with the help of an appraiser or accountant. Such a study need not be as thorough as that prepared by an engineer. You could focus on easy to identify and value personal property items like appliances and carpeting, and land improvements such as fences or decks. You need to identify the personal property and land improvements you wish to depreciate separately from the building and determine their fair market value when you placed them into service in your rental activity. If the property is new, or fairly new, you base the fair market value on the cost. The new prices for most types of personal property can easily be researched on the internet. If the property is older, you'll need to figure out the value based on the new price minus an amount for the wear and tear the property has undergone. Look at listings for similar property online or call people who buy and sell the type of property involved. If you think the property is extremely valuable, get an appraisal from an expert. Keep records of how you calculated the property's value.

Identifying Personal Property and Land Improvements

The goal of the cost segregation is to identify and value the personal property and land improvement elements of your rental property. These elements need not be depreciated over 27.5 years. As explained above, for a five-year period, 100% of the cost of these items can be fully deducted in one year with bonus depreciation.

Personal Property

Experts estimate that anywhere from 20% to 35% of the property in apartments and other residential properties is personal property that can be depreciated much more quickly than the building itself. It is to your advantage to identify as many of these items of personal property inside and outside your rental building as you can. This way, you can depreciate them separately from your building using bonus depreciation. Each component that is reclassified as personal property must be treated as an individual unit of property for depreciation purposes. (In Chapter 4, see "Defining the 'Unit of Property' (UOP).")

It can be surprisingly difficult to determine whether an asset is personal property or part of a rental building. Many items you might not think of as personal property have been classified as such by the engineers who perform cost segregation studies. However, in some cases IRS auditors have determined that cost segregation studies have gone too far in classifying property in buildings as personal property and have reclassified items as structural components instead. Remember, the IRS can impose a stiff 20% penalty if you use cost segregation too aggressively and overvalue personal property and/or land improvements by 200% or more. (I.R.C. § 6662(a).)

The general rule is that any tangible property inside, or attached to, your rental building, that is not a structural component, is personal property for depreciation purposes. IRS regulations define structural components as:

- "all parts of a building," and
- "all other components relating to the operation or maintenance of a building." (IRS Reg. § 1.48-1(e)(2).)

Ordinarily, a building is planned, designed, and constructed with the expectation that the structural components will remain in place indefinitely. They are usually integrated with the building during the construction phase and are permanent parts of the building. They are not installed merely to meet the peculiar needs of a tenant. They are for the operation or maintenance of a building and "cannot be removed or relocated without doing at least temporary damage to the building itself." (*Metro Nat'l. Corp. v. Comm'r.*, T.C. Memo 1987-38.)

The tax court developed six questions designed to determine whether a particular asset qualifies as personal property:

1. Can the property be moved and has it been moved? A "Yes" indicates the item is personal property.
2. Is the property designed or constructed to remain permanently in place? A "Yes" indicates the property is a building component.
3. Are there circumstances that show that the property may or will have to be moved? A "Yes" indicates the item is personal property.
4. Is the property readily movable? A "Yes" indicates the item is personal property.
5. How much damage will the property sustain when it is removed? The less damage, the more likely the property is personal property.
6. How is the property affixed to land? The more permanently affixed, the more likely the property is a building component. (*Whiteco Industries, Inc. v. Comm'r.*, 65 T.C. 664, 672–673 (1975).)

The following tables list common types of assets inside rental buildings that are structural components and personal property.

Personal Property
Kitchen appliances, such as stoves, refrigerators, dishwashers, microwaves, and trash compactors (IRS Reg. § 1.48-1(c))
Removable partitions (Senate Report 95-163; *Metro Nat'l. Corp. v. Comm'r.,* T.C. Memo 1987-38)
Carpeting that is tacked down, not glued to the floor (Senate Report 95-163)
Tile flooring applied with adhesives designed to ease its removal—not cemented, mudded, or otherwise permanently affixed to the building floor (Senate Report 95-163)
Clothes washers and dryers (*Mandler v. Comm'r.,* 65 T.C. 586)
Furniture owned by the landlord (Rev. Rul. 81-133)
Ornamental fixtures (Senate Report 95-163)
Drapes, curtains, and window blinds (IRS Reg. § 1.48-1(c))
False balconies (Senate Report 95-163)
Awnings and canopies (PLR 7102269400A)
Fire extinguishers (Rev. Rul. 67-417)
Portable space heaters (Rev. Rul. 70-103)
Lighting to illuminate the exterior of a building, but not lighting for parking areas (Senate Report 95-163)
Decorative lighting, such as chandeliers and décor wall lights (*Morrison, Inc. v. Comm'r.,* T.C. Memo 1986-129)
Plants inside a building (*Texas Instruments, Inc. v. Comm'r.,* T.C. Memo 1992-306)
Advertising signs (*Whiteco Industries, Inc. v. Comm'r.,* 65 T.C. 664, 672–673 (1975))
Portable window air conditioners (*Film N' Photos v. Comm'r.,* 37 T.C. Memo 1978-162)
Movable storage sheds (PLR 7102269400A)
Walls and nonmovable partitions and permanent coverings for them, such as paneling (IRS Reg. § 1.48-1(e)(2))

Building Components
Floors and permanent coverings for them, such as tiling that has been cemented or glued to the floor (IRS Reg. § 1.48-1(e)(2))
Ceilings, including suspended ceilings (IRS Reg. § 1.48-1(e)(2); *Boddie-Noelle Enters. v. United States*, 96-2 USTC ¶ 50,627 (Fed. Cl. 1996))
Windows and doors (IRS Reg. § 1.48-1(e)(2))
All components of a central air conditioning or heating system, including motors, compressors, pipes, and ducts (whether in, on, or adjacent to the building) (IRS Reg. § 1.48-1(e)(2))
Plumbing and plumbing fixtures, such as sinks and bathtubs (IRS Reg. § 1.48-1(e)(2))
Electric wiring and lighting fixtures (IRS Reg. § 1.48-1(e)(2))
Chimneys and fireplaces (IRS Reg. § 1.48-1(e)(2))
Stairways and elevators (IRS Reg. § 1.48-1(e)(2))
Sprinkler systems (IRS Reg. § 1.48-1(e)(2))
Fire escapes (IRS Reg. § 1.48-1(e)(2))

Land Improvements

Land improvements aren't personal property. Instead, they are usually classified as real property. However, unlike residential rental buildings and their structural components, land improvements are depreciated over 15 years, not 27.5 years, making them eligible for bonus depreciation. Land improvements consist of such elements as:

- site walls
- landscaping and shrubbery
- driveways and walks
- fencing
- decks and patios, and
- other site improvements directly associated with a building, such as grading and excavating (see Chapter 5 for a detailed discussion).

Cost Segregation Example

Landlord Jack purchases a ten-year-old rental duplex for $300,000 in 2022 (including closing costs, fees, and other expenses). He elects to employ cost segregation to maximize his 2022 depreciation deductions. He determines that his improvement ratio is 80%, based on the replacement cost of the duplex. So, the depreciable basis of the duplex (cost minus land value) is $240,000. He has a cost segregation study prepared, which provides the following data on how much of the $240,000 basis consists of the building (and building components), personal property, and land improvements.

Jack may use 100% bonus depreciation to deduct in 2022 the entire cost of the duplex's land improvements and personal property, giving him an additional $64,445 deduction. He may not use bonus depreciation or any other form of accelerated depreciation for the building and its structural components—they must be depreciated over 27.5 years. But he may use the values in the report if he later replaces a structural component, such as the roof, and elects to make a partial disposition election on his tax return. This enables him to fully deduct the unrecovered basis (original cost minus depreciation deductions) in the replaced component. For example, if he replaces the $17,395 roof ten years from now, he'll have $11,386 in unrecovered basis he can fully deduct.

Jack creates separate depreciation schedules for the personal property, land improvements, and building and components. The following chart summarizes his depreciation deductions.

Year	Building ($178,555 basis; 27.5-year recovery period; straight-line method; property placed in service in January)	Land Improvements ($37,195 basis; 15-year recovery period; 100% bonus depreciation)	Personal Property ($24,250 basis; 5-year recovery period; 100% bonus depreciation)	Total
1	$5,681	$37,195	$24,250	$67,126
2–28	$6,493	0	0	$6,493

Building (Real Property)	
Description	Allocated Purchase Cost
Foundation and framing	$56,785
Interior walls and ceilings	$40,385
Roof	$17,395
HVAC	$13,330
Wood flooring	$11,664
Bathroom plumbing fixtures	$10,984
Lighting	$7,934
Electrical	$5,458
Windows	$5,193
Doors	$4,797
Bathroom vanities	$2,539
Water and waste utility services	$2,091
Total	$178,555
Land Improvements	
Description	Allocated Purchase Cost
Driveway and walks	$11,613
Landscaping	$9,997
Deck/patio	$7,751
Site fencing	$3,070
Site walls	$2,282
Other site improvements	$1,962
Total	$37,195
Personal Property	
Description	Allocated Purchase Cost
Carpet	$7,195
Kitchen cabinets and countertops	$6,448
Appliances	$5,357
Kitchen sink and plumbing	$2,347
Removable flooring	$1,195
Ceiling fans	$1,168
Blinds and curtains	$598
Total	$24,250

In contrast, if Jack simply depreciated the building, land improvements, and personal property together, his depreciation schedule would look like this:

80% improvement ratio × $300,000 cost = $240,000 basis

Year	Depreciation
1	$7,636
2–28	$8,727

As you can see, Jack gets a huge first-year deduction by using cost segregation and deducting all his rental's personal property and land improvements with 100% bonus depreciation—$67,126 versus $6,493 with regular depreciation alone. This enormous depreciation deduction helps him end up with a $40,000 rental loss on the duplex for 2022 for tax purposes—that is, his total expenses including depreciation exceed his rental income by $40,000. Fortunately, Jack is a real estate broker and qualifies as a real estate professional for purposes of the passive loss rules. So, he's able to deduct his rental loss from his other nonrental income for 2022. The additional total $60,633 deduction for 2022 saves him $21,222 in federal income taxes at his top 35% tax rate.

The Pass-Through Tax Deduction

The Tax Cuts and Jobs Act established a new income tax deduction for owners of pass-through businesses, which includes most landlords. This deduction is commonly referred to as the "pass-through deduction" or "qualified business income (QBI) deduction."

If you qualify, you may be able to deduct up to 20% of your net rental income from your income taxes, reducing your effective income tax rate on such income by 20%. This deduction began in 2018 and is scheduled to last through 2025. This deduction is available for all types of pass-through businesses, but this chapter focuses on how it works for residential landlords.

Landlords must satisfy the following basic requirements to qualify for this complex deduction.

Your Rental Activity Must Be a Business

To qualify for the pass-through deduction, your rental activity must constitute a business, not an investment or a not-for-profit activity. This determination is made under the general rules used to determine whether any activity is a business. (I.R.C. § 162; IRS Reg. 1.199A-1(b)(14).) These rules are discussed in detail in Chapter 2.

Most landlords should have little trouble qualifying as a business for purposes of the pass-through deduction. The IRS and courts have both found that ownership of even one rental property can constitute a business for tax purposes. However, landlords who rent their property at below-market rates or make no effort to rent it at all are likely to run afoul of this requirement. Also, questions might arise where a landlord spends very little time managing a rental property.

To provide absolute certainty, the IRS has created a safe harbor rule. Landlords who satisfy the rule are automatically deemed to be in business solely for purposes of the pass-through deduction. Use of the safe harbor is purely optional, and most landlords don't need it. This safe harbor rule is covered at the end of this chapter. (See "Landlord Business Safe Harbor Rule," below.)

You Must Have a Pass-Through Business

You have to have a pass-through business to qualify for this deduction. A "pass-through business" is one in which the profits (or losses) are passed through the business and the owners pay tax on the money on their individual tax returns at their individual tax rates. Luckily, virtually all landlords operate as a pass-through business whether they own rental property:

- individually
- jointly with one or more individuals as tenants in common, or as a joint tenancy with your spouse
- as an owner of a one-member or multimember limited liability company (LLC)
- as a partner in a partnership, or
- as an S corporation shareholder (S corporations are rarely used for rental property).

Regular C corporations don't qualify for the pass-through deduction; but, for a variety of tax reasons, C corporations are almost never used for rental property.

You Must Have Qualified Business Income

Landlords may qualify to deduct from their income tax up to 20% of their "qualified business income" (QBI). QBI is the net income (profit) your rental business earns during the year. You determine this by subtracting all your regular rental deductions from your total rental income. Your net rental income or loss is listed in the "Total rental real estate and royalty income (or loss)" line at the bottom of Schedule E.

QBI does not include:

- short-term or long-term capital gain or loss—for example, you do not include capital gain (or loss) earned from selling your rental property
- dividend income
- interest income
- wages paid to S corporation shareholders

- guaranteed payments to partners in partnerships or LLC members, or
- business income earned outside the United States—thus, if you own rental property outside the United States, you may not include income it earns in your QBI.

EXAMPLE 1: Landlord Ann owns a rental home. This year, her tenants paid her $12,000 in rent, and she incurred $6,000 in total deductible expenses, including depreciation. Her QBI is $6,000.

EXAMPLE 2: Landlord Will owns two rental properties. One earns a profit of $10,000 and the other incurs a loss of $4,000. His QBI for his rental business is $6,000.

If you're a member of a multimember LLC, partnership, limited liability partnership (LLP), or S corporation, your QBI is determined at the member-partner-shareholder level. This means each partner, member, shareholder, or other owner takes into account their pro rata share of the pass-through business's income, deductions, gains, and losses.

EXAMPLE: Landlord Carla is a member of an LLC that owns an apartment building. The LLC has five members and Carla has a 20% ownership interest. This year, the LLC has $50,000 in income and Carla's pro rata share is $10,000. So, her QBI for the year is $10,000.

Rental Losses Reduce or Eliminate the Pass-Through Deduction

It should be clear that you can benefit from the pass-through deduction only if your rental business earns a profit for the year. You get no deduction if your rental activity shows a net loss because your QBI will be zero. If you have suspended passive losses (losses you were unable to deduct because of the passive loss rules covered in Chapter 16), they are carried forward to future years and "released" in any year you have net rental income. These may reduce or completely offset your net rental income even though you had a profitable year—the result, little or no QBI.

EXAMPLE: Assume that Landlord Will from the above example had $20,000 in suspended passive losses from prior years. His $6,000 in net profit this year releases $6,000 of the suspended losses to completely offset his profit, resulting in a QBI of zero.

Look at your last year's tax return. If it includes IRS Form 8582 listing substantial suspended passive losses, your real estate business may not generate taxable income for some time and you won't be able to benefit from the pass-through deduction.

Landlords With Multiple Businesses

Ordinarily, if you have other nonrental businesses, QBI is determined separately for each separate business you own. If one or more of your businesses lose money, you deduct the loss from the QBI from your profitable businesses. If you have a "qualified business loss"—that is, your net QBI is zero or less—you get no pass-through deduction for the year. Any loss is carried forward to the next year and the pass-through deduction for that year (or the next future year with positive QBI) is reduced (but not below zero) by 20% of the loss.

EXAMPLE: During 2022, George earned $20,000 in QBI from his rental business and had a $50,000 loss from his Bitcoin mining business. He had a $30,000 qualified business loss, so he gets no pass-through deduction for 2022 and his loss must be carried forward to 2023. His pass-through deduction for 2023 must be reduced by 20% of his $30,000 loss, or $6,000.

You Must Have Taxable Income

To determine your pass-through deduction, you must first figure your total taxable income for the year (not counting the pass-through deduction). This is your total taxable income from all sources (rental and other business, investment, and job income) minus deductions, including the standard deduction ($12,950 for singles and $25,900 for marrieds filing jointly in 2022) or your itemized deductions. However, you do not include net capital gains for the year in your taxable income (such amounts already receive preferential tax treatment). If you're married and file jointly, include your spouse's income in your taxable income.

Your pass-through deduction can never exceed 20% of your taxable income. This limitation will apply and reduce your pass-through deduction to less than 20% of QBI, if you don't have enough nonbusiness income to offset your personal deductions which reduce your taxable income below the amount of your qualified business income.

> **EXAMPLE:** Larson earned $100,000 in profit from his rental business in 2022. He had no other income and took the standard deduction. His taxable income is $87,050 ($100,000 – $12,950 standard deduction = $87,050). Even though Larson had $100,000 in QBI, his pass-through deduction can't exceed 20% of $87,050, or $17,410. If Larson had $12,950 in additional nonbusiness income (such as employee income), he would have had $100,000 in taxable income and qualified for the full 20% of QBI deduction, or $20,000.

Calculating Your Pass-Through Deduction

How you calculate the pass-through deduction depends on your annual taxable income. The rules differ for 2022 taxable income:

- up to $170,050 ($340,100 for marrieds)
- between $170,051 and $220,050 ($340,101–$440,100 for marrieds), and
- above $220,050 ($440,100 for marrieds).

Taxable Income Up to $170,050 ($340,100 If Married)

If your 2022 taxable income is at or below $170,050 if single or $340,100 if married filing jointly, your pass-through deduction is equal to 20% of your QBI. However, as discussed above, the deduction may not exceed 20% of your taxable income.

> **EXAMPLE:** Tom is single and earned $100,000 in QBI during the year from his rental business in 2022. He also earned $32,950 in investment income and took the $12,950 standard deduction. His total taxable income for the year is $120,000 (($100,000 + $32,950) − $12,950 = $120,000). His pass-through deduction is 20% × $100,000 = $20,000. He may deduct $20,000 from his taxable income.

If your taxable income is at or below the $170,050/$340,100 thresholds, that's all there is to the pass-through deduction. You're effectively taxed on only 80% of your rental business income.

Taxable Income Above $220,050 ($440,100 If Married)

If your 2022 taxable income exceeds $220,050 (single) or $440,100 (married filing jointly), your maximum possible pass-through deduction is 20% of your QBI, just like at the lower income levels. However, when your income is this high, a W-2 wages/business property limitation takes effect. Your deduction is limited to the greater of:

- 50% of your pro rata share of W-2 employee wages paid by your rental business, or
- 25% of W-2 wages *plus* 2.5% of the acquisition cost of your pro rata share of the depreciable property owned by your business.

Most small landlords (and many larger ones) have no employees. They manage their properties themselves or hire property management companies that are not W-2 employees. So, they have zero wages upon which to base their pass-through deduction. Fortunately, the pass-through deduction may alternatively be based on 2.5% of the acquisition cost of your depreciable property plus 25% of W-2 wages (which will likely be zero). This provision was added to the Tax Cuts and Jobs Act at the last minute to enable more rental property owners to benefit from the pass-through deduction.

The business property must be depreciable long-term property used in the production of income. This would include your rental property and any other depreciable long-term property you use in your rental business, such as gardening and office equipment. The cost is its unadjusted basis —the original acquisition cost, minus cost of land in the case of rental buildings. If you added improvements after you purchased the property, you should add their acquisition cost to the unadjusted basis of the property.

In the case of personal property (not your rental buildings), it makes no difference whether you deducted the full cost the first year with bonus depreciation or Section 179. But you can't count any long-term property you deducted with the de minimis safe harbor, safe harbor for small taxpayers, or routine maintenance safe harbors. Such property is not considered depreciable property for tax purposes.

You can include any property you acquire during the year and still own at the end of the year. You can't include any property you sell any time during the year.

The 2.5% deduction can be taken during the entire depreciation period for the property—this is 27.5 years for residential rental property. Personal property has a shorter depreciation period—five or seven years. However, for purposes of the pass-through deduction, the depreciation period can be no shorter than ten years. So, the cost of personal property can be included in your 2.5% deduction a full ten years after purchase.

> **EXAMPLE:** Hal and Wanda are married and file jointly. Their taxable income for 2022 is $500,000, including $100,000 in QBI they earned from their rental business they own through an LLC. They have no employees. They own an apartment building they bought four years ago for $600,000. The land is worth $100,000, so its unadjusted acquisition basis is $500,000. Their maximum possible pass-through deduction is 20% of their $100,000 QBI, which equals $20,000. However, because their taxable income was above $440,100, their pass-through deduction is limited to the greater of (1) 50% of W-2 wages, or (2) 25% of W-2 wages plus 2.5% of their apartment building's $500,000 basis. (1) is 0. (2) is $12,500 (2.5% × $500,000) + (25% × 0) = $12,500. Their pass-through deduction is $12,500.

Rental property that is fully depreciated can't be included in the 2.5% property calculation. So, landlords at these income levels who purchased their rental property many years ago and have fully depreciated all or most of it might end up with little or no pass-through deduction.

> **EXAMPLE:** Monica is a single taxpayer with a total income of $250,000 in 2022, including $10,000 from a rental duplex she bought in 1990 for $100,000. The duplex has been fully depreciated. However, she replaced the appliances in 2021 for $3,000. Monica's taxable income for 2022 after subtracting the $12,950 standard deduction is $237,050. At this income level, her pass-through deduction is limited to the greater of 50% of W-2 wages she pays employees, or 25% of W-2 wages plus 2.5% of her depreciable property's acquisition basis. She has no employees. The only depreciable property she can include in the 2.5% property calculation is the appliances she purchased in 2021. Her duplex can't be included because it was fully depreciated. Her pass-through deduction is limited to $75 (2.5% × $3,000 = $75).

If you're in this situation, you can vastly increase your pass-through deduction by purchasing new rental property. Indeed, the more property you own, the greater your pass-through deduction can be. But remember that your pass-through deduction can never exceed 20% of your QBI or 20% of your taxable income.

> **EXAMPLE:** Assume that Monica bought a rental home across the street from her duplex for $250,000 in 2022. She broke even on the home that year, so her QBI remained $10,000. The home's acquisition cost, not counting the land, was $200,000. Monica's pass-through deduction is now limited to 2.5% × $203,000 = $5,075. However, she may not deduct this full amount because it is more than 20% of her $10,000 QBI. She may deduct $2,000 for 2022 (20% × $10,000 = $2,000).

Taxable Income $170,051 to $220,050 ($340,101 to $440,100 If Married)

If your 2022 taxable income is $170,051 to $220,050 (single) or $340,101 to $440,100 (married filing jointly), the W-2 wages/property limitation is phased in—that is, only part of your deduction is subject to the limit and the rest is based on 20% of your QBI. The phase-in range is $50,000 for singles, and $100,000 for marrieds. For example, the limit would be 50% phased in for married taxpayers with taxable income of $390,100 ($50,000 over $340,100) which equals 50% of the $100,000 phase-in range. At the top of the income range ($220,050 for singles, $440,100 for marrieds), your entire deduction is subject to the W-2 wages/business property limit.

To calculate the phase-in, first determine what the amount of your deduction would be if the W-2 wages/property limit didn't apply at all—this is 20% × your QBI. Next, calculate your deduction as if the W-2 wages/property limit applied in full. Your phase-in amount is based on the difference between the two multiplied by your phase-in percentage.

> EXAMPLE: Sid and Nancy are married landlords whose taxable income for 2022 is $370,100, including $100,000 in QBI from their rental business. They own an apartment building with an unadjusted basis of $400,000 and have no employees. Their phase-in percentage is 30% because their $370,100 taxable income is $30,000 over the $340,100 limit ($30,000 ÷ $100,000 phase-in range = 30%). Their deduction if the W-2 wages/property limit didn't apply would be 20% of their $100,000 QBI, which equals $20,000. Their fully limited deduction based on depreciable property is $10,000 (2.5% × $400,000 basis = $10,000). The difference between the two is $10,000. They should lose 30% of the difference between the full deduction of $20,000 and the fully limited deduction of $10,000. The difference amounts to $3,000 (30% × ($20,000 − $10,000) = $3,000). So, they should lose $3,000 from the full $20,000 deduction. Sid and Nancy can take a $17,000 pass-through deduction on their return.

Pass-Through Deduction Thresholds, Limits, and Phase-Ins (2022)

Taxable Income: Single: Up to $170,050 Married: Up to $340,100	Taxable Income: Single: $170,051–$220,050 Married: $340,101–$440,100	Taxable Income: Single: $220,051 or more Married: $440,101 or more
Full 20% deduction No W-2/property limit	20% deduction subject to phase-in of W-2/property limit	20% deduction permitted but fully subject to W-2/property limit

Landlords Who Own Multiple Properties

If a landlord personally owns multiple rental properties or owns them through the same legal entity, the properties are all part of a single rental business. So, they're all grouped together for purposes of the pass-through deduction.

> EXAMPLE: Landlord Larson personally owns two rental homes. One earned a profit of $15,000; one incurred a loss of $5,000. He groups the two together for purposes of the pass-through deduction. This results in a $10,000 rental profit for the year, making him eligible for a maximum $2,000 pass-through deduction.

If multiple properties are owned through separate legal entities, the owners may always treat them as separate businesses for purposes of the pass-through deduction. However, they may also have the option of grouping ("aggregating") them into one business for the deduction.

There is no benefit in doing this if your taxable income is no more than $170,050 for singles and $340,100 for married joint filers. But if your income is higher, the pass-through deduction is based wholly or partly on the depreciable basis (cost) of your property and how much you pay your employees (if any). So, combining multiple properties at these income levels can result in a larger pass-through deduction than computing the deduction separately for each property. For example, if one rental property generates substantial rental income but has little depreciable basis, grouping it with another property with little income and more basis can result in a larger deduction.

You can group (aggregate) multiple rental businesses only if the same person or group of people owns 50% or more of each business for a majority of the year, which must include the last day of the year. The businesses must share the same tax year. In addition, at least two of the following requirements must be satisfied:

- The businesses provide products, property, or services that are the same or customarily offered together.
- The businesses share facilities or significant centralized business elements, such as personnel, accounting, legal, manufacturing, purchasing, human resources, or information technology resources.
- The businesses are operated in coordination with, or reliance upon, one or more of the businesses in the combined group. (IRS Reg. 1.199A-4(b)(1).)

The same people do not need to own an interest in each business that is being grouped. Commercial properties may not be grouped with residential properties.

> **EXAMPLE:** Landlord Lucy, a single taxpayer, had taxable income of $250,000 in 2022. She owns two single-member limited liability companies (SMLLCs). LLC1 owns and operates a 30-year-old small apartment building. LLC2 owns a brand new rental triplex. Lucy can treat each LLC as a separate rental business for purposes of the pass-through deduction.
>
> **Apartment building.** The apartment building earned a $125,000 profit in 2022. Because Lucy's income is over $220,050, her pass-through deduction is limited to the greater of (1) 50% of the W-2 wages Lucy pays her employees, or (2) 25% of W-2 wages plus 2.5% of the depreciable basis of her building. Both (1) and (2) are zero: Lucy has no employees and the depreciable basis of her apartment building is zero because the 30-year-old building has been fully depreciated. So, Lucy's pass-through deduction for the building is zero.
>
> **Triplex.** The triplex, which Lucy bought last year, has a depreciable basis of $500,000. Unfortunately, the building incurred a $25,000 loss. So, Lucy has no net rental income from the building. She gets no pass-through deduction for the triplex, despite the large cost of the building.

Apartment and triplex aggregated. Lucy may elect to group the two LLCs into one rental business for the pass-through deduction. She may do this because (1) she owns over 50% of each LLC, (2) the LLCs provide similar services—residential rental services, and (3) the two LLCs share legal and accounting resources—Lucy provides these services for each LLC. When she groups the two LLCs, she has $100,000 in rental income for the year ($125,000 apartment income minus $25,000 triplex loss). Because she has no employees, her pass-through deduction is equal to 2.5% of the depreciable basis in her rental property (2.5% × $500,000 basis in the triplex) for a $12,500 deduction.

You must file an election with your tax return each year listing the businesses being aggregated. Despite the annual election requirement, the election is irrevocable. This means it can't be changed from year to year unless there is a material change in circumstances. However, new businesses can be added to the existing group if they meet the above requirements. For this reason, you must think carefully before using this strategy. It might be beneficial one year, but result in smaller pass-through deductions in future years if your circumstances change.

Taking the Pass-Through Deduction

The pass-through deduction is a personal deduction you may take on your Form 1040 whether or not you itemize. You don't take it on Schedule E. To compute and claim the deduction, you must complete IRS Form 8995, *Qualified Business Income Deduction Simplified Computation*. But if your taxable income exceeds the applicable threshold amount, you should file Form 8995-A, *Qualified Business Income Deduction*. You then transfer the amount of the deduction to your Form 1040.

The pass-through deduction is not an "above-the-line" deduction on the first page of Form 1040 that reduces your adjusted gross income (AGI). So, for example, it doesn't reduce your income for purposes of qualifying for Affordable Care Act health insurance credits. Moreover, the deduction only reduces income taxes, not Social Security or Medicare taxes.

Strategies to Maximize the Pass-Through Deduction

Landlords can increase their pass-through deduction in several ways.

Increase Rental Income

First, your pass-through deduction is always limited to 20% of your net rental income (QBI). So, the more rental income you have, the greater your deduction will be. You can increase your net rental income by paying off some or all of the debt in your rental property, so you will have smaller (or no) mortgage payments on the property, thereby increasing your net income from the property. You can also avoid maximizing your annual depreciation deductions for the first years you own the property. To do this, don't use cost segregation, bonus depreciation, or Section 179 expensing. This way, you spread your depreciation deductions over more years.

Buy New Rental Property

Second, as shown above, the maximum pass-through deduction is 20% of your net rental income (your QBI). But if your 2022 taxable income exceeds $220,050 if you're single or $440,100 if you're married filing jointly, your deduction will be limited to the greater of (1) 50% of W-2 wages you pay to employees, or (2) 25% of W-2 wages plus 2.5% of the unadjusted basis (acquisition cost) of your rental property. In between these two thresholds the W-2/property limit is phased in. Most small landlords have no employees, so the limit will usually be based on 2.5% of your unadjusted basis in your rental property. If this amount is equal to or more than 20% of QBI, there's no problem—your deduction will still be equal to 20% of your QBI. But, if it's less, you'll lose part of your deduction. If, for example, you have $100,000 unadjusted basis in your rental property, your deduction will be limited to $2,500 (2.5% × 100,000 = $2,500). If you earned $20,000 in profit from the property, you'd lose $1,500 you could have deducted had the W-2/property limit not applied—your deduction would have been 20% × $20,000 = $4,000.

If you're in this situation, you can increase your deduction by buying new rental property, which will increase your total unadjusted basis to be multiplied by 2.5%. You could also hire one or more employees to work in your rental business. You can count 25% of the W-2 wages you pay along with the 2.5% of unadjusted basis. Obviously, you shouldn't hire an employee solely to increase your pass-through deduction.

Keep Your Taxable Income Under W-2/Property Thresholds

If the W-2/property limitation reduces or eliminates your deduction, you could seek to keep your taxable income for the year below the full W-2/property phase-in amount: for 2022, $220,050 for singles or $440,100 for marrieds filing jointly. If you keep your 2022 taxable income at or below $170,050 (single) or $340,100 (married), you'll completely avoid the phase-in of the W-2/property limitation and qualify for the full 20% of QBI deduction. Your taxable income is your total income (not including capital gains) minus your deductions. If you don't itemize, this would include your standard deduction ($12,950 for singles, $25,900 for marrieds in 2022). So, if you take the standard deduction, you could have $183,000 (single) or $366,000 in income (married) and come within the income limits to qualify for the 20% of QBI deduction.

If your income is at or near these limits, you can do a lot of things to reduce your taxable income for the year. For example, you can:

- contribute to retirement accounts such as IRAs and 401(k)s—your contributions are deducted from your taxable income subject to annual limits (in 2022, business owners can contribute up to $61,000 to retirement plans)
- give money to charity if you're so inclined (make sure you're able to itemize your personal deductions), or
- buy new rental property that generates losses (hopefully, only temporarily).

Landlord Business Safe Harbor Rule

As discussed at the beginning of this chapter, your rental activity must constitute a business to take the pass-through deduction. It can't be an investment activity or a not-for-profit activity.

Most landlords are in business, but questions can arise when a landlord owns one or only a few rental units and spends relatively little time managing them. To provide clarity and certainty, the IRS has created a safe harbor rule solely for the pass-through deduction. If you satisfy the rule, the IRS will assume your rental activity is a business for purposes of the pass-through deduction—but for no other purpose.

Use of the safe harbor is purely optional. Most landlords don't need it. And you'll be better off if you ensure that your rental activity qualifies as a business under the general rules covered in Chapter 2, rather than relying on the safe harbor. This is because the safe harbor won't help you to qualify for the other tax benefits that come from being in business, such as taking the home office deduction; using Section 179 expensing; or avoiding the net investment income tax (see Chapter 19).

Also, you can't use this safe harbor if you or family members live in the property more than 14 days during the year, which eliminates many Airbnb hosts. You also can't use the safe harbor for properties leased under a triple net lease arrangement in which the tenant pays for taxes, fees, and insurance, and is responsible for maintenance (these leases are rarely used for residential properties).

The safe harbor requirements are fairly onerous. You must do three things:
- perform 250 hours of real estate rental services each year
- keep records documenting the real estate services performed, and
- keep separate books and records showing income and expenses for each rental real estate enterprise you own (something you should already be doing). (IRS Notice 2019-7.)

One thing you are not required to do to qualify for the safe harbor is file all required IRS Forms 1099-NEC (Form 1099-MISC for 2020 and earlier) when you hire independent contractors to work in your rental activity.

250 Hours of Real Estate Rental Services

You or others working on your behalf must work 250 hours each year providing rental services. The 250-hour requirement applies year by year for 2018 through 2022. For 2023 and later, you satisfy the requirement if 250 or more hours of services are performed in any three of five consecutive years ending with the current year.

Real estate rental services include the following:

- advertising to rent the property
- negotiating and signing leases
- verifying information in tenant applications
- collecting rent
- daily operation, maintenance, and repair of the property
- managing of the real estate
- purchasing of materials, and
- supervising employees and independent contractors.

Such services don't all have to be performed by you, the property owner. They may also be performed by your employees, agents, or independent contractors. For example, if you hire a real estate management company, the time they spend managing your property counts toward the 250-hour requirement. Because rental services performed by managers, agents, employees, and independent contractors count toward the 250-hour requirement, you should ask such workers to keep track of the time they work on your rentals.

> EXAMPLE: Brandon owns a single-family home he rents out. In 2022, he personally spends 50 hours managing the rental. He also hired painters to paint the home inside and out. They spent 300 hours painting, giving him 350 total hours for the year.

The following types of activities do *not* count toward the 250 hours:

- financial or investment management activities, such as arranging financing
- procuring property
- studying and reviewing financial statements or reports on operations

- planning, managing, or constructing long-term capital improvements to your property, or
- hours spent traveling to and from the real estate.

Record of Real Estate Services

Starting in 2019, you must maintain contemporaneous time reports, logs, or other records, showing:
- hours of all services performed
- descriptions of all services performed
- dates on which such services were performed, and
- who performed the services.

You don't need to file these records with your tax return. Keep them available for inspection at the IRS's request.

Combining Properties for the Safe Harbor

If you own multiple rental properties, you can treat each separate property as a separate rental enterprise for purposes of the safe harbor rule. But you have the option of combining similar properties together and treating them all as a single enterprise. Residential rental properties may only be combined with other residential properties, and commercial with other commercial properties. Combining your properties can put you over the 250-hour threshold because it allows you to combine the time you work on each.

> **EXAMPLE:** Lila owns six rental homes. She spends 50 hours per year managing each home. If she treats each home as a separate residential rental enterprise, she won't exceed the 250-hour threshold for any of them. If she combines all six homes into a single rental enterprise, she'll have 300 hours.

Once you make such a combination, you must use it for all future years unless there is a significant change in circumstances; it is unclear what such a change would be.

Signed Statement Filed With Tax Return

If you elect to use the safe harbor, you must include in your tax return the following statement signed under penalty of perjury:

Under penalties of perjury, I (we) declare that I (we) have examined the statement, and, to the best of my (our) knowledge and belief, the statement contains all the relevant facts relating to the revenue procedure, and such facts are true, correct, and complete.

If you electronically file your return, this statement should be included as a pdf.

What If You Don't Qualify for the Safe Harbor?

If you don't qualify for the safe harbor because you can't meet the 250-hour requirement, you by no means have to abandon the pass-through deduction. You'll just have to qualify as a business under the normal rules covered in Chapter 1. The fact that you don't qualify for the safe harbor should not be held against you. Neither the IRS nor courts have ever held that there is a minimum 250-hour annual work requirement for a rental activity to qualify as a business. You could qualify as a business with substantially fewer than 250 hours. How many fewer is not really clear.

Interest

nterest is often a landlord's single biggest expense. This chapter explains when and how it can be deducted.

Interest Landlords Can (and Can't) Deduct

As a general rule, you may deduct interest on money you borrow for a business or an investment activity, including being a landlord. A landlord's most common deductible interest payments are:

- mortgage interest payments to banks and other financial institutions on loans used to acquire rental property
- mortgage interest payments to financial institutions on loans used to improve rental property
- interest on credit cards for goods or services used in a rental activity
- interest on government loans, and
- personal loans for any item used in a rental activity.

The limitations on when and how these interest payments may be deducted are explained in more detail below.

CAUTION

No deduction for money kept in the bank. You get no rental deduction for interest you pay on loan proceeds that you keep in the bank. Your rental interest deduction begins only when you spend the money on your rental activity. Money kept in the bank is considered an investment—at best you might be able to deduct the interest you pay on the money as investment interest.

Certain types of interest can't be deducted under any circumstances:

- **Interest on money you don't owe.** You may only deduct interest for money you legally owe. If you are liable for part of a debt, you can deduct only your share of the total interest paid or accrued.

    EXAMPLE: Sandra and her daughter, Sophie, purchase a rental house together. Both their names are on the deed, but only Sophie's name is on the promissory note for the mortgage loan. Because Sandra is not legally liable for the mortgage loan, she can't deduct any interest she pays on it; only Sophie gets this deduction.

- **Interest paid with funds borrowed from original lender.** You can't deduct interest you pay with funds borrowed from the original lender through a second loan, an advance, or any other arrangement similar to a loan. You can deduct the interest expense once you start making payments on the new loan. When you make a payment on the new loan, you first apply the payment to interest and then to the principal.

  EXAMPLE: Patrick obtains a $20,000 high-interest, short-term loan from the Acme Finance Company to pay for repairs to get his aged rental building up to code and avoid a condemnation. Patrick is personally liable for the loan. He falls behind in his loan payments. To avoid having Acme take his bank accounts or personal property, he obtains a second loan from Acme for $5,000, secured by his own house. He uses the second loan to pay $5,000 in overdue payments on his original loan from Acme. The $5,000 payment, which is almost all for interest charges, is not a deductible interest payment. Six months later, Patrick pays back the $5,000 loan with interest. He can deduct the interest he pays on this loan.

- **Interest on income tax.** Interest charged on income tax assessed on your individual income tax return is not deductible even though the tax due is related to income from your rental activity.

Mortgage Interest

Landlords typically borrow money from banks or other financial institutions to purchase their rental properties. The ability to borrow so much to purchase real estate is one of its great attractions as an investment. The more leverage you have, the more money you can make for each dollar invested. (Leverage means using borrowed funds to increase your total purchasing power.)

You can deduct the mortgage interest you pay for a rental property each year as it is paid. You list the deduction on Schedule E, on the line labeled "Mortgage interest paid to banks, etc."

Interest, Not Principal, Is Deductible

You only deduct the interest you pay on a loan to purchase or improve a rental property. You may not deduct payments of principal—that is, your repayments of the amount you borrowed. The principal is ordinarily added to the basis of your property and depreciated over 27.5 years. (See Chapter 5.)

> **EXAMPLE:** Kasem takes out a $10,000 second mortgage on his rental house to remodel the kitchen. This loan is a home improvement loan. The $10,000 loan amount isn't deductible. Instead, it is added to Kasem's basis in the home and depreciated over 27.5 years.

In contrast, if you borrow money and use it to repair your rental property, you may deduct the principal amount of the loan in the year in which it is incurred as an operating expense. You deduct the interest as it is paid each year. (See Chapter 4 for a detailed discussion of the difference between a repair and an improvement.)

> **EXAMPLE:** Kasem later takes out a $10,000 third mortgage on his rental home to repair the roof. This expense is a repair, not an improvement. The $10,000 principal amount of the loan is deductible in full in the year Kasem takes out the loan. He deducts the interest on the loan as he pays it each year.

It's easy to keep track of how much of your loan payment is for interest and how much for principal. If you paid $600 or more of mortgage interest (including certain points) during the year on any one mortgage, you will receive an IRS Form 1098 from the lender listing how much you paid in interest during the year.

Depending on the length of the loan, your first few years' payments will be mostly for interest, not principal. However, as a loan becomes "seasoned" (gets older) more and more of the loan payments are for repayment of principal, not interest, and are therefore not deductible. When your loan is paid off, you'll get no more interest deductions. This fact is something to keep in mind when you figure the value of your tax deduction for a rental property.

Expenses to Obtain a Mortgage

You can't deduct as interest any expenses you pay to obtain a mortgage on your rental property. Instead, such expenses are deducted in equal annual amounts over the period of the loan. These expenses include:

- points (see "Points and Prepaid Interest," below)
- private mortgage insurance (see below)
- loan assumption fees
- costs of a credit report
- fees for an appraisal and/or inspection required by a lender, and
- mortgage commissions and fees.

Private Mortgage Insurance

Private mortgage insurance (PMI) is a special insurance policy that protects the lender if the borrower defaults on the loan. A landlord can deduct any PMI premiums the landlord pays on rental property as they are paid each year. You list the deduction on Line 9 of Schedule E—write "PMI" on the dotted line.

Mortgage Refinancing

One way to use real estate to get cash is to do a "cash-out refinancing"—obtain a new loan to pay off your old loan, plus borrow more money to end up with cash in your pocket. However, you may not deduct the interest on the cash-out portion of the loan unless you use the money to do real estate improvements (or to pay for certain medical or education expenses).

> EXAMPLE: Tim owes $100,000 on his rental duplex, which has a fair market value of $200,000. He obtains a new $150,000 loan on the property. He pays off the original $100,000 loan and puts the other $50,000 in his pocket to use for a vacation, new car, and other personal purposes. He may only deduct two-thirds of the interest he pays on the new loan because the other third was a cash-out that he used for personal purposes. However, if Tim used the $50,000 to pay for new improvements to his duplex, he could deduct all of the interest.

Mixed-Use Properties

If you live in a multiunit building and rent out the other units, you claim the home mortgage deduction for the portion you live in and deduct the remainder as a landlord expense on your Schedule E. If you receive one bill, you should prorate the rental portion based on square footage.

> EXAMPLE: Samantha owns a duplex and lives in one unit and rents out the other. She has a $100,000 home loan on the entire property, for which she paid $6,000 in interest this year. Both units are the same size, so Samantha deducts 50% of her interest payment as a personal itemized deduction on her Schedule A, and the other 50% as a landlord expense on her Schedule E.

Other Interest Expenses

Landlords aren't limited just to deducting interest on mortgages. Other interest is also deductible.

Credit Cards and Loans

If you use your credit card or take out a loan to purchase goods or services for your rental activity, you can deduct the interest you pay to the credit card company or lender, even if you have to depreciate the principal amount of the purchase. This interest is considered trade or business interest because the borrowed money is used to help carry on your business. A typical example is interest on a credit card (or bank loan) used to purchase supplies for your rental activity.

Business interest is fully deductible in the year in which it is paid (or incurred in the case of accrual basis taxpayers; see Chapter 17).

> EXAMPLE: Andre uses his credit card to purchase and install a $900 dishwasher in a rental duplex he owns. The credit card interest he pays on the $900 is deductible as it is paid. However, the $900 cost of the dishwasher must be depreciated over five years. (See Chapter 5.)

It's a very good idea to use a separate credit card to buy things for your rental activity. If you use a credit card to buy rental-related items and personal items, you'll have to figure out how much of the monthly credit card interest you pay is for the rental items and how much for the personal items—often, a math nightmare.

Car Loans

If you use your car for your rental activity, you can deduct the interest that you pay on your car loan as an interest expense. You can take this deduction whether you deduct your car expenses using the actual expense method or the standard mileage rate, because the standard mileage rate was not intended to encompass interest on a car loan. The amount you can deduct depends on how much you use the car for business—for example, if you use it 25% of the time for your rental business, you may deduct 25% of your car loan interest payments. (See Chapter 11.)

Home Offices

If you take the home office deduction, you can deduct the home office percentage of your home mortgage interest as a business expense, instead of an itemized personal deduction. (See Chapter 10 for more on the home office deduction.) This deduction can be advantageous because the Tax Cuts and Jobs Act limited the annual mortgage interest deduction to interest on total loans up to $750,000, lowered from loans up to $1 million under prior law. Any mortgage interest amounts you deduct as part of the home office deduction don't count toward the limits on deducting the home mortgage interest as a personal itemized deduction.

Home Equity Loans

Before 2018, interest on home equity loans of less than $100,000 was deductible as an itemized personal deduction regardless of how the money was spent—for example, you could spend the money on your rental activities and still deduct the interest as a personal deduction.

This could be favorable for a landlord because these loans are not subject to the passive activity rules discussed in Chapter 16. However, during 2018 through 2025, interest on home equity loans is deductible as a personal itemized deduction only if it is used to purchase or improve a first or second home—that is, a home where you live, not a rental property. So, you may not deduct the interest on a home equity loan used for rental property as a personal itemized deduction on Schedule A.

But, you may deduct interest on a home equity loan you use for your rental activity as a rental deduction, not a personal itemized deduction. You take this deduction on Schedule E, and it is subject to the passive loss rules. Such a home equity loan does not count toward the $750,000 loan limit on the home mortgage deduction in effect for homes purchased during 2018 through 2025 ($1 million for homes purchased before 2018).

Government Loans

During the COVID-19 pandemic, many landlords got loans from the federal government to help tide them over. Such loans included Paycheck Protection Program (PPP) loans and Economic Injury Disaster Loans (EIDLs) from the Small Business Administration. The interest paid on all such loans is tax deductible the year it's paid. The loans themselves are not taxable income.

Points and Prepaid Interest

If you are a cash basis taxpayer (the vast majority of small landlords are—see Chapter 17), you may not deduct interest that you prepay in a single year. Instead, you must allocate the interest over the tax years to which it applies and deduct it in those years.

The most common type of prepaid interest is points. The term "points" is often used to describe some of the charges paid by a borrower when the borrower takes out a loan or a mortgage. A point is equal to 1% of the loan amount—for example, one point on a $100,000 loan is $1,000. These charges are also called "loan origination fees," "maximum loan charges," "loan discounts," or "premium charges." If any of these charges (points) are solely for the use of money, they are interest for tax purposes. Because points are prepaid interest, you can't deduct the full amount in the year paid. (However, there is an exception for points paid on your home mortgage—see IRS Publication 936, *Home Mortgage Interest Deduction*, for details.) Instead, you must allocate the interest payment portion over the term of the loan and only deduct for payments allocated for that tax year.

Points for a mortgage on rental property are deductible each year according to the original issue discount (OID) rules. To determine how to deduct points, you must first determine whether they are de minimis (Latin for minimal). Points are de minimis if they are less than ¼ of 1% (0.0025%) of the amount borrowed multiplied by the number of full years of the loan term. For example, if you borrow $100,000 for 30 years, the points are de minimis if they are less than $100,000 × 30 × 0.0025 = $7,500. If the points are de minimis, you can use any of the following ways to figure the amount of points to deduct each year:

- in equal amounts (straight-line basis) over the term of the loan
- in proportion to the mortgage interest payments
- on a constant-yield basis over the term of the loan, or
- deduct them at the end of the loan period.

> EXAMPLE: Carol paid $1,500 in points for a $100,000 30-year loan to purchase a rental property. The points are de minimis and Carol elects to deduct them in equal amounts over the loan period. A 30-year loan has 360 monthly payments: $1,500 ÷ 360 = $4.17. So, she may deduct $4.17 for every month she pays off the loan, which comes to $50 per year.

If the points are not de minimis, you must use the constant-yield method to deduct them. This method is complicated. You should have a tax pro help you with the computations.

If the loan ends early because you pay it off, refinance, or lose the property through foreclosure, the remaining undeducted points can be deducted the final year. But no deduction is allowed if the loan is refinanced with the same lender. In this event, the remaining points are deductible over the term of the new mortgage.

The first year you deduct points, you must list the amount in the amortization section of IRS Form 4562, *Depreciation and Amortization (Including Information on Listed Property)*. You then add the amount to your other mortgage interest deductions you list on IRS Schedule E (see Chapter 18).

Interest on Construction Loans

If you borrow money to construct a rental property, you may currently deduct as an operating expense the interest you pay before, during, and after construction, provided that your rental business gross receipts for the previous three years averaged $26 million or less. Such smaller real estate businesses are exempt from the tax code's uniform capitalization rules that require certain interest and other expenses of constructing buildings and other property be capitalized—that is, added to the property's basis and depreciated.

However, if your rental business gross receipts were more than $26 million, you become subject to the uniform capitalization rules. Under these rules, you may not deduct the interest you pay during the construction period. Instead, this cost must be added to the basis of your property and depreciated over 27.5 years. (See Chapter 5.) (I.R.C. § 263A(f)(1).)

The construction period for real property begins when physical construction starts. Physical construction includes:

- clearing, grading, or excavating land
- demolishing or gutting an existing building
- construction of infrastructure such as sidewalks, sewers, cables, and wiring
- structural, mechanical, or electrical work on a building, and
- landscaping.

The construction period ends when all production activities reasonably expected to be done are completed and the property is placed in service —that is, made available for rent.

Activities such as planning and design, preparing architectural blueprints, or obtaining building permits don't constitute physical construction. So, interest paid while these activities are going on, but before physical construction is done, can be currently deducted as an operating expense.

A limited de minimis exception applies to the uniform capitalization rules for larger real estate businesses with $26 million or more in gross receipts. Property with a production period of 90 days or less is exempt from the interest capitalization requirements if the total cost of production is no more than $1 million divided by the number of days in the production period. (IRS Reg. 1.263A-8(b)(4).) For example, if you build a structure in 90 days, it will be exempt from the interest capitalization rules if the total cost is $11,111 or less ($1 million ÷ 90).

Loans With Low or No Interest

One way a person who sells real property and finances all or part of the sale themselves can save on taxes is to charge little or no interest on the amount the buyer borrows. To make up for the low or no interest, the seller increases the property's purchase price. This tactic is advantageous for the seller because interest payments are taxed at ordinary income tax rates, while the gain on the sale of real property owned for more than one year is taxed at lower capital gains rates (usually 20%).

> **EXAMPLE:** Joe owns a rental house with a fair market value of $100,000. He sells the property to Jenn. Jenn pays $120,000. She puts down $20,000 and Joe finances the remainder himself, charging Jenn only 2% interest. He pays 20% capital gains tax on his gain on the sale ($120,000 minus his $60,000 basis), and ordinary income tax on the interest payments Jenn will make— taxed at Joe's top 24% income tax rate. Joe comes out ahead on the deal by getting a higher sales price for the property and charging less interest.

Unfortunately for sellers, the IRS is well aware of this scheme. If an installment sale contract doesn't provide for adequate interest, part of the sales price must be treated as interest for tax purposes. This amount is called "unstated interest" or "original issue discount," depending upon the circumstances. The seller must reduce the stated sales price, and increase their annual interest income, by this interest amount. For the buyer, the property's basis is the stated purchase price, less the amount considered to be unstated interest.

How much interest is too little? Generally, an interest rate is inadequate if it is less than the applicable federal rate of interest (AFR). The AFR is set by the IRS each month. You can find it on the IRS website at www.irs.gov (look for the Index of Applicable Federal Rates).

Calculating how much additional interest must be paid is very complicated. Refer to IRS Publication 537, *Installment Sales*, for more information; or, better yet, see an accountant.

Loans on Rental Property Used for Nonrental Purposes

You can take out a loan secured by your rental property and use the proceeds for nonrental purposes. If you do this, you can't deduct interest you pay on the loan as a rental expense. Whether it is deductible at all, and to what extent, depends on what you use the money for:

- **Personal purposes.** You get no deduction if you use the loan proceeds to buy something for your personal use—for example, you take a vacation or buy new appliances for your residence. Personal interest is not deductible, except for interest paid for a mortgage to purchase or improve a personal residence or second home, subject to a loan ceiling ($750,000 for homes acquired 2018 through 2025; $1 million for homes purchased before 2018), and some interest on student loans.
- **Investment purposes.** You may get a deduction if you use the loan for investment purposes—for example, to purchase stocks or bonds

or some other investment. You can deduct investment interest as an itemized personal deduction. But you can deduct investment interest only from investment income. So, if you have no investment income, you get no deduction. If your interest expense exceeds your investment income, you can't deduct the overage. You must carry it forward to deduct in a future year when you have enough investment income.

- **Business purposes.** You can deduct the interest if you use the loan proceeds for a business other than renting residential property— for example, a landlord borrows money on his rental property to purchase equipment for his construction business. You can fully deduct business interest as a business expense in the year in which it is paid. Sole proprietors (people who individually own their businesses) deduct interest expenses on IRS Schedule C, *Profit or Loss From Business (Sole Proprietorship)*.

Limitation on Interest Deductions by Landlords Earning $27 Million or More

During 2017 and earlier, businesses could deduct all the interest they paid without limit. However, the Tax Cuts and Jobs Act limited this deduction. Starting in 2018, all businesses with average gross receipts of $25 million or more over the prior three years could deduct interest payments only up to 30% of their adjusted taxable income. (I.R.C. § 163(j).) Undeductible interest must be carried forward to be deducted in any number of future years.

However, due to the COVID-19 pandemic, Congress increased the limit for deducting interest to 50% of adjusted taxable income for 2019 and 2020 (2020 only for partnerships). A taxpayer could also elect to use their adjusted taxable income from 2019 to calculate their interest deduction for 2020, which could provide a larger deduction because the COVID-19 pandemic severely impacted many landlords' 2020 income.

Businesses whose average gross receipts over the prior three years are less than $27 million are not subject to this limitation and can deduct 100% of their interest expense each year (the ceiling is adjusted for inflation each year). Obviously, this includes most landlords.

Landlords (and other real property businesses) who earn $27 million and more can get out of this prohibition, and thereby deduct 100% of their interest expenses each year, by filing an election with their tax return (which is irrevocable). Thereafter, they must depreciate their real property under the longer periods required by the alternative depreciation system (ADS)—30 years (instead of 27.5) for residential property and 40 years (instead of 39) for nonresidential property. Also, such electing businesses may not use bonus depreciation for commercial property, but it can still be used for residential property. Landlords who elect out of the interest deduction limitation must apply the 30-year ADS depreciation period to all their residential rental property, even property placed in service in their rental business before 2018, when the interest limitation went into effect.

Start-Up Expenses

L andlords often need to spend money to get their rental business started. Costs you incur before you are actually in business are called "start-up expenses." Special tax rules govern the deduction of these costs. As long as your rental activity qualifies as a business, these expenses are fully deductible. If you are a landlord who is already actively engaged in the residential rental business, you might not need to read this chapter. But if you aren't yet in business or are considering expanding your residential rental business into new geographic areas, this material explains what type of expenditures are start-up expenses and how you can deduct these costs.

What Are Start-Up Expenses?

"Start-up expenses" are the costs you incur to get your rental business up and running. Any expense that would be deductible as an operating expense by an ongoing business is a start-up expense when it's incurred before a business begins. Common start-up expenses for landlords include:

- minor or incidental repairs to get a rental property ready to rent
- outside office expenses paid for before a rental business begins, such as office rent, telephone service, utilities, office supplies, and office equipment rental
- home office expenses
- the cost of investigating what it will take to create a successful residential rental business, including research on potential real estate markets
- insurance premiums (but not title insurance)
- maintenance costs for a rental property paid for before the property is offered for rent—for example, landscaping and utilities (but not the cost of connecting utilities)
- costs for recruiting and training employees before the business opens—for example, hiring and training an apartment manager
- costs to create and set up a website
- fees paid to a market research firm to analyze the demographics, traffic patterns, and general economic conditions of a neighborhood
- business licenses, permits, and other fees, and

- fees paid to lawyers, accountants, consultants, and others for professional services; however, legal and other fees paid to purchase a rental property are not start-up expenses.

Unlike operating expenses, start-up expenses can't automatically be deducted in a single year because the money you spend to start a rental (or any other) business is a capital expense—a cost that will benefit you for more than one year. Normally, you can't deduct these types of capital expenses until you sell or otherwise dispose of the business. However, a special tax rule allows you to deduct up to $5,000 in start-up expenses the first year you are in business, and then deduct the remainder, if any, in equal amounts over the next 15 years.

> **EXAMPLE:** Ed, a Los Angeles resident, is thinking about purchasing a rental house in Las Vegas. He has never been a landlord before, but he thinks it might be a good investment. He starts looking for a house to buy. But he discovers that it is not so easy to find a suitable property. He makes six trips to Las Vegas over the next year. He incurs substantial travel expenses but finds no property he likes. Then, on the seventh trip, he discovers his dream rental house. He quickly buys it and takes title on September 1. The house is vacant but requires some repairs. Ed hires a handyman to do the work and arranges for a gardener to take care of the lawn and landscaping on a weekly basis. On November 1, he lists the property for rent by taking out an ad in the local newspaper. He finds a tenant who moves in on December 1.
>
> Before November 1 (the date he offered the house for rent) Ed paid the following expenses during the year:
>
> | | |
> |---|---:|
> | Travel, lodging, and food for six unsuccessful trips to Las Vegas | $3,800 |
> | Travel, lodging, and food for one successful Las Vegas trip | 500 |
> | Gardener | 100 |
> | Utilities | 100 |
> | Repairs | 7,000 |
> | Total | $11,500 |

All of these expenses are start-up expenses except for the $500 travel costs to find the property Ed ended up buying. Those costs must be added to the property's tax basis and depreciated. This leaves $11,000 in deductible start-up expenses. Ed may deduct $5,000 of the $11,000 on his tax return for the current year. He can deduct the remaining $6,000 in equal installments over the first 180 months (15 years) he's in business, starting with the month his rental business began (November). He deducts $33.33 for every full month he's in business until he has completely deducted the $6,000 (assuming his rental business lasts that long).

Obviously, you want to spend no more than the first-year limit on start-up expenses so you don't have to wait 15 years to get all of your money back. Some ways you can avoid spending more than the limit are described in more detail below. But first, you need to understand when a rental business begins for tax purposes.

Determining Your Business Start Date

A crucial moment in your tax life as a landlord is when your rental business begins. Once your business is up and running, the start-up expense rule will not apply. Until then, you need to count every penny you spend to make sure you don't go over the limit for currently deductible start-up expenses.

Rental Business Begins When You Offer Property for Rent

The general rule is that a new business begins for tax purposes when it starts to function as a going concern and performs the activities for which it was organized. (*Richmond Television Corp. v. United States*, 345 F.2d 901 (4th Cir. 1965).) For a rental business, this is when you first offer property for rent. You don't have to actually rent out your property—that is, have it occupied by tenants—you only have to put it on the rental market. (*Francis v. Comm'r.*, T.C. Memo 1977-170.)

Obviously, you must actually own a rental property before you can rent it out. So, your rental business doesn't begin until you take ownership of the property, make the building available for immediate occupancy, and offer it for rent. In other words, a rental business does not begin when you make an offer to buy, put a deposit on, or sign a sales contract for a property you plan to rent.

The date you offer your property for rent is an important one that you should plan for and make careful note of. You should also be prepared to prove you offered your property for rent on the date you claim.

Expanding an Existing Rental Business

If you've never owned a rental property, it's easy to tell when your rental business begins—the date you offer your first property for rent. But what if you already own rental property and decide to purchase additional rental property? The cost of expanding an existing business is a business operating expense, not a start-up expense. As long as business expansion costs are ordinary and necessary, they are currently deductible.

> **EXAMPLE:** Alex owns an apartment building that he has rented out for over two years. This rental (which qualifies as a business) has been so successful that he decides to purchase another apartment building. He spends $4,000 in travel expenses looking for properties to buy. Because Alex is already in business, these costs are currently deductible as business operating expenses—they aren't start-up expenses.

However, your expenses will be currently deductible only if the expansion involves an activity that is "within the compass" of your existing rental business. In other words, it must be part of "the normal expansion" of your business. (*Malmstedt v. Comm'r.*, 578 F.2d 520 (4th Cir. 1978).) The costs of expanding into a *new* business are start-up expenses, not operating expenses.

The IRS and tax court have taken a very narrow view of what constitutes a rental business. They have held that a landlord's rental business only exists in the geographic area where the property is located. So, a landlord who buys (or seeks to buy) property in a different area is starting a new rental business, which means the expenses for expanding in the new location are start-up expenses.

EXAMPLE: Patrick O'Donnell was a Chicago resident who owned two apartments in Las Vegas. He took a two-day trip to Miami to investigate buying a rental property there. However, he decided not to go through with the deal. Both the IRS and tax court denied him a deduction for his travel expenses. The court found that, even though O'Donnell was in the rental business in Las Vegas, his business did not extend to Miami, so he couldn't deduct the trip as an operating expense. (*O'Donnell v. Comm'r.*, 62 T.C. 781.)

In another case, the tax court held that a husband and wife who owned several rental properties in North Carolina started a new rental business (as opposed to expanded their existing rental business) when they purchased a rental house in Richmond, Virginia—even though they lived in Richmond. (*Odom v. Comm'r.*, T.C. Memo 1982-531.)

Forming New Business Entities

Another situation where a landlord could be viewed as starting a new rental business, not expanding an existing one, is where a new business entity such as an LLC or partnership is formed to own the new property. This is often done in an attempt to limit a landlord's legal liability. (See Chapter 1.)

EXAMPLE: Hayley and her husband own an LLC that, in turn, owns an apartment building. They decide to purchase a new apartment building. They form a second LLC, unrelated to the first, to own this property, hoping separate ownership entities will insulate each property from debts or lawsuits arising from the other property. The second LLC could be viewed by the IRS as an entirely new rental business. Any costs the second LLC incurs before the new apartment building is offered for rent would be start-up expenses.

How to Deduct Start-Up Expenses

The amount of start-up expenses you're allowed to deduct the first year you're in business is limited. For the past several years, the limit has been $5,000. You'll have to deduct any expenses in excess of the first-year limit in equal amounts over the first 180 months (15 years) you're in business. This process is called "amortization." The 180 months is the minimum amortization period; you can choose a longer period if you wish (almost no one does).

But you won't be entitled to the full $5,000 first-year deduction if you have more than $50,000 in start-up expenses. Your first-year deduction is reduced by the amount by which such start-up expenditures exceed the $50,000 limit. For example, if you have $53,000 in start-up expenses, you may only deduct $2,000 the first year, instead of $5,000. If you have $60,000 or more in start-up expenses, you get no current deduction. The whole amount must be deducted over 180 months.

> **CAUTION**
> **Investors can't deduct start-up expenses.** Only people engaged in a business can deduct start-up expenses. Investors in real estate are not considered to be "in business" for tax purposes. (*Sorrell v. Comm'r.,* 882 F.2d 484 (11th Cir. 1989).) (See Chapter 2 for a detailed discussion of investors versus landlords for tax purposes.)

You used to have to attach a separate written statement to your tax return electing to claim start-up expenses as a current deduction. This step is no longer required. Instead, you are automatically deemed to have made the election for the year in which your business began. All you must do is list your start-up costs as "Other expenses" on your Schedule E (or another appropriate return). You don't have to specifically identify the deducted amounts as start-up expenditures for the election to be effective. However, if you have more than $5,000 in start-up expenses, you must amortize (deduct) the excess over 180 months. To do so, you must complete and attach IRS Form 4562 to your return for the first tax year you are in business.

If you don't want to currently deduct your start-up expenses, you can forgo the deemed election by clearly capitalizing your start-up expenses instead. You must do this on your federal income tax return for the tax year in which your business began. Your return must be filed on time (including any extensions) and this election is irrevocable. If you do this, your start-up costs become part of the tax basis of your business.

Expenses You Can Deduct

You can deduct as start-up expenses any costs that would be currently deductible as operating expenses after your rental business begins. So, the expenses must be ordinary, necessary, directly related to the business, and reasonable in amount. (See Chapter 3 for a discussion of operating expenses.) For example, you can't deduct the cost of pleasure travel unrelated to your rental business. These expenses would not be deductible as operating expenses by an ongoing rental business, so you can't deduct them as start-up expenses either. (See "What Are Start-Up Expenses?" above, for common examples of deductible start-up expenses for landlords.)

Costs That Are Not Start-Up Expenses

Some costs related to opening a rental business are not considered start-up expenses. Many of these costs are still deductible, but different rules apply to them.

Real Property and Other Long-Term Assets

Real property and other long-term assets you purchase for your rental business that will last for more than one year are not considered part of your start-up costs. This category includes the property you buy to rent and any long-term personal property you purchase for your rental property, such as appliances, carpeting, furniture, or lawn mowers. It also includes any long-term property you buy to run your business, such as computers, office furniture and equipment, and cars and other vehicles. These items are capital assets and their costs are capital expenses.

You must depreciate the cost of this property over its useful life—
27.5 years for residential real property and five or seven years for most
personal property. (In the case of some personal property, you have
the option of deducting the cost in one year under Section 179—see
Chapter 5 for more on Section 179.) Chapter 5 explains how to depreciate long-term assets. However, you can't take depreciation deductions
until your property is placed in service—for example, you can't begin
to depreciate a rental building until you make it available for rent.

Ordinarily, the largest single expense you will have that you can't
deduct as a start-up expense is the cost of your rental property—for
example, the house or apartment building that you purchase to rent.
For tax purposes, the cost of the rental property includes not just the
purchase price, but expenses related to the purchase, including:

- bidding costs, application fees, and similar expenses
- costs to appraise or otherwise determine the property's value
- architectural, engineering, environmental, geological, or inspection
  services for the property—for example, termite inspection fees
- expenses for preparing or reviewing the property's acquisition
  documents, such as bids, offers, sales agreements, or purchase
  contracts
- costs to negotiate the purchase terms or structure, including
  tax advice
- expenses for evaluating and examining the property's title—
  for example, abstract fees and attorneys' fees
- costs to obtain regulatory approval or secure permits
- property conveyance costs, including sales and transfer taxes
  and title registration costs—for example, recording fees and title
  insurance fees
- finders' fees and brokers' commissions, including amounts
  contingent on successful closing of the purchase, and
- the cost of services provided by a qualified intermediary in a
  like-kind exchange. (IRS Reg. § 1.263(a)-2.)

You can't deduct any of these expenses as start-up expenses. Instead,
you add these costs to the rental property's basis (the property's value for
tax purposes) and then depreciate the property's cost (including these
amounts) over 27.5 years.

> **TIP**
>
> **Some costs associated with purchasing property might be start-up expenses.** You can deduct certain expenses related to buying real property as start-up expenses if you meet all the requirements. These expenses include casualty insurance premiums (for example, fire insurance), and charges for utilities or other services for the property before closing.

Real Property Improvements

The costs of improvements you make to rental property are not start-up or operating expenses. Instead, these costs are capital expenses that you must depreciate. The costs of any repairs you make to rental property, on the other hand, are start-up expenses before your rental business begins and operating expenses after you are in business. (*Gordon v. Comm'r.* and *Jarrett v. Comm'r.*, T.C. Summ. Op. 2013-91.) The difference between an improvement and a repair is that a repair merely keeps property in good operating condition, while an improvement makes it more valuable, useful, or long-lived. For example, fixing a crack in an existing foundation is a repair; but adding a new foundation to a building is an improvement. Telling the difference between a repair and an improvement can be difficult. (See Chapter 4.)

Travel Expenses

Travel expenses to get your rental business going are deductible start-up expenses with one important exception: Travel costs to buy a particular rental property are not start-up expenses. Instead, they are capital expenses that must be added to the cost of the property and depreciated. (See Chapter 12.)

Interest and Taxes

You can't deduct interest on a rental property mortgage (or any other interest) or real estate taxes as start-up expenses. Points you pay to obtain a mortgage are considered interest. You can deduct these costs as you pay them, once your real estate business begins. (See Chapter 8.)

Organizational Costs

Costs you pay to form a partnership, limited liability company, or corporation are not part of your start-up costs. But under a different rule, you can deduct $5,000 of these costs the first year you're in business and any amount remaining over the first 180 months you are in business. (I.R.C. § 248.)

> **CAUTION**
>
> **If you form a single-member LLC, don't spend more than $5,000 in organizational expenses.** Because single-member LLCs are considered "disregarded entities" for tax purposes, the IRS doesn't allow these entities to deduct organizational expenses over $5,000. Instead, any expenses over that amount must be capitalized, which means they would not be deductible until the LLC is dissolved. (Treas. Reg. §§ 1.263(a)-5(d)(1), (3).) So, if you're forming a single-member LLC, it's best to avoid spending over $5,000 in organizational expenses, which generally should not pose a problem.

If Your Business Doesn't Last 15 Years

Many rental businesses don't last for 180 months. If you had more than the first-year limit in start-up expenses and are in the process of deducting the excess amount, you don't lose the value of your deductions if you sell or close your rental business before you have had a chance to deduct all of your start-up expenses. You can deduct any leftover start-up expenses as ordinary business losses. (I.R.C. § 195(b)(2).) So, you might be able to deduct them from any income you have that year, deduct them in future years, or deduct them from previous years' taxes. However, rules limit deductions for losses from a real estate activity. (See Chapter 16.)

If Your Business Never Begins

Many people investigate starting a rental business, but the venture never gets off the ground. General start-up costs are expenses you pay before you decide to start a new business or acquire a specific existing business. They include all of the costs of doing a general search for, or preliminary investigation of, a business—for example, costs to analyze potential markets. If you never start the business, these costs are personal (and not deductible). In other words, they are a dead loss.

One intended effect of this rule is that you can't deduct travel or other "fun" expenses by claiming that you incurred them to investigate a rental business unless you actually start the business. Otherwise, it would be pretty tough for the IRS to figure out whether you were really considering a new venture or just having a good time.

> EXAMPLE: Kam spends $5,000 on a two-week Hawaii vacation. While there, she spends two days looking at rental properties for sale, but doesn't buy anything. She has never been a landlord, so owning rental property would be a new business. The cost of her trip isn't a start-up expense.

To get a deduction for a rental business that never begins, you must enter into a transaction for profit and later abandon the transaction. To do this, you must go beyond a general investigatory search and focus on acquisition of a specific rental property. For example, you'd be able to take a deduction if you entered into a contract to purchase a rental property, but the sale fell through. You could deduct the acquisition costs you incurred in the failed purchase on IRS Form 4797, *Sales of Business Property*. These costs would have been added to the property's basis, and not deducted, had the acquisition been successful. These costs could include, for example, the cost of inspection and termite reports, earnest money or deposits that were lost, and the cost of traveling to the property.

The Home Office Deduction

The federal government helps business owners by letting them deduct their home office expenses from their taxable income. This deduction is available whether you own your home or apartment or are a renter. If your rental activity qualifies as a business, you're entitled to a full home office deduction.

Qualifying for the Home Office Deduction

In the past, the IRS took the position that landlords couldn't take the home office deduction. However, the tax court has held that landlords who meet the requirements may take the deduction, and landlords have successfully done so.

> **EXAMPLE:** Edwin Curphey, a dermatologist, owned six rental properties in Hawaii that he managed by himself. He converted a bedroom in his home into an office that he used exclusively for bookkeeping and other activities related to management of his rental properties. The room was furnished with a desk, bookcase, filing cabinet, calculators, and answering machine. The closet of the room was used only to store items used for the rental properties, such as lamps, carpets, and other furnishings, For Rent signs, and a toolbox. Because Curphey met the requirements for the deduction, the tax court held he could deduct his home office expenses. (*Curphey v. Comm'r.*, 73 T.C. 766 (1980).)

Still, the IRS doesn't go out of its way to encourage landlords to take the deduction. Indeed, you won't find a single word about it in any IRS publication or form.

You must meet strict requirements to qualify for the home office deduction. You're entitled to the home office deduction if:

- your rental activities qualify as a business
- you use your home office exclusively for your rental business, and
- you use your home office for rental business on a regular basis.

After you meet these three threshold requirements, you must also satisfy *any one* of the following four requirements:

- you regularly and exclusively use your home office for administrative or management activities for your rental business and have no other fixed location where you regularly perform such activities

- you perform your most important rental activities at your home office
- you meet business-related visitors, such as tenants, at your home office, or
- you use a separate structure on your property exclusively for rental business purposes.

Threshold Requirements

To take the home office deduction, you must have a home office—that is, an office or other workplace in your home that you use regularly and exclusively for your rental business. Your home may be a house, apartment, condominium, mobile home, or even a boat. Your home can even be a part of your rental property—for example, an apartment in a multiunit apartment building you own, or one-half of a duplex—but you must actually live in it.

Your office may be all or part of a bedroom, den, or other space in your home that is physically and functionally part of your residence. You can also take the deduction for separate structures on your property that you use for business, such as an unattached garage or workshop. Any space that is not part of your residence is not subject to these rules—for example, space inside your rental building that you use for office work, maintenance, storage, or other landlord purposes.

Your Rental Activities Must Be a Business

Your rental activities must qualify as a business for tax purposes if you want to take the home office deduction. The deduction is not available if your rental activity qualifies only as an investment. Whether your rental activity is a business depends on how much time and effort you put into it. To be a business, you must be actively involved in managing your property on a regular, systematic, and continuous basis. You don't have to work full time as a landlord—in fact, you can have only a single rental unit and still be a business for tax purposes. You just must be able to show that you are actively involved in managing the rental. (See Chapter 2 for more on when a rental activity constitutes a business for tax purposes.)

You Must Use Your Home Office Exclusively for Business

You can't take the home office deduction unless you use part of your home exclusively for your rental business. In other words, you must use your home office *only for your rental business.* The more space you devote exclusively to your business, the more your home office deduction will be worth.

If you use part of your home—such as a bedroom—as your rental business office, and you use that same space for personal purposes, you won't qualify for the home office deduction.

You Must Use Your Home Office Regularly

It's not enough to use a part of your home exclusively for business; you must also use it regularly. For example, you can't place a desk in a corner of a room and claim the home office deduction if you almost never use the desk for your business.

Unfortunately, the IRS doesn't offer a clear definition of regular use. The agency has stated only that you must use a portion of your home for business on a continuing basis—not just for occasional or incidental business. One court has held that 12 hours of use a week is sufficient. (*Green v. Comm'r.*, 79 T.C. 428 (1982).)

Many landlords probably spend less than 12 hours per week working in their home offices. As long as they work regularly, they probably pass muster with the IRS. So, for example, even in the case of Edwin Curphey (see example at the beginning of "Qualifying for the Home Office Deduction," above), who owned only six rental units but had clearly defined home office space, the IRS didn't raise the issue of how much time he spent in his home office (it couldn't have been much).

Additional Requirements

Using a home office exclusively and regularly for your rental business is not enough to qualify for the home office deduction: You must also satisfy at least one of the additional three tests described below.

You Perform Administrative and Management Work at Your Home Office

You qualify for the home office deduction if:

- you regularly and exclusively use your home office for administrative or management activities for your rental business, and
- there is no other fixed location where you regularly conduct these activities.

Home offices that meet these requirements are deemed to qualify as the principal place of business for your rental activity. Administrative or management activities include, but are not limited to, keeping books and records, ordering supplies, scheduling appointments, talking to tenants or a resident manager on the phone, arranging for repairs, and writing a rental advertisement. Provided you have no other fixed location where you regularly do these things—for example, an outside office—you'll get the deduction. This makes it easy for almost any landlord to qualify for the deduction. All you have to do is set up a home office that you regularly and exclusively use to manage or administer your rental business.

Under these rules, you can even have an outside office or workplace and still qualify for the home office deduction, as long as you use your home office to perform management tasks and you don't perform substantial management tasks at your outside office.

You Perform Your Most Important Rental Activities at Home

If you can't satisfy the requirements discussed above, you can still qualify for the home office deduction if you perform your most important rental business activities—those activities that most directly generate your rental income—at home.

If the work landlords do at their home offices and at their rental properties is of equal importance, then their principal place of business is where they spend more than half of their time. If you can show that you spend more time at your home office than at your rental properties, your home should qualify as your principal place of business.

You Meet Business Visitors at Home

Even if your home office is not your principal place of business, you may deduct your expenses for any part of your home that you use exclusively to meet with tenants, maintenance workers, vendors, or others involved with your rental business. You must physically meet with others in this home location—phoning them from there is not sufficient. And the meetings must be a regular part of your rental business; occasional meetings don't qualify.

It's not entirely clear how often you must meet these people at home for those meetings to be considered regular. However, the IRS has indicated that meeting people one or two days a week is sufficient. Exclusive use means you use the space where you meet tenants and others only for your rental business. You are free to use the space for business purposes other than meeting tenants—for example, doing your rental business bookkeeping or other paperwork. But you cannot use the space for personal purposes, such as watching television.

If you want to qualify under this part of the rule, keep a log or appointment book showing all the visits by your tenants and others.

You Use a Separate Structure for Rental Business

You can also deduct expenses for a separate freestanding structure, such as a garage or shed, if you use it exclusively and regularly for your rental business. The structure does not have to be your principal place of business, and you do not have to meet tenants there.

Exclusive use means that you use the structure only for your rental business.

> EXAMPLE: Gina uses a storage shed in the rear of her house exclusively to store tools and supplies she uses for her rental business. She may take the home office deduction for the shed.

Calculating the Home Office Deduction

Figuring out how much the home office deduction will save you in taxes is the fun part. You can always use the actual expense method discussed below. However, you have the option of using a new simplified method of calculating your deduction. (See "Simplified Home Office Deduction Method," below.)

How Much of Your Home Is Used for Your Rental Business?

To calculate your home office deduction, you need to determine what percentage of your home you use for your rental business. The law says you can use "any reasonable method" to do this. The most common method is to divide the square footage of your home office by the square footage of your entire home. For example, if your home office is 400 square feet, and your entire home is 1,600 square feet, 25% of your home is used for your office. Alternatively, if the rooms in your home are about the same size, you can divide the number of rooms used for business by the total number of rooms in your home. This calculation will often give you a larger deduction than the square footage method.

What Expenses Can You Deduct?

The home office deduction is not one deduction, but many. Most costs associated with maintaining and running your home office are deductible. However, because your office is in your home, some of the money you spend also benefits you personally. For example, your utility bill pays to heat your home office, but it also keeps the rest of your living space warm. The IRS deals with this issue by dividing home office expenses into two categories: direct expenses, which benefit only your home office, and indirect expenses, which benefit both your office and the rest of your home.

You Can Deduct Business Expenses Even If You Don't Qualify for the Home Office Deduction

Many business owners believe that they can't deduct any expenses they incur while working at home unless they qualify for the home office deduction. This belief isn't correct and has cost many taxpayers valuable deductions. Even if you don't qualify for or take the home office deduction, you can still take tax deductions for expenses you incur while working at your rental business at home. These are expenses that arise from the fact that you are doing business as a landlord, not from your use of the home itself.

Possible deductions include business equipment and furniture, a second phone you use for your rental business, and supplies.

Direct Expenses

You have a direct home office expense when you pay for something just for the home office portion of your home. This kind of expense includes, for example, the cost of painting your home office, carpeting it, or hiring someone to clean it. The entire amount of a direct home office expense is deductible.

Virtually anything you buy for your office is deductible. But you might have to depreciate permanent improvements to your home over 39 years, rather than deduct them in the year when you pay for them. Permanent improvements are changes that go beyond simple repairs, such as adding a new room to your home to serve as your office. (See Chapter 4 for more information on improvements versus repairs.)

Indirect Expenses

An indirect expense is a payment for something that benefits your *entire home*, including both the home office portion and your personal space. You may deduct only a portion of this expense—the home office percentage of the total.

Most of your home office expenses will be indirect expenses, including:

- **Rent.** If you rent your home or apartment, you can use the home office deduction to deduct part of your rent—a substantial expense that is ordinarily not deductible.

- **Mortgage interest and property taxes.** Whether or not you have a home office, you might be able to deduct your monthly mortgage interest and property tax payments as a personal itemized income tax deduction on your Schedule A, *Itemized Deductions* (the tax form where you list your personal income tax deductions). However, the Tax Cuts and Jobs Act lessened the value of this deduction and made it impossible for many taxpayers to take it at all. You can take a personal deduction for mortgage interest and property tax only if you itemize your personal expenses on your return. You should itemize only if your mortgage interest, property taxes, and other personal deductions exceed the standard deduction. The Tax Cuts and Jobs Act almost doubled the standard deduction. So, only about 10% of all taxpayers are able to itemize, compared with 30% in past years. In addition, starting in 2018 and continuing through 2025, the itemized deduction for property taxes is limited to $10,000 per year. Also, for homes purchased in 2018 through 2025, the deduction for home mortgage interest is limited to acquisition loans for a main and second home totaling a maximum of $750,000. The amount is $1 million for homes purchased before 2018. If you have a home office, you have the option of deducting the home office percentage of your mortgage interest and property tax payments on Schedule E as part of your home office deduction. If you do this, you may not deduct this amount on your Schedule A (you can't deduct the same item twice). So, you can deduct this amount without itemizing. If you do itemize, these amounts don't count toward the limits on deducting property tax and home mortgage interest as a personal itemized deduction.

EXAMPLE: Landlord Ed pays $12,000 per year in property tax on his home. He uses 25% of the home as an office for his residential rental business. This use enables him to deduct $3,000 of his property tax (25%) as part of his home office deduction. He deducts the remaining $9,000 as a personal itemized deduction on his Schedule A. Had he not had a home office, he could have deducted only $10,000 of his $12,000 in property tax.

- **Depreciation.** If you own your home, you're also entitled to a depreciation deduction for the office portion of your home. (See Chapter 5 for a detailed discussion of depreciation.)
- **Utilities.** You may deduct your home office percentage of your utility bills for your entire home, including electricity, gas, water, heating oil, and trash removal.
- **Insurance.** Both homeowners' and renters' insurance are partly deductible as indirect home office expenses. However, special insurance coverage you buy just for your home office—for example, insurance for your computer or other rental business equipment—is fully deductible as a direct expense.
- **Home maintenance.** You can deduct the home office percentage of home maintenance expenses that benefit your entire home, such as housecleaning of your entire house, roof and furnace repairs, and exterior painting. Home maintenance costs that don't benefit your home office—for example, painting your kitchen—are not deductible at all.
- **Casualty losses.** Casualty losses that affect your entire house—for example, a leak that floods your entire home—are deductible in the amount of your home office percentage. Casualty losses that affect only your home office, for example, a leak that floods only the home office area of the house, are fully deductible direct expenses. Casualty losses that don't affect your home office—for example, if only your kitchen floods—are not deductible as business expenses. A personal deduction is available for uninsured casualty losses to the nonoffice portions of a home, but during 2018 through 2025 it is limited to losses that occur in a presidentially declared disaster area. (See Chapter 14 for a detailed discussion of casualty losses.)

- **Condominium association fees.** These fees (often substantial) are partly deductible as an indirect expense if you have a home office.
- **Security system costs.** Security system costs are partly deductible as an indirect expense if your security system protects your entire home. If you have a security system that protects only your home office, the cost is a fully deductible direct expense.
- **Local travel expenses.** If your home office is your principal place of business, you can deduct the cost of traveling from your home to other work locations for your rental business. For example, you can deduct the cost of driving from home to perform maintenance at your rental property. If you don't have a home office, these costs are not deductible. (See Chapter 11 for a detailed discussion of the business mileage deduction.)

Profit Limit on Deductions

The tax code significantly limits the size of any home office deduction: You can't deduct more than the net profit you earn from a business you run from your home office. If your rental business earns a substantial profit, this limitation won't pose a problem. But if your business earns very little or loses money, the limitation could prevent you from deducting part or even all of your home office expenses in the current year.

If your deductions exceed your profits, you can deduct the excess in the following year and in each succeeding year until you deduct the entire amount, assuming you earn profits in these years. No limit applies to how far into the future you can deduct these expenses; you can claim them even if you're no longer living in the home where they were incurred.

So, whether or not your business is making money, you should keep track of your home office expenses and claim the deduction on your tax return. The profit limitation applies only to the home office deduction. It does not apply to rental business expenses that you can deduct under other provisions of the tax code.

For these purposes, your profit is the gross income you earn from your rental business minus your rental business deductions other than your home office deduction. You must also subtract the home office portion of your mortgage interest, real estate taxes, and casualty losses.

Special Concerns for Homeowners

As long as you live in your home for at least two out of the five years before you sell it, the profit you make on the sale—up to $250,000 for single taxpayers and $500,000 for married taxpayers filing jointly— is not taxable. (See IRS Publication 523, *Selling Your Home*.)

But you'll have to pay a capital gains tax on the depreciation deductions you took after May 6, 1997 for your home office. This is the deduction you are allowed for the yearly decline in value due to wear and tear of the portion of the building that contains your home office. (See Chapter 5 for more information on depreciation deductions.) These recaptured deductions are taxed at a 25% rate (unless your income tax bracket is lower than 25%).

> **EXAMPLE:** Sally bought a $200,000 home in 2009 and used one of her bedrooms as her home office for her rental business. She sold her home this year for $300,000, realizing a $100,000 gain (profit). Her depreciation deductions for her home office totaled $2,000. She must pay a tax of 25% of $2,000, or $500.

Having to pay a 25% tax on the depreciation deductions you took in the years before you sold your house is actually not a bad deal. This tax is probably no more—and is often less—tax than you would have had to pay if you hadn't taken the deductions in the first place and instead paid tax on your additional taxable income at ordinary income tax rates.

You can avoid such depreciation recapture if you use the new simplified method of calculating the home office deduction. (See "Simplified Home Office Deduction Method," below.) When you use this method, you deduct $5 per square foot of your home office and your depreciation deduction for the home office is deemed to be zero for the year. So, you have no depreciation recapture when you sell your home. Also, the adjusted basis of your home doesn't change.

Simplified Home Office Deduction Method

As long as you meet all the requirements to qualify for the home office deduction discussed above, you have the option of using a much simpler method to calculate your home deduction. Using this method, you just deduct $5 for every square foot of your home office. All you need to do is get out your measuring tape.

For example, if your home office is 200 square feet, you'll get a $1,000 home office deduction. That's all there is to it. You don't have to figure out what percentage of your home your office occupies. You also don't need to keep records of your direct or indirect home office expenses, such as utilities, rent, mortgage payments, real estate taxes, or casualty losses. These expenses aren't deductible when you use the simplified method. Nor do you get a depreciation deduction for your home office.

Sounds great, but what's the catch? The catch is that when you use the simplified method your home office deduction is capped at $1,500 per year. You'll reach the cap if your home office is 300 square feet. Even if your home office is 400 square feet, you'll still be limited to a $1,500 home office deduction if you use the simplified method. You can't carry over any part of the deduction to future years. Also, if you use the regular method to calculate your deduction, the total amount you can deduct could come out to more than if you deduct $5 per square foot of your home office.

IRS Reporting Requirements

Reporting your home office deduction is simple. First, you figure out the amount of your deduction. You can do this by using the IRS worksheet contained in Publication 587, *Business Use of Your Home*. If you have enough rental income to take a home office deduction this year (Line 32 of the worksheet), report the amount (up to the profit limit) on Line 19 of your Schedule E. Write "Business Use of Home" on the dotted line beside the entry. If you don't have enough rental income to take a home office deduction this year, write nothing in your Schedule E. Keep your record of your home office expenses to use in a future year when you have more rental income.

You need not file IRS Form 8829, *Expenses for Business Use of Your Home*. This form is only filed by taxpayers who file IRS Schedule C, *Profit or Loss From Business (Sole Proprietorship)*. Landlords ordinarily do not file Schedule C. However, there is an exception: If your rental activity qualifies as a hotel business because you engaged in short-term rentals, you may have to file Schedule C. (See Chapter 18 for more information.) If so, include Form 8829 with it if you claim the home office deduction.

Deducting an Outside Office

If you have an outside office for your rental activities, your tax life is simpler than if you use a home office. In addition, landlords who are investors, as well as business owners, can deduct expenses for an outside office.

Renting an Office

The rent and other expenses you pay for an outside office or other work space you use for your rental activity may be deducted the year they are paid as ordinary and necessary business expenses. None of the home office deduction rules apply to outside offices. You may deduct the rent you pay your landlord to use the property during the year. You may also deduct other expenses you pay the landlord, such as a portion of the landlord's property taxes or utility bills. Of course, you can deduct your own utility bills. You may deduct the cost of repairs you pay for, but permanent improvements to the property must be depreciated over several years. For example, you can currently deduct the cost of fixing the furnace, but you'd have to depreciate the cost of buying a new furnace. (See Chapter 5.)

Rental expenses for an outside office are reported on your Schedule E, the same as any other rental operating expense. List them on Line 18.

Using an Office in Your Rental Building

Many landlords use space inside their rental buildings as an office, as a workshop, or for storage. You may deduct the utilities you pay for the space, but you get no deduction for the rent you lose by not renting the space to tenants. You may depreciate the space along with the rest of your building. Use the 27.5-year depreciation period for residential property, if 80% of your total rentals from the building come from the dwelling units. Otherwise, you must use the 39-year term for nonresidential property. When you use a space in your building as an office, you use the fair rental value of the space to calculate this percentage.

> **EXAMPLE:** Sam owns several rental properties, including a duplex with two small one-bedroom units of equal size. He rents one side of the duplex to a tenant to live in and uses the other side as his office for his rental activities. He charges his tenant $800 per month rent, which is also the fair rental value of his office. Less than 80% of the gross rental income from the duplex comes from dwelling units—$800 is 50% of $1,600. As a result, Sam must depreciate the entire duplex using the 39-year term for nonresidential property. He may deduct the full amount he spends for utilities for his office and for repairs.

(See Chapter 5 for a detailed discussion of depreciation.)

Buying a Separate Office Building

If you buy a separate building that is not a residential rental to use as your office, you may currently deduct as ordinary and necessary business expenses your mortgage interest, real estate taxes, and expenses associated with the sale. In addition, you may depreciate the value of the real estate (not including the land) over 39 years. The cost of repairs may be currently deducted, but permanent improvements to the property must be depreciated. (See Chapter 4 for more on repairs versus improvements.)

CHAPTER

11

Car and Local Transportation Expenses

This chapter shows you how to deduct expenses for local transportation—that is, trips that don't require you to stay away from home overnight. These rules apply to local trips using any means of transportation, but this chapter focuses primarily on car expenses, the most common type of deduction for local travel. Overnight trips (whether by car or other means) are covered in Chapter 12.

> **CAUTION**
>
> **Transportation expenses are a red flag for the IRS.** Car and other local transportation expenses are always a key item for IRS auditors. It is easy to overstate them, so, if you're audited, the IRS will probably look carefully to make sure that you're not bending the rules. Your first line of defense against an audit is to keep good records to back up your deductions. Keeping good records is something no tax preparation software or accountant can do for you—you must develop good record-keeping habits and follow them faithfully to stay out of trouble with the IRS.

Deductible Local Transportation Expenses

Local transportation costs are deductible in the year in which they are incurred as operating expenses if they are ordinary and necessary for your rental activity—meaning common, helpful, and appropriate for your activity. (See Chapter 3 for a detailed discussion of the ordinary and necessary requirement.) It makes no difference what type of transportation you use to make the local trips—car, van, pickup, truck, motorcycle, taxi, bus, or train—or whether the vehicle you use is owned or leased. You can deduct these costs as long as they are ordinary and necessary and meet the other requirements discussed below.

You can deduct local transportation expenses if your rental activity qualifies as a business or an investment for tax purposes. (*Horowitz v. Comm'r.*, T.C. Memo 1979-27.) If you do a lot of driving for your rental activity, however, there's a good chance you are engaged in a business, not an investment. Investors usually don't do much driving to or from their rental properties or for other business purposes because (by definition) they are not actively involved in the management of their rental properties. (See Chapter 2 for a detailed discussion of whether you qualify as a business or an investor for tax purposes.)

Travel Costs Before You Become a Landlord

The cost of local travel you do before you become a landlord, such as travel to investigate purchasing a rental property, is not a currently deductible operating expense. If your rental activity becomes a business, such travel is a start-up expense. Up to $5,000 in start-up expenses may be deducted the first year your rental business is in operation. Any amount over $5,000 must be deducted in equal installments over the first 180 months you're in business. Landlords who are only investors may not deduct such start-up expenses. (See Chapter 2.)

Travel Must Be for Rental Activities

You can deduct only local trips that are for your rental activities—for example, to collect rental income or to manage, conserve, or maintain your rental property. Personal trips—for example, to the supermarket or the gym—are not deductible as transportation expenses. You can deduct the cost of driving to:

- your rental property
- where you have your principal place of business for your rental activity, including a home office
- places where you meet with tenants, suppliers, vendors, repair people, attorneys, accountants, real estate brokers, real estate managers, and other people who help in your rental activity
- the garbage dump where you haul refuse from your rental property
- a local college where you take landlord-related classes (educational expenses are deductible only if your rental activities qualify as a business; see Chapter 15), or
- a store where you buy supplies or materials for your real estate activity.

Moreover, you don't have to do all the driving yourself to get a car expense deduction. Any use of your car by another person qualifies as a deductible business expense if it is directly connected with your business. So, for example, you can count as business mileage a car trip your employee, spouse, or child takes to deliver an item for your rental business or for any other business purpose.

Driving From and to Home

Most local trips that landlords make for their rental activities start and end at home. Whether driving from home is deductible as an operating expense depends on whether you have a home office for your rental activity, and where you drive to.

You Have a Home Office

If you have a home office that qualifies as your principal place of business, you can deduct the cost of any trips you make from home to another location for your rental activity. You can get a lot of travel deductions this way. For example, you can deduct the cost of driving from home to your rental property or to the bank.

To deduct the cost of driving to and from your home office, it must qualify as your principal place of business. The rules for the home office deduction are used to determine whether a home office is a person's principal place of business. Under these rules, a home office qualifies if it is the place where you perform management or administrative tasks. Practically any landlord can set up a home office to perform such tasks—but you may not use the office for any other purpose.

> **EXAMPLE:** Kam owns five rental houses scattered throughout Southern California. She maintains a home office where she does bookkeeping and other administrative and management work for her rental business. She can deduct all of her rental-business-related trips from her home office, including trips she makes from home to any of her rental properties. Thanks to her home office, she can usually deduct 200 miles per month as a business trip expense.

You might think that landlords whose rental activities qualify as an investment (not a business) have no principal place of business because they are not in business. This isn't the case, though. Landlords who are investors get the same transportation deductions as landlords who are in business, as long as their home office meets the requirements for the home office deduction. If it does, then their home office is treated as their principal place of business for the transportation deduction. This is so, even though the home office deduction itself is limited to landlords who are in business. (See Chapter 10 for more on the home office deduction.)

You Don't Have a Home Office

If you don't have a home office that qualifies as your principal place of business, your transportation deductions will be limited by the commuting rule. Commuting expenses are nondeductible personal expenses. Commuting means driving from where you live to your main or regular place of work for your rental activity. For landlords, this means driving from home to their rental properties or to their outside office (if they have one).

> EXAMPLE: Sue, an accountant, lives in a Chicago suburb and owns a five-unit apartment building in downtown Chicago, about ten miles away. Sue does no work for her rental activity from home. Instead, she does all of her rental-related bookkeeping and other management tasks from her accounting office. Because of the commuting rule, Sue may not deduct the cost of driving from her home to her rental properties, or to her accounting office to perform rental-related work.

Even if a trip from home has a business purpose—for example, to haul tools or supplies from home to your rental property—it is still considered commuting and is not deductible. (You may, however, deduct the cost of renting a trailer or any other extraordinary expenses you incur to haul the tools or supplies from your home.)

Once you arrive at your rental office or rental property, you may deduct trips to other rental-related locations, but not trips back home.

> **EXAMPLE:** Sue drives directly from home to her rental property to supervise a repair. She then drives directly to her office, and drives back home later that day. She may deduct the trip from her rental property to her rental office, but none of her other trips.

Travel to a Temporary Work Location

Even if you don't have a home office, some trips from home may be deductible. Remember, commuting occurs when you go from home to a permanent work location—either:

- your office or other principal place of business for your rental activity, or
- your rental property, or any other place where you have worked or expect to work for more than one year.

Travel between your home and a temporary work location is not considered commuting and is therefore deductible. A temporary work location is any place where you perform work for your rental activity on an irregular basis with the reasonable expectation that the work there will last one year or less.

> **EXAMPLE:** Sue travels from home to her local college to attend a three-day seminar on rental property management. This trip isn't commuting, so she can deduct the travel expense.

Places like the bank and supply stores do not qualify as temporary work locations because you don't perform work there. You're a customer at these locations.

The Standard Mileage Rate

If you drive a car, SUV, van, pickup, or panel truck for your rental activity (as most landlords do), you have two options for deducting your vehicle expenses: You can use the standard mileage rate or you can deduct your actual expenses. You can figure your deduction both ways the first year before deciding which method to use on your tax return. Let's start with the easy one—the standard mileage rate.

How the Standard Mileage Rate Works

To use the standard mileage rate, you deduct a specified number of cents for every mile you drive for your rental activity. The IRS sets the standard mileage rate each year. Due to rapidly rising inflation, two standard mileage rates are in effect for 2022. For January 1, 2022 through June 30, 2022 the standard rate is 58.5 cents per mile. For July 1, 2022 through December 31, 2022, the rate is 62.5 cents per mile. To figure out your deduction, simply multiply your business miles by the applicable standard mileage rate.

> **EXAMPLE:** Ed drove his car 5,000 miles for his rental activity during January through June 2022 and 5,000 miles during July through December. His car expense deduction is (58.5 cents × 5,000) + (62.5 cents × 5,000) = $6,050.

The big advantage of the standard mileage rate is that it requires very little record keeping. You only need to keep track of how many rental activity miles you drive, not the actual expenses for your car, such as gas, maintenance, or repairs. However, unless you drive a very inexpensive car that qualifies for very little depreciation, the standard mileage rate will usually give you a smaller deduction than the actual expense method.

If you choose the standard mileage rate, you can't deduct actual car operating expenses—for example, maintenance and repairs, gasoline and its taxes, oil, insurance, and vehicle registration fees. All of these items are factored into the rate set by the IRS. And you can't deduct the cost of the car through regular or bonus depreciation or Section 179 expensing, because the car's depreciation is also factored into the standard mileage rate (as are lease payments for a leased car).

The only actual expenses you can deduct (because these costs aren't included in the standard mileage rate) are:
- parking fees and tolls for rental-related trips (but you can't deduct parking ticket fines or the cost of parking your car at your place of work)
- interest on a car loan (deductible as business interest), and
- personal property tax you paid when you bought the vehicle, based on its value—this tax is often included as part of your auto registration fee.

If, like most landlords, you use your car for both rental-related and personal trips, you can deduct only the rental use percentage of the abovementioned interest and taxes.

> **EXAMPLE:** Riley uses his car 50% for his rental activity and 50% for personal trips. He uses the standard mileage rate to deduct his car expenses. He pays $3,000 a year in interest on his car loan. He may deduct 50% of this amount, or $1,500, as an operating expense in addition to his rental activity mileage deduction.

Requirements to Use the Standard Mileage Rate

Not everyone can use the standard mileage rate. You won't be able to use it (and will have to use the actual expense method instead) if you can't meet the following two requirements.

First-Year Rule

You must use the standard mileage rate in the first year you use a car for your rental activity or you are forever foreclosed from using that method for that car. If you use the standard mileage rate the first year, you can switch to the actual expense method in a later year. But as a practical matter, once you switch from the standard rate to the actual expense method it's nearly impossible to switch back to the standard rate. If you're not sure which method you want to use, it's a good idea to use the standard mileage rate the first year you use the car for business. This choice leaves all your options open for later years.

Five-Car Rule

You can't use the standard mileage rate if you have five or more cars that you use for your rental activity simultaneously.

The Actual Expense Method

Instead of using the standard mileage rate, you can deduct the actual cost of using your car for your rental activity. Although it requires more record keeping, you can get a larger deduction if you use the actual expense method instead of the standard mileage rate. A larger deduction is most likely if your car is more expensive than average to operate.

Nevertheless, many taxpayers choose the standard mileage rate because it's easier. You only need to keep track of how many miles you drive for your rental activity, instead of keeping track of how much you spend for gas, oil, repairs, and all your other car expenses. Moreover, if you don't drive many miles each year for your rental activity, the extra deduction you get from the actual expense method may not be worth the record keeping required.

How the Actual Expense Method Works

As the name implies, under the actual expense method, you deduct the actual costs you incur each year to operate your car, plus depreciation. If you use this method, you must keep careful track of all of your car expenses during the year, including:

- gas and oil
- repairs and maintenance
- depreciation of your original vehicle and improvements
- car repair tools
- license fees
- parking fees for rental activity trips
- registration fees
- tires
- insurance
- garage rent
- tolls for rental activity trips
- car washing

- lease payments
- interest on car loans
- towing charges, and
- auto club dues.

Watch Those Tickets

You may not deduct the cost of driving violations or parking tickets, even if you were on rental-related business when you got the ticket. Government fines and penalties are never deductible as a matter of public policy.

When you do your taxes, add up the cost of all these items. For everything but parking fees and tolls, multiply the total cost of each item by your car's business use percentage. You determine your business use percentage by keeping track of all the miles you drive for your rental activity during the year and the total mileage driven. You divide the business mileage by your total mileage to figure your business use percentage. For parking fees and tolls that are rental-activity related, include (and deduct) the full cost. The total is your deductible transportation expense for the year.

> EXAMPLE: Lara owns several rental houses in the Miami area. In one recent year, she drove her car 1,000 miles for her rental activity and 10,000 miles total. Her business use percentage is 10% (1,000 ÷ 10,000 = 10%). She can deduct 10% of the actual costs of operating her car, plus the full cost of any rental-related tolls and parking fees. Her expenses amount to $10,000 for the year, so she gets a $1,000 deduction, plus $50 in tolls and parking.

Record-Keeping Requirements

When you deduct actual car expenses, you must keep records of all the costs of owning and operating your car. This requirement includes keeping track of not only the number of rental activity miles and total miles you drive, but also gas, repair, parking, insurance, tolls, and any other car expenses. (You'll find more information on record-keeping requirements in Chapter 17.)

Vehicle Depreciation Deductions

Using the actual expense method, you can depreciate the cost of your vehicle over several years. Although the general concept of depreciation is the same for every type of property, special rules apply to depreciation deductions for cars. These rules can give you a lower annual deduction for cars than you'd be entitled to using the normal depreciation rules.

Your annual depreciation deduction is limited to the amounts listed in the charts below if your vehicle is a passenger automobile as defined by the IRS. A passenger automobile is any four-wheeled vehicle made primarily for use on public streets and highways that has an unloaded gross weight of 6,000 pounds or less. This definition includes virtually all automobiles, including cars, trucks, pickups, vans, and SUVs.

The Tax Cuts and Jobs Act greatly increased the annual limits for passenger vehicles placed into service during 2018 and later. The amounts for vehicles placed into service during 2022 are shown in the following chart, which applies to all passenger vehicles, including automobiles, trucks, and vans. The chart shows that if you place a passenger vehicle into service in your business in 2022, you may take a maximum depreciation deduction of $11,200. The second year, you may deduct a whopping $18,000. That's $29,200 in depreciation deductions in the first two years—$37,200 if bonus depreciation is also claimed. These are by far the highest annual limits for passenger vehicle depreciation that have ever been allowed. The annual limits are now so high they only impact vehicles that cost $50,000 or more.

Depreciation Limits for Passenger Vehicles (must be reduced by percentage of personal use)				
Year Placed in Service	1st tax year	2nd tax year	3rd tax year	4th and later years
2022	$11,200 ($19,200 if $8,000 bonus depreciation used)	$18,000	$10,800	$6,460

Bonus depreciation can be applied to vehicles, but the bonus amount is fixed at $8,000, no matter how much the vehicle costs. So, by using bonus depreciation, you can depreciate $19,200 for a passenger vehicle the first year when it is placed in service in 2022 instead of $11,200. However, you can use bonus depreciation only if you use your used or new vehicle more than 50% of the time for business purposes (because vehicles are classified as listed property for depreciation purposes).

The deduction limits above are based on 100% rental activity use of the vehicle. If, like most landlords, you don't use your car solely for your rental activity, the limits are reduced based on your percentage of personal use. In addition, if, like most landlords, you use your car less than 51% for your rental business, you'll have to use the slowest method of depreciation —the straight-line method—and you won't qualify for bonus depreciation. You must continue to use this method even if your business use rises over 50% in later years. The following chart shows how much of your vehicle's depreciable basis you can deduct each year using the straight-line method, up to the maximum limits.

Straight-Line Depreciation Table	
Year	Depreciation Percentage
1	10%
2	20%
3	20%
4	20%
5	20%
6	10%

EXAMPLE: Jenn purchases a $60,000 passenger automobile in 2022 that she uses 25% of the time for her residential rental business. Her depreciable basis in the vehicle is $15,000 (25% × $60,000 = $15,000). If Jenn uses the actual expense method, she qualifies for a $1,500 depreciation deduction for 2022 (10% × $15,000 = $1,500). She'll be able to deduct $3,000 per year the following four years (20% × $15,000 = $3,000). She also gets to deduct 25% of what she spends to drive her car each year, including gas and repairs.

Special Rule for Heavy Vehicles

The annual dollar limits in the charts above don't apply to trucks, pickups, RVs, vans, SUVs, and other vehicles that don't come within the passenger automobile definition—that is, vehicles with less than a gross loaded weight of 6,000 pounds. Using bonus depreciation and/or Section 179, you might be able to deduct a substantial portion of the cost of such a vehicle in a single year. But you must use the vehicle at least 51% of the time to take advantage of bonus depreciation or Section 179. The Section 179 deduction for SUVs and other vehicles up to 14,000 pounds is limited to a maximum of $27,000 for 2022. However, no such limits apply to bonus depreciation, which is set at 100% during 2018 through 2022, and 80% for 2023.

So, you could buy an SUV (or van, truck, pickup, or RV) weighing more than 6,000 pounds for your rental business and deduct the entire cost in the first year if you used it 100% for your rental business. For example, suppose Terry pays $100,000 for a 7,000-pound SUV in 2022 that she uses 100% of the time for her rental business. Terry may deduct the entire $100,000 cost in 2022 using bonus depreciation. If Terry used the vehicle 60% for her rental business, she could deduct $60,000. If Terry purchases the SUV in 2023, her bonus depreciation percentage would be reduced to 80% of the vehicle's cost.

Auto Repairs and Improvements

Auto repairs and maintenance costs are fully deductible in the year you pay them. Add these costs to your other annual expenses when you use the actual expense method. (You get no extra deduction for repairs when you use the standard mileage rate.) If you fix your car yourself, you may deduct the cost of parts and depreciate or deduct tools, but you can't take a deduction for your time or labor.

Unlike repairs, improvements to your car must be depreciated over several years, not deducted all in the year when you pay for them.

Improvements must be depreciated separately from the vehicle itself— that is, they are treated as a separate item of depreciable property. The same rules, however, apply to depreciating improvements as regular auto depreciation. Combine the cost of the original vehicle and the improvements for purposes of the annual automobile depreciation limit. The recovery period begins when the improvement is placed in service.

Leasing a Car

If you lease a car that you use in your rental activity, you can use the actual expense method to deduct the portion of each lease payment that reflects the rental activity percentage use of the car. You can't deduct any part of a lease payment that is for commuting or personal use of the car.

> **EXAMPLE:** John pays $600 a month to lease a Lexus. He uses it 10% for his rental activity and 90% for personal purposes. He may deduct 10% of his lease payments ($60 a month) as a local transportation expense for his sales business.

Leasing companies typically require you to make an advance or down payment to lease a car. You can deduct the business use percentage of this cost as well, but you must spread the deduction out equally over the entire lease period.

You may use either the actual expense method or the standard mileage rate when you lease a car for business. However, if you want to use the standard mileage rate, you must use it the first year you lease the car and continue to use it for the entire lease term. If you use the standard mileage method, you can't deduct any portion of your lease payments. Instead, this cost is covered by the standard mileage rate set by the IRS.

When you lease a car for more than 30 days and use the actual expense method, you are required to reduce your deduction by a relatively small amount, called the "inclusion amount," if the car exceeds a certain value. For vehicles placed into service in 2022, the inclusion amount will only apply to vehicles that cost over $50,000. The inclusion amount is calculated to make the lease deduction about the same as the depreciation deduction that would have been available if the automobile had been purchased. The IRS recalculates it each year. You can find the inclusion amount for the current year in the tables published in IRS Publication 463, *Travel, Gift, and Car Expenses.*

Other Local Transportation Expenses

You don't have to drive a car or another vehicle to get a tax deduction for local trips. You can deduct the cost of travel by bus or other public transit, taxi, train, ferry, motorcycle, bicycle, or any other means. However, all the rules limiting deductions for travel by car also apply to other transportation methods. The same record-keeping requirements apply as well.

Reporting Transportation Expenses on Your Tax Return

Report your local transportation deduction on Line 6 of IRS Schedule E. Combine it with your travel expenses (see Chapter 18). You must also complete and file Part V of IRS Form 4562, *Depreciation and Amortization (Including Information on Listed Property)*. This form requires that you answer the following questions about your vehicle use:

- total business/investment miles driven during the year
- total commuting miles driven during the year
- total other personal (noncommuting) miles driven during the year, and
- whether you had another vehicle available for personal use.

As you can see, by looking at your answers to these questions, the IRS can determine what percentage of the time you claim to use your car for your rental activity and for personal use. The IRS will likely think something is wrong if you claim to use your car 100% of the time for your rental activity, but say you have no other car available for personal use.

Travel Expenses

I f you travel overnight for your rental activity, you can deduct your airfare, hotel bills, meals, and other expenses. If you plan your trip carefully, you can even mix landlord business with pleasure and still take a deduction. However, IRS auditors closely scrutinize deductions for overnight travel and many taxpayers get caught claiming these deductions without proper records to back them up. To stay within the law (and avoid unwanted attention from the IRS), you need to know how this deduction works and how to properly document your travel expenses.

What Are Travel Expenses?

For tax purposes, "travel expenses" are the amounts you spend when you travel away from your tax home overnight for your business (rental) activity. You don't have to travel any set distance to take a travel expense deduction. But you can't take this deduction if you just spend the night in a motel across town. You must travel outside your city limits. If you don't live in a city, you must go outside the general area where your tax home is located.

You must stay away overnight or at least long enough to require a stop for sleep or rest. You can't satisfy the rest requirement by merely napping in your car.

> EXAMPLE: Phoebe lives in Los Angeles. She flies to San Francisco to deal with a repair problem in a rental house she owns there. She spends the night in a hotel, and returns home the following day. Her trip is a deductible travel expense.

If you don't stay overnight, your trip won't qualify as travel. But you might still be able to take a tax deduction. Local trips for your rental activity are also deductible (see Chapter 11), but you're entitled to deduct only your transportation expenses—the cost of driving or using some other means of transportation. You may not deduct meals or other expenses like you can when you travel and stay overnight.

EXAMPLE: Philip drives from his home in Los Angeles to San Diego to show his rental property to prospective tenants and returns home that same day. His 200-mile round trip is a deductible local trip. He may deduct his expenses for the 200 miles he drove, but he can't deduct the breakfast he bought on the way to San Diego.

RELATED TOPIC

How to deduct local travel. For a detailed discussion of tax deductions for local travel, see Chapter 11.

Where Is Your Tax Home?

Your "tax home" is the entire city or general area where your principal place of business for your rental activity is located. If you run your rental activity out of your residence, your tax home is the city or area where you live.

The IRS doesn't care how far you travel for business. You'll get a deduction as long as you travel outside your tax home's city limits and stay overnight. So, even if you're just traveling across town, you'll qualify for a deduction if you manage to stay outside your city limits.

EXAMPLE: Pete's tax home is in San Francisco. He drives to Oakland to check up on an apartment building he owns. He decides to spend the night in an Oakland hotel rather than brave the traffic back to San Francisco. Pete's stay qualifies as a deductible travel expense even though the distance between San Francisco and Oakland is only eight miles. Pete can deduct his hotel and meal expenses.

If you don't live in a city, your tax home covers the general area where you typically reside—the area within about 40 miles of your home.

Your Trip Must Be for Rental Business

To deduct the cost of your trip, it must be primarily for your rental activity. So, you must have a rental purpose in mind before starting out, and you must actually do something for your rental activity while you're away. Examples of rental business purposes include:

- traveling to your rental property to deal with tenants, maintenance, or repairs
- traveling to building supply stores or other places to obtain materials and supplies for your rental activity
- traveling to your rental property to show it to prospective tenants
- learning new skills to help in your rental activity, by attending landlord-related classes, seminars, conventions, or trade shows, and
- traveling to see people who can help you operate your rental activity, such as attorneys, accountants, or real estate brokers.

On the other hand, rental-related activities do not include:

- sightseeing
- recreational activities that you attend by yourself or with family or friends, or
- attending personal investment seminars or political events.

Use common sense when deciding whether to claim that a trip is for your rental activity. If you're audited, the IRS is likely to question any trip that doesn't have some logical connection to your rental activity.

> ! CAUTION
> **Travel for building improvements is not deductible.** You cannot deduct the cost of traveling away from home if the primary purpose of the trip is to improve your rental property. The cost of travel for improvements must be added to the cost of the improvement and recovered by taking depreciation over many years. In contrast, travel costs for repairs are currently deductible operating expenses. (See Chapter 4 for a detailed discussion of how to tell the difference between repairs and improvements for tax purposes.)

Travel Must Be Ordinary and Necessary

To be deductible, your travel expenses must be ordinary and necessary. So, the trip and the expenses you incur must be helpful and appropriate for your rental activity, not necessarily indispensable. Traveling to a rental property isn't always ordinary and necessary.

> **EXAMPLE:** Rayford Strickland owned two parcels of real estate about 500 miles from his tax home in Texas. During a two-year period, he made 80 trips to the property at a claimed cost of $11,000. The properties generated a total of $1,653 in income during this time. The IRS and tax court disallowed Strickland's travel expense deductions. The court found that the 80 trips were not an ordinary and necessary expense because Strickland was unable to provide any explanation of why it was necessary to make so many trips to the two properties. (*Strickland v. Comm'r.*, 43 T.C. Memo 1061.)

Travel Before You Become a Landlord

You must be involved in an ongoing rental activity to deduct your business trips. Trips you take to investigate acquiring your first rental property are not currently deductible business travel expenses.

> **EXAMPLE:** Michelle, a San Francisco resident, has never owned any rental property, but would like to buy some. She has heard that there are good buys in Reno, Nevada, so she takes several trips there to search for income properties. She can't currently deduct her travel expenses because she is not yet in business.

Travel to View Rental Properties for Sale

You must clear several hurdles to deduct travel expenses you incur while looking at rental properties to purchase. You may not deduct expenses you incur to find new properties to buy if your rental activity is an investment, instead of a business, for tax purposes. Investors may not deduct expenses incurred to find new investments. Most landlords are in business. (*Frank v. Comm'r.*, 20 T.C. 511.) (See Chapter 2 for a detailed discussion of whether a rental activity qualifies as a business or an investment.)

If your rental activity is a business, travel costs to look for properties to purchase fall into two categories:

- expenses incurred to look at properties you purchase, and
- expenses incurred to look at properties you don't purchase.

Expenses you incur to look at a property you end up buying must be added to the basis of your property and depreciated over 27.5 years along with the rest of the property. (Rev. Rul. 77-254.) This means it will take a long time to fully deduct your travel expenses for a property you buy.

If you look at rental property on a trip, but don't buy it, your travel expenses can be currently deductible as an operating expense, but only if you are already engaged in a rental business in the geographic area where the property is located. Unfortunately for landlords who like to travel, the IRS and courts have taken a restrictive view of the geographic area in which a small landlord is in business, holding that it extends only to the area where the landlord already owns property.

> **EXAMPLE:** Patrick O'Donnell, a Chicago resident who owned two apartments in Las Vegas, took a two-day trip to Miami to investigate buying a rental property there. However, he decided not to go through with the deal. Both the IRS and tax court denied him a deduction for his travel expenses. The court found that, even though O'Donnell was in the rental business in Las Vegas, his business did not extend to Miami. Because he was not in business in Miami, he couldn't deduct as a business operating expense his costs to travel there to look at properties. If he had actually bought a rental property in Miami, his travel expenses to purchase it would still not be currently deductible. Instead, he would have to add the cost to the property's basis and depreciate it over 27.5 years. However, if he had also incurred expenses to look at properties he didn't buy before finding the property he did buy, those expenses could be deducted as business start-up expenses. (See Chapter 9.) (*O'Donnell v. Comm'r*, 62 T.C. 781.)

It's unclear exactly how large an area the IRS and tax court would say a small landlord does business in. For example, would O'Donnell in the above example have been able to deduct the expenses of looking for rental properties in Reno, Nevada, or Los Angeles? No one knows. It is clear, however, that your best case for being able to deduct travel expenses is where you look for property in or near an area where you already own rental real estate. Once you start traveling outside of the area where you already own rental property, you'll have a tougher time claiming the deduction with the IRS, especially if you travel to a vacation destination like Miami or Hawaii.

If you travel outside your area of business to look at new rental properties and decide to take your chances with the IRS and claim the deduction, be sure to properly document your expenses and the time you spend looking for rental properties on your trip. You'll have a problem only if you're audited. But, claiming large travel deductions as a landlord will definitely increase your chance of getting audited.

Deductible Travel Expenses

Subject to the limits covered in "How Much You Can Deduct," below, virtually all of your travel expenses are deductible. These costs fall into two broad categories: your transportation expenses and the expenses you incur at your destination.

Transportation expenses are the costs of getting to and from your destination—for example:

- fares for airplanes, trains, or buses
- driving expenses, including car rentals, and
- shipping costs for your personal luggage or other things you need for your rental activity.

If you drive your own car to your destination, you may deduct your costs using the standard mileage rate, or you can deduct your actual expenses. You may also deduct your mileage while at your destination. (See Chapter 11 for more on mileage deductions.)

You may also deduct your food and lodging expenses while at your destination. Destination expenses include:

- hotel or other lodging expenses for days you work at your rental activity
- 50% of meal and beverage expenses
- taxi, Uber/Lyft, public transportation, and car rental expenses at your destination

- telephone, internet, and fax expenses
- computer rental fees
- laundry and dry-cleaning expenses, and
- tips you pay on any of the other costs.

You may deduct meals you eat alone while traveling on business or meals with business associates while traveling. Business associates include current or potential customers, consultants, clients, or similar business contacts. You (the business owner) or an employee must be present at the meal, but you don't have to eat anything if a business associate does. Ordinarily, meals are only 50% deductible, but restaurant meals are 100% deductible for 2021–2022 (see "Limits on Meal Expense Deduction," below).

You may not deduct entertainment expenses when you travel, even if you incur them for your rental activity. So, you can't deduct the cost of a nightclub, concert, or ball game while on the road, even if you take a business associate along. The Tax Cuts and Jobs Act eliminated all such entertainment deductions starting in 2018. You can deduct the cost of a meal at an event, like a ball game, if you're separately billed for it.

Traveling First Class or Steerage

You may not deduct lavish or extravagant expenses, but the IRS gives you a great deal of leeway here. You may, if you wish, travel first class, stay at four-star hotels, and eat at expensive restaurants. On the other hand, you're also entitled to be a cheapskate—for example, you could stay with a friend or relative at your destination to save on hotel charges and still deduct your meals and other expenses.

Taking People With You

You may deduct the expenses you pay for a person who travels with you only if that person:

- is your employee
- has a genuine business reason for going on the trip with you, and
- would otherwise be allowed to deduct the travel expenses.

These rules apply to your family as well. So, you can deduct the expense of taking your spouse, child, or other relative only if the person is your employee and his or her presence is essential to your rental activity.

> **EXAMPLE:** Jason lives in Dallas and owns an apartment building in Tulsa, Oklahoma. He hires his son Dave to assist him in doing repairs for his property. He may deduct the cost of traveling to Tulsa with Dave to do repairs.

In addition, you may deduct the travel costs of your spouse or any other relative who is a co-owner of the rental property you travel to visit, provided that person spends sufficient time on rental activities.

If you bring your family along simply to enjoy the trip, you may still deduct your own business expenses as if you were traveling alone—and you don't have to reduce your deductions, even if others get a free ride with you. For example, if you drive to your destination, you can deduct the entire cost of the drive, even if your family rides along with you. Similarly, you can deduct the full cost of a single hotel room even if you obtain a larger, more expensive room for your whole family.

How Much You Can Deduct

If you spend all of your time at your destination on rental business, you may deduct 100% of your expenses (except meal expenses, which can be either 50% or 100% deductible—see "Limits on Meal Expense Deduction," below). However, things get more complicated if you mix business and pleasure. Different rules apply to your transportation expenses and the expenses you incur while at your destination (destination expenses).

Travel within the United States is subject to an all-or-nothing rule: You may deduct 100% of your transportation expenses only if you spend *more than half of your time* on rental activities while at your destination. In other words, your rental activity days must outnumber your personal days. If you spend more time on personal activities than on rental activities, you get no transportation deduction.

You may also deduct the destination expenses you incur on days when you do rental-related tasks. Expenses incurred on personal days at your destination are nondeductible personal expenses. (The rules used to determine what constitutes a rental activity day are discussed below.)

> **EXAMPLE:** Tom's tax home is in Atlanta, but he owns an apartment building in New Orleans. He takes the train to New Orleans to supervise extensive remodeling of his property. He spends six days in New Orleans, where he spends all of his time on rental business, and spends $900 for his hotel, meals, and other living expenses. On the way home, he stops in Mobile for three days to visit his parents and spends $100 for lodging and meals there. His round-trip train fare is $250. Tom's trip consisted of six rental activity days and three personal days, so he spent more than half of the trip on rental activities. He can deduct 100% of his train fare and the entire $900 he spent while on business in New Orleans. He may not, however, deduct the $100 he spent while visiting his parents.

If your trip is primarily a vacation—that is, you spend more than half of your time on personal activities—the entire cost of the trip is a nondeductible personal expense. But you may deduct destination expenses that are directly related to your rental activity, like phone calls. It doesn't include transportation, lodging, or food.

As long as your trip is primarily for your rental activity, you can add a vacation to the end of the trip, make a side trip purely for fun, or enjoy evenings at the theater or ballet, and still deduct your entire airfare. What you spend while having fun is not deductible, but you can deduct all of your rental activity and transportation expenses.

> **EXAMPLE:** Will flies to Miami, where he spends four days working on his rental property. He spends three extra days in Miami swimming and enjoying the sights. Because he spent over half his time on rental business—four days out of seven—the cost of his flight is entirely deductible, as are his hotel and meal costs while he worked on his rental property. He may not deduct his hotel, meal, or other expenses during his vacation days.

Calculating Time Spent on Rental Activities

To calculate how much time you spend on rental activities while on a trip, compare the number of days you spend on rental-related work to the number of days you spend on personal activities. You spend a day on rental activities if you:

- spend more than four hours doing rental-related work
- are not at a particular place for your rental activity—for example, to show a vacant rental unit even if you spend most of the day on personal activities
- spend more than four hours on travel for your rental activity (travel time begins when you leave home and ends when you reach your hotel, or vice versa)
- drive at least 300 miles for your rental activity (you can average your mileage, like if you drive 600 miles to your destination in two days, you may claim two 300-mile days, even if you drove 500 miles on one day and 100 miles on the other)
- spend more than four hours on some combination of travel and your rental activities
- are prevented from working rental activities because of circumstances beyond your control, such as a transit strike or terrorist act, and
- stay at your destination between days you work on rental activities, if it would have cost more to go home and return than to remain where you are. This sandwich rule allows you to count weekends as rental activity days, if you work at your travel destination during the previous and following week.

Be sure to keep track of your time while you're away. You can do this by taking notes on your calendar or travel diary. (See Chapter 17 for a detailed discussion of record keeping while traveling.)

Limits on Meal Expense Deduction

There are two ways to calculate your meal expense deduction: You can keep track of your actual expenses or use the standard meal allowance set by the federal government. During 2021–2022, the actual expense method can give you a much larger deduction.

Deducting Actual Meal Expenses

If you use the actual expense method, you must keep track of what you spend on meals, including tips and tax, en route to and at your business destination. When you do your taxes, you add these amounts together to determine your total deduction.

> **EXAMPLE:** Frank lives in Santa Fe, New Mexico, and owns a rental home in Albuquerque. He travels to Albuquerque by car to perform repairs and maintenance on the property and stays overnight in a motel. On the way, he spends $200 on meals. While in Albuquerque, he spends another $200 for food. His total meal expense for the trip is $400.

If you combine a rental-related trip with a vacation, you may deduct only those meals you eat while on rental business—for example, meals you eat while performing repairs, showing a vacant unit, or doing other rental-related work. Meals that are part of business entertainment are subject to the rules on entertainment expenses, covered in Chapter 15.

Ordinarily, you may only deduct 50% of the total cost of a business meal. For example, if a meal costs $100, you may deduct $50. But in the wake of the economic devastation that the COVID-19 pandemic caused to restaurants, Congress enacted a special rule for 2021 and 2022. During these years, you may deduct 100% of the cost of business meals and beverages purchased from restaurants. (I.R.C. § 274(n)(2)(D).) This rule is intended to help restaurants get back on their feet.

For these purposes, a "restaurant" is a business that prepares and sells food or beverages to retail customers for immediate consumption, which includes everything from high-end French restaurants to McDonald's and Starbucks.

However, you don't have to eat the food at the restaurant to get the 100% deduction. You can order restaurant takeout while traveling and deduct the full cost. Likewise, you can deduct 100% of the cost of business meals ordered from restaurants through delivery services like Grubhub or Uber Eats.

"Restaurants" do not include businesses that predominantly sell prepackaged food or beverages for later consumption, like grocery stores, liquor stores, drugstores, specialty food stores, and vending machines. So, food or beverages purchased from these places while traveling are still subject to the 50% limitation. Hotel room service should qualify for the 100% deduction. But food or beverages you grab from a hotel minibar should be subject to the 50% limit.

> **EXAMPLE:** Frank from the above example spent $375 on food from restaurants and $25 for prepackaged sandwiches from grocery stores. He may deduct the entire $375 for restaurant meals, but only 50% ($12.50) of the cost of the grocery store food.

You do not necessarily have to keep all your receipts for your business meals, but you need to keep careful track of what you spend, and you should be able to prove that the meal was for business. Also, during 2021–2022, you should separately track your total costs for meals and beverages purchased from restaurants and those for meals from other places like grocery stores. See Chapter 15 for a detailed discussion of record keeping for meal expenses.

Using the Standard Meal Allowance

Instead of deducting your actual expenses, you can deduct a set amount for each day of your business trip. This amount is called the "standard meal allowance." It covers your expenses for business meals, beverages, tax, and tips.

The amount of the allowance varies depending on where and when you travel. For 2022, the standard meal allowance ranged from $59 per day for travel in the least expensive areas to up to $79 for high cost areas, which includes most major cities. Unfortunately, when you use the standard meal allowance, you may only deduct one-half (50%) of the allowance amount. You may not deduct 100% of the allowance amount for meals purchased from restaurants during 2021–2022 as you can with the actual expense method. As a result, you'll usually get a larger deduction if you deduct your actual expenses.

Note that if you use the standard meal allowance, you must use it for all of the business trips you take during the year. You can't use it for some trips and then use the actual expense method for others. If you travel to more than one location in one day, you must use the rate in effect for the area where you spend the night.

The standard meal allowance is revised each year. You can find the current rates for travel within the United States on the internet at the U.S. General Services Administration website at www.gsa.gov.

Hiring Help

Whenever you hire a worker to help you with your rental business, you'll face a number of tax-related questions:

- Are your payments to the worker deductible?
- Is the worker an employee or independent contractor?
- If the worker is an independent contractor, what tax-reporting requirements do you have?
- If the worker is an employee, what payroll tax rules must you comply with?
- Do special rules apply when you hire a family member?

This chapter goes over the tax rules that apply to landlords who hire people to help them with their rental business and explains how you can comply with those rules.

Your Employees and Independent Contractors Should Track Their Time

As discussed in detail in Chapter 7, landlords may qualify for a pass-through deduction equal to 20% of their rental income if their rental activity qualifies as a business. For purposes of the pass-through deduction only, the IRS says that landlords who work 250 hours per year are automatically deemed to be in business. The 250 hours includes work performed on your behalf by employees and independent contractors. So, whenever you hire employees or independent contractors, such as rental agents or repair people, to work in your rental activity, you should require them to keep track of their time and report it to you, and you should keep a record of it. This is so even if you don't pay them by the hour.

Deducting Payments to Workers

You may deduct all or most of what you pay a person who performs services for your rental activity. It doesn't matter how you measure or make the payments. You can pay a salary or a set fee for a job, or you can pay by the hour. You can even provide free rent in exchange for services.

The money you pay a worker will fall into one of the following three categories of deductible rental expenses:

- operating expenses
- start-up expenses, or
- depreciation.

The general rules for each of these types of expenses are discussed in earlier chapters; this section explains how workers' pay falls into all of these categories.

Operating Expenses

Most of the time, amounts you pay workers will be operating expenses. These expenses are currently deductible as long as they are:

- ordinary and necessary
- reasonable in amount
- paid for services actually performed, and
- actually paid or incurred in the year the deduction is claimed (as shown by your payroll records).

A worker's services are ordinary and necessary if they are common, accepted, helpful, and appropriate for your rental activity—they don't have to be indispensable. A worker's pay is reasonable if the amount is within the range that other landlords pay for similar services. These requirements usually won't pose a problem when you hire a worker to perform any legitimate function for your rental activity.

EXAMPLE: Ken hires Karen, a gardener, to perform gardening work on his three rental houses. He pays her $200 per month—what similar workers are typically paid in the area. Ken can deduct his monthly payments to Karen as an operating expense. If Karen works a full year, Ken will get a $2,400 deduction.

Payments to workers for personal services are not deductible as business expenses.

EXAMPLE: Ken also hires Karen to perform gardening services for his personal residence. These services are personal, not related to Ken's rental activity. So, Ken may not deduct her pay as an operating expense. Indeed, such payments are not deductible at all.

Special rules (described below) apply if you hire family members to work in your rental activity. (See Chapter 3 for more on operating expenses.)

Start-Up Expenses

Amounts you pay workers for services performed during the start-up phase of your rental activity are start-up expenses. Up to $5,000 in start-up expenses may be deducted in the first year in which your rental activity is in operation. Any amount over the limit must be deducted in equal installments over the first 180 months you're in business. (See Chapter 9 for more on deducting start-up costs.)

EXAMPLE: Michelle purchases her first rental property—a small house in need of a new paint job. She hires Al, a professional painter, to paint the house. After Al completes his work, Michelle lists the house for rent. Michelle paid Al $2,000 to paint her house. His fee is a start-up expense because it was incurred before Michelle's rental activity had begun—that is, before she offered the property for rent. Michelle may deduct the $2,000 the first year she is in business.

Depreciation Expenses

Amounts you pay workers to help purchase, transport, install, or improve long-term assets are not business operating expenses. Instead, these costs are added to the basis (cost) of the asset and get depreciated over time with the asset. In certain situations, you may be able to currently deduct these costs using bonus depreciation or Section 179 expensing.

> **EXAMPLE:** John buys a dilapidated apartment building for $250,000. He pays Janelle, a licensed contractor, $50,000 to refurbish the building. John paid Janelle the money to improve a long-term asset—a building. So, he may not currently deduct the $50,000. Instead, once the building is offered for rent, he may depreciate the cost over 27.5 years. He gets to deduct $1,818 per year, except for the first and last years.

Employees Versus Independent Contractors

As far as the IRS is concerned, the only two types of people you can hire to help in your rental activity are employees and independent contractors (ICs). It's very important to understand the difference between these two categories because the tax rules for each are very different. If you hire an employee, you become subject to a wide array of state and federal tax requirements. You might have to withhold taxes from your employees' earnings and pay other taxes for them out of your own pocket. You must also comply with complex and burdensome bookkeeping and reporting requirements. If you hire an IC, none of these requirements apply. On the other hand, if your taxable 2022 income is over $170,050 if single, or $340,100 if married filing jointly, any pass-through deduction you qualify for will be based in part on how much you pay your employees, but not ICs. So, classifying workers as employees can help maximize this deduction. (See Chapter 7.)

Initially, it's up to you to determine whether any person you hire to help in your rental activity is an employee or an IC. However, your decision about how to classify a worker is subject to review by various government agencies, including:

- the IRS
- your state's tax department
- your state's unemployment compensation insurance agency, and
- your state's workers' compensation insurance agency.

These agencies are mostly interested in whether you have classified workers as independent contractors when you should have classified them as employees. The reason is that you must pay money to each of these agencies for employees, but not for independent contractors. As more workers are classified as employees, the more money flows into the agencies' coffers. In the case of taxing agencies, employers must withhold tax from employees' paychecks and hand it over to the government; ICs pay their own taxes, which means the government must wait longer to get its money and faces the possibility that ICs won't declare their income or will otherwise cheat on their taxes. If an agency determines that you misclassified an employee as an IC, you might have to pay back taxes, fines, and penalties.

Tests to Determine Workers' Tax Status

Scrutinizing agencies use various tests to determine whether a worker is an IC or an employee. The determining factor is usually whether you have the right to control the worker. If you have the right to *direct and control* the way a worker performs—both the final results of the job and the details of when, where, and how the work is done—then the worker is your employee. On the other hand, if you have only the right to accept or reject the final results the worker achieves, then that person is an IC.

An employer might not always exercise its right of control. For example, if an employee is experienced and well trained, the employer might not feel the need to closely supervise that employee. But the employer still has the right to step in at any time, which distinguishes an employment relationship from an IC arrangement.

EXAMPLE: Aria hires Jon to serve as resident manager for her triplex. Jon works ten hours per week. Aria has full control over the work Jon does. She must approve any repair he makes and provide any tools or supplies he needs to perform his maintenance duties. Aria has the right to fire Jon at any time if she is unhappy with his performance.

If Jon proves to be an able and conscientious worker, Aria may choose not to supervise him very closely. But Aria has the right to do so at any time. Jon is Aria's employee.

In contrast, a worker is an independent contractor if the landlord does not have the right to control the person on the job. Because the worker is an independent businessperson not solely dependent on you (the hiring party) for a living, your control is limited to accepting or rejecting the final results the IC achieves.

EXAMPLE: Aria hires Moriah, a real estate manager, to keep track of her rental income and expenses and to help with her taxes. Aria is only one of Moriah's many clients. Aria doesn't tell Moriah how to do her accounting tasks; Moriah is a professional who already knows how to do her work. Moriah sets her own hours, provides her own equipment, and works from her own home office. Moriah is an independent contractor.

Because Moriah is clearly running her own business, it's virtually certain that Aria doesn't have the right to control the way Moriah performs her accounting services. Aria's control is limited to accepting or rejecting the final result. If Aria doesn't like the work Moriah has done, she can refuse to pay her.

Auditors have no clear way to figure out whether you have the right to control a worker you hire. After all, they can't look into your mind to see whether you are controlling a worker (or whether you believe that you have the right to do so). They rely instead on indirect or circumstantial evidence indicating control or lack of it—for example, whether you provide a worker with tools and equipment, where the work is performed, how the worker is paid, and whether you can fire the worker.

CAUTION

Part-time workers and temps can be employees. Don't assume that a person you hire to work part time or for a short period automatically qualifies as an IC. People who work for you only temporarily or part time are your employees if you have the right to control the way they work.

Common Classifications for Workers

Let's apply the IRS rules for worker status to the type of people landlords commonly hire.

People Who Offer Services to the Public

People who offer their services to the general public are almost always independent contractors. This includes most of the people landlords hire—for example:

- repair people
- construction contractors
- gardeners
- plumbers
- electricians
- carpet layers
- painters
- roofers, and
- people who provide professional services to the public, such as real estate brokers, real estate appraisers, architects, real estate management companies, lawyers, accountants, and bookkeepers.

Virtually all the factors considered by the IRS will ordinarily point to IC status whenever a person provides services such as these to the public at large.

People Who Work Solely for You

Any person who works just for you will likely be your employee. These will often be family members, but not always.

RESOURCE

Need more information about independent contractors? For a detailed discussion of the practical and legal issues business owners face when hiring ICs, see *Working With Independent Contractors*, by Stephen Fishman (Nolo).

Tax Rules When Hiring Independent Contractors

As far as taxes are concerned, hiring independent contractors is very simple. When you hire an independent contractor, you don't have to withhold or pay any state or federal payroll taxes on the IC's behalf. In contrast, when you hire an employee you must withhold federal and state taxes and pay one-half of the worker's Social Security and Medicare taxes out of your own pocket. (See "Tax Rules for Employees," below.) This is one of the great benefits of hiring ICs.

But if your rental activity is a business for tax purposes, you'll have to take care of some tax details when you hire an IC: If you pay an unincorporated IC $600 or more during the year by cash, check, or direct deposit for business-related services, you must:

- file IRS Form 1099-NEC (Form 1099-MISC was filed in 2020 and earlier for payments made in 2019 and before) telling the IRS how much you paid the worker, and
- obtain the IC's taxpayer identification number.

Complying with the 1099 filing requirement is more important now than it has ever been because the IRS has recently said that issuance of all required 1099s by landlords is an important factor that should be considered in determining whether a landlord's rental activity is a business for purposes of the pass-through deduction. (Preamble to Section 199A Regulations.) This can be especially important for landlords who wish to benefit from the deduction, but who don't qualify for the special landlord business safe harbor rule the IRS has established for it. (See Chapter 7 for a detailed discussion.)

No Form 1099-NEC for Payments Through PayPal or Credit Card

If you pay an independent contractor through an online payment service like PayPal, credit card, or any other type of electronic payment, you don't need to file a Form 1099-NEC reporting the payment to the IRS. Instead, PayPal, the credit card company, or the payment company you use is supposed to report the payments to the IRS by filing IRS Form 1099-K, *Payment Card and Third Party Network Transactions*. Copies of the form are sent by the processing company to the independent contractor, the IRS, and the contractor's state tax department. No copy is sent to you, the payor.

Rental Agents Must Report IC Payments

If a rental agent manages your rental property, the agent must comply with the reporting requirements explained in this section. The agent must also report to the IRS the gross (total) amount of rent collected each year, without subtracting fees, commissions, or other expenses. (IRS Reg. § 1.6041-1.)

For example, suppose Gale is a rental agent who manages rental property for Harper. Gale finds tenants, arranges leases, collects rent, deals with tenant complaints, and hires and makes payments to repair people. Gale subtracts her commission and any maintenance payments from the rental payments and remits the remainder to Harper. Gale must comply with the IC reporting requirements when she hires repair people and others to perform services for Harper's property. In addition, she must file a 1099-NEC form with the IRS each year reporting the total amount of rent she collected from the property, without deducting her commission and payments. Harper may deduct these expenses on her own tax return.

The IRS imposes these requirements because it is very concerned that to avoid paying taxes, many ICs don't report all the income they earn. To help prevent this, the IRS wants to find out how much you pay ICs you hire and make sure it has their correct taxpayer ID numbers.

This requirement applies only to landlords whose rental activities qualify as a business for tax purposes. Landlords who are merely investors need not comply. However, most landlords qualify as business owners and it is to your advantage to do so. (See Chapter 2 for a detailed discussion.)

The IRS can impose monetary penalties on landlords who fail to comply with the reporting requirements. The penalty ranges from $50 to $290, depending on how quickly you fix the error by filing the 1099-NEC.

Complying with this requirement might help you avoid future problems with the IRS. Here's why: the IRS has an Automated Underreporter program in which IRS computers match information that landlords report on Schedule E about expenses paid with the Form 1099-NECs the landlords file reporting payments to independent contractors. If you claim a deductible expense for a payment to an independent contractor, but have not filed the required Form 1099-NEC, the IRS may send you a notice asking you to explain the discrepancy or pay additional taxes. Your return could also be flagged for an audit.

Threshold for IC Income Reporting

You need to obtain an unincorporated IC's taxpayer ID number and file a 1099-NEC form with the IRS only if you pay the IC $600 or more during a year for rental-related services. It makes no difference whether the sum was one payment for a single job or the total of many small payments for multiple jobs.

> **EXAMPLE:** Andre hires Leslie to paint a rental house and pays her $1,000. Because Andre paid Leslie more than $600 for rental-related services, Andre must file Form 1099-NEC with the IRS reporting the payment, and obtain Leslie's taxpayer ID number.

In calculating whether the payments made to an IC total $600 or more during a year, you must include payments you make for parts or materials the IC used in performing the services. For example, if you hire an electrician to rewire a rental building and he charges you separately for the electrical wiring and other materials he installs, the cost must be included in the tally. However, not all payments you make to ICs are counted toward the $600 threshold.

Payments for Merchandise

Under current law, you don't need to include in the $600 threshold payments you make solely for merchandise.

> **EXAMPLE:** Brenda hires AJ, an IC electrician, to rewire her apartment building. She pays him $1,000 for new lighting fixtures. The payment doesn't have to be counted toward the $600 threshold because the fixtures are merchandise.

Payments for Personal Services

You only have to count payments you make to ICs for services they perform in the course of your rental activity. You don't count payments for services you make to ICs for personal or household services or repairs —for example, payments to babysitters or gardeners and housekeepers for your personal residence. Running your home is not a rental activity.

> **EXAMPLE:** Landlord Joe pays Mya a total of $1,000 during the year for gardening services for his residence. None of the payments count toward the $600 threshold because they don't relate to Joe's rental activity. Joe doesn't have to get Mya's taxpayer ID number or file a 1099-NEC form reporting the payments to the IRS.

Obtaining Taxpayer Identification Numbers

Some ICs work in the underground economy—that is, they're paid in cash and never pay any taxes or file tax returns. The IRS might not even know they exist. The IRS wants you to help it find these people by supplying the taxpayer ID numbers of all ICs who meet the requirements explained above.

If an IC won't give you their number or the IRS informs you that the number the IC gave you is incorrect, the IRS assumes the person isn't going to voluntarily pay taxes. So it requires you to withhold taxes from the compensation you pay the IC and remit them to the IRS. This is called "backup withholding." If you fail to backup withhold, the IRS will impose an assessment against you equal to 24% of what you paid the IC.

How to Avoid Backup Withholding

Backup withholding can be a bookkeeping burden for you. Fortunately, it's very easy to avoid it. Have the IC fill out and sign IRS Form W-9, *Request for Taxpayer Identification Number and Certification*, and retain it in your files. (You can download it from the IRS website at www.irs.gov.)

You don't have to file the W-9 with the IRS. This simple form merely requires the IC to list the IC's name and address and taxpayer ID number. Partnerships and sole proprietors with employees must have a federal employer identification number (EIN), which they obtain from the IRS. In the case of sole proprietors without employees, the taxpayer ID number is the IC's Social Security number.

If the IC doesn't already have an EIN, but promises to obtain one, you don't have to backup withhold for 60 days after the IC applies for one. Have the IC fill out and sign the W-9 form, stating "Applied For" in the space where the ID number is supposed to be listed. If you don't receive the IC's ID number within 60 days, start backup withholding.

Backup Withholding Procedure

If you are unable to obtain an IC's taxpayer ID number or the IRS informs you that the number the IC gave you is incorrect, you'll have to do backup withholding. You must begin doing so after you pay an IC $600 or more during the year. You need not backup withhold on payments totaling less than $600.

To backup withhold, deposit with your bank 24% of the IC's compensation every quarter. You must make these deposits separately from any payroll tax deposits you make for employees. Report the amounts withheld on IRS Form 945, *Annual Return of Withheld Federal Income Tax*. This form is an annual return you must file by January 31 of the following year. (See the instructions to Form 945 for details.) You can download it from the IRS website at www.irs.gov.

Filing IRS Form 1099-NEC

The IRS wants to know how much ICs earn each year so it can make sure they are reporting all their income. The IRS accomplishes this goal by requiring people and companies that hire ICs to report the amount of their payments to the IRS on IRS Form 1099-NEC. Form 1099-NEC must be filed, starting in 2021, for payments made in 2020 and later. Form 1099-MISC was filed before 2021 for payments made in 2019 and earlier. You must file a 1099-NEC form for each IC you paid $600 or more by cash, check, or direct deposit during the year. You don't have to file a Form 1099 if you pay an independent contractor electronically through a third-party payment organization— for example, through PayPal—or by credit or debit card. The IRS may impose a $290 fine per violation if you intentionally fail to file a Form 1099 when required.

To order the official IRS forms (which are scannable), go to Online Ordering for Information Returns and Employer Returns (www.irs.gov/ Businesses/Online-Ordering-for-Information-Returns-and-Employer-Returns) and the IRS will mail them to you. You can also use tax preparation, accounting, or property management software to prepare your 1099-NECs. Alternatively, there are inexpensive online services you can use to complete and file the forms (see "Filing 1099-NECs Electronically," below).

Filling out Form 1099-NEC is easy. Follow this step-by-step approach:

1. List your name and address in the first box titled "PAYER'S name."

2. Enter your taxpayer identification number in the box entitled "PAYER'S TIN."

3. The IC you have paid is called the "RECIPIENT" on this form, meaning the person who received the money. Provide the IC's taxpayer identification number, name, and address in the boxes indicated. For sole proprietors, you list the individual's name first, and then you may list a different business name, though this is not required. You may not enter only a business name for a sole proprietor.

4. Enter the amount of your payments to the IC in Box 1 entitled "Nonemployee compensation."

5. Finally, if you've done backup withholding for an IC who has not provided you with a taxpayer ID number, enter the amount of federal tax withheld in Box 4. Enter any state tax withheld in Box 5.

Form 1099-NEC contains five copies. These must be filed as follows:

- Copy A, the top copy, must be filed with the IRS no later than February 1 of the year after payment was made to the IC. If you don't use the remaining two spaces for other ICs, leave those spaces blank. Don't cut the page.

- Copy 1 must be filed with your state tax department if your state has a state income tax. The filing deadline is likely February 1, but check with your state tax department to make sure. Your state may also have a specific transmittal form or cover letter you must obtain.

- Copy B and Copy 2 must be given to the worker no later than February 1 of the year after payment was made.

- Copy C is for you to retain for your files.

File all the IRS copies of each 1099-NEC form together with Form 1096, a simple transmittal form. Add up all the payments reported on all the 1099-NEC forms and list the total in the box indicated on Form 1096. File the forms with the IRS Service Center listed on the reverse of Form 1096.

Filing 1099-NECs Electronically

You have the option of filing your 1099-NECs with the IRS electronically instead of by postal mail.

You can fill out Copies B, C, 1, and 2 of Form 1099-NEC online in a pdf format on the IRS website at www.IRS.gov/Form1099NEC. You can furnish copies of these completed forms to ICs and your state tax agency, and for your own files. However, you can't electronically file this copy of the form with the IRS. To file Form 1099-NEC electronically with the IRS, you must use software that meets IRS requirements. You have three options:

- You can use accounting software such as *QuickBooks* or *Xero*.
- You can use online 1099 filing services like efilemyforms.com, efile4biz.com, tax1099.com, and efile1099now.com.
- You can electronically file 1099-NEC forms directly with the IRS yourself by using its FIRE Production System at https://fire.irs.gov. To do so, you must get permission from the IRS by filing IRS Form 4419, *Application for Filing Information Returns Electronically (FIRE)*. This form need only be filed one time, and can be filed online. You must obtain a Transmitter Control Code (TCC) from the IRS and create a user ID, password, and 10-digit PIN for your account. For more details, visit the IRS Filing Information Returns Electronically (FIRE) website at www.irs.gov/tax-professionals/e-file-providers-partners/filing-information-returns-electronically-fire.

You can also send 1099-NECs to independent contractors electronically —that is, by email. But you may do this only if the contractor agrees. If the contractor doesn't agree, you must deliver a printed copy of the 1099-NEC by mail or in person.

Reporting Requirements Don't Apply to Corporations

Under current law, the filing and ID requirements discussed above don't apply to corporations. This has long been one of the advantages of hiring incorporated ICs—no need to file anything with the IRS.

> **EXAMPLE:** Landlord Bob pays $5,000 to Yvonne, a CPA, to perform accounting services. Yvonne has formed her own one-person corporation called Yvonne's Accounting Services, Inc. Bob pays the corporation, not Yvonne personally. Because Bob is paying a corporation, he doesn't need to report the payment on Form 1099-NEC or obtain Yvonne's personal taxpayer ID number.

Two exceptions apply to the rule that you don't have to file 1099-NEC forms for payments to corporations. You must report all payments of $600 or more you make to a doctor or lawyer who is incorporated. This is necessary only where the payments are for your landlord activity—for example, you hire an incorporated attorney to handle a tenant eviction. You don't need to report payments you make to incorporated doctors or lawyers for personal services.

New Hire Reporting Requirements for ICs

Several states require that businesses that hire independent contractors file a report with a state agency providing the contractors' contact information and how much they pay the workers. The purpose of these requirements is to aid in the enforcement of child support orders issued against independent contractors.

The following states impose reporting requirements for those hiring independent contractors: Arizona, California (if paid over $600 per year), Connecticut (if paid over $5,000 per year), Iowa, Maine (if paid $2,500 or more), Massachusetts, Nebraska, New Hampshire (if paid $2,500 per year), New Jersey, Ohio (if paid over $2,500 per year), Texas, Utah, Virginia, and West Virginia. Find the state agency to contact at the U.S. Department of Health & Human Services website at www.acf.hhs.gov/css/contact-information/state-new-hire-reporting-websites.

Paying Independent Contractors' Expenses

Independent contractors often incur expenses while performing services for their clients or customers—for example, for travel or materials. Although many ICs want their clients to separately reimburse them for such expenses, it's better for you not to do so. ICs who pay their own expenses are less likely to be viewed as your employees by the IRS or other government agencies. Instead of reimbursing expenses, pay ICs enough so they can cover their own expenses.

However, it's customary in some businesses and professions for the client to reimburse the IC for expenses. For example, a lawyer who handles an eviction or other legal matter for your rental business will usually seek reimbursement for expenses such as photocopying, court reporters, and travel. If this is the case, you may pay these reimbursements without concern about misclassification problems.

When you reimburse an IC for a business-related expense, you get the deduction for the expense, not the IC. You should not include the amount of the reimbursement on the 1099-NEC form you file with the IRS reporting how much you paid the IC, because the reimbursement is not considered income for the IC.

Tax Rules for Employees

Whenever you hire an employee other than your spouse or child, you become an unpaid tax collector for the government. You are required to withhold and pay both federal and state taxes for the worker. These taxes are called "payroll taxes" or "employment taxes." Federal payroll taxes consist the following.

Social Security and Medicare taxes (FICA). The employer and employee must each pay Social Security and Medicare (FICA) taxes. The employer must deduct the employee's share from each wage payment. The FICA tax rate for both employer and employee is 7.65% of taxable wages (6.2% for the Social Security tax and 1.45% for the Medicare tax). The Social Security tax (old age, survivors and disability insurance or "OASDI") is subject to an annual taxable wage base limit ($147,000 for 2022). There is no wage base limit for the Medicare tax (hospital insurance or "HI").

Payment of Deferred 2020 Employer FICA Contributions

Due to the COVID-19 pandemic, employers (including landlords with employees) had the option of deferring their 2020 FICA payments. All such payments due beginning on March 27, 2020 (the date the Coronavirus Aid, Relief, and Economic Security Act, also known as the "CARES Act," was signed into law) and ending on December 31, 2020 could be deferred. Half of the deferred payroll taxes were due on December 31, 2021, with the remainder due on December 31, 2022. The deferral applied only to the employer portion of FICA taxes. Employers were required to continue to withhold their employees' contributions and deposit the money with the IRS.

Federal income tax withholding (FITW). The employer must also withhold federal income tax from each wage payment made to an employee. The amount to be withheld depends on the employee's marital status and number of withholding allowances and exemptions claimed.

Federal unemployment tax (FUTA). An employer must also pay federal unemployment tax on the employee's wages up to an annual FUTA wage base ($7,000 in 2022). The FUTA tax rate is 6%, but employers obtain a 5.4% credit for timely payment of state unemployment taxes. So, the FUTA tax rate is generally 0.6%, or $42 per year per employee. This tax must be paid if an employer (1) pays at least $1,500 in total wages to employees in any three-month period, or (2) has at least one employee during any day of a week during 20 weeks in a calendar year (the 20 weeks need not be consecutive).

You must periodically pay FICA, FUTA, and FITW to the IRS, electronically. You are entitled to deduct as a business expense payroll taxes that you pay yourself. You get no deductions for taxes you withhold from employees' pay.

Every year, employers must file IRS Form W-2, *Wage and Tax Statement*, for each of their workers. The form shows the IRS how much the worker was paid and how much tax was withheld.

However, if you hire your spouse or child to work in your rental activity, you might not have to pay some or all of the payroll taxes you must pay when you hire nonrelatives.

> **RESOURCE**
> **Find out more about payroll taxes.** IRS Publication 15, Circular E, *Employer's Tax Guide*, provides detailed information on payroll tax requirements. You can download it from the IRS website at www.irs.gov.

State Payroll Taxes

Employers in every state are required to pay and withhold state payroll taxes. These taxes include:

- state unemployment compensation taxes in all states
- state income tax withholding in most states, and
- state disability taxes in a few states.

Unemployment Compensation

Employers in every state are required to contribute to a state unemployment insurance fund. Employees make no contributions, except in Alaska, New Jersey, Pennsylvania, and Rhode Island, where employers must withhold small employee contributions from employees' paychecks. The employer contributions are a deductible expense.

If your payroll is very small—less than $1,500 per calendar quarter—you probably won't have to pay unemployment compensation taxes. In most states, you must pay state unemployment taxes for employees if you're paying federal unemployment taxes. But some states have stricter requirements. Contact your state labor department for the exact rules and payroll amounts.

Income Taxes

All states except Alaska, Florida, Nevada, South Dakota, Tennessee, Texas, Washington, and Wyoming have income taxation. If your state has income taxes, you must withhold the applicable amount from your employees' paychecks and pay it to the state taxing authority. Each state has its own income tax withholding forms and procedures. Contact your state tax department for information. Of course, employers get no deductions for withholding their employees' state income taxes.

Disability Insurance

California, Hawaii, New Jersey, New York, and Rhode Island have state disability insurance programs that provide employees with coverage for injuries or illnesses that are not related to work. Employers in these states must withhold their employees' disability insurance contributions from their pay. Employers must also make their own contributions in Hawaii, New Jersey, and New York—these employer contributions are deductible.

Workers' Compensation Insurance

Employers in all states (subject to some important exceptions) must provide their employees with workers' compensation insurance to cover work-related injuries. Workers' compensation is not a payroll tax. Employers purchase a workers' compensation policy from a private insurer or the state workers' compensation fund. Your workers' compensation insurance premiums are deductible as an insurance expense (see Chapter 15).

Paid Family Leave

The following states have implemented paid family leave programs: California, Connecticut, Massachusetts (only for employers with 25 or more employees), New Jersey, New York, Oregon, Rhode Island, and Washington. In some of these states both employers and employees must make contributions. In others, employers must withhold contributions from their employees' pay, but need make no contributions themselves. Check with your state for details.

TIP
Bookkeeping expenses are deductible. Figuring out how much to withhold, doing the necessary record keeping, and filling out the required forms can be complicated. If you have a computer, software programs such as *QuickBooks* can help with all the calculations and print out your employees' checks and IRS forms. The cost of such software is deductible—you can deduct the full cost in one year using bonus depreciation or Section 179 or depreciate the cost over three years (see Chapter 5). You can also hire a bookkeeper or payroll tax service to do the work. Amounts you pay a bookkeeper or payroll tax service are deductible operating expenses. You can find these listed in the phone book or on the internet under "payroll tax services." You can also find a list of payroll service providers on the IRS website. Be aware, however, that even if you hire a payroll service, you remain personally liable if your payroll taxes are not paid on time. The IRS recommends that employers: (1) keep their company address on file with the IRS, rather than the address of the payroll service provider, so that the company will be contacted by the IRS if there are any problems; (2) require the payroll service provider to post a fiduciary bond in case it defaults on its obligation to pay any penalties and interest due to IRS deficiency notices; and (3) ask the service provider to enroll in and use the Electronic Federal Tax Payment System (EFTPS) so the employer can confirm payments made on its behalf.

Hiring Your Family

Whoever said "never hire your relatives" must never have read the tax code. The tax law promotes family togetherness by making it highly advantageous for landlords to hire family members.

Employing Your Children

Believe it or not, your children can be a great tax savings device. If you hire your children as employees to do legitimate work in your rental activity, you may deduct their salaries from your rental income as an operating expense. Your child will have to pay tax on their salary only to the extent it exceeds the standard deduction amount for the year—$12,950 in 2022. Moreover, if your child is under the age of 18, you won't have to withhold or pay any FICA (Social Security or Medicare) tax on the salary (subject to a couple of exceptions).

These rules allow you to shift part of your income from your own tax bracket to your child's bracket, which should be much lower than yours (unless you earn little or no income). This approach can result in substantial tax savings.

No Payroll Taxes

One of the advantages of hiring your child is that you don't have to pay FICA taxes for your child under the age of 18 who works in your trade or business, or your partnership, if it's owned solely by you and your spouse.

Moreover, you don't have to pay federal unemployment (FUTA) taxes for services performed by your child who is under 21 years old.

But these rules don't apply—and you must pay both FICA and FUTA—if you hire your child to work for:

- your partnership, unless all the partners are parents of the child, or
- your corporation (few small landlords are incorporated).

No Withholding

In addition, if your child has no unearned income (for example, interest or dividend income), you must withhold income taxes from your child's pay only if it exceeds the standard deduction for the year. The standard deduction was $12,950 in 2022 and is adjusted every year for inflation. Children who are paid less than this amount don't have to pay any income taxes on their earnings. However, you must withhold income taxes if your child has more than $400 in unearned income for the year and their total income exceeds $1,150 (in 2022).

Employing Your Spouse

You don't get the benefits of income shifting when you employ your spouse in your business, because your income is combined when you file a joint tax return. You'll also have to pay FICA taxes on your spouse's wages, so you get no savings there either.

The real advantage of hiring your spouse is in the realm of employee benefits. You can provide your spouse with employee benefits such as health and accident insurance. You can take a tax deduction for the cost of the benefit and your spouse doesn't have to declare the benefit as income, provided the IRS requirements are satisfied. This is a particularly valuable tool for health insurance—you can give your spouse health insurance coverage as an employee benefit.

Another benefit of hiring your spouse is that you can take rental-related trips together and deduct the cost as a travel expense, as long as your spouse's presence was necessary (for your rental activity, not for you personally).

Rules to Follow When Employing Your Family

The IRS is well aware of the tax benefits of hiring a child or spouse, so it's on the lookout for taxpayers who claim the benefit without meeting the requirements. If the IRS concludes that your spouse or children aren't really employees, you'll lose your tax deductions for their salary and benefits—and they'll have to pay tax on their benefits. To avoid this, you should follow these simple rules.

Rule 1: Your Child or Spouse Must Be a Real Employee

First of all, your child or spouse must be a bona fide employee. Their work must be ordinary and necessary for your rental activity, and their pay must be compensation for services actually performed. Their services don't have to be indispensable, but they must be common, accepted, helpful, and appropriate for your business. Any real work for your rental can qualify—for example, you could employ your child or spouse to perform yard work or routine maintenance for your rental properties; or they could clean your office, answer the phone and emails, maintain your website, and help with bookkeeping. You get no business deductions when you pay your child for personal services, such as babysitting or mowing your lawn at home.

The IRS won't believe that an extremely young child is a legitimate employee. How young is too young? The IRS has accepted that a seven-year-old child may be an employee (see "Hardworking Seven-Year-Old Was Parents' Employee," below), but probably won't believe that children younger than seven are performing any useful work for your rental activity.

Hardworking Seven-Year-Old Was Parents' Employee

Walt and Dorothy Eller owned three trailer parks and a small strip mall in Northern California. They hired their three children, ages seven, 11, and 12, to perform various services for their businesses including pool maintenance, landscaping, reading gas and electric meters, delivering leaflets and messages to tenants, answering phones, doing minor repairs, and sweeping and cleaning trailer pads and parking lots. The children worked after school, on weekends, and during their summer vacations.

The Ellers paid their children a total of $17,800 over a three-year period and deducted the amounts as business expenses. The IRS tried to disallow the deductions, claiming that the children's pay was excessive. The court allowed most of the deductions, noting that these hardworking children performed essential services for their parents' businesses. The court found that the seven-year-old was a bona fide employee, but ruled that he should earn somewhat less than his older brother and sister because 11- and 12-year-old children can generally handle greater responsibility and do more work than seven-year-old children. So, while the older siblings could be paid $5,700 for their services over the three years in question, the seven-year-old could reasonably be paid only $4,000. (*Eller v. Comm'r*, 77 T.C. 934 (1981).)

You should keep track of the work and hours your spouse or children perform by having them fill out time sheets or timecards. You can find these in stationery stores, you can create a timesheet yourself, or you can use a timesheet app. It should list the date, the services performed, and the time spent performing the services. Although not legally required, it's also a good idea to have your spouse or child sign a written employment agreement specifying their job duties and hours. These duties should only be related to your business.

Rule 2: Compensation Must Be Reasonable

When you hire your children, it is advantageous (taxwise) to pay them as much as possible. That way, you can shift more of your income to your children, who are probably in a much lower income tax bracket. Conversely, you want to pay your spouse as little as possible, because you get no benefits from income shifting; you and your spouse are in the same income tax bracket (assuming you file a joint return, as the vast majority of married people do). Moreover, your spouse will have to pay Social Security tax on your spouse's salary—an amount that isn't tax deductible. (As your spouse's employer, you'll have to pay employment taxes on your spouse's salary as well, but these taxes are deductible business expenses.)

On the other hand, if your 2022 taxable income exceeds $170,050 if single, or $340,100 if married filing jointly, the pass-through tax deduction is based in part on the amount you pay your employees; so, to maximize this deduction, you might want to pay your spouse more. (See Chapter 7.)

However, you can't just pay whatever amount will result in the lowest tax bill: Your spouse's and/or your child's total compensation must be reasonably related to the value of the work performed. Total compensation means the sum of the salary plus all the fringe benefits you provide, including health insurance and medical expense reimbursements, if any. You shouldn't have a problem as long as you don't pay more than you'd pay a stranger for the same work. In other words, don't try paying your child $100 per hour for yard work just to get a big tax deduction. Find out what workers who perform similar services in your area are being paid.

To prove how much you paid (and that you actually paid it), you should pay your child or spouse by check or electronic deposit, not cash. Do this once or twice a month, just as you would for any other employee. The funds should be deposited in a bank account in your child's or spouse's name. Your child's bank account may be a trust account.

Rule 3: Comply With Legal Requirements for Employers

You must comply with most of the same legal requirements when you hire a child or spouse as you do when you hire a stranger.

These rules are explained in detail in Publication 15, Circular E, *Employer's Tax Guide*, and Publication 929, *Tax Rules for Children and Dependents*. You can download them from the IRS website at www.irs.gov or get free copies by calling the IRS at 800-TAX-FORM.

Hiring a Resident Manager

Landlords who don't want to do all the work themselves often hire a resident manager (also called an "apartment manager") to handle the day-to-day details of running an apartment building, such as dealing with repairs, showing and renting vacant units, and collecting rent. As the name implies, a resident manager lives at the rental property. In some states and cities resident managers are required if an apartment building exceeds a certain size (16 or more units in California; nine or more units in New York City).

You should have a resident manager sign an employment agreement spelling out the job's duties and pay. Detailed guidance on how to hire a resident manager, including a sample employment agreement, can be found in *Every Landlord's Legal Guide*, by Marcia Stewart, Janet Portman, and Ann O'Connell (Nolo).

Management Companies Are Not Employees

Instead of, or in addition to, hiring a resident manager, some landlords hire property management companies to manage their rentals. Such companies are often used by owners of large apartment complexes or absentee landlords who live far away from their rental property. Typically, you sign a contract spelling out the management company's duties and fees. Such companies normally charge a fixed percentage—typically 5% to 10%—of the rent collected. Such fees are a deductible rental expense. Schedule E contains a line where they are deducted.

A management company is an independent contractor, not your employee. The people who work for the company are its employees or independent contractors—you are not responsible for their payroll taxes. The rules for independent contractors covered above apply to management companies.

Resident or apartment managers are employees of the landlords who hire them. This is so, whether they are paid a regular salary or are compensated wholly or partly with reduced rent. Not a single court decision or IRS ruling has ever held otherwise. (PLR 8128117.) All of the tax rules for hiring employees discussed in "Tax Rules for Employees," above, apply to resident managers, but there are a couple of special rules you need to know about.

No Payroll Taxes for Free Lodging

If you pay a resident manager a regular salary, you must pay and withhold federal payroll taxes, which consist of Social Security and Medicare taxes, unemployment taxes, and federal income taxes. However, you need not pay or withhold any federal payroll taxes on the value of free lodging you provide a resident manager for a rental property if:

- the lodging is at your rental property—that is, the manager lives in a unit at your rental building
- the lodging is furnished for your convenience, and
- you require the manager to live there as a condition of employment—in other words, the manager has no choice in the matter. (I.R.C. § 119.)

It is not difficult for any landlord who hires a resident manager to satisfy these requirements.

Under the rules, you furnish lodging for your convenience if you do it for a substantial business reason, other than providing the employee with additional pay. Obviously, landlords have a substantial business reason to have someone living at their rental property—they need a person there 24 hours a day to take care of tenants, maintenance, and security. Moreover, as mentioned above, resident managers are required by law in some states.

The condition of employment test is met if you require the employee to accept the lodging because the employee needs to live at your rental property to properly perform the job's duties. The very nature of resident managers' duties requires that they live at the rental property. It's a good idea to have a written employment agreement with a resident manager, including a clause requiring the manager to live at your rental property. This clause can simply say: "In order to properly accomplish the duties of Resident Manager, Employee is required to live at Employer's rental property at [address] as a condition of employment."

> **EXAMPLE:** Anne owns a triplex. She rents two of the units to regular tenants, but she gives John, the tenant of the third unit, an $800 per month reduction in rent in return for his working as her resident manager. John takes care of repairs, maintenance, and gardening for the building. Although John is Anne's employee, she doesn't have to withhold or pay any payroll taxes on the $800 in free monthly rent she pays John.

The value of the free lodging you provide to a resident manager need not be reported on the W-2 form you file with the IRS. This means that it does not count for purposes of calculating the pass-through tax deduction that went into effect in 2018. If your 2022 taxable income is over $340,100 if you're married, or $170,050 if you're single, the pass-through tax deduction is based in part on the amount you pay your employees—only W-2 income counts. For most landlords at these income levels the deduction would be equal to 25% of what they pay their W-2 employees plus 2.5% of the value of their real property. To maximize this deduction, you might want to pay your resident manager more W-2 wages and provide less free lodging. (See Chapter 7.)

EXAMPLE: Anne from the above example pays her resident manager John $800 per month, instead of reducing his rent by $800. She classifies him as her part-time employee and pays payroll tax on the salary she pays John. Anne, a single taxpayer, has $200,000 in taxable income. She'll be able to deduct up to 25% of what she pays John—$2,400—as part of her pass-through tax deduction. She'll also be able to deduct the full amount of the salary she pays as a rental expense deduction on Schedule E.

COVID-19 Tax Credits for Landlord Employers

Congress established two temporary tax credits for employers who suffered economically during the COVID-19 pandemic or provided their employees with COVID-19-related paid sick and family leave. These were the Employee Retention Credit (ERC) and the sick and family leave credit. Landlords with employees could qualify for either or both credits.

The ERC was available during March 13, 2020 through September 30, 2021 (December 31, 2021 for rental businesses that began after February 15, 2020). The 2020 ERC was equal to 50% of employee wages up to $10,000 for a maximum credit of $5,000 per year. The 2021 ERC was equal to 70% of employee wages up to $7,000 per employee per quarter (available through September 30, 2021) for a maximum credit of $21,000.

Your rental business qualified for the ERC if:

- it fully or partially suspended operations due to government limits on commerce during COVID-19, or
- quarterly revenue declined by 20% or more in 2021 compared with the same quarter in 2019, or 50% or more in 2020 when compared with the same quarter in 2019.

If your rental business qualified for the ERC but didn't claim it, you may still do so by amending your payroll tax returns using IRS Form 941-X.

You have until April 15, 2024, to file for the 2020 credit and April 15, 2025, for the 2021 ERC.

Payroll tax credits were also available to employers who provided COVID-related paid sick and family leave to their employees during April 2020 through September 2021. Again, if you failed to claim these credits during 2020 or 2021, you may do so by filing amended payroll tax returns.

Both of these credits were refundable, meaning you get the full amount even if it exceeded your tax liability for the year. So, the IRS pays the excess amount to you as a refund.

For detailed IRS guidance on the ERC, see www.irs.gov/coronavirus/employee-retention-credit.

For information on the sick and family leave credits, see the IRS FAQs at:

- www.irs.gov/newsroom/tax-credits-for-paid-leave-under-the-families-first-coronavirus-response-act-for-leave-prior-to-april-1-2021, and
- www.irs.gov/newsroom/tax-credits-for-paid-leave-under-the-american-rescue-plan-act-of-2021-for-leave-after-march-31-2021.

14

Casualty and Theft Losses

Bad things can happen to good rental property. If your rental property is damaged or destroyed by a sudden event like a fire or flood, or if you have a loss due to vandalism or theft, you might be able to obtain a tax deduction for all or part of your loss. These types of losses are called "casualty losses."

What Is a Casualty?

A "casualty" is damage, destruction, or loss of property due to an event that's sudden, unexpected, or unusual. Deductible casualty losses can result from many different causes, including, but not limited to:

- earthquakes
- fires
- floods
- government-ordered demolition or relocation of a building that is unsafe to use because of a disaster
- landslides
- oil spills
- sonic booms
- storms, including hurricanes and tornadoes
- terrorist attacks
- theft
- vandalism, including vandalism to rental property by tenants, and
- volcanic eruptions.

One thing all the events in the list above have in common is that they're sudden—they happen quickly. Suddenness is the hallmark of a casualty loss. So, loss of property due to slow, progressive deterioration isn't deductible as a casualty loss. For example, the steady weakening or deterioration of a rental building due to normal wind and weather conditions is not a deductible casualty loss.

Although damage to property due to routine wear and tear over time isn't a deductible casualty loss, routine wear and tear can result in a sudden event that causes a casualty loss.

> **EXAMPLE:** Patrick owns a rental home with an aged water heater that has deteriorated over time due to routine wear and tear. One day the water heater suddenly bursts, causing rust and water damage to rugs and drapes in Patrick's property. The damage to the water heater itself isn't a casualty loss because it was due to routine wear and tear. But the damage to the rugs and drapes is a deductible casualty loss because it was caused by a sudden, unexpected, and unusual event—a burst water heater.

External Force Required

Some external force must be involved in a casualty loss. So, you get no deduction if you simply lose property or it is damaged or destroyed due to your own negligence. But a deductible casualty loss can be caused by another person's carelessness or negligence. For example, you can deduct as a casualty loss sudden damage caused by a negligent contractor or worker.

> **EXAMPLE:** Richard and Ruth Marx noticed that the roof to their house was leaking and hired a building contractor to repair it. Not long afterward, the roof leaked again during a storm, but this time the leak was much worse: It caused the drywall ceiling of the home to fall in, resulting in substantial damage to the interior. The tax court permitted the Marxes to claim a casualty loss for the damage, finding that the massive leaks were sudden and unexpected, were caused by the contractor's negligence, and were independent of the preexisting minor leak. (*Marx v. Comm'r.*, T.C. Memo 1991-598.)

Theft or Vandalism

You may also obtain a casualty loss deduction if anything on or in your rental property is stolen or vandalized. The taking of property must be illegal under the laws of the state where it occurred and it must have been done with criminal intent. You should file a police report when a theft occurs or if your property is vandalized. You must deduct losses from a theft or vandalism in the tax year in which the loss is discovered.

> **EXAMPLE:** Lillia, the owner of a four-unit apartment building, is forced to evict one of her tenants for nonpayment of rent. After the tenant moves out, she discovers that he has completely trashed the apartment—among other things, stopping the toilet with diapers, breaking mirrors, staining carpets, and punching holes in the walls. Lillia can deduct the uninsured portion of the cost of the vandalism as a casualty loss.

A Presidentially Declared Disaster Isn't Required

The casualty doesn't have to be a presidentially declared disaster for a loss to rental business property to be deductible. This differs from casualty losses to personal property, which are deductible during 2018–2025 only if due to presidentially declared disasters. For example, you can deduct property losses from a localized accidental fire in an apartment building. But personal property losses because of a fire in your home are deductible only if the fire is declared a federal disaster, not likely for a small house fire.

Calculating a Casualty Loss Deduction

You usually won't be able to deduct the entire cost of property damaged or destroyed by a casualty. How much you may deduct depends on whether the property involved was stolen, completely destroyed, or partially destroyed, and whether the loss was covered by insurance. You must always reduce your casualty losses by the amount of any insurance proceeds you receive, or reasonably expect to receive in the future. If more than one item is stolen, damaged, or destroyed, you must figure your deduction separately for each.

One good thing about casualty losses is that they are not subject to the restrictions on deducting passive losses discussed in Chapter 16. You can simply ignore the complex passive loss rules when determining how much you may deduct.

Casualty Loss Limited to Adjusted Basis

The basic rule is that you can deduct the amount of a property's decline in value up to its adjusted basis. The adjusted basis is always the ceiling for the deduction.

Your adjusted basis is usually the property's original cost, plus the value of any improvements, minus all deductions you took for the property, including depreciation or Section 179 expensing. (See Chapter 5.) You determine the basis for a building, land improvements, and landscaping separately. The basis is reduced by the amount of claimed casualty losses and insurance recoveries. The cost of the land is not part of a building's basis.

Rental business personal property (appliances, furniture, computers, and other equipment, for example) often has a zero adjusted basis because 100% of the cost can be deducted the year of purchase with 100% bonus depreciation (through 2022) or Section 179 expensing. In this event, the casualty loss deduction is zero.

But, your repair costs may be currently deductible (see below).

> **EXAMPLE:** Sara purchased a refrigerator for $2,000 two years ago for her rental home. She deducted the entire cost that year with bonus depreciation. Her adjusted basis in the refrigerator is zero. A tenant completely destroyed the refrigerator before he was evicted. Sara's casualty loss deduction is zero.

However, bonus depreciation and Section 179 are not available for real property. Residential real property must be depreciated over 27.5 years. So, it rarely has a zero adjusted basis when a casualty occurs.

Insurance

In addition to the adjusted basis ceiling, you must reduce your casualty loss deduction by the amount of any insurance proceeds or other reimbursement you actually receive or reasonably expect to receive. Unlike the case with personal casualty losses, you don't have to file an insurance claim to qualify for a rental business casualty loss deduction. In some cases, you could be better off not filing a claim if it would result in substantial increases in your insurance premiums or cancellation of your policy.

Other reimbursement includes any of the following payments or services you receive or expect to receive:

- the cost of any repairs made by a tenant that you don't pay for
- payments to you by the tenant to cover the cost of repairs
- any part of a federal disaster loan that is forgiven
- court awards for damage or theft loss, minus any attorneys' fees or other expenses incurred to obtain the award, and
- the value of repairs, restoration, or cleanup services provided for free by a relief agency such as the Red Cross.

If the insurance or other reimbursement turns out to be less than you expected, you can claim a loss the year you determine you'll receive no further reimbursement. Don't amend your original return for the prior year. If the reimbursement is larger than expected, you must include the amount in income for the year received to the extent a tax benefit was obtained from the excess loss claimed in the earlier year.

If you're uncertain about the amount of insurance or other reimbursement you'll likely receive, the IRS advises waiting to deduct the amount about which you're uncertain until the year you're reasonably certain you'll receive no reimbursement.

Property a Total Loss

If the property is completely destroyed or stolen, your deduction is calculated as follows:

$$
\begin{array}{l}
 \text{Adjusted basis} \\
- \text{ Salvage value} \\
- \underline{\text{ Insurance proceeds}} \\
= \underline{\text{ Deductible loss}}
\end{array}
$$

"Salvage value" is the value of whatever remains after the property is destroyed. This value usually won't amount to much. For example, if a rental house burns down completely, some bricks, building materials, personal property, and other items might remain with some scrap value. Obviously, if a personal property item is stolen, no salvage value exists at all.

> EXAMPLE: Sean's rental house burns down and is completely destroyed. The house had an adjusted basis of $100,000. Sean only had $50,000 of fire insurance coverage. The house's salvage value is $2,000. Sean's deductible casualty loss is $48,000, calculated as follows:
>
> | | | |
> |---|---|---|
> | Adjusted basis | $ | 100,000 |
> | Salvage value of building | – | 2,000 |
> | Insurance recovery | – | 50,000 |
> | Deductible loss | $ | 48,000 |

Property a Partial Loss

If the property is only partly destroyed, your casualty loss deduction is the *lesser* of:

- the decrease in the property's fair market value (FMV), or
- its adjusted basis.

You must reduce both amounts by any insurance you receive or expect to receive. Unless you've owned the property for many years, the FMV measure is usually less and is the one you must use.

You can hire a qualified appraiser to determine the reduction in FMV of your partly damaged property. The appraiser should determine the property's FMV just before and just after the casualty event. The decline in FMV doesn't include any general decline of property values in the area due to the event, like a large fire.

However, it is often too expensive or impractical to hire an appraiser. You can use the cost of repairing the property to measure the decline in its FMV, but only if:

- the repairs are actually completed by the due date for your tax return
- the repairs are necessary to bring the property back to its condition before the casualty
- the amount spent for repairs is not excessive
- the repairs take care of the damage only, and
- the value of the property after the repairs is not, due to the repairs, greater than its value before the casualty. (IRS Reg. § 1.165-7(a)(2)(ii).)

Note that the cost of repairs is not the casualty loss; it's only used as evidence of the decline in the property's FMV. If you obtain an appraisal, you don't have to repair or replace the property to claim a casualty loss deduction.

> **EXAMPLE:** The chimney in Safiya's rental duplex collapses during an earthquake. She has no earthquake insurance coverage. She pays $5,000 to a building contractor to repair the chimney back to the condition it was in before the earthquake. She figures her casualty loss deduction as follows:
>
> | | | |
> |---|---|---:|
> | 1. | Adjusted basis of duplex before earthquake | $ 96,000 |
> | 2. | Fair market value before earthquake | 225,000 |
> | 3. | Fair market value after earthquake | − 220,000 |
> | 4. | Decrease in fair market value (based on cost of repair) | 5,000 |
> | | | |
> | 5. | Amount of loss (line 1 or line 4, whichever is less) | 5,000 |
> | 6. | Insurance reimbursement | − 0 |
> | 7. | Deductible loss | $ (5,000) |

Deducting Separate Components

You must calculate casualty loss to rental property separately for each item that is damaged or destroyed. (IRS Reg. § 1.165-7(a)(2)(i).) This may include a building, land improvements under the building, landscaping, and other land improvements apart from the building. However, you don't need to separately deduct personal property items inside a rental property, such as stoves and refrigerators, that were included in the original purchase price for the property.

> **EXAMPLE:** Tim's rental house is damaged by a tornado. The twister not only damaged the building, but tore up his landscaping—trees and shrubs—as well. Tim must separately calculate his casualty loss for the building and the landscaping. The adjusted basis of the building is $166,000. The trees and shrubs have an adjusted basis of $4,500. Tim hires an appraiser who determines that the fair market value of the building immediately before the tornado was $200,000, and was $152,000 immediately afterwards. The fair market value of the trees and shrubs immediately before the casualty was $4,000 and afterwards was $400. Tim received $40,000 in insurance to cover the loss to the building.
>
> Tim calculates his casualty loss for the building as follows:

1. Adjusted basis of house before tornado	$ 166,000
2. Fair market value before tornado	200,000
3. Fair market value after tornado	− 152,000
4. Decrease in fair market value	48,000
5. Amount of loss (line 1 or line 4, whichever is less)	48,000
6. Insurance reimbursement	− 40,000
7. Deductible loss	$ 8,000

Tim separately calculates his loss for the landscaping as follows:

1. Adjusted basis of landscaping before tornado	$ 4,500
2. Fair market value before tornado	4,000
3. Fair market value after tornado	− 400
4. Decrease in fair market value	3,600
5. Amount of loss (line 1 or line 4, whichever is less)	3,600
6. Insurance reimbursement	− 0
7. Deductible casualty loss	$ 3,600

Effect of Casualty Losses on Basis

Any casualty loss you claim on your taxes reduces the basis of the property. Insurance or other reimbursements you receive also reduce your basis. This will increase your gain when you sell the property (see Chapter 5).

> EXAMPLE: Paola owns an apartment building with a $500,000 adjusted basis. It suffers a $50,000 uninsured casualty loss from a storm. Paola deducts the $50,000 casualty loss and reduces the basis in the apartment building to $450,000. If Paola had insurance covering the loss, she would have gotten no casualty loss deductions and still would have had to reduce the basis of her building by $50,000.

Federally Declared Disaster Area Losses

As mentioned above, you can deduct a casualty loss to rental property whether or not the damage is due to a federally declared disaster. However, if you suffer a deductible casualty loss in an area that the President declares a federal disaster, you may elect to deduct the loss for your taxes for the previous year. This deduction will provide you with a quick tax refund because you'll get back part of the tax you paid for the prior year.

If you have already filed your return for the prior year, you can claim a disaster loss against that year's income by filing an amended return (see Chapter 16). You must do so within six months after the regular due date for filing your original return for the disaster year. For example, you have until October 15, 2023, to amend your 2021 return to claim a federally declared disaster loss that occurred during 2022.

> EXAMPLE: Tom's apartment building is damaged by a flood in August of 2022. Tom suffers a deductible casualty loss of $10,000. The area in which his building is located is declared a federal disaster area. Tom may deduct his $10,000 casualty loss on his 2021 taxes, even though he has already paid them, by filing an amended return for the year. As a result, he gets a $2,500 tax refund for that year.

You can determine if an area has been declared a disaster area by checking the Federal Emergency Management Administration (FEMA) website at www.fema.gov/disasters.

Casualty Gains

If the total insurance compensation and/or other reimbursement you receive is more than the adjusted basis in the destroyed or damaged property, you'll have a casualty gain, not a loss. This situation is common.

> **EXAMPLE:** Sara purchased an apartment building 20 years ago. Its adjusted basis is $250,000. The building is completely destroyed in a fire. Sara receives an insurance recovery of $500,000. She has a $250,000 casualty gain.

Such a gain is taxable income. It is taxed at ordinary income rates to the extent of the depreciation deductions taken on the property. The remaining gain is taxed at capital gains rates.

However, under the involuntary conversion rules, you can defer the gain by purchasing replacement property of equal or greater value. Your basis in the replacement property is its cost reduced by the amount of unrecognized casualty gain.

> **EXAMPLE:** Sara purchases a new apartment building for $750,000 six months after the fire. She doesn't have to pay any tax on her casualty gain. Her basis in the new building is $500,000 ($750,000 cost − $250,000 gain).

If the cost of the replacement property is less than the reimbursement received, you must recognize the gain to the extent the reimbursement exceeds the cost of the replacement property.

If the casualty loss is not due to a federally declared disaster, the replacement property must be "similar or related in service or use to the property destroyed." Alternatively, you may purchase a controlling interest (at least 80%) in a corporation owning such property. The property must be replaced within two years after the close of the first taxable year in which any part of the gain is realized.

If the property was damaged or destroyed in a federally declared disaster, you have four years to purchase the replacement property. Additionally, any business-use property will qualify.

Repair and Replacement Costs for Casualty Losses

The cost of repairing or replacing business property damaged or destroyed in a casualty event is not part of a casualty loss; neither are cleanup costs. The cost of restoring property destroyed or damaged due to a casualty event ordinarily must be capitalized (depreciated) and added to the property's basis. (IRS Reg. § 1.263(a)-3(k)(1)(iii).)

> **EXAMPLE:** Landlord Jason owns an apartment building with an adjusted basis of $500,000 that suffers extensive uninsured damage due to a flood. Jason deducts a casualty loss of $140,000. The amount of the loss is based on the cost to restore the damage caused by the flood: $100,000 to completely replace the roof and an additional $40,000 for debris cleanup, patching drywall, painting, and replacing three broken windowpanes. The adjusted basis of the property is reduced by $140,000. Jason must depreciate over 27.5 years the entire $140,000 because it is less than the property's adjusted basis. This is so even though $40,000 is for repairs that would otherwise be currently deductible.

However, under the IRS repair regulations that took effect in 2014, a building owner is only required to depreciate restoration costs to the extent of the property's adjusted basis immediately before the casualty event that damaged or destroyed the building. Any costs over this amount may be currently deducted if they constitute repairs under the IRS repair regulations discussed in Chapter 4. (IRS Reg. § 1.263(a)-3(k)(4)(ii).)

Most of the time, such deductible expenses will be cleanup costs following the casualty event.

> **EXAMPLE:** Assume that the adjusted basis of Jason's building in the previous example was $100,000. Jason must depreciate $100,000 to replace the roof (as a restoration or a major building component). The remaining $40,000 paid for debris cleanup, patching drywall, painting, and replacing the three broken windowpanes exceeds the adjusted basis in the building. These expenses qualify as a repair under the repair regulations and may be currently deducted in one year by Jason.

Tax Reporting and Record Keeping for Casualty Losses

Casualty losses are a hot-ticket item for the IRS. Claiming them will increase your chances of being audited. Make sure you can document your losses. You'll need to have:

- documents showing that you owned each asset you claimed was damaged, stolen, or destroyed—for example, a deed or receipt
- contracts or purchase receipts showing the original cost of the item, plus any improvements you made to it
- copies of your old tax returns showing all your regular and bonus depreciation and Section 179 deductions for the property, and
- evidence of the property's fair market value, such as insurance records, an appraisal, or receipts for the cost of repairing it.

You report casualty losses to rental property on Part B of IRS Form 4684, *Casualties and Thefts*, and then transfer the deductible casualty loss to Form 4797, *Sales of Business Property*, and the first page of your Form 1040. The amount of your deductible casualty loss is subtracted from your adjusted gross income for the year. These reporting requirements differ from those for other deductions covered in this book, which are reported on IRS Schedule E, Form 1040.

Additional Deductions

This chapter looks at some common deductible operating expenses that you're likely to incur in the course of your rental activity, such as real estate taxes, insurance, and legal fees. You can deduct these costs as operating expenses as long as they are ordinary, necessary, and reasonable in amount—and meet the additional requirements discussed below.

Dues and Subscriptions

Dues you pay to professional, business, and civic organizations are deductible expenses, as long as the organization's main purpose is not to provide entertainment facilities to members. You can deduct dues paid to:

- apartment owner associations
- real estate boards
- local chambers of commerce and business leagues, and
- civic or public service organizations, such as a Rotary or Lions Club.

You get no deduction for dues you pay to belong to other types of social, business, or recreational clubs—for example, country clubs or athletic clubs. For this reason, it's best not to use the word "dues" on your tax return because the IRS might question the expense. Use other words to describe the deduction—for example, if you're deducting membership dues for an apartment owners' organization, list the expense as "apartment owners' association membership fees."

You may also deduct the cost of publications you read for your rental activity—magazines or journals on real estate, taxation, law, or finance. Subscription websites dealing with real estate are also deductible. (Don't forget to deduct the cost of this book!)

Education Expenses

You may deduct your expenses for landlord-related education—for example, a seminar or course on buying or operating rental property. You may also deduct the cost of attending a real-estate-related convention or meeting as an education expense. To qualify for an education deduction, you must be able to show the education:

- maintains or improves skills required to be a successful landlord, or
- is required by law or regulation to maintain your professional status.

EXAMPLE 1: Jeremy owns three rental houses. He attends a one-day seminar on how to make more money from rental property offered by The Learning Annex, a company that produces educational seminars on various subjects. The cost is deductible as an education expense.

EXAMPLE 2: Hamzah is a landlord and licensed real estate broker. Every year, he is required by his state real estate licensing board to take 30 hours of continuing education to maintain his status as a licensed broker. He may deduct the cost as an education expense.

Deductible education expenses include tuition, fees, books, and other learning materials. They also include transportation and travel (see below). You may also deduct expenses you pay to educate or train your employees.

Before You Are in Business

You can't currently deduct education expenses you incur before your rental activity begins. For example, if you have never owned rental property and attend a course on how to be a successful landlord, you may not deduct the expense as an education expense. However, if you do end up buying rental property, you may deduct the expense as a start-up expense. You can deduct up to $5,000 in start-up expenses the first year your rental activity is in operation. You must deduct any amount over the applicable limit in equal installments over the first 180 months you're in business. (See Chapter 9.)

Likewise, if you're not already involved in the real estate field, you may not deduct the cost of attending courses to become a licensed real estate broker. (IRS Reg. § 1.162-5(a).)

Lifetime Learning Credit

Instead of taking a tax deduction for your rental-business–related education expenses, you may qualify for the lifetime learning credit. A tax credit is a dollar-for-dollar reduction in your tax liability, so it's even better than a tax deduction.

The lifetime learning credit can be used to help pay for any undergraduate- or graduate-level education, including nondegree education to acquire or improve job skills (for example, a continuing education course). If you qualify, your credit equals 20% of the first $10,000 of postsecondary tuition and fees you pay during the year, for a maximum credit of $2,000 per tax return. But the credit is phased out and then eliminated at certain income levels: It begins to go down if your modified adjusted gross income (MAGI) is above $80,000 ($160,000 for a joint return) and you cannot claim the credit at all if your MAGI is above $90,000 ($180,000 for a joint return). The limits are adjusted for inflation each year. These are the limits starting in 2021.

You can take this credit not only for yourself, but for a dependent child (or children) for whom you claim a tax exemption, or your spouse as well (if you file jointly). And it can be taken any number of times. However, you can't take the credit if you've already deducted the education cost as a business expense.

> EXAMPLE: Bill, a self-employed real estate broker with a $75,000 AGI, spends $2,000 on continuing real estate education courses. He may take a $400 lifetime learning credit (20% × $2,000 = $400).

Traveling for Education

Transportation expenses you pay to travel to and from a deductible educational activity are deductible. This includes transportation between your home and the educational activity. Going to or from home to an educational activity does not constitute nondeductible commuting.

If you drive, you may deduct your actual expenses or use the standard mileage rate. (See Chapter 11 for more on deducting car expenses.)

No law that says you must take your education courses as close to home as possible. You can travel outside your geographic area for education, even if the same or a similar educational activity is available near your home or place of business. Companies and groups that sponsor educational events are well aware of this rule and take advantage of it by offering courses and seminars at resorts and other enjoyable vacation spots such as Hawaii and California. Deductible travel expenses can include airfare or other transportation, lodging, and meals. (See Chapter 12 for more on deducting travel expenses.)

Gifts

You may deduct the cost of gifts you make in the course of your rental business—for example, to thank or maintain goodwill with a vendor, tenant, or employee, including holiday gifts to tenants. But the gift expense deduction is limited to $25 per person per year. Any amount over the $25 limit isn't deductible. If this amount seems low, that's because it was established in 1954. In addition, special record-keeping requirements apply to gifts. (See Chapter 17.)

> **EXAMPLE:** Landlord Lisa gives a $60 Christmas gift to the gardener who takes care of her rental properties. She may deduct $25 of the cost.

The $25 limit applies only to gifts to individuals. It doesn't apply if you give a gift to an entire company. Such companywide gifts are deductible in any amount, as long as they are reasonable. However, the $25 limit does apply if the gift is intended for a particular person or group of people within the company.

If you give a gift to a family member of a tenant, the gift is considered to be an indirect gift to the tenant and is subject to the $25 limit. So, you're limited to a single $25 gift deduction for each tenant and his or her entire family.

Insurance for Your Rental Activity

You can deduct the premiums you pay for almost any insurance related to your rental activity, including fire, theft, and flood insurance for rental property, as well as landlord liability insurance. If you have employees, you may deduct the cost of their health and workers' compensation insurance. Unemployment insurance contributions you make for your employees are deducted either as insurance costs or as taxes, depending on how they are characterized by your state's laws.

The one type of insurance that may not be deducted as an operating expense is title insurance you obtain when you purchase rental property. Its cost is added to the basis of the property and depreciated over 27.5 years. The same rule applies to insurance premiums you pay on property under construction. (See Chapter 5.)

Homeowners' Insurance for Your Home Office

If you have a home office and qualify for the home office deduction, you may deduct the home office percentage of your homeowners' or renters' insurance premiums. For example, if your home office takes up 20% of your home, you may deduct 20% of the premiums. You can deduct 100% of any coverage that you add to your homeowners' policy specifically for your home office and/or rental property. For example, if you add an endorsement to your policy to cover business property, you can deduct 100% of the cost.

Car Insurance

If you use the actual expense method to deduct your car expenses, you can deduct the cost of insurance that covers liability, damages, and other losses for vehicles used in your rental activity as an operating expense. If you use a vehicle only for your rental activity, you can deduct 100% of your insurance costs. If you operate a vehicle both for your rental activity and for personal use, you can deduct only the part of the insurance premiums that applies to the rental use of your vehicle.

For example, if you use a car 10% for your rental activity and 90% for personal reasons, you can deduct 10% of your insurance costs.

If you use the standard mileage rate to deduct your car expenses, you can't take a separate deduction for insurance. The standard rate is intended to cover all your automobile costs, including insurance. (See Chapter 11 for more on vehicle deductions.)

Prepaying Your Insurance Premiums

Many landlords make a single payment for an entire year of insurance coverage. This type of prepayment is fully deductible in the year it was made, provided it complies with the 12-month rule. Under this rule, cash basis taxpayers (which includes most small landlords) may deduct a prepaid expense such as insurance in the current year, if the term of the insurance coverage extends no longer than the earlier of 12 months, or the end of the tax year after the tax year in which the payment was made.

There is one small catch: If you previously followed the old rule under which expenses prepaid beyond the calendar year were not currently deductible, you must get IRS approval to use the 12-month rule. Approval is granted automatically by the IRS upon filing of IRS Form 3115, *Application for Change in Accounting Method.* You should attach one copy of the form to the return for the year of the change and send another copy to the IRS national office (not the service center where you file your return). The address is on the instructions for the form.

It is a good idea to get a tax pro to help you with this form because it might require some adjustment of the deductions you've taken for prepaid expenses in previous years under the old rule.

Legal and Professional Services

You can deduct fees that you pay to attorneys, accountants, property management companies, real estate investment advisers, and other professionals as operating expenses if the fees are for work related to your rental activity.

> **EXAMPLE:** Landlord Ian hires attorney Jake to evict a deadbeat tenant. The legal fees Ian pays Jake are a deductible operating expense.

Legal and professional fees that you pay for personal purposes generally are not deductible. For example, you can't deduct the legal fees you incur if you get divorced or you sue someone for a traffic accident injury. Nor are the fees that you pay to write your will deductible, even if the will covers rental property that you own.

Buying Long-Term Property

If you pay legal or other fees in the course of buying real estate or other long-term property, you must add the amount of the fee to the tax basis (cost) of the property. You deduct this cost over several years, through depreciation. This rule also applies to attorneys' fees incurred in legal disputes over who holds title to real estate, or in boundary disputes or condemnation proceedings.

Management Fees

The fees you pay a real estate management company to manage your property are deductible operating expenses. But be careful if you hire your child, spouse, or other relatives to serve as your manager. If you pay a relative more than the going market rate and you are audited, the IRS can deny your deduction for the excess amount. (IRS Reg. § 1.162-1(a).)

Starting a Business

Legal and accounting fees that you pay to start a rental business are deductible only as business start-up expenses. You may deduct them over the first 60 months you are in business. The same holds true for incorporation fees or fees that you pay to form a partnership or an LLC. You may not deduct such fees if your rental activity is an investment for tax purposes, not a business. (See Chapter 9 for more on deducting start-up costs.)

Accounting Fees

You may deduct any accounting fees that you pay for your rental activity as a deductible operating expense—for example, fees you pay an accountant to set up or keep your books, prepare your tax return, or give you tax advice for your rental activity.

You may also deduct the cost of having an accountant or other tax professional complete the rental portion of your tax return—Schedule E and other rental activity tax forms—but you can't deduct the time the preparer spends on the personal part of your return. Make sure that you get an itemized bill showing the portion of the tax preparation fee allocated to preparing your Schedule E.

Meals and Entertainment

Meal and entertainment expenses are usually not a big deduction item for a person running a small rental business, which is good because the Tax Cuts and Jobs Act imposed new restrictions on these deductions starting in 2018.

Entertainment

The Tax Cuts and Jobs Act eliminated almost all deductions for business-related entertainment. (I.R.C. § 274(a).) So, you may not deduct country club or skiing outings, theater or sporting event tickets, entertainment at nightclubs, hunting or fishing or similar trips, or vacation trips even if such expenses result in a specific business benefit. Nondeductible entertainment expenses also include membership fees and dues for any club organized for business, pleasure, recreation, or other social purposes, and any entertainment facility fees.

Meals

The IRS has adopted regulations providing that most business-related food and beverage expenses are deductible. (IRS Reg. 1.274-12.) Under the IRS regulations, food and beverage costs are deductible as a business expense if:

- the expense is not lavish or extravagant under the circumstances
- the taxpayer, or an employee of the taxpayer, is present when the items are consumed, and
- the food or beverages are provided to a business associate.

You or an employee needs to be present at the meal to take this deduction. Moreover, the food or beverages must be furnished to a "business associate," who is any person you could reasonably expect to engage or deal with in the active conduct of your rental business. This category includes customers, consultants, clients, or similar business contacts. Presumably, this category would also include tenants or prospective tenants. The IRS doesn't require that you actually close a transaction or get some other specific business benefit to take this deduction.

Ordinarily, you may only deduct 50% of the total cost of a business meal, including food, beverages, tax, and tip. For example, if a meal costs $100, you may deduct $50. However, Congress enacted a special rule for 2021 and 2022 to help restaurants recover from the COVID-19 pandemic. During these years, you may deduct 100% of the cost of business meals and beverages purchased from restaurants. (I.R.C. § 274(n)(2)(D).)

For these purposes, a "restaurant" is a business that prepares and sells food or beverages to retail customers for immediate consumption, which includes everything from high-end French restaurants to McDonald's and Starbucks.

You don't have to eat the food at the restaurant to get the 100% deduction. You can order restaurant takeout and deduct the full cost. Likewise, you can deduct 100% of the cost of business meals ordered from restaurants through delivery services like Grubhub or Uber Eats.

"Restaurants" do not include businesses that predominantly sell prepackaged food or beverages for later consumption, such as grocery stores, liquor stores, drugstores, specialty food stores, and vending machines. Food or beverages purchased from these places are still subject to the 50% limitation.

Because of these rules, you should separately track your total costs for meals and beverages purchased from restaurants and those for meals from other places like grocery stores.

What about meals you pay for during an entertainment activity, like a sporting event? These meals are deductible if they are purchased separately from the entertainment or listed separately on the receipt.

Taxes

Most taxes that you pay in the course of your rental activity are currently deductible operating expenses.

Real Property Taxes

You can fully deduct your current year state and local property taxes on rental real property as an operating expense. However, if you prepay the next year's property taxes, you may not deduct the prepaid amount until the following year.

When you buy your rental property, the property taxes due for the year must be divided between the buyer and seller according to how many days of the tax year each held ownership of the property. You'll usually find information on this in the settlement statement you receive at the property closing.

Local Benefit Taxes and Special Assessments

Water bills, sewer charges, and other service charges assessed against your rental property are not real estate taxes, but they are deductible as operating expenses. (If a tenant pays these expenses, as sometimes happens with single-family house rentals, the landlord gets no deduction unless the landlord reimburses the tenant. The tenant gets no deduction because these are personal expenses for the tenant.)

But real estate taxes imposed to fund specific local benefits for property, such as streets, sidewalks, sewer lines, and water mains, are not currently deductible as operating expenses where they are imposed only on the property owners who will benefit from them. Because these benefits increase the value of your property, you must add what you pay for them to the tax basis of your property and depreciate them. (I.R.C. § 164(c)(1).) Most of these improvements can be depreciated over 15 years as land improvements (see Chapter 5).

However, this rule has an exception: Any part of a special assessment you pay that is for maintenance, repairs, or an interest charge for a local benefit for your property is deductible as an operating expense. You may claim this deduction only if the taxing authority sends you an itemized tax bill separately listing the amounts you must pay for construction, interest, and maintenance. (IRS Reg. § 1.164-4(b)(1).)

> EXAMPLE: A city assessed a front-foot benefit charge against property benefited by the construction of a water system. The city's tax bill itemized the charge, showing how much was assessed for construction of the water system, interest, and maintenance costs. Taxpayers were allowed to currently deduct the amounts for interest and maintenance. (Rev. Rul. 79-201.)

Real Estate Transfer Taxes

When you purchase rental property, you must ordinarily pay state and local real estate transfer taxes. You can't deduct these taxes in the year in which you paid them. Instead, add them to the basis of your property and depreciate them over time, as explained in Chapter 5.

State Income Taxes

If you live in one of the 41 states with state income taxes, you'll have to pay that tax on your net rental income when you file your state tax return. The state income taxes you personally pay on your rental income are deductible on your federal income tax return as an itemized personal deduction.

However, the personal federal income tax deduction for state and local income taxes and property taxes (SALT) is capped at $10,000 per year through 2025.

Deducting State Income Taxes with a Pass-Through Entity

Due to the $10,000 cap on deducting state and local taxes, many landlords with profitable rentals can't deduct their income taxes on their federal income tax return. For example, if you live in a high-tax state, like California or New York, and owe $10,000 or more in property taxes, that tax alone will use up your $10,000 deduction. You'll get no federal deduction at all for the state income taxes you pay.

But some landlords can get around the $10,000 SALT limit. A majority of states have adopted an optional pass-through entity (PTE) tax that effectively enables many landlords to deduct state income tax on their rental income without limit. In these states, a PTE's owners can elect to have the PTE pay the state income tax due on the PTE's rental income that would otherwise be paid on their personal tax returns. The PTE then claims a federal business expense deduction for the state income tax payments. The $10,000 SALT cap doesn't apply to such payments by a PTE. The PTE's owners then get a state income tax credit for the state income tax the PTE paid or pay state income tax on the reduced amount of PTE income. The IRS has approved this arrangement. (IRS Notice 2022-75.)

> **EXAMPLE:** ABC, LLC is a two-member California LLC that owns an apartment building earning $400,000 in net rental income. Both members make the PTE tax election, and the LLC pays a 9.3% PTE tax to California. This $37,200 payment is a deductible business expense by the LLC, reducing its net income to $362,800. Each LLC member reports $181,400 of net income ($362,800 × 50%) on their federal K-1, resulting in a $43,536 federal income tax bill. Without the PTE tax deduction, they would have had to pay $48,000. When the members file their individual California income tax returns, they each report $200,000 of net income from ABC, LLC and take a tax credit of $18,600 against their individual California income tax. So, they pay no individual California income tax on their LLC income. Meanwhile, they each save $4,464 in federal income tax.

> ### Deducting State Income Taxes with
> ### a Pass-Through Entity (continued)
>
> State PTE taxes are only for landlords who own rental properties
> through PTEs: partnerships, limited partnerships, multimember LLCs,
> and S corporations. Landlords who are sole proprietors or owners of
> single-member LLCs can't pay them.
>
> PTE taxes have been enacted in the following states: Alabama, Arizona,
> Arkansas, California, Colorado, Connecticut, Georgia, Idaho, Illinois, Kansas,
> Louisiana, Maryland, Massachusetts, Michigan, Minnesota, Missouri,
> Mississippi, New Jersey, New Mexico, New York, North Carolina, Ohio,
> Oklahoma, Oregon, Rhode Island, South Carolina, Utah, Virginia, and
> Wisconsin. If you own rental property through a multiowner PTE, such as
> a partnership or LLC, in one of these states, check your state tax agency's
> website for information on its PTE tax. The tax rates and procedures for
> making the PTE tax election and paying the tax vary from state to state.
> Your PTE will usually have to pay estimated tax to the state, which is due
> before the PTE's tax return is filed.

Employment Taxes

If you have employees, you must pay half of their Social Security and
Medicare taxes from your own funds and withhold the other half from
their pay. These taxes consist of a 12.4% Social Security tax, up to an
annual salary cap ($147,000 in 2022); and a 2.9% Medicare tax up to
an annual ceiling—$200,000 for single taxpayers and $250,000 for
married couples filing jointly. Net self-employment or wage income
above the ceiling is taxed at a 3.8% rate. You may deduct half of this
amount as a business expense. You should treat the taxes you withhold
from your employees' pay as wages paid to your employees on your tax
return. However, you don't have to pay employment taxes when you hire
your children. (See Chapter 13.)

Tax Break for Accessibility Changes

A special tax law provision allows businesses (including landlords) to currently deduct up to $15,000 of the cost of making their buildings or other facilities—such as roads, walks, and parking lots—accessible to the elderly or disabled. (I.R.C. § 190.) These changes would ordinarily constitute improvements for tax purposes that would have to be depreciated over many years. This tax break is intended to encourage landlords and other business owners to make their facilities more accessible to the disabled and elderly. You may take this deduction whether or not the improvements you make are required by law.

The most you can deduct as a cost of removing barriers to the disabled and the elderly for any tax year is $15,000. But you can add any costs over this limit to the basis of the property and depreciate them.

To qualify for the deduction, your renovations must comply with applicable accessibility standards. Detailed standards are set forth in the ADA Accessibility Guidelines, which can be found at www.access-board.gov. IRS Publication 535, *Business Expenses*, also contains a summary of these standards.

You may claim the deduction on your income tax return for the tax year you paid for the work, or the year you incurred the expenses. Identify the deduction as a separate item. The choice applies to all of the qualifying costs you have during the year, up to the $15,000 limit. You must maintain adequate records to support your deduction—keep your receipts.

> EXAMPLE: Jason owns an 80-year-old apartment building that isn't wheelchair accessible. He installs four wheelchair ramps at a cost of $5,000. Ordinarily, this installation would be an improvement that Jason would have to depreciate. But due to the special rule, he may deduct the entire $5,000 in one year.

Unpaid Rent

If tenants fail to pay the rent owed you, can you deduct the loss? The short answer for the vast majority of small landlords is no. (Some bad debts are deductible, but unpaid rent is almost never one of them.) Here's why.

IRS regulations provide that a worthless debt arising from unpaid rent is deductible only if you report the amount of rent you were supposed to be paid as income for that year (or a prior year). (IRS Reg. § 1.166-1(e).) Landlords who can report this kind of not-yet-collected rent are operating on an accrual accounting basis (if you are an accrual basis taxpayer, you report rent as income as it becomes due, not when it's actually paid). The great majority of small landlords operate on a cash basis, which means they report rent as income only when it is actually paid to them by their tenants. Because cash basis landlords don't report rent that has never been paid on their tax returns, it's not deductible. (See Chapter 17 for a detailed discussion of accounting methods.)

> **EXAMPLE:** John and Margaret Kopunek rented a house in Sarasota, Florida, to a new tenant who stopped paying rent after a few months and moved out. After they kept the tenant's security deposit, the Kopuneks were left with $750 in unpaid rent. Because they were cash basis taxpayers, they did not report the $750 of rent that they never received as income on their tax return for the year. When they deducted the $750 from their taxes for the year as a bad debt, they were audited by the IRS and the deduction was denied. The tax court held that the IRS had acted properly. Having never reported the unpaid rent as income, the hapless Kopuneks could not deduct it as a bad debt. (*Kopunek v. Comm'r.*, T.C. Memo 1987-417.)

So, in order to deduct unpaid rent, you must report unpaid rent as income on your tax return for the year the rent was due—in other words, you'd have to adopt an accrual method of accounting. However, the deduction merely offsets the income you've already reported. Thus, there is no point in switching to the accrual method of accounting just to be able to write off unpaid rent; you won't save an extra penny in taxes.

Nor can you deduct unpaid rent as a casualty loss (see Chapter 14). The Kopuneks, from the example above, tried this and failed. (*Kopunek v. Comm'r.*, T.C. Memo 1987-417.)

If you have a tenant who can't pay the rent, you may choose to evict that tenant and find a new one. It can easily cost $10,000 or more to evict a tenant; even the cheapest evictions usually cost at least $3,500. Fortunately, the legal fees and other expenses you incur to evict a tenant are deductible (see "Legal and Professional Services," above).

An often quicker and cheaper alternative to evicting a tenant is to offer "cash for keys." The landlord pays the tenant a specific amount of money if the tenant moves out on an agreed-upon date. This kind of agreement can be good for both the landlord and tenant. The tenant avoids having an eviction on record and gets money to help move. The landlord gets the tenant to leave without going through the stress and expense of an eviction. Cash for keys is perfectly legal in all 50 states. (But restrictions could be in place if a unit is subject to local rent control laws.) It's wise to put a cash-for-keys agreement in writing, which the landlord and tenant both sign.

The amounts landlords pay tenants to move is a deductible rental expense. If the payment to the tenant is over $600 by cash or check, the landlord should file a Form 1099-NEC with the IRS reporting the payment, which is taxable income for the tenant.

Whether you evict a tenant or do a "cash-for-keys repossession," you can get a court judgment against the tenant for the amount of the unpaid rent, less any security deposit you've retained. However, unless the tenant has money, earns a salary, or has assets you can get your hands on, the judgment will be worthless. A court won't collect a judgment for you; you must do it yourself.

Normal Rules Applied to Unpaid Rent During the COVID-19 Pandemic

The rules discussed above applied during the COVID-19 pandemic. Rent unpaid during the pandemic was not deductible by cash basis landlords even though many tenants stopped paying rent during the pandemic, and landlords in many states and cities weren't allowed to evict them for nonpayment.

Likewise, landlords who offered tenants a rent holiday or reduction during the pandemic aren't entitled to a bad debt tax deduction. Such a rent holiday or reduction would also not qualify as a deductible charitable contribution. First, you never qualify for a charitable tax deduction when you give something of value to an individual, even if the person is needy. You can only get a deduction when you give money or property to a tax-qualified 501(c)(3) charity. However, even if you make a rental available for free to a charity, you likely still won't get a charitable deduction. IRS rules generally don't allow a charitable deduction for a contribution of less than your entire interest in property. The IRS says that a contribution of the right to use property is a contribution of less than your entire interest in that property and is not deductible. For example, the IRS doesn't allow a deduction when owners of vacation homes make them available as prizes in charity auctions.

Deducting Rental Losses

I f, like many landlords, your tax deductions from your rental properties exceed your rental income, this section is the single most important chapter in this book. Complex IRS rules might prevent you from deducting all or part of your rental losses from the other income you earn during the year, which could end up costing you thousands of dollars in extra taxes. However, important exceptions to the rules help small landlords and others in the real estate industry.

Even if you're fortunate enough to earn a profit each year from your rentals, you still need to know about these rules and how they affect you. This chapter explains the rules in detail.

What Are Rental Losses?

You have a rental loss if all the deductions from a rental property you own exceed the annual rent and other money you receive from the property. If you own multiple properties, the annual income or losses from each property are combined (netted) to determine if you have income or loss from all your rental activities for the year. You report your rental income and deductible expenses on IRS Schedule E.

EXAMPLE: Tanya owns two rental houses. She receives $24,000 annually in rent from each house. She reports her annual expenses for the properties on Schedule E as follows:

Expense	Amount—House A	Amount—House B
Advertising	$ 100	$ 0
Auto and travel	200	200
Cleaning and maintenance	1,500	500
Insurance	2,000	1,800
Mortgage interest	10,000	7,000
Other interest	700	0
Repairs	600	1,000
Supplies	2,000	1,500
Taxes	2,400	2,000
Utilities	2,500	2,000
Depreciation	+ 8,000	+ 7,000
Total expenses	$ 30,000	$ 23,000
Rents received	$ 24,000	$ 24,000
Total expenses	− 30,000	− 23,000
Income or (loss)	$ (6,000)	$ 1,000

Tanya's deductible expenses for House A exceeded the $24,000 in rent she received by $6,000. So, she had a $6,000 rental loss for the year for the property. She had $1,000 of income on House B—her expenses for that property were $23,000 and she received $24,000 rent. Tanya subtracts her rental losses (the $6,000 loss on House A) from her rental income (the $1,000 profit on House B), leaving her with a $5,000 loss for the year from all her rental activities.

It is extremely common for landlords to have rental losses, especially in the first few years. Indeed, IRS statistics show that in one recent year, over half of the filed Schedule E forms reporting rental income and expenses showed a loss. This amounted to over 5.2 million taxpayers. If you have a rental loss, you have plenty of company.

Often, you have a loss for tax purposes even if your rental income exceeds your operating expenses. This is because your depreciation deduction is included as an expense for these purposes (even though depreciation is not an operating expense—see Chapter 3 for more on operating expenses). Without the depreciation deduction, Tanya (in the above example) would have had income of $2,000 from House A, instead of a $6,000 loss.

If you have a rental loss for the year, you become subject to two sets of tax rules:

- the passive loss rules, and
- the at-risk rules.

The passive loss rules are by far the most important for most landlords, so we will discuss those rules first.

Overview of the Passive Loss Rules

Fasten your seat belts: We are about to embark on one of the most complicated, confusing, and frightening journeys a rental property owner can take—into the realm of the passive activity loss rules (PAL rules, for short). These rules can make you or break you come tax time.

RESOURCE

Need more information? The IRS has created a very useful, highly detailed guide to passive activity losses for its auditors called the *Passive Activity Loss Audit Technique Guide.* If you want more information on the passive loss rules, this is a good place to look. It's available to the public at the IRS website at www.irs.gov.

What Are the PAL Rules For?

Thirty-five years ago, landlords could freely deduct their rental losses from all of the other income they or their spouses earned during the year (assuming they filed a joint return). However, the unfettered deductibility of real estate losses led to enormous abuses. In the 1980s, wealthy individuals invested in real estate limited partnerships and other tax shelters created solely to generate large losses through depreciation, interest, and other deductions. The investors in these tax shelters would use the losses to offset their other income. The tax benefits obtained could far exceed the amount of money invested in the tax shelter.

All this came to an abrupt end in 1986, when Congress enacted the PAL rules. (I.R.C. § 469.) These rules were designed to limit a taxpayer's ability to use rental or business losses to offset other income. The PAL rules apply to all business activities, but are particularly strict for rental real estate because real estate was the primary tax shelter.

How the PAL Rules Work

Most landlords earn income and incur expenses from more than one source—in addition to income and expenses from their rental property, they might earn a salary from a job, or make money from a business they own. They might also have investments other than rental property, such as stocks and bonds.

For purposes of the PAL rules, all the income you earn and losses you incur are divided into three separate categories:

- **Active income or loss.** Income or loss from any business activity, other than real estate rentals, in which you materially participate (actively manage); see "The Real Estate Professional Exemption," below, for a detailed discussion of material participation. This includes salary and other income from a job or a business you run, or the money you earn from selling your personal services. Social Security benefits are included as well.

- **Passive income or loss.** Income or loss from (1) businesses in which you don't materially participate, and (2) all rental properties you own. Under the rules, income and loss from rental activities are automatically passive, whether or not the landlord materially participates in the rental activity. (Casualty losses from rental property are not passive losses—see Chapter 14.)

- **Portfolio income or loss.** Income or loss from investments, such as interest earned on savings, or dividends earned on stocks; gains or losses when investments are sold; expenses paid for investments.

Imagine three buckets, one for each of the three kinds of income or loss. Every penny you earn during the year must go into one of these three buckets. In addition, all the money you spend on investments or business activities, such as a rental real estate business, any business you actively manage, or any self-employment activity, goes into one of the buckets. Money you spend for personal purposes, such as food and clothing, is not counted.

- **Active income or loss.** Income or loss from your job or business activities (other than real estate rentals) in which you materially participate.

- **Passive income or loss.** Income or loss from rental properties or businesses in which you don't materially participate.

- **Portfolio income or loss.** Income or loss from any investments.

Here's the key to the PAL rules: The contents of the passive bucket must always stay in that bucket. You can't use passive losses to offset income in the other two buckets. Nor can you use passive income to offset losses from the other buckets.

> **EXAMPLE:** Sidney is a successful doctor. This year, he has $200,000 in income from his practice and also earns $50,000 in income from invest-ments. Sidney invests $25,000 in a real estate limited partnership tax shelter. The partnership owns several rental properties that operate at a substantial loss. At the end of the year, the partnership informs Sidney that his share of the partnership's annual operating loss is $75,000. Sidney's three buckets look like this:

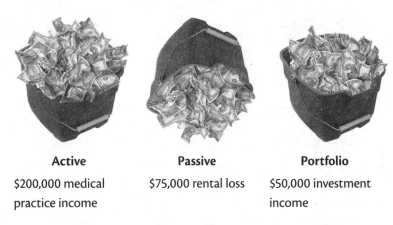

Active	**Passive**	**Portfolio**
$200,000 medical practice income	$75,000 rental loss	$50,000 investment income

Sidney invested in the limited partnership because he wanted to use his share of the losses it generated to reduce his taxable income from his medical practice. However, at tax time, he's in for a shock. Because passive income or loss must stay in the passive bucket, Sidney can't deduct his $75,000 passive loss from his medical practice income or his investment income. Because he earned no passive income during the year, he can't use his passive loss at all this year. His real estate tax shelter turned out to be useless.

This is what the PAL rules are intended to do: prevent you from deducting your passive losses (such as from rental activities) from your active or portfolio income. So, there is no point in investing in real estate rentals just to incur tax losses because you won't be able to use these losses to offset your other non–real-estate income.

The PAL rules have accomplished their purpose of preventing wealthy people from investing in rental real estate solely to create tax losses. But the rules apply to all owners of rental property, even landlords who are in the business of renting properties to earn a living and have no interest in obtaining tax losses. To prevent undue economic hardship to these people, special rules were created that wholly or partly exempt many small landlords and people active in the real estate industry from the PAL rules. These are:

- the $25,000 offset, and
- the real estate professional exemption.

The $25,000 Offset

Congress felt it was unfair to prevent landlords with moderate incomes from deducting their rental losses from their nonrental income. So, a special exception—the $25,000 offset—was fashioned for them. It permits landlords to deduct up to $25,000 in rental losses from any other nonpassive income they earn during the year. The offset applies to all rental properties that a landlord owns—that is, you don't get a separate $25,000 for each property you own. (I.R.C. § 469(i).)

> EXAMPLE: Recall Tanya from the example at the beginning of the chapter. She owned two rental houses and had a $6,000 loss from one and $1,000 in income from the other. She also has a job that pays her an $80,000 salary. In addition, Tanya earned $10,000 in dividends from stocks and incurred $1,000 in investment expenses (stockbroker commissions), leaving her with $9,000 in investment income. Her three buckets look like this:

Active	Passive	Portfolio
$80,000 income from job	$5,000 loss from rentals	$9,000 investment income

If Tanya were not a landlord, the PAL rules would bar her from deducting her passive loss from her rentals from her active or portfolio income. However, if Tanya qualifies for the $25,000 offset, which is available only for landlords, she can deduct her $5,000 loss from her nonpassive income that includes her salary and investment income.

The $25,000 offset is particularly important to small landlords. If your income isn't much over $100,000 and your annual rental losses are less than $25,000, it can give you complete relief from the onerous PAL rules.

If you have more than $25,000 in annual losses, you don't lose the excess amount. Instead, they become suspended losses you can deduct the following year or years provided you qualify for the offset during those years. You can also deduct them when you sell the property.

> **EXAMPLE:** Landlord Mario qualified for the $25,000 offset and had $35,000 in rental losses this year. He may deduct $25,000 of the $35,000 from his other nonrental income for the year. The remaining $10,000 in losses are suspended. He may deduct them the following year using the $25,000 offset if he qualifies for it. If he does, that would leave another $15,000 in losses he could deduct that year using the offset.

Requirements

To qualify for the $25,000 offset, you must:

- actively participate in your rental activity
- come within the income limits, and
- be at least a 10% owner of the rental activity.

Any individual who meets these requirements may use the $25,000 offset. This is so whether the individual owns rental property alone or with one or more co-owners. General partners in partnerships that own rental property may use the exemption, but not limited partners. Nor can it be used for property owned by a corporation or trust.

Active Participation

You qualify for the $25,000 offset only if you actively participate in the running of your rental real estate, which is very easy to do. You don't have to work any set number of hours to actively participate; you simply have to be the person who makes the final decisions about approving tenants, arranging for repairs, setting rents, and other management tasks. If you manage your rentals yourself, you'll satisfy this requirement without any problem. The IRS probably won't even raise the issue if you're audited. Management tasks performed by your spouse are also counted in determining if you actively participate. (I.R.C. § 469(i)(6)(D).)

The only time you could have trouble with this requirement is if you hire a resident or nonresident manager or management company to manage your property for you. You can't simply let the manager do everything. To actively participate, you or your spouse must exercise independent judgment, and not simply okay the actions of a manager or management company. For example, you must be the one who makes such important decisions as what the rent will be and whether to do a major repair or improvement. The manager can make recommendations about such matters, but the final decision must be yours. (S. Rep. No. 313, 99th Cong., 2d Sess. 738 (1986).)

Some management firms automatically issue letters to their clients stating that the client is "actively involved in management of the rental" and approves tenants, arranges for repairs, sets rental fees, and so on. IRS training materials advise IRS auditors to ignore such letters. Instead, if an IRS auditor questions whether you actively participate, the auditor is instructed to ask to see a copy of your contract with your management company—the contract should show who has the right to make the final decisions. (*Passive Activity Loss Audit Technique Guide*, pp. 2–7.)

Read your management contract and make sure it provides that you make the final decisions on important rental matters. It should read something like this: "Client shall make all major management decisions for the property, including final approval of all new tenants, rental rates, and repairs over $_____."

Although a well-drafted contract will help show that you actively participate, be sure to document and keep copies of any correspondence with the management company (including emails) that establish your involvement in decision-making and the management of the property.

Income (MAGI) Limits

The $25,000 offset is intended for landlords who earn moderate incomes. If your modified adjusted gross income (MAGI) is less than $100,000, you're entitled to the full $25,000 offset. It goes down as your MAGI increases, and is eliminated completely once your modified adjusted gross income exceeds $150,000. (I.R.C. § 469(i)(3).) While $100,000–$150,000 might not sound like a lot, 43.5% of all landlords make less than $125,000, and 30% earn less than $90,000.

Your MAGI consists of all your taxable income for the year, not including taxable Social Security benefits and passive activity income or loss, minus the following expenses:

- self-employed health insurance premiums paid during the year
- contributions to IRAs and pension plans
- one-half of self-employment taxes paid, and
- student loan interest. (I.R.C. § 469(i)(3)(E).)

For most taxpayers, their MAGI is all of their income, not counting their passive income or loss. If you get Social Security, you also deduct this amount from your income, except for any amount you must pay income tax on. Not being able to deduct passive losses from your MAGI can make it more difficult to fall within the $100,000 to $150,000 MAGI range.

EXAMPLE: Raul, a self-employed person, earned $150,000 in net income from his engineering consulting business this year and $5,000 in investment income. He also owned an apartment building that had a $25,000 loss. He can't deduct the $25,000 passive loss from the apartment building from his business or investment income. Because his MAGI is $155,000, he is not eligible for any offset.

The offset amount is $25,000 for both single and married taxpayers filing joint returns. Married people who file separate tax returns and live separately for the entire year are each entitled to a $12,500 offset. However, married people who file separate returns and live together *any time* during the year get no offset at all. (I.R.C. § 469(i)(5)(B).)

$25,000 Limit Applies to Tax Credits

Some rental property owners can obtain tax credits by rehabilitating their rental property or from the low-income housing tax credit. A tax credit is subtracted from your tax liability after you calculate your taxes. (See Chapter 1.) Because these credits come from your rental property, they go into your passive income or loss bucket, and are subject to the same passive loss rules as the rental property deduction. However, they get particularly favorable treatment when it comes to the $25,000 offset. You don't need to satisfy the active participation requirement to deduct these credits as part of your offset. In addition, for these credits, the phaseout of the $25,000 offset starts when your modified adjusted gross income exceeds $200,000 ($100,000 if you are a married individual filing a separate return and living apart at all times during the year). There is no phaseout of the $25,000 offset for low-income housing credits for property placed in service after 1989. But there's a catch: You can deduct these credits only to the extent you have taxable passive income for the year—no income, no credit. The credits are suspended to a future year when you have net passive income you must pay income tax on. Use IRS Form 8582-CR, *Passive Activity Credit Limitations*, to figure your allowable annual credit. (I.R.C. § 469(j)(5).)

The phaseout of the $25,000 offset works as follows. For every dollar your MAGI exceeds $100,000, you reduce your $25,000 offset by 50 cents. For example, if your MAGI is $110,000, you reduce your offset by $5,000 (0.5 × $10,000 = $5,000). In that case, you could deduct only $20,000 in passive losses for the year ($25,000 − $5,000 = $20,000). Once your MAGI is $150,000 or more, your offset disappears entirely (50 cents × $50,000 = $25,000).

You might be able to reduce your MAGI if it exceeds $150,000, or if you want to increase the amount of offset you're eligible for. One way is to defer some of the compensation you're owed to the following year. Another way is to make contributions to an IRA or tax qualified retirement plan, which you can deduct from your MAGI.

> EXAMPLE: Raul's MAGI for the year is $155,000—he has $150,000 in net income from his engineering consulting business and $5,000 in investment income. He also has a $25,000 loss from an apartment building that he owns. Raul makes a $15,000 contribution to his 401(k) retirement plan and tells one of his clients not to pay the $40,000 the client owes him until the following year. Raul thereby reduces his MAGI from $155,000 to $100,000 and can now deduct the full $25,000 offset amount.

Ownership Requirement

To qualify for the offset, you must own at least 10% of all interests in your real estate activity for the entire year. If you're married, your spouse's ownership interests can be counted too. The ownership percentage is determined by the value of the property. For example, if the rental property is worth $100,000, you must own at least $10,000. If you own more than one rental building, you must own 10% or more of each building. (I.R.C. § 469(i)(6)(A).)

This rule should not pose a problem for most small landlords. However, it eliminates most owners of vacation time-shares, because a person who buys a time-share usually obtains less than a 10% interest in the property. (*Toups v. Comm'r.*, 66 T.C. Memo 370.)

If you own a condominium, you need own only 10% of the value of your particular condominium unit, not 10% of the entire building that contains many separate condominium units.

Determining Your Offset Deduction

Here's how to determine your deduction from the offset:

1. First, subtract your passive activity deductions from your passive income. You should have a net loss; otherwise, you won't need the offset. For example, suppose Tess has two apartment buildings. One earned a $5,000 profit; the other had a $15,000 loss. Tess has a $10,000 passive loss for the year.

2. Next, determine the amount of the offset you're eligible for. This amount will be $25,000 if your MAGI is $100,000 or less. Your offset will be less than $25,000 if your MAGI is $100,000 to $150,000. You get no offset at all if your MAGI is $150,000 or more. Suppose Tess's MAGI is $75,000. She qualifies for the full $25,000 offset. But she only has $10,000 in passive losses this year, so she can't use the remaining $15,000 of the offset.

3. Then, deduct the applicable amount of your offset from your active or portfolio income. Tess deducts her $10,000 passive loss from her active income, reducing it to $65,000 in taxable income for the year.

The Real Estate Professional Exemption

People in the real estate industry moaned and groaned about the passive loss rules. Because the PAL rules were intended to curtail passive investors' use of real estate tax shelters, those actively engaged in the real estate business felt it was unfair to have the rules apply to them. Congress agreed and created a special exemption from the passive loss rules for real estate professionals. This rule provides substantially more relief than the $25,000 offset because there is no maximum offset amount or income limit requirements.

Landlords who qualify for the real estate professional exemption get extraordinary tax benefits unavailable to other people who earn income from rental property:

- First, real estate professionals can treat all of their losses from rental properties as active losses. So, they can deduct any rental activity losses they have for the year from all of their other income for the year, including active income and portfolio income. (I.R.C. § 469(c)(7).) However, during 2021 through 2026, a maximum of $270,000 in losses can be deducted each year by singles, and $540,000 by married taxpayers (see "Annual Loss Limits," below).

- Second, real estate professionals are not subject to the 3.8% Medicare tax on rental income that went into effect in 2013. This tax is imposed on all landlords with adjusted gross income over $200,000 for singles and $250,000 for married taxpayers filing jointly. Real estate professionals are specifically exempted from the 3.8% tax, provided that they materially participate in the rental activity and such activity qualifies as a business. (See Chapter 19 for a detailed discussion of this tax.)

These tax benefits are particularly valuable for landlords with high incomes or large rental losses. They can give real estate professionals who invest in real property a substantial financial advantage over landlords who don't qualify for them.

You don't have to be a real estate broker or developer to qualify for the real estate professional exemption. Any person who can pass the test discussed below will qualify. This includes full-time landlords and some part-time landlords as well.

Make sure the exemption applies to your type of business entity. The real estate professional exemption can be used by landlords who are individuals (including joint tenants and tenants in common), general partnerships, limited liability companies taxed like partnerships (most are), and S corporations. C corporations qualify only if 51% or more of their gross receipts come from real property businesses in which they materially participate. The exemption does not apply to limited partnerships, estates, and most types of trusts.

You must meet two separate and distinct requirements to obtain the real estate professional exemption—you have to:

- qualify as a real estate professional, and
- materially participate in your rental activities.

Real Estate Professional Test

To qualify as a real estate professional, you must:

- participate in one or more real property businesses
- "materially participate" in one or more of such businesses
- spend at least 51% of your annual work time at your real property business or businesses in which you materially participate, and
- spend at least 751 hours per year working at your real property businesses in which you materially participate. (I.R.C. § 469(c)(7).)

Participate in Real Property Businesses

Logically enough, to qualify as a real estate professional, you must work at one or more real property trades or businesses during the year. You don't have to work solely as a landlord; other real estate businesses can count as well. Indeed, the more such businesses you have, the easier it can be to qualify as a real estate pro.

A real property trade or business means any real property development, redevelopment, construction, reconstruction, acquisition, conversion, rental, operation, management, leasing, or brokerage business. (I.R.C. § 469(c)(7)(C).) This covers virtually any real estate business activity. Most people who qualify for the exemption are engaged in one of the following activities:

- real estate rentals
- construction (contractor or builder)
- real estate brokerage work, or
- real property management.

You must be directly involved in one or more of these real property businesses to qualify for the exemption. So, for example, an attorney or accountant is not in the real property business, even if the attorney or accountant advises people who are in the business. Mortgage brokers, lenders, and bankers don't qualify either, because the IRS views them as involved in the financial services industry, not real estate. (IRS Chief Counsel Advice 2015-04010.) Real estate sales agents, on the other hand, can qualify for the exemption because they're usually paid on a straight commission basis, which makes them independent contractors, not employees, for tax purposes. As independent contractors, they are in business and, therefore, can qualify for the exemption.

If you are an employee in someone else's real property business, you do not qualify for the real estate professional exemption. You must own your own real property business or be a part owner of a business with more than a 5% ownership interest. If you work as an employee for a corporation, you must own more than 5% of your employer's outstanding stock.

You Don't Have to Be a Licensed Broker to Be in the Brokerage Business

You don't have to be licensed by your state as a real estate broker to be in the real estate brokerage business for tax purposes. Any person who engages in one or more of the following activities is in the real estate brokerage business:

- selling, exchanging, purchasing, renting, or leasing real property
- offering to do the activities mentioned above
- negotiating the terms of real estate contracts
- listing real property for sale, lease, or exchange, or
- procuring prospective sellers, purchasers, lessors, or lessees.

It makes no difference whether a person who engaged in these activities is licensed as a real estate broker, agent, or salesperson. In one case, the tax court held that a person licensed as a real estate salesperson in California was engaged in a brokerage business for tax purposes because she sold, exchanged, leased, and rented property, and solicited listings. It made no difference that under California law a person must be licensed as a broker to be in the brokerage business. (*Agarwall v. Comm'r.*, T.C. Summ. Op. 2009-29.)

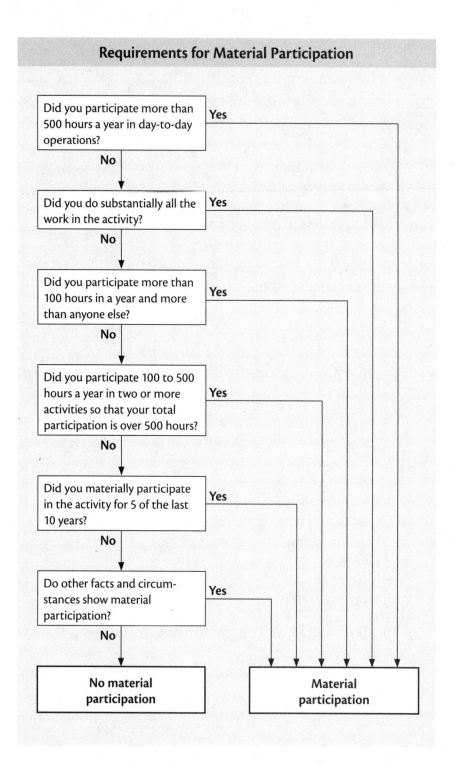

Material Participation Test

You must "materially participate" in any of the real property businesses described above for the time you spend at it to count toward qualifying as a real estate professional. For example, if you're a landlord and also work as a real estate broker, you can count the brokerage activity only if you materially participate in it.

You materially participate in a business only if you are involved with its day-to-day operations on a regular, continuous, and substantial basis. (I.R.C. § 469(h).) The IRS has created several tests to determine material participation, based on the amount of time you spend working in real estate activities. You only need to pass one of the tests to show material participation in an activity.

Most people use one of the first three tests. These three tests are based on the number of hours you work at your rental activity. As explained below, you can count your spouse's hours as well as your own.

500-hour test. You (and your spouse) participated in the activity for more than 500 hours during the year. This is the simplest test. If you have more than one real estate activity, you can often satisfy this test by grouping them together.

Substantially all test. You (and your spouse) did substantially all the work in the activity during the year. You don't have to do 100% of the work, but others may only do an insubstantial amount.

101-hour test. You (and your spouse) participated in the business for more than 100 hours during the year, and you participated at least as much as any other person (including employees and independent contractors, such as property managers). This test is also frequently used by real estate professionals.

Significant participation activities test. You can use this test if you have two or more "significant participation activities" that you combine to equal 500 or more hours. A significant participation activity is real estate business activity in which (1) you spend more than 100 hours, and (2) such activity does not count as material participation under any of the other six tests—for example, you can't count an activity in which you work more than 500 hours because you materially participate in such an activity. This test is rarely used for real estate.

Past performance test. You satisfy any of the IRS tests for material participation for any five of the last ten years. This test is rarely used.

Facts and circumstances test. The facts and circumstances show that you materially participated. You can't use this test if (1) you didn't participate in the activity for at least 101 hours; (2) anyone worked more than you; or (3) anyone was paid to manage the activity.

When computing your hours, do not treat work you do in your capacity as an investor as participation in your real estate activity. This includes:

- studying and reviewing financial statements or reports on the activity's operations—including time spent reading this book!
- preparing or compiling summaries or analyses of the finances or operations of the activity for your own use, or
- monitoring the activity's finances or operations in a nonmanagerial capacity—for example, reviewing rental statements you receive from a rental management company that manages your property for you. (IRS Reg. § 1.469-5(f)(2)(ii).)

Courts have held that the time you spend organizing your personal records, preparing your taxes, paying bills, and reviewing monthly statements prepared by a real estate management company all constitute investor activities. (*Barniskis v. Comm'r.*, T.C. Memo 1999-258.) Time you spend doing these tasks can't be counted to pass the material participation tests.

Absentee landlords who hire real property managers to do all of their work for them might have difficulty passing the material participation test. To materially participate, a landlord must be involved with the day-to-day operation of the rental property, something absentee landlords often don't do. If you live a substantial distance away from your rental property, the IRS will likely question whether you are really involved in day-to-day operations.

> EXAMPLE: Josephine owns two five-unit apartment buildings in Las Vegas, but lives in Houston. She hires a real property management company to manage the properties. She is not involved with the day-to-day management of the buildings. Her involvement is limited to approving the management company's decisions. This year, she spent 50 hours dealing with her management company. She spent another 25 hours reading

financial statements and otherwise dealing with her investment. Josephine has not materially participated in her rental activity. None of the time she spends reading financial statements counts as material participation. This leaves her with just 50 hours of work during the year, not enough to materially participate under any of the tests. She clearly doesn't satisfy the 500-hour or 101-hour test. Nor does she meet the "you-did-all-the-work" test because the management company did most of the work.

If you're married, you combine the time your spouse spends materially participating in the business with your own time whether or not you and your spouse file a joint return. Nor is it necessary for the spouse to have an ownership interest in the business. (IRS Reg. § 1.469-9(c)(4).) This can make it much easier to pass one of the material participation tests.

EXAMPLE: Frank and Felicia are married and file a joint return. They own a four-unit apartment building they manage themselves. Felicia does most of the work, spending 400 hours a year dealing with tenants, showing vacant units, handling bookkeeping chores, and so forth. Frank does most of the repair work for the property, spending 120 hours a year on it. Together, Frank and Felicia spent 520 hours materially participating in their rental real estate activity—more than enough to pass the 500-hour test.

If you have multiple real estate businesses, you can group them together for purposes of the material participation tests. This way, you can combine the hours you work at them—for example, if you group two activities in which you work 300 hours per year, you'll end up with 600 hours (more than the 500 hours you need to materially participate).

IRS regulations provide that you can combine your activities for these purposes just about any way you want, so long as the result is reasonable under the circumstances. (IRS Reg. § 1.469-9(d).) One example the IRS has provided is that of an individual who owns two rental properties and a separate real property development business. He combines all three activities for purposes of the material participation rules and spends a total of 750 hours working at them during the year. Because this number of hours is more than 500, he materially participated in them and qualifies as a real estate professional. (IRS Chief Counsel Memo 201427016 (7/3/2014).)

If you own more than one rental property, you'll ordinarily want to group them all together so you can combine the hours you spend on each.

You can also group multiple properties together for purposes of the pass-through deduction discussed in Chapter 7. Note that grouping your properties for purposes of the material participation test does not affect any groupings you make for the pass-through deduction. The two are completely unrelated.

51% Test

Now that you've figured out which real property business or businesses you participated in during the year, you can apply the 51% test. This test requires that you spend more than half of your total working hours during the year working in all the real property businesses in which you materially participated. Again, be sure only to count the time at the real property business in which you materially participate. For example, if you materially participate in real estate management, but not at real estate brokerage, you can't use your brokerage hours to help pass the 51% test.

If you work full time at something other than one or more real property businesses, it will be next to impossible to pass the 51% test. For example, if you work 40 hours per week at a non–real-property business, you would have to work an average of 41 hours per week at one or more real estate activities in which you materially participate to pass the test. So, you'd have to put in an 81-hour week. The IRS isn't likely to believe you work this much unless you have extremely convincing documentation. IRS auditors are instructed to look carefully at W-2 forms when they audit taxpayers who claim real estate professional status. If the W-2 shows that a taxpayer has a job not in real estate, the auditor will question whether the 51% test has been satisfied.

Fortunately, if you're married and file a joint return, it's sufficient for either spouse to pass the 51% test (and the 751-hour test discussed below). If one spouse passes both tests, both spouses are deemed to pass. Note that the same spouse must pass both tests. So, if you're married, you can work full time at a non–real-property business and still meet the test if your spouse spends all (or at least over half) of his or her work time managing your rental properties.

> **EXAMPLE:** Leo and Leona are married and file a joint return. Leo is a physician and doesn't spend any time working on real estate. Leona spends 100% of her annual work time managing apartment buildings the couple owns. The test is satisfied because Leona spends more than half of her time working in the real property business. If Leo spends 20% of his time managing their rental property and Leona spends 40% of her time on real property business, they will not satisfy the 51% test. To meet the 51% test, one spouse must spend at least 51% of his or her time working at a real property business—you can't combine time to reach the 51%.

If you or your spouse is involved in more than one real property business in which one of you materially participates, you can add the time you spend in each of the businesses to see if you pass the 51% test.

> **EXAMPLE:** John works 800 hours per year as a part-time bookkeeper. He owns rental property on which he works 100 hours per year. He also works 701 hours per year as a real estate broker. John passes the 51% test because he spent a combined 801 hours working in real estate businesses and 800 hours in other activities.

751-Hour Test

It's not enough that you (or your spouse) spend more than half of your work time in a real property business. After all, if you had no other work, you'd spend more than half your work time on real estate if you spent only one hour a year on it. To avoid this result, you or your spouse must spend at least 751 hours per year working at your real property business or businesses in which you materially participate—the same spouse must pass both the 751-hour and 51% tests. 751 hours amounts to only 14.5 hours a week. As with the 51% requirement, you can combine the time you spend working at multiple real estate activities in which you materially participate.

> **EXAMPLE:** John worked 200 hours per year on his rental properties (which was enough to materially participate in them) and 601 hours as a real estate broker. By combining both of these real estate business activities, John exceeds the 751-hour limit.

People like John, who work full or part time as a real estate broker, contractor, developer, or other real estate professional, will likely have little trouble meeting the 751-hour requirement. The people who have trouble passing this test are those whose sole real property business is managing their rentals. If you own only a few units, it's unlikely you will need to spend 751 hours per year dealing with them. (And, ironically, if you have stable, long-term tenants who place few demands on their landlord, you'll have less reason to spend time on that rental.) One real property management expert estimates that landlords who manage their rental properties themselves must spend four hours working on each unit per month. At that rate, you would need to own at least 16 rental units to work 751 hours per year.

Materially Participate in Rental Activity

If you passed the previous four tests, you qualify as a real estate professional. However, this doesn't mean you get to treat the income or loss from your real estate rentals as nonpassive. You're allowed to do so only for those rentals in which you materially participate during the year.

The material participation rules covered above apply here as well. However, the time you spend on real estate businesses other than rentals is not considered when you determine if you materially participated in your rental activity.

Most real estate professionals use one of the following three material participation tests.

500-hour test. You (and your spouse) participated in the rental activity for more than 500 hours during the year. You might not be able to spend this much time if you own only a single rental property. But landlords with multiple properties can often satisfy this test by grouping them together (see below).

> EXAMPLE: Bill owns eight rental houses. He spends 70 hours per year managing each house. He combines the properties for purposes of material participation, resulting in 560 total hours.

Substantially all test. You (and your spouse) did substantially all the work in the rental activity during the year. This test is frequently used by real estate professionals who own a single property or don't wish to group multiple properties together. You can materially participate in a business under this test even if you devote much less than 500 hours to it during the year.

To qualify for this test, you must do "substantially all" the work required to manage the rental property. This doesn't mean you have to do 100% of the work yourself. You can hire repair people or contractors to do occasional work on the property. But their work can only be occasional—it should not make up a substantial portion of the total time spent managing the property.

> **EXAMPLE:** Jon is a real estate broker who owns one rental property. During the year he spent 70 hours managing the property. He did all the work required, except he hired a plumber one time to fix a leak. The plumber billed Jon one hour for the job. Jon satisfies the substantially all test.

If you hire others to help with repairs or other tasks, it's wise to keep track of the work they perform and how much time they spend.

101-hour test. You (and your spouse) participated in the rental activity for more than 100 hours during the year, and you participated at least as much as any other person (including employees and independent contractors, such as property managers). This test is also frequently used by real estate professionals.

> **EXAMPLE:** David and Lisa are married and own one rental property. During the year, David worked 80 hours on the property and Lisa 25 hours. They also hired a gardener who worked 36 hours for the year. They pass the 101-hour test because they have 105 combined total hours, which is more than the gardener.

If you own more than one rental property, the default rule is that each one is a separate rental activity in which you must materially participate to treat it as nonpassive.

Fortunately, you don't have to stick with this default rule. You can file a statement (called an "election") with your tax return stating that you want all of your rental activities grouped together as one single activity. This way, you can combine the time you spend working on each rental property to satisfy the material participation tests. If you fail to file the election, you'll have to show that you materially participated in each rental property you own to treat that property's income or loss as nonpassive. For most landlords, this is impossible to do, which makes filing a timely election very important.

> **EXAMPLE:** Donald Trask owned 33 rental properties in California. He combined all of his income and losses from all of the properties on one Schedule E and claimed a loss of over $27,000 for the year 2001. Trask established that he was a real estate professional—he worked full time in his rental business and spent more than 750 hours at it. However, Trask failed to file an election to treat all of his 33 rental activities as one activity. So, he had to materially participate in each rental property. Trask admitted that he did not materially participate in any of his many rentals when viewed separately. Thus, he didn't qualify for the exemption for any of his properties. (*Trask v. Comm'r.*, T.C. Memo 2010-78 (2010).)

To make an election to treat all your rental activities as one activity, you'll need to draft a statement like the one below and attach it to your tax return.

Tax Year: _____Taxpayer Name: _____

Taxpayer Identification Number: _____

In accordance with Regulation 1.469-9(g)(3), taxpayer states that he/she is a qualifying real estate professional, and elects under I.R.C. § 469(c)(7)(A) to treat all interests in rental real estate as a single rental real estate activity.

_____

Your Signature

You Might Be Able to File Your Election Late

Unfortunately, many landlords, and many tax preparers, are unaware of the need to file an election to group their rental activities to qualify for the PAL exemption. Many have been treating all their rental properties as a single activity on their tax returns without filing the election. If they get audited by the IRS, their failure to file this simple piece of paper can cost them their PAL exemption and force them to give back all or part of the rental losses they claimed on their return.

Fortunately, the IRS allows real estate professionals in this situation to file a retroactive PAL election and keep their exemption. To do so, you must have filed returns consistent with a single-activity election for all the years to which the late election is to apply. You must also show the IRS that you had "reasonable cause" for the late election. Reasonable cause could be that you reasonably relied on a qualified tax professional and that person failed to advise you to make the election. The election is made by filing Form 1040-X to amend your most recent return and attaching a statement with the required information. The amended return should show zero tax if you meet all the eligibility requirements because the return should have been filed consistently with having made a grouping election that enabled you to pass the material participation test. If you're currently under examination by the IRS, a copy of the amended return should also be filed with the examiner. (For more details, see Rev. Proc. 2011-34, available at www.irs.gov/pub/irs-drop/rp-11-34.pdf.)

Note that this election is an all-or-nothing proposition: You must group all of your rental properties together as a single activity, or group none of them. You can't pick or choose which properties to include.

The election can be filed in any year in which you qualify for the real estate professional exemption. It only needs to be filed once—it applies automatically to all future years that you qualify for the exemption. It may be revoked only if you have a material change in circumstances. The fact that the election is less advantageous to you in a particular year is not a material change in circumstances. (IRS Reg. § 1.469-9(g).)

You can also group multiple properties together for purposes of the pass-through deduction discussed in Chapter 7. Filing an election to treat all your real interests as a single rental activity for purposes of the passive loss rules has no effect on any groupings you make for the pass-through deduction. The two are completely unrelated.

> **CAUTION**
>
> **Filing an election could cause problems if you have suspended losses.** Suspended losses are unused passive losses from prior years. If you have substantial suspended losses from multiple rental properties, think carefully before filing an election to treat them as a single activity. The election could make it difficult for you to deduct your suspended losses when you sell your property.

Applying the Test

Let's take a look at a couple of examples applying the real estate professional exemption tests.

> **EXAMPLE 1:** Max and Maxine are married and own two duplexes they rent out. They have filed an election with their tax return to treat both properties as a single rental activity for tax purposes. Max works full time (1,800 hours per year) as an accountant. Maxine is a licensed real estate agent. She spends 1,000 hours per year working in this real property business. Max and Maxine both work at managing their rental property. This doesn't take much time. Max spent 70 hours this year, and Maxine 80 hours. The tests can be answered as follows:
>
> - Do they participate in one or more real property businesses? Yes. Maxine works as an agent and they both work at being landlords.
> - Do they "materially participate" in one or more of such businesses? Yes. Maxine spent 1,000 hours working at real estate brokerage—more than enough to materially participate under the more-than-500-hour test. Together, the couple spent 150 hours managing their rental property. This is far too little for the 500-hour material participation test; but they qualify under the 101-hour test because no one else worked on their rentals as much as they did.

- Did the same person spend at least 51% of their annual work time at a real property business in which they materially participated? Yes. Max can't pass the test. He spent almost all his time working at accounting. But Maxine passes the test because she spent 100% of her time working on real property activities in which she materially participated.
- Did the same person spend at least 751 hours per year working at a real property business they materially participated in? Yes. Maxine easily passes—she put in 1,080 hours on real property activities. Because Maxine passes the 51% and 751-hour tests, both Max and Maxine are deemed to pass.
- Did they materially participate in their rental activities? Yes. Together the couple materially participated in their duplexes because they spent 150 hours managing them during the year and no one else spent more time.

Max and Maxine may treat as nonpassive any income or loss from their rental activity for the year. So, if they incur a loss, they may deduct it from other income they earn, such as Max's accountant income. If they earn a profit, it won't be subject to the net investment income tax.

EXAMPLE 2: Bill is a retired teacher who owns a small apartment building. He spent 600 hours managing the building this year, and worked at no other activity. His wife does not work and is not involved with the rental. Their test answers follow:

- Do they participate in one or more real property businesses? Yes. Bill worked at being a landlord.
- Do they "materially participate" in one or more of such businesses? Yes. Bill spent 600 hours managing his rental—more than enough to materially participate under the 500-hour test.
- Did one person spend at least 51% of their annual work time at a real property business in which they materially participated? Yes. Bill easily satisfies this test because he worked at no non–real-estate activities.
- Did one person spend at least 751 hours per year working at a real property business they materially participated? No. Bill had to spend at least 751 hours working at real property activities to qualify for the exemption. He fails the test because he spent only 600 hours working at his rental.

Bill does not qualify for the exemption. Had he been able to spend an additional 151 hours working at his rental activity, he would have passed the 751-hour test. Alternatively, he could have worked at least 501 hours per year at some other real estate activity, such as selling real estate, and combined those hours with his rental activity hours to satisfy the 751-hour threshold. Had he done either, he could have treated his rental activity as nonpassive because he materially participated in it by working over 500 hours per year at it.

What Happens If You Qualify for the Exemption?

You must determine anew each year whether you qualify for the real estate professional exemption by applying the three tests discussed above. Any year you qualify, the income or loss from your rental property no longer goes into the passive bucket. It is now nonpassive income or loss. Any loss you have from the property may be deducted from your active or portfolio income, but not from any passive income. Likewise, any income from the property may be placed in the active or portfolio bucket and you can use it to offset any losses in those buckets. However, you may not use the exemption to reduce your income for the year to below zero—that is, to create a net operating loss for the year (see "Overview of the Passive Loss Rules," above).

Now, suppose you incurred passive losses from the property in previous years that you weren't able to deduct because you didn't qualify for the exemption or couldn't use the $25,000 offset. These unused passive losses are called "suspended passive losses." They remain passive losses—they stay in your passive bucket. However, you may deduct them from income from your now-exempt rental property income. You can also deduct them from passive income in your passive bucket for the current year, or if you sell the exempt rental property (see "Deducting Suspended Passive Losses," below). Because they're in your passive bucket, you can't deduct these suspended losses from your active or portfolio income. (I.R.C. § 469(f)(1)(C).)

EXAMPLE: Jill owns an apartment building. She has $20,000 of rental income in one year. For the first time, she qualifies for the real estate professional exemption. Jill has $10,000 in suspended rental losses from the property from prior years when she did not qualify for the exemption. She may deduct her $10,000 in suspended losses from her rental property income, leaving her with $10,000 in rental income for the year.

The Real Estate Professional Exemption Is Not Optional

Usually, qualifying for the real estate professional exemption is highly beneficial taxwise. Indeed, real estate professionals who qualify can have a huge financial advantage over those who aren't so lucky, because they can deduct all their rental losses from any nonpassive income.

However, qualifying for the exemption will not benefit you if you have substantial passive income from non–real-estate rental businesses because you can't use your rental losses to offset such passive income. It's left to sit and you can't deduct it until a future year, when you have enough passive losses. If you don't have enough losses, it could sit forever.

EXAMPLE: This year, Felix earns $20,000 in passive income from two limited partnerships. His rental properties have a $20,000 loss. Unfortunately for Felix, he qualifies for the real estate broker exemption from the passive loss rules. This means he must treat the $20,000 in rental losses as nonpassive loss. As a result, he may not deduct it from his $20,000 in passive income.

Unfortunately for people like Felix, the real estate professional exemption is mandatory, not optional. If you qualify, you are not allowed to deduct your losses from your exempt rental real property from passive income. The only way to avoid this is to make sure you don't qualify for the exemption. This is not hard to do—for example, you can hire a management company to manage your rentals for you so you will not materially participate in them. Or, you could just make sure you work less than 751 hours per year in real estate activities.

EXAMPLE: Assume that Felix makes sure he does not qualify for the real estate professional exemption by working less than 751 hours in real estate this year. Now, his $20,000 in rental losses is passive. He may deduct this amount from his $20,000 in passive income from limited partnerships, leaving him with zero passive income to pay tax on.

Record Keeping for the Real Estate Professional Exemption

To know whether you qualify for the real estate professional exemption, you must know how many hours you (and your spouse, if you're married) spent during the year working in (1) real estate businesses of all kinds, (2) rental real estate activities, and (3) all non–real-estate work activities.

If the IRS audits you, you'll need good records of your annual work hours to preserve your real estate professional exemption. Under IRS regulations, you may use any "reasonable means" to keep track of your work time, including daily time reports, logs, appointment books, calendars, or narrative summaries. (IRS Reg. § 1.469-5T(f)(4).) The regulations don't require you to keep contemporaneous records—that is, records made at or near the time you did the work involved—but it is a good practice to do so.

> **CAUTION**
> **You're an IRS target.** The real estate professional exemption has been receiving much attention from the IRS lately. Tax pros report that many of their real estate professional clients are being audited on this issue. This attention is likely to increase in future years because even more landlords seek to qualify for the real estate professional exemption in order to avoid the net investment income tax (see Chapter 19). The best way to protect yourself from the IRS is to keep adequate records.

Many taxpayers keep few or no records of their time. When they get audited, they sit down and write a narrative summary of work they did during the year, with estimates of the time they spent; or they rely on their oral testimony. This approach is a good way to lose your exemption.

> EXAMPLE: Judy Bailey kept a daily calendar for 1997 that listed the number of visits she made to her many rental properties, but the calendar did not quantify the number of hours that she spent on her rental activities. When the IRS audited Judy, she wrote a summary report, in which she generally explained the activities she performed at the rental properties and estimated the number of hours she spent on each rental property. Both the IRS and tax court found this summary to be inadequate. The court noted that Bailey's estimates were uncorroborated by any other evidence. She assigned hours to activities years after the fact, based solely on her judgment and experience as to how much time the activities must have taken her. The court concluded, therefore, that the summary was an unreliable "ballpark guesstimate." Bailey lost her exemption. (*Bailey v. Comm'r.*, T.C. Memo 2001-296.)

You should learn from Judy Bailey's mistakes. Keep careful track of the actual number of hours you (and your spouse) spend working on each activity during the year. You can note your time on a calendar, appointment book, log, or timesheet. It doesn't matter, as long as your records are accurate and believable. Get in the habit of initialing and dating tenant files, financial records, contracts, applications, and other documents you review. This will help document your participation.

If you work a regular job, you should have no problem keeping track of those hours. If you work about the same number of hours each week, you can even dispense with a calendar or other record of this time. Make every effort, however, to keep close track of the time you spend on real estate business activities. Remember, to qualify for the exemption, you'll have to show that you spent at least 51% of your time on real estate activities, and that these activities amounted to at least 751 hours.

Get into the habit of writing down the time you perform *any task* related to a real estate activity. This includes, of course, all the time you spend working on your rental properties. For example, you should include the time you spend:

- showing the property for rental
- taking tenant applications
- screening tenants (including ordering credit reports and evaluating them, and calling references)

- preparing and negotiating leases and other rental agreements
- cleaning and preparing units for rent, including "initiation" time you spend welcoming the tenant to the property and explaining your policies
- doing repairs yourself
- doing improvements yourself or arranging for others to do them
- hiring and supervising a resident manager
- purchasing supplies and materials for your rental business
- inspecting the property
- responding to tenant complaints and inquiries
- collecting and depositing rents
- evicting tenants
- writing and placing advertisements
- creating and maintaining a website you use to promote your rentals attending seminars or other educational events on how to manage rental property, such as educational events sponsored by your local landlord association
- time spent attending landlord association meetings, and
- traveling for any of the activities listed above—however, you can't count travel that constitutes personal commuting (see Chapter 11).

According to the IRS, time you spend traveling to look for new rental properties to purchase can't be included in your rental activity hours because it is an investment activity. Moreover, the IRS also claims that time spent with real property managers does not count either.

If you buy or sell a rental property during the year, keep track of the time involved as well—for example, finding the property, negotiating the purchase, arranging for financing, dealing with escrow, and so forth.

If you have a real estate business other than rentals, keep track of that time as well. For example, if you're a real estate broker, track the time you spend showing properties, marketing your services, and dealing with buyers and sellers.

Deducting Suspended Passive Losses

Rental property passive losses you aren't allowed to deduct the year they are incurred are called "suspended passive losses." They are not lost. Rather, they are carried forward indefinitely until either of two things happen: You have rental income, or you sell the property.

You Must Have Passive Income

You can deduct your suspended losses in any year in which you earn enough passive income. Because they are passive losses, they can't be deducted from your active or portfolio income.

> EXAMPLE: Joe has $10,000 in suspended passive losses from prior years. This year, he had $25,000 in income from his rental properties, and only $20,000 in deductions. So, he has $5,000 in passive income for the year. He may deduct his prior suspended losses from this income, leaving him no rental income to pay tax on for the year. He also earned $80,000 in salary from his job, but he can't deduct his suspended losses from this active income. He must carry forward his remaining $5,000 in suspended losses to future years.

The $25,000 Offset

Suspended losses may also be deducted by using the $25,000 offset. You can do this for any suspended loss from a property in which you actively participated during the year the loss was incurred.

> EXAMPLE: Tom had a $10,000 loss from his rental activities this year. He has $15,000 in suspended losses from the last two years (in both years, he actively participated in his rental activity). Because he qualifies for the $25,000 offset this year, he may deduct his $10,000 passive loss from this year and his $15,000 suspended losses from prior years.

The Real Estate Professional Exemption

If you qualify for the real estate professional exemption to the PAL rules, you may deduct your suspended losses from income you earn from the property.

Profits From Sale of Property

Finally, you may deduct your suspended passive losses from the profit you earn when you sell your rental property. To deduct your suspended losses upon sale, you must:

- sell "substantially all" of your interest in the rental activity
- sell to an unrelated party—that is, a person other than your spouse, brothers, sisters, ancestors (parents, grandparents), lineal descendants (children, grandchildren), or a corporation or partnership in which you own more than 50% (100% of your ownership interest), and
- the sale must be a taxable event—that is, you must recognize income or loss for tax purposes; this means tax-deferred Section 1031 exchanges don't count, except to the extent you recognize any taxable income. (I.R.C. § 469(g).)

To deduct your suspended losses from your profit, you must sell substantially all of your rental activity. If you own only one rental property, that property is your entire rental activity. If you own two or more properties, each property will be a separate rental activity unless you elected to group them together. As discussed above, such grouping can help you satisfy the material participation requirement if you want to qualify for the real estate professional exemption from the PAL rules. But it can lead to problems when you sell only one of your grouped properties and try to deduct any suspended losses you have for the property.

> **EXAMPLE:** Callie buys three rental houses in 2016. By 2022, she has $20,000 in suspended losses for each house. She decides she's had enough of the PAL rules and qualifies for the real estate professional exemption

by becoming a real estate sales agent. To meet the material participation requirements, she elects in 2022 to treat all three houses as one rental activity. This year, she sells one of the houses. She can't deduct her $20,000 in suspended losses because she hasn't sold substantially all her rental activity—the activity consists of three houses, and she has sold only one. Had Callie not elected to group her three houses into one activity, each one would be its own rental activity and she could deduct her suspended losses when she sold each one.

It's not entirely clear how much of your activity you must sell to sell substantially all of it—for example, if you own three properties you have elected to group together as one activity, must you sell all three or will two do? If you're presented with this problem, consult a tax professional.

If you meet the requirements for deducting profits from a sale, deduct your suspended losses in the following order:

- first, against income the passive rental activity earned during the year and any gain from its sale
- then, against net income earned during the year from all other passive activities, and
- lastly, from any other income—that is, income from nonpassive activities (active and portfolio income). (I.R.C. § 469(g)(1).)

EXAMPLE: Jason owns a rental house from which he has $60,000 in suspended losses. This year, Jason received $5,000 in income from the house, which was passive income. He also earned $90,000 in salary for the year, and $5,000 in passive income from a limited partnership interest he owns. Jason sells his house for a $30,000 profit. He deducts his $60,000 in suspended losses as follows:

First, against the $5,000 passive income he earned from the house and his $30,000 profit from its sale. This leaves $25,000 in suspended losses ($60,000 − $35,000 = $25,000); next, against the income from his other passive activities—this is the $5,000 income he had from his limited partnership interest. This leaves $20,000 in suspended losses; and finally, from his $90,000 salary income, reducing his taxable income to $70,000 for the year.

As you can see from the example, if you have enough suspended losses, you may be able to deduct them from nonpassive income, such as salary income, that you earned during the year you sold your rental property.

Tax Reporting for Passive Rental Losses

The IRS wants to know if you have rental losses. They designed Schedule E to show them. The form requires you to separately deduct your expenses from your income for each rental property you own. The form will show if you have net income or loss for each rental property.

You might also have to complete IRS Form 8582, *Passive Activity Loss Limitations*. This complex tax form requires you to list your current and suspended losses for each rental property, and any other passive activities you are engaged in. You then go through several calculations to figure your deductible passive loss for the year, and the amount of passive loss you must carry forward to future years.

If you qualify for the $25,000 offset, you might not have to file Form 8582. This permits you to deduct up to $25,000 in passive losses from rental property, but your adjusted gross income (modified by some special rules) must be below $150,000. If you qualify for the offset, you don't need to file Form 8582 so long as the following are true:

- Your rental real estate activities were your only passive activities.
- Your have no suspended losses or tax credits from prior years for your rental.
- Your total losses from your rentals were not more than $25,000.
- Your modified adjusted gross income was not more than $100,000.
- You don't own any rental real estate as a limited partner.

So, before you go to the trouble of filling out Form 8582, determine if you qualify for the $25,000 offset and meet the above requirements.

Strategies for Dealing With the Passive Loss Rules

If you are unable to get full relief from the PAL rules through the $25,000 offset and/or real estate professional exemption, there are some things you can do to limit their impact.

Lower Your Rental Expenses

The PAL rules bar you from deducting your rental expenses from non-passive income—income from your rental properties or other passive activities. If you don't have enough passive income to deduct all your losses, you can reduce your losses by lowering your expenses. For example, you could:

- pay less mortgage interest on your rental properties by borrowing less money—make a larger down payment when you buy the property or pay down your mortgage. (If you have substantial investments that generate portfolio income, such as stocks and bonds, you could sell them and use the money for this purpose.)
- spend less on repairs and other operating expenses, or
- defer expenses to future years when you might have more passive income.

Generate More Passive Income

Generate more passive income to soak up your passive losses. The two ways to do this are:

- invest in a rental property or other business that produces passive income (only businesses in which you don't materially participate produce passive income), or
- sell your rental property or another passive activity you own, such as a limited partnership interest.

CAUTION

Passive income may be subject to net investment income tax.
If you have passive losses, passive income is a great thing to have. However, passive income can be too much of a good thing. If your passive income exceeds your passive losses, you'll have to add it to your taxable income for the year. It will be subject not only to regular income tax, but to the new 3.8% net investment income tax if your adjusted gross income exceeds $200,000 if you're single and $250,000 if you're married and filing jointly. (See Chapter 19.)

Some investments are especially designed to produce passive income to soak up passive losses—these are called "passive income generators"—PIGs for short. Limited partnerships that invest in real estate that generates substantial annual income, such as conference centers, golf courses, and ski resorts, often fall into this category. Such PIGs are syndicated—that is, they're offered to the public through public offerings—and are actively marketed by brokers. If you're interested in investing in a PIG, you'll have no trouble finding out about them from stockbrokers, financial planners, financial publications, or the internet. Of course, you should be careful when making any investment.

One way you can't generate more passive income to absorb your rental income is to rent to a business you own or materially participate in. Under the "self-rental rule," such income is recharacterized as nonpassive and can't be used to offset real estate rental losses. (*Beecher v. Comm'r.*, 481 F.3d 717 (9th Cir. 2007); Treas. Reg. 1.469-2(f)(6).)

> EXAMPLE: Gary and Dolores Beecher are a married couple who owned two corporations engaged in the business of repairing automobile interiors and exteriors. They also owned five rental properties that resulted in substantial annual losses. The Beechers had a great idea: Because they worked out of their home, they would lease their home office to their corporation. They would use this lease income—ordinarily, passive income—to offset the losses from their rentals. As a result of this combination of income and losses, the Beechers paid no tax on the rental income paid to them by their corporations—this amounted to over $85,000 of tax-free income over three years. Unfortunately, the IRS audited the Beechers and recharacterized their rental income from their corporations as active, not passive, income.

So, it could not be used to offset their rental losses. Under the self-rental rule, income from the rental of property for use in a trade or business in which the taxpayer materially participates is treated as nonpassive income. The courts upheld the IRS's ruling.

Annual Loss Limits

Depending on the year involved, an annual limit could apply to the total losses you are allowed to deduct on your tax return. The limits are quite high, so they don't affect most small landlords.

Losses Before 2018

Before 2018, real estate professionals who materially participated in their rental activities could deduct an unlimited amount of rental losses each year from their other nonrental (nonpassive) income.

Losses Incurred 2018–2020

The Tax Cuts and Jobs Act (TCJA) established a new limit on deducting business losses by taxpayers other than regular C corporations, which affected the vast majority of rental property owners. As originally enacted, the TCJA provided that, starting in 2018 and continuing through 2025, single taxpayers could deduct no more than $250,000 per year in business losses, including rental business losses, over their rental and other business income. Married taxpayers filing jointly could deduct no more than $500,000. These numbers are adjusted for inflation—for 2022, the limits were $270,000/$540,000.

In other words, a landlord could deduct losses equal to his or her total income from the rental business and any other businesses and an additional $250,000 or $500,000. The effect was that no more than $250,000/$500,000 in rental losses could be deducted from nonrental income in any one year during 2018 through 2025 (plus an amount for the inflation adjustment). Excess losses had to be deducted in future years as part of the taxpayer's net operating loss (NOL).

However, the CARES Act that Congress enacted in 2020 eliminated the annual limit for losses incurred during 2018 through 2020. Such losses were fully deductible (subject to the passive loss and at-risk rules). Taxpayers who were unable to deduct part of their losses for 2018 or 2019 due to the limit may amend their returns for the years involved to claim them.

Losses Incurred 2021–2026

Losses incurred during 2021 through 2026 are subject to an annual limit, which is adjusted for inflation each year. For 2022, the limit was $270,000 for singles and $540,000 for married taxpayers filing jointly. Unused losses—called "excess business losses"—must be deducted in future years as part of the taxpayer's net operating loss (NOL) carryforward.

Excess business losses are calculated as follows:

4. Add all your income for the year from all your businesses, rental and nonrental, plus wage income.
5. Add to this total $270,000 if single or $540,000 if married filing jointly—this is the total amount of losses you may deduct.
6. Subtract this amount from your total rental and other business losses for the year—any positive number is an excess business loss.

> **EXAMPLE:** Sheila, a single taxpayer, is a successful real estate broker who also owns multiple rental properties, which she has grouped together for passive loss purposes. She qualifies as a real estate professional and materially participates in her rental activity. So, the passive loss rules don't prevent her from deducting her losses from her nonpassive income. In 2022, she earned $100,000 from her real estate brokerage business (and had no other income) and she had $400,000 in rental losses. Her excess business loss is $30,000 ($400,000 − (100,000 + $270,000) = $30,000).

If rental property is owned through a multimember LLC taxed as a partnership or an S corporation, the $270,000/$540,000 limit applies to each owner's or member's share of the pass-through's losses.

The limit applies after the passive loss rules are applied. Presumably, if a rental loss is disallowed under the passive loss rules, any deductions or income from the activity would not be considered in calculating an excess business loss.

The excess business loss limitation applies to the total (aggregate) income and deductions from all of a taxpayer's trades or businesses, including rental and nonrental businesses. If spouses filing jointly have separate businesses, the $524,000 limit applies to the total income and deductions from all of their businesses, rental and nonrental.

Losses Incurred 2027 and Later

The loss rules are scheduled to revert to their pre-2018 form starting in 2027, with no limits on loss deductions (unless the law is changed again).

At-Risk Rules

Yet another set of rules, in addition to the passive loss rules, might limit your deductions for your rental real estate losses. These rules are the at-risk rules. Fortunately, these rules aren't nearly as complicated as the PAL rules and they don't apply to most landlords. You usually don't have to worry about the at-risk rules unless you obtain seller financing or a loan from a relative at unusually favorable terms. The rules don't apply at all to rental property placed in service before 1987.

To prevent abusive tax shelters, the at-risk rules limit your annual deductible losses to the amount of money that you have at risk. At risk has nothing to do with insurance, and having insurance will not render you not at risk. At risk means how much money you could lose if a business activity goes belly-up. You are at risk to the extent of your investment in the activity.

In the case of rental real estate activities, you are at risk for:

- the total amount of cash you invest—for example, your cash down payment to purchase a rental property
- the adjusted basis of property you contribute to the activity, and
- most loans you obtain to purchase or otherwise operate your rental activity. (I.R.C. § 465.)

Most landlords borrow money to purchase their rental properties, and it is these borrowed funds that make up the great bulk of their at-risk amounts. You may include in your at-risk amount the amount of any type of loan you use for your real estate activity, except for nonrecourse loans from:

- the seller of the property or a person related to the seller
- a person who is related to you and gives you a loan at below-market rates or with other unusually favorable terms, or
- a person who receives a fee due to your investment in the real property or a person related to that person—for example, a real estate broker.

A "nonrecourse loan" is a loan for which you are not personally liable. The lender's only recourse if you fail to pay is to foreclose on the property. The mortgage document for a nonrecourse loan will contain an exculpatory clause providing that the borrower is not personally liable for the loan. A loan is a "recourse loan" if you are personally liable if it is not repaid on time—that is, the lender can not only foreclose on the property, but also get a deficiency judgment against you for the difference between the property's value at foreclosure and the amount you owe. With this deficiency judgment in hand, the lender can then go after your personal assets, such as your personal bank accounts.

However, you may include in your at-risk amount nonrecourse loans you obtain from banks, savings and loans, and other companies in the business of making real estate loans, or loans obtained from or guaranteed by the government. What all this means is that you may include all your borrowed funds in your at-risk amount unless you obtain seller financing or get a below-market nonrecourse loan from a relative. A person is related to you for these purposes if that person is your spouse, brother, sister, ancestor (parent, grandparents), or lineal descendant (child or grandchild).

> EXAMPLE 1: Stuart buys a rental home by making a $20,000 down payment and borrowing $180,000 from a bank. He is at risk for $200,000. This year, he loses $10,000 on the property. This amount is far less than his at-risk amount, so it doesn't affect his ability to deduct the loss.

EXAMPLE 2: Assume that, instead of using conventional financing as in the example above, Stuart purchases his home using creative financing. He gives the seller $1,000 cash and a car with an adjusted basis of $4,000. He borrows the remaining $195,000 from the seller, agreeing to a nonrecourse loan. Now, Stuart is at risk for only $5,000, because the $195,000 loan is not included in his at-risk amount. If he loses $10,000 on his property this year, he may only deduct $5,000. The remaining $5,000 loss is suspended and must be carried over to a future year when he has a sufficient amount at risk.

The at-risk rules are applied before the passive loss rules. So, Stuart in the example above would be left with a $5,000 passive loss. He would then determine if he could deduct this loss by applying the PAL rules and exceptions discussed above.

If the at-risk rules prevent you from deducting a loss, you'll have to fill out IRS Form 6198, *At-Risk Limitations.*

If you purchase a rental property with seller financing, you need to carefully consider the effect of the at-risk rules. You might consider avoiding or limiting their application by obtaining at least some conventional financing, or by borrowing less by making a larger down payment.

How to Deduct Rental Losses

If, after applying the PAL rules and at-risk rules discussed above, you have a deductible loss from your real estate rentals, transfer it from your Schedule E to Schedule 1, Part 1 of your IRS Form 1040. Use the loss to reduce the taxable income you report on your Form 1040 for the year. The loss can be deducted from any income—active, passive, or portfolio. If you have other losses, you can deduct those losses from your income for the year as well. Other losses could include:

- casualty losses (see Chapter 14)
- deductible losses from other businesses you're involved in other than real estate, and
- losses incurred when you sell or otherwise dispose of rental or business property.

If your total losses for the year exceed all your annual income from whatever source, you have an NOL.

> **EXAMPLE:** Maya lost $100,000 from her rental business this year and had $50,000 in total nonrental income. Her NOL for the year is $50,000. However, figuring the amount of an NOL is not always as simple as deducting your losses from your annual income. Tax preparation software can do the calculations for you.

The rules for deducting NOLs differ according to the years they were incurred. For this reason, you need to track each year's NOL separately.

NOLs for 2017 and Earlier

For 2017 and earlier, landlords could "carry a loss back"—that is, they could apply an NOL to past tax years by filing an application for a refund or an amended return. Carrying an NOL back means you deduct the NOL amount from your taxable income for prior years. This enables you to get a refund for all or part of the taxes you paid in past years. NOLs could generally be carried back two years, and then carried forward 20 years. Moreover, NOLs could reduce taxable income to zero in the carryback or carryforward years. You also had the option to elect to only carry an NOL forward to future years.

> **EXAMPLE:** Maya incurred a $50,000 NOL for 2017. She could carry the full amount back to 2015. So, she deducts $50,000 from her 2015 income, reducing her 2015 taxable income and resulting in a refund of all or part of the tax she paid that year. If part of the $50,000 NOL is left after reducing her 2015 income to zero, the remaining amount is carried forward to 2016 and then to 2018 and future years. She also had the option of waiving the carryback and carrying the $50,000 forward to 2018 where it could offset up to 100% of her income. Any unused amount could be carried forward up to 20 years.

These rules continue to apply for NOLs incurred in 2017 and earlier.

NOLs for 2018 Through 2020

The Tax Cuts and Jobs Act (TCJA) radically changed NOL deductions starting in 2018. However, Congress temporarily delayed these restrictive new rules in response to the COVID-19 pandemic.

The TCJA eliminated all carrybacks of NOLs. Instead, taxpayers were only allowed to deduct them in any number of future years. Moreover, an NOL could only offset up to 80% of taxable income (before the pass-through deduction) for any year.

> **EXAMPLE:** Assume that Maya from the previous example incurred her $50,000 NOL in 2018. Because of the TCJA, she could not carry it back to 2016 and obtain a refund of the tax she paid that year. She could only carry it forward to 2019, when it could only offset a maximum of 80% of her income. Any remaining amount had to be deducted in 2020 and later.

Due to the economic devastation that the COVID-19 pandemic caused, Congress amended the NOL rules for 2018 through 2020 to make it easier to deduct NOLs. For these years, an NOL could be carried back five years and then carried forward indefinitely until used up. Ordinarily, you must carry an NOL back to the earliest year within the carryback period in which there is taxable income, then to the next earliest year, and so on. Also, NOLs for these years may offset 100% of taxable income to reduce the tax liability to zero.

> **EXAMPLE:** Assume that Maya from the previous examples incurred her $50,000 NOL in 2020. She may carry it back to 2015 to reduce her taxable income for that year and obtain a refund of up to 100% of the tax she paid. If she has any NOL amount remaining after reducing her 2015 taxable income to zero, it is applied to tax years 2016 through 2019 in turn. Any remaining NOL is then applied to 2021 and any number of future years until used up. Alternatively, Maya could elect only to carry her NOL forward to 2021 and future years.

You didn't have to carry back an NOL for 2018 through 2020 for five years if you didn't want to. You could elect to apply the NOL only to future years by attaching a statement to your tax return for the year. To do so, you had to affirmatively waive the carryback by attaching a statement to your tax return. You had to include a separate statement for each year for which you waived the NOL carryback and state that you elected to apply Revenue Procedure 2020-24.

The decision to carry back an NOL was made on a year-by-year basis. For example, if you had NOLs for 2018 and 2019, you could carry back the 2018 NOL but elect to only carry forward the 2019 NOL. For 2018 and 2019 NOLs, you had to make this election on your 2020 tax return. For 2020, you made it with your 2021 return.

NOLs for 2021 and Later

The NOL rules the TCJA initially put in place in 2018, and then postponed for 2018–2020, returned for 2021 and later. So, for 2021 and later years, you may only deduct NOLs for the current year and any number of future years. You may not carry them back to deduct in past years. In addition, NOLs for these years may only offset up to 80% of taxable income (before the pass-through deduction) for any year.

If, in addition to carrying forward a regular NOL, you have suspended passive activity losses from prior years you're carrying forward, the PAL carryforward is applied first against passive income before the regular NOL is applied against all your income.

Annual Dollar Limit on NOL Deduction

Another change the TCJA made was to limit deductions of "excess business losses" by individual business owners during 2018 through 2025. Married taxpayers filing jointly could deduct no more than $519,000 per year in total business losses. Individual taxpayers could deduct no more than $259,000. Unused losses had to be deducted in any number of future years as part of the taxpayer's NOL carryforward.

Congress eliminated this dollar limitation for losses incurred during 2018 through 2020. So, taxpayers with very large losses for any of these years could deduct them in full.

The excess business loss limit returned for 2021 and was extended through 2026. For 2022, NOLs are limited to $270,000 for individual taxpayers and $540,000 for married taxpayers filing jointly. Losses over these amounts must be carried forward and deducted in future years.

Claiming an NOL Refund

There are two ways to claim a refund for prior years' taxes due to an NOL. The quickest way is to file IRS Form 1045, *Application for Tentative Refund.* If you file Form 1045, the IRS is required to send your refund within 90 days. Additionally, the IRS makes only a limited examination of the claim for omissions and computational errors.

You must file Form 1045 within one year after the end of the year in which the NOL arose.

The other way to deduct an NOL is to amend your tax return for the year involved by filing IRS Form 1040-X, *Amended U.S. Individual Income Tax Return.* You have three years after the end of the tax year to file Form 1040-X.

RESOURCE

Need to know more about NOLs? Refer to IRS Publication 536, *Net Operating Losses (NOLs) for Individuals, Estates, and Trusts,* for more information. You can download it from the IRS website at www.irs.gov, or obtain a paper copy by calling the IRS at 800-TAX-FORM.

Record Keeping and Accounting

Your deductions for your rental activities are only as good as the records you keep to back them up. Any deduction you forget to claim on your tax return, or lose after an IRS audit because you lack adequate records, costs you dearly. Every $100 in unclaimed deductions costs the average midlevel-income landlord (in a 24% tax bracket) $24 in additional federal income taxes. This chapter shows you how to document your expenditures and other deductions so you won't end up paying more tax than you have to.

What Records Do You Need?

If, like most small landlords, you haven't formed a separate business entity to own your property and have no employees, you need just two types of records for tax purposes:

- a record of your rental income and expenses, and
- supporting documents for your income and expenses.

You need records of your income and expenses to figure out whether your rental activity earned a taxable profit or incurred a deductible loss during the year. You'll also have to summarize your rental income and expenses for each rental property in your tax return (IRS Schedule E).

You need receipts and other supporting documents, such as credit card records and canceled checks, to serve as insurance in case you're audited by the IRS. These supporting documents enable you to prove to the IRS that your claimed expenses are genuine. Some expenses—travel, for example—require particularly stringent documentation. Without this paper trail, you'll lose valuable deductions in the event of an audit. Remember, if you're audited, it's up to you to prove that your deductions are legitimate.

If you own more than one rental property, you must separately keep track of your income and expenses for each property—don't mix them together. One reason for this inconvenient rule is that the IRS requires that you separately list your income and expenses for each property on your Schedule E. Also, you'll never know how much money you're making or losing on each property unless you separately track your income and expenses.

Paper Versus Electronic Records

The first choice you need to make is whether to keep paper records you create by hand or to use computerized electronic record keeping. Either method is acceptable to the IRS.

Although it might seem old-fashioned, many small landlord owners keep their records by hand on paper, especially when they are first starting out. You can use a columnar pad, notebook paper, or blank ledger books. Also, "one-write systems" allow you to write checks and keep track of expenses simultaneously.

Manual bookkeeping might take a bit more time than using a computer, but it has the advantage of simplicity. You'll always be better off using handwritten ledger sheets, which are easy to create and understand and simple to keep up to date, instead of a complicated computer program that you don't understand or use properly.

If you want to use electronic record keeping, many options are available to choose from. These options range from simple checkbook programs to sophisticated property management software. We won't discuss how to use these programs in detail. You'll need to read the manual or tutorial that comes with the program you choose. However, if you're not prepared to invest the time to use a computer program correctly, don't use it!

Create Your Own Spreadsheet

You can create your own spreadsheet to keep track of your expenses and income with a program such as *Excel*. Use one spreadsheet per rental and then total them all at the end of the year. See the discussion on how to track business expenses to see what you should include in your spreadsheet.

Software

You can use different software options to help you track your finances. Before getting one, make sure you understand what it offers and how you would use it. You don't want to get something too advanced if a simpler program will do because the more advanced programs can be harder to use and understand. Try to find the one that best suits your needs.

Personal Finance Software

A personal finance program, such as *Quicken*, might be perfectly adequate for a landlord with just a few units. These programs are easy to use because they work off of a computerized checkbook. When you buy something for your rental, you write a check using the program. It automatically inputs the data into a computerized check register, and you print out the check using your computer (payments can also be made online). You'll have to input credit card and cash payments separately.

You create a list of expense categories just like you do when you create a ledger sheet or spreadsheet. Programs like *Quicken* come with preselected categories, but these are not adequate for landlords, so you'll probably have to create your own. The expense category is automatically noted in your register when you write a check.

The program can then take this information and automatically create income and expense reports—that is, it will show you the amounts you've spent or earned for each category, serving the same purpose as the expense journal. It can also create profit and loss statements.

Small Business Accounting Software

Small business accounting programs, such as *QuickBooks* by Intuit, can do everything personal financial software can do and much more, including create bills, reconcile bank accounts, generate sophisticated reports, create budgets, track employee time, calculate payroll withholding, and generate and maintain fixed asset records.

These programs are more expensive than personal finance software and are harder to learn to use. If you don't need their advanced features, there is no reason to use one of them. A list and comparison of most available accounting software packages and online subscription services can be found at http://en.wikipedia.org/wiki/Comparison_of_accounting_software.

Property Management Software

Many software applications are designed specifically for rental property management, including *Quicken Rental Property Manager, Buildium, Yardi*, and *VMS*. These applications can be particularly helpful if you own more than ten units. In addition, Apartments.com has a free online landlord expense tracking app. These applications have features designed specifically with landlords in mind. For example, they can:

- identify tax-deductible rental property expenses
- track income and expenses by property
- create a Schedule E report to save you time on taxes
- show which rents have been paid
- show how rental properties are doing, and
- store lease terms, rental rates, and security deposits for each tenant.

If you're interested, you should visit the websites for these applications, try a demo, and see if you need and like their advanced features.

Special Concerns When You Hire Employees

If you have employees—such as a resident manager—you must create and keep a number of records, including payroll tax records, withholding records, and employment tax returns. And you must keep these records for four years.

For detailed information, see IRS Publication 15, Circular E, *Employer's Tax Guide*. You can download it from the IRS website at www.irs.gov. Also, contact your state tax agency for your state's requirements. A list of all 50 state tax agency websites can be found at the Federation of Tax Administrators website, at www.taxadmin.org.

A Simple Record-Keeping System

Here's a simple record-keeping system you can use if you own only a few rental units. You can implement it entirely by hand, or combine it with software applications such as spreadsheets.

An Easy Filing System

You will need to establish a system to deal with all your receipts, canceled checks, credit card statements, income and expense journals, and other records. Here's one way to do this:

- Each year, get a separate accordion folder for each rental property you own and label it with the name of the property—for example, 123 Main Street. This folder will contain your records for all your rental units at a single address. (If you choose, you can use a filing cabinet instead of an accordion folder.)
- Place several manila folders in the accordion folder: one for each expense category you have and one folder for your asset records.
- Once a month, file your receipts in the proper manila folders in chronological order—do this at the same time you complete your expense journal. If a receipt applies to more than one property, make copies to file with your receipts for each property.
- Keep the bank statement for your rental checking account and credit card statements for your rental credit card together in chronological order. Use a separate accordion folder for this with files for each month of the year.
- Keep your income and expense journals and depreciation worksheet in your accordion folder for the appropriate property.
- At the end of the calendar year, safely store your accordion folders to use when you (or your accountant) prepare your tax returns. Make sure it contains all your receipts, income and expense journals, depreciation worksheet, car mileage records, listed property journal, appointment book or calendar, and any other records you'll need to prepare your tax returns.
- Get a new accordion folder and create a new set of records for the new year. (The folders are a tax-deductible supplies expense.)

Separate Checkbook and Credit Cards

One of the first things you should do (if you haven't done it already) is set up a separate checking account for your rental activity. Your rental checkbook will serve as your basic source of information for recording your rental expenses and income. Deposit all of your rental income into the account and make rental-related payments by check from the account. Don't use your rental account to pay for personal expenses or your personal account to pay for rental activity items.

Using a separate account will provide these important benefits:

- It will be much easier for you to keep track of your rental income and expenses if you pay them from a separate account.
- Your rental account will clearly separate your personal and rental activity finances; this will prove very helpful if the IRS audits you.
- Your rental account will help convince the IRS that your rental is a for-profit activity. People with not-for-profit activities don't generally have separate bank accounts to fund their pursuits. (See Chapter 2 for more on establishing your tax status.)

 CAUTION
Some states require landlords to use a separate account for tenants' security deposits. Check your state's laws, available online at www.nolo.com and in *Every Landlord's Legal Guide,* by Marcia Stewart, Janet Portman, and Ann O'Connell (Nolo). If your state requires a separate account, you might need to establish two accounts for your business—one for general rental activity, and one for security deposits.

Use a Separate Credit Card for Rental Activity Expenses

Use a separate credit card for rental activity expenses instead of putting both personal and rental items on one card. Credit card interest for rental activity purchases is 100% deductible, while interest for personal purchases is not deductible at all (see Chapter 8). Using a separate card for rental-related purchases will make it much easier for you to keep track of how much interest you've paid for such purchases. If you have more than one personal credit card, you can use one for your rental activity only—you don't need to get a special business credit card.

Dealing With Receipts, Canceled Checks, and Other Supporting Documents

The IRS lives by the maxim "Figures lie and liars figure." It knows very well that you can claim anything in your books and on your tax returns, because you create or complete them yourself. For this reason, the IRS requires that you have documents to support the deductions you claim on your tax return. In the absence of a supporting document, an IRS auditor may conclude that an item you claim as a rental activity expense is really a personal expense, or that you never bought the item at all. Either way, your deduction will be disallowed or reduced.

The supporting documents you need depend on the type of deduction. However, at a minimum, every deduction should be supported by documentation showing:

- what you purchased for your rental activity
- how much you paid for it, and
- whom (or what company) you bought it from.

You must meet additional record-keeping requirements for local transportation, travel, meal, and gift deductions, as well as for certain long-term assets that you buy for your rental activity. (These rules are covered below.)

You can meet the basic requirements by keeping the following types of documentation:

- canceled checks
- sales receipts
- account statements
- credit card sales slips
- invoices, and
- petty cash slips for small cash payments (these are preprinted receipts that say you paid in cash; you can get them at any stationery store).

Canceled Check + Receipt = Proof of Deduction

We're about to disabuse you of a commonly held belief—that a canceled check will prove that you purchased the item it paid for, especially if you note on the check (or on your register) what the check was for. For example, suppose Manny owns three rental houses. He buys a $500 snowblower to use at his rental properties from the local home supply store. He writes a check for the amount and gets a receipt. How does he prove to the IRS that he has a $500 rental expense?

Make Digital Copies of Your Receipts

According to an old Chinese proverb, the palest ink is more reliable than the most retentive memory. But when it comes to receipts, ink is no longer so reliable. Receipts printed on thermal paper (as most are) fade over time. By the time the IRS audits your return, you might find that all or most of the paper receipts you've carefully retained in your files are unreadable.

Because of the fading problem, you should photocopy your receipts if you intend to rely on hard copies. Obviously, this process is time consuming and annoying. But an easier alternative is available: Make digital copies of your receipts and throw away the hard copies.

Many inexpensive smartphone applications can help you copy and keep track of receipts. Two of the most popular are Shoeboxed.com and Expensify.com. Using these and other similar apps, you can add notes and then upload the digital photos to an online account for permanent storage. These apps can even automatically categorize your expenses, and you can export your data to *QuickBooks*, *Quicken*, *Excel*, *Freshbooks*, and other accounting software.

Manny assumes that if he saves his canceled check when it's returned from his bank, that's all the proof he needs. He's wrong. All a canceled check proves is that he spent money for something. It doesn't prove what he bought. Of course, Manny can write a note on his check describing what he purchased, but why should the IRS believe what he writes on his checks himself?

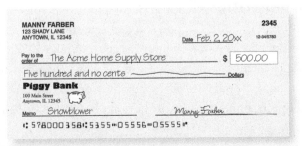

Does Manny's sales receipt prove that he bought his snowblower for his rental activity? Again, no. A sales receipt proves only that somebody purchased the item listed in the receipt. It doesn't show who purchased it. You could write a note on the receipt stating that you bought the item, but you could easily lie. Indeed, for all the IRS knows, you could hang around stores and pick up receipts people throw away to give yourself tax deductions.

Acme Home Supply Store 4546 Main Street Anytown, IL 12345						**509257**	
CUSTOMER'S ORDER NO. 14601				DATE February 1, 20xx			
NAME							
ADDRESS							
CITY, STATE, ZIP							
SOLD BY SF	CASH	C.O.D.	CHARGE	ON ACCT.	MDSE. RETD.	PAID OUT	
QUAN.		DESCRIPTION				PRICE	AMOUNT
1	1	Snow Blower 500				500	500
2							
3							
4							
5							
6							
7							
8							
9							
10							
11						Total	500
12							
RECEIVED BY							
KEEP THIS SLIP FOR REFERENCE							

However, when you put a canceled check together with a sales receipt (or an invoice, a cash register tape, or a similar document), you have concrete proof that you purchased the item listed in the receipt. The check proves that you bought something, and the receipt proves what that something is.

This two-step process doesn't necessarily prove that you bought the item for your rental, but it's a good start. Often, the face of a receipt, sales slip, or the payee's name on your canceled check will strongly indicate that the item you purchased was for your rental activity. But if it's not clear, note the purpose of the purchase on the document. Such a note is not proof of how you used the item, but it will be helpful.

For some types of items that you use for both rental and personal purposes—computers are one example—you might be required to keep careful records of your use. (See "Asset Records," below, for the stricter rules that apply to these types of expenses.)

Credit Cards

Using a credit card is a great way to pay rental expenses. The credit card slip will prove that you bought the item listed on the slip. You'll also have a monthly statement to back up your credit card slips.

Account Statements

Sometimes, you'll need to use an account statement to prove an expense. Some banks no longer return canceled checks, or you might pay for something with an ATM card, PayPal, or another electronic funds transfer method. Moreover, you might not always have a credit card slip when you pay by credit card—for example, when you buy an item over the internet. In these situations, the IRS will accept an account statement as proof that you purchased the item. The chart below shows what type of information you need on an account statement.

Proving Payments With Bank Statements	
If payment is by:	**The statement must show:**
Check	Check number Amount Payee's name Date the check amount was posted to the account by the bank
Electronic funds transfer	Amount transferred Payee's name Date the amount transferred was posted to the account by the bank
Credit card	Amount charged Payee's name Transaction date

Filing Your Receipts

If you pay an expense with a check, note the check number on the receipt. If you pay by credit card, mark it with the code CC. If you own multiple rental properties, indicate which property the receipt is for by marking it with a code. Make up any code that makes sense to you—for example, "Main St." You don't need to note the unit number, even if a check was for an expense for a specific unit. If a receipt applies to all your properties, say so on it (and make duplicates to place in each property's folder). File your receipts by expense category.

Expense Journal

You need to keep track of what you spend on your rental properties. Track your expenses by creating an expense journal—a listing of all your expenses by category. This will show what you buy for your rental activity and how much you spent. It's very easy to do this. You can write your journal out on paper, or you can set up a computer spreadsheet program, such as *Excel*, to do it. Or, if you already have or would prefer to use a financial computer program, such as *Quicken*, you can do that instead. You can also use programs especially designed for landlords, such as *Quicken Rental Property Manager* or *Buildium*.

Creating an Expense Journal

You can easily create an expense journal by using paper divided into columns, or by using a professional multicolumn book you can get from any stationery or office supply store. These multicolumn pages are also called "ledger sheets." Get ledger sheets with at least 14 columns. Devote a separate column to each major category of expense you have. Alternatively, you can purchase accounting record books with the rental expense categories already printed on them.

Your rental expense categories in your expense journal should be keyed to the categories on IRS Schedule E, the tax form you file to report your rental expenses and income. This is how the IRS wants you to categorize your expenses when you report them on your taxes, so you should use these categories in your records. This way, you simply transfer the totals from your records to your Schedule E when you do your taxes.

Schedule E lists 13 expense categories:

- advertising
- auto and travel
- cleaning and maintenance
- commissions
- insurance
- legal and other professional fees
- management fees
- mortgage interest paid to banks
- other interest
- repairs
- supplies
- taxes, and
- utilities.

The ins and outs of Schedule E are discussed in Chapter 18. Refer to that chapter if you need more information about these categories. You might not need to use all of these categories—for example, if you manage your rentals by yourself, you probably don't need the management fees or commissions categories.

The Schedule E categories probably include most of your expenses, but you might have others that are not listed—for example:

- home office expenses
- gifts
- homeowners' association dues for rental condominiums and planned-unit developments
- start-up expenses
- telephone expenses
- employee expenses
- education expenses
- casualty losses, and
- equipment rental.

You should also have one final category called "miscellaneous" for occasional expenses that don't fit any existing category. But don't use a miscellaneous category on your Schedule E—it's not allowed. You must have a descriptive category for each expense; you can't claim an expense as miscellaneous.

Don't list your depreciation expenses in your expense journal. These belong in your separate asset records.

You won't need a category for your car expenses unless you use the actual expense method to figure your deduction.

Now, sit down with your bills and receipts and sort them into categorized piles to determine which categories you need in your expense journal. In separate columns, list the check number, date, and name of the person or company paid for each transaction. If you pay by credit card or check, indicate it in the check number column.

Once a month, go through your check register, credit card slips, receipts, and other expense records and record the required information for each transaction. Also, total the amounts for each category when you come to the end of the page and keep a running total of what you've spent for each category for the year to date. After recording the expense, you should file the receipts, checks, and so on in the appropriate manila folder.

Rental Income Journal

Of course, you must also keep track of how much money you earn from your rentals and report it to the IRS on your Schedule E. This amount will primarily consist of the rent you collect. But it could also include:

- fees you charge tenants for paying rent late
- garage or other parking charges
- interest you earn on tenant security deposits
- security deposits you retain to pay for repairs, unpaid rent, or other expenses
- laundry income
- the value of services tenants provide in lieu of rent, or
- payments tenants make to you for repairs or other expenses. (See Chapter 4.)

Allocating Expenses Among Multiple Properties

If you own more than one rental property, some of the items you buy will benefit more than just one property. Good examples are tools and office supplies you use for all your properties, or legal, accounting, or other professional services that apply to all your properties. In this event, you'll have to allocate the expense among your properties. The IRS doesn't require that you use any particular method to do this task. But whatever method you use must be reasonable and used consistently.

One allocation method is simply to divide the expense involved equally among your properties. This approach makes sense where the properties generate about the same rental income each year.

For example, suppose Stuart owns three rental houses. He pays $300 for a new lawn mower he will use for all three houses. He allocates $100 of the cost to each rental house.

If your rental properties vary greatly in size, a more reasonable way to allocate expenses is by the gross income they generate. For instance, suppose Marjorie owns a rental house, a duplex, and a four-unit apartment building. She allocates expenses for all the properties according to the monthly rental income she receives from each one, as follows:

House	$1,000
Duplex	2,000
Apartments	+ 4,000
Total	$7,000

She determines an allocation percentage for each property by dividing its monthly rental by the total rental income she receives:

House	$1,000 ÷ $7,000	=	14%
Duplex	$2,000 ÷ $7,000	=	29%
Apartments	$4,000 ÷ $7,000	=	57%

She pays $300 for a lawn mower she will use for all the properties. She allocates the cost as follows:

House	14% × $300	=	$42
Duplex	29% × $300	=	$87
Apartments	57% × $300	=	$171

Any interest you earn on your tenants' security deposits is also rental income, unless state or local law requires you to repay it to your tenants on a yearly basis or when they move out.

Interest you earn on your rental checking account, if any, is not rental income. It is personal interest. Do not include it in your rental income on Schedule E.

As with your rental expenses, you can keep track of your rental income manually by using ledger sheets. You may also use computer spreadsheets, accounting programs like *Quicken*, or programs specially designed for landlords.

Whatever method you use, you must keep separate track of the income you earn for each rental property you own. So, you'll have separate ledger sheets, spreadsheets, or computer listings for each property.

Asset Records

You need a separate set of records for your long-term assets. These assets consist primarily of your rental building or buildings, but they also include property such as computers and office furniture, appliances you separately depreciate, and real property improvements. Such long-term property is ordinarily depreciated over several years, not deducted in a single year as are operating expenses. Depreciation is covered in detail in Chapter 5.

When you purchase any property with a useful life of more than one year, you must keep records to verify:

- when and how you acquired the asset
- the purchase price
- how you used the asset
- the cost of any improvements—for example, adding a new roof to a rental building
- Section 179 deductions taken (see Chapter 5)
- deductions taken for regular and bonus depreciation
- when and how you disposed of the asset
- the selling price, and
- expenses of the sale.

You should create a depreciation worksheet showing this information for all your long-term assets, and update it each year. The instructions to IRS Form 4562, *Depreciation and Amortization (Including Information on Listed Property)*, contain a blank worksheet. You can also use a spreadsheet or computer accounting program such as *QuickBooks*. You don't need to file the worksheet with your tax returns, but it will provide you with all the information you need to claim your depreciation deductions on your taxes. And you will need it if you are audited.

Listed Property

The IRS is especially interested in certain kinds of property that tax-payers can easily use personally—yet claim that they purchased for their business. To minimize the chances of abuse, the IRS separates these properties into a list—which is called "listed property." Listed property gets extra scrutiny and has special documentation requirements. Listed property includes:

- cars, boats, airplanes, motorcycles, and other vehicles, and
- any other property generally used for entertainment, recreation, or amusement—for example, cameras and camcorders.

Your paper or electronic mileage logbook (see below) provides an adequate record of your use of your car or other vehicle. For other listed assets, keep an appointment book, logbook, rental diary, or calendar showing the dates, times, and reasons for which the property is used—for both rental and personal purchases. You also can purchase logbooks for this purpose at stationery or office supply stores.

Asset Files

You should establish an asset file where you keep all your records supporting your depreciation deductions. This file doesn't have to be anything fancy. An accordion file will work fine. Make a separate file for each rental property you own.

Keep your real property closing statements and any documentation showing the cost of the land, such as appraisals and property tax statements.

File your receipts for each long-term asset you purchase, as well as canceled checks or credit card statements proving how much you paid. It's particularly important to keep receipts for real property improvements because these will affect the tax basis of your real property. (See Chapter 5.)

You don't have to file any of these supporting documents with your tax returns, but you must have them available in case the IRS audits you and questions your depreciation deductions.

Records Required for Local Travel

If you use a car or another vehicle for rental business purposes, you're entitled to take a deduction for gas and other auto expenses. You can either deduct the actual cost of your gas and other expenses, or take the standard rate deduction based on the number of rental miles you drive.

Either way, you must keep a record of:

- your mileage
- the dates of your rental business trips
- the places you drove for rental business, and
- the rental business purpose for your trips.

The last three items are relatively easy to keep track of. You can record the information in your appointment book, calendar, or day planner. Or, you can record it in a paper or electronic mileage log.

Calculating your mileage takes more work. The IRS wants to know the total number of miles you drove during the year for rental business, commuting, and personal driving other than commuting. Commuting is travel between home and your office or other principal place where you conduct your rental activity. If you work from a home office, you'll have no commuting mileage. Personal miles include, for example, trips to the grocery store, personal vacations, or visits to friends or relatives.

To keep track of your business driving, you can use either a paper mileage logbook that you keep in your car or an electronic application. Logbooks are available in any stationery store. There are many smartphone apps that you can use to record your mileage; the most popular is *MileIQ*.

Keeping Track of Actual Expenses

If you take the deduction for your actual auto expenses instead of using the standard rate (or if you are thinking about switching to this method), keep receipts for all of your auto-related expenses, including gasoline, oil, tires, repairs, and insurance. Create a category for auto expenses in your expense journal. Also, when you figure your depreciation deduction for the year, you'll need to include the amount you're entitled to deduct for depreciation of your auto. (See Chapter 11 for more on using the actual expense method, including vehicle depreciation.)

Allocating Your Rental Miles

You're required to list on Schedule E your car expenses for each rental property you own. This task poses no problem if you only own one property. But things can get more complicated if you own more than one, because you might make some trips that benefit more than one property at the same time—for example, a trip to the hardware store to purchase supplies you'll use for all your properties. In this event, you must allocate your mileage among your properties. You can split your mileage equally or use a percentage based on the income your properties earn.

Records Required for Long-Distance Travel and Gifts

Deductions for travel (including meals while traveling) and gifts are hot-button items for the IRS because they have been greatly abused by many taxpayers. You need to have more records for these expenses than for almost any others, and they will be closely scrutinized if you're audited.

Whenever you incur an expense for rental-related travel (including meals while traveling) or gifts, you must document the following facts:

- **The date.** The date you incurred the expense will usually be listed on a receipt or credit card slip; appointment books, day planners, and similar documents have the dates preprinted on each page, so entries on the appropriate page automatically date the expense.

- **The amount.** You'll need to be able to prove how much you spent, including tax and tip for meals. Document the amount of each separate travel expense, such as airfare, lodging, and meals. However, the cost of meals and incidental expenses may be combined on a daily basis by category—for example, daily meal, gas, taxi, or Uber/Lyft expenses.
- **The place.** Where you incurred the expense will usually be shown on a receipt, or you can record it in an appointment book.
- **The rental activity purpose.** You'll have to be able to show that the expense was incurred for your rental activity—for example, that you took an out-of-town trip to inspect or repair one of your rental properties.
- **The rental activity relationship.** If meals or gifts are involved, show the business relationship of the people receiving the gift or at the meal—for example, list their names and occupations and any other information needed to establish their relation to you as a landlord.

Business Meals When You're Not Traveling

Meals and beverages you purchase other than while traveling on business are no longer subject to the strict substantiation rules described above. Instead, they are now subject to the same record-keeping rules as any business deduction. So, you're still supposed to have records of the amount and business purpose. But, if you lack adequate records, you can ask the IRS and/or tax court to permit you at least a partial deduction under the *Cohan* rule. Under this rule, taxpayers who lack all required records are permitted to make an estimate of how much they must have spent. The IRS has discretion to allow such taxpayers to deduct all or part of the estimated amount. But, you must provide at least some credible evidence on which to base this estimate, such as receipts, canceled checks, notes in your appointment book, or other records.

The chart below shows the information your records must contain for travel, meals while traveling, and gift expenses.

Receipts to Keep	
Type of Expense	**Receipts to Save**
Travel	Airplane, train, or bus ticket stubs; travel agency receipts; rental car; and so on
Meals While Traveling	Meal check, credit card slip
Lodging	Statement or bill from hotel or other lodging provider; your own written records for cleaning, laundry, telephone charges, tips, and other charges not shown separately on hotel statement

The IRS does not require you to keep receipts, canceled checks, credit card slips, or any other supporting documents for travel, meal, and gift expenses that cost less than $75. *However, you must still document the five facts listed above.* This exception does not apply to lodging—that is, hotel or similar costs—when you travel for your rental activity. You do need receipts for these expenses, even if they cost less than $75.

All this record keeping is not as hard as it sounds. You can record the five facts you have to document in a variety of ways, and the information doesn't have to be all in one place. Information that is shown on a receipt, a canceled check, or another item need not be duplicated in a log, an appointment book, a calendar, or an account book. So, for example, you can record the five facts with:

- a receipt, credit card slip, or similar document alone
- a receipt combined with an appointment book entry, or
- an appointment book entry alone (for expenses less than $75).

However you document your expense, you are supposed to do it in a timely manner. You don't need to record the details of every expense on the day you incur it. It is sufficient to record them on a weekly basis. But if you're prone to forget details, it's best to get everything you need in writing within a day or two.

Proof Required for Travel and Gift Deductions				
Records must show:	**Amount**	**Time**	**Place or Description**	**Business Purpose and Relationship**
Travel	Cost of each separate expense for travel, lodging, and meals. Incidental expenses may be totaled in categories such as taxis, daily meals, and so on.	Dates you left and returned for each trip, and the number of days spent on business	Name of city, town, or other destination	Business purpose for the expense, or the benefit gained or expected to be gained
Gifts	Cost of gift	Date of gift	Description of gift	Same as for travel
Meals	Cost	Date of meal	Place of meal	Same as for travel

How Long to Keep Records

You need to have copies of your tax returns and supporting documents available in case the IRS or another taxing agency (such as your state income tax agency) audits you. You might also need them for other purposes—for example, to get a loan, a mortgage, or insurance. Keep your records for as long as the IRS has to audit you after you file your returns for the year. These statutes of limitation range from three years to forever—they are listed in the table below.

To be on the safe side, keep your tax returns indefinitely. They usually don't take up much space, so it's normally not a big hardship. Your supporting documents probably take up more space. Hang on to these for at least six years after you file your return.

Keep your long-term asset records for as long as you own the property and for three years after you sell or otherwise dispose of it.

Scanning Your Records

If you don't want to keep paper copies of your tax records, you can make digital copies by scanning them and storing them on a computer or in the "cloud." The IRS has approved the use of electronic storage systems for this purpose. (Rev. Proc. 97-22, 1997-1 CB 652.)

IRS Statutes of Limitations

If:	The limitations period is:
You failed to pay all the tax due.	3 years
You underreported your gross income for the year by more than 25%.	6 years
You filed a fraudulent return.	No limit
You did not file a return.	No limit

Accounting Methods

An "accounting method" is a set of rules that you'll use to determine when and how to report your income and expenses.

You must choose an accounting method when you file your first tax return for your rental activity. If you later want to change your accounting method, you must get IRS approval. The two basic methods of accounting are cash basis and accrual basis. Almost all small landlords use the cash method because it's, by far, the simpler of the two.

With the cash method, you record income only when the money is received and expenses only when you actually pay them. If you borrow money to pay rental activity expenses, you incur an expense under the cash method only when you make payments on the loan. Using the cash method, then, is like maintaining a checkbook. Although it's called the cash method, this method for paying business expenses includes payments by check, credit card, or electronic funds transfer, as well as payments by cash.

All About Schedule E

T his chapter shows how to fill out IRS Schedule E, the tax form landlords use to report their income and deductions to the IRS.

Who Must File Schedule E?

You must file Schedule E if, like most landlords, you receive rental income from property that you own as an individual. It doesn't matter whether you own the rental property alone, with your spouse, or with one or more co-owners.

However, if you own or use your rental property in one of the following manners, you do not use Schedule E to report rental income or deductions for the property:

- **Ownership through a business entity.** Partnerships, limited partner-ships, multimember LLCs, and S corporations file IRS Form 8825, *Rental Real Estate Income and Expenses of a Partnership or an S Corporation*, to report rental income and deductions. This form is very similar to Schedule E. The individual LLC or partnership members (or S corporation shareholders) are each given a Schedule K-1 by the entity reporting their individual shares of annual income or loss from the rental activity. The individuals then list this amount on Part II of Schedule E, on Page 2.

  But a single-member LLC is ordinarily not treated as a separate entity for federal income tax purposes. So, if you are the sole member of an LLC, you normally file Schedule E, Part I.

- **Schedule C business.** Do not file Schedule E if your rental activity is classified as a regular business instead of a rental activity, which will be the case if you provide substantial services to your guests, such as maid service and food service. (See Chapter 1.) If you are an individual owner or owner of a one-person LLC, file Schedule C, *Profit or Loss From Business (Sole Proprietorship)*.

Married Landlords

Spouses often co-own residential rental properties. The long-standing rule has been that married couples who file a joint tax return can report their rental income and expenses on a single Schedule E that they file with their joint Form 1040 tax return. (See "Co-Ownership by Spouses" in Chapter 1 and IRS Reg. § 301.7701-1(a)(2) ("mere co-ownership of property that is maintained, kept in repair, and rented or leased does not constitute a separate entity for federal tax purposes").)

Like other co-owners of rental property, landlord spouses are not considered partners in a partnership (and don't have to file a partnership tax return) unless they provide significant personal services with the rental, such as maid service or food service. However, if landlord spouses were to be considered partners because of the services they provide with their rental, they might have an option that is not available to other co-owners of property. Under an IRS rule, a married couple may elect to be taxed as a "qualified joint venture." If they qualify for the election, they're treated as sole proprietors for tax purposes and each spouse files a separate Schedule C reporting their share of rental income and expenses. (See "Co-Ownership by Spouses" in Chapter 1.) This election doesn't reduce their taxes, but it does result in a much simpler tax return.

Filling Out Schedule E

Completing Schedule E is a relatively straightforward process. You fill out only the first page, which is called "Part I." (Part I is also used for royalties, which have nothing to do with rental property.) Parts II–V on the second page are only used by partnerships, S corporations, estates, trusts, and real estate mortgage investment conduits (REMICs, a type of real estate investment).

You separately list on the schedule your income and expenses for each rental property you own. A rental property comprises all the rental units you have at a single address. If you own a multiunit building, you must add together the income and expenses from all the units and list the totals on Schedule E.

Schedule E is designed to be used by up to three rental properties, labeled A, B, and C; there are separate columns for each property. If you have more than three rental properties, complete and attach as many Schedule Es as you need for them all. But fill in Lines 23a through 26 on only one Schedule E. The figures there as reported on one of your Schedule Es should be the combined totals for all properties reported.

If you own only a part interest in a rental property, report only your share of the property's income and expenses.

> **EXAMPLE:** Betty and Bettina each own a 50% interest in a duplex they rent out. Betty reports 50% of the property's income and expenses on her Schedule E, and Bettina reports the other 50% on her Schedule E.

If you and your spouse elect qualified joint venture status, you must divide all income, expenses, losses, and credits between you according to your respective interests in the venture—for example, if you're equal co-owners, you each get 50% of these items. You only file one Schedule E, but each of you must report your interest as separate properties on Line 1. On Lines 3 through 22 for each separate property interest, you must enter your share of the applicable income, deduction, or loss. (See Chapter 1 for a detailed discussion of qualified joint ventures.)

Filing IRS Forms 1099 (Lines A and B)

Line A asks whether you made any payments during the year that required you to file IRS Forms 1099. If you answer yes, you have to answer in Line B whether you have already filed, "or will you file," the forms. Obviously, you should answer "yes" on Line B if you answered "yes" on Line A. If you haven't filed the required 1099 forms, you should do so as soon as possible.

When does a landlord have to file Forms 1099? Several types of 1099 forms exist. The one that usually has to be filed by landlords is Form 1099-NEC (Form 1099-MISC was filed before 2021). You must file Form 1099-NEC if (1) your rental activity constitutes a business for tax

SCHEDULE E
(Form 1040)

Department of the Treasury
Internal Revenue Service (99)

Supplemental Income and Loss

(From rental real estate, royalties, partnerships, S corporations, estates, trusts, REMICs, etc.)

▶ Attach to Form 1040, 1040-SR, 1040-NR, or 1041.

▶ Go to *www.irs.gov/ScheduleE* for instructions and the latest information.

OMB No. 1545-0074

2021

Attachment
Sequence No. **13**

Name(s) shown on return | Your social security number

Part I | **Income or Loss From Rental Real Estate and Royalties** **Note:** If you are in the business of renting personal property, use **Schedule C.** See instructions. If you are an individual, report farm rental income or loss from **Form 4835** on page 2, line 40.

A Did you make any payments in 2021 that would require you to file Form(s) 1099? See instructions . . . . . ☐ Yes ☐ No
B If "Yes," did you or will you file required Form(s) 1099? . . . . ☐ Yes ☐ No

1a Physical address of each property (street, city, state, ZIP code)

A
B
C

1b	Type of Property (from list below)	**2** For each rental real estate property listed above, report the number of fair rental and personal use days. Check the **QJV** box only if you meet the requirements to file as a qualified joint venture. See instructions.		Fair Rental Days	Personal Use Days	QJV
A			A			☐
B			B			☐
C			C			☐

Type of Property:
1 Single Family Residence   3 Vacation/Short-Term Rental   5 Land   7 Self-Rental
2 Multi-Family Residence   4 Commercial   6 Royalties   8 Other (describe)

Income:	**Properties:**		**A**	**B**	**C**
3 Rents received		3			
4 Royalties received		4			
Expenses:					
5 Advertising		5			
6 Auto and travel (see instructions)		6			
7 Cleaning and maintenance		7			
8 Commissions.		8			
9 Insurance		9			
10 Legal and other professional fees		10			
11 Management fees		11			
12 Mortgage interest paid to banks, etc. (see instructions)		12			
13 Other interest.		13			
14 Repairs.		14			
15 Supplies		15			
16 Taxes		16			
17 Utilities		17			
18 Depreciation expense or depletion		18			
19 Other (list) ▶ _____		19			
20 Total expenses. Add lines 5 through 19		20			
21 Subtract line 20 from line 3 (rents) and/or 4 (royalties). If result is a (loss), see instructions to find out if you must file **Form 6198**		21			
22 Deductible rental real estate loss after limitation, if any, on **Form 8582** (see instructions)		22 (	)(	)(	)

23a Total of all amounts reported on line 3 for all rental properties	23a		
b Total of all amounts reported on line 4 for all royalty properties	23b		
c Total of all amounts reported on line 12 for all properties	23c		
d Total of all amounts reported on line 18 for all properties	23d		
e Total of all amounts reported on line 20 for all properties	23e		
24 **Income.** Add positive amounts shown on line 21. **Do not** include any losses	24	
25 **Losses.** Add royalty losses from line 21 and rental real estate losses from line 22. Enter total losses here .	25 (	)
26 **Total rental real estate and royalty income or (loss).** Combine lines 24 and 25. Enter the result here. If Parts II, III, IV, and line 40 on page 2 do not apply to you, also enter this amount on Schedule 1 (Form 1040), line 5. Otherwise, include this amount in the total on line 41 on page 2 .	26	

For Paperwork Reduction Act Notice, see the separate instructions. | Cat. No. 11344L | **Schedule E (Form 1040) 2021**

Schedule E (Form 1040) 2021   Attachment Sequence No. **13**   Page **2**

Name(s) shown on return. Do not enter name and social security number if shown on other side.	Your social security number

Caution: The IRS compares amounts reported on your tax return with amounts shown on Schedule(s) K-1.

Part II   **Income or Loss From Partnerships and S Corporations** — **Note:** If you report a loss, receive a distribution, dispose of stock, or receive a loan repayment from an S corporation, you **must** check the box in column **(e)** on line 28 and attach the required basis computation. If you report a loss from an at-risk activity for which **any** amount is **not** at risk, you **must** check the box in column **(f)** on line 28 and attach **Form 6198**. See instructions.

27   Are you reporting any loss not allowed in a prior year due to the at-risk or basis limitations, a prior year unallowed loss from a passive activity (if that loss was not reported on Form 8582), or unreimbursed partnership expenses? If you answered "Yes," see instructions before completing this section . . . . ☐ **Yes**   ☐ **No**

28	(a) Name	(b) Enter P for partnership; S for S corporation	(c) Check if foreign partnership	(d) Employer identification number	(e) Check if basis computation is required	(f) Check if any amount is not at risk
A			☐		☐	
B			☐		☐	
C			☐		☐	☐
D			☐		☐	☐

	Passive Income and Loss		Nonpassive Income and Loss		
	(g) Passive loss allowed (attach **Form 8582** if required)	(h) Passive income from **Schedule K-1**	(i) Nonpassive loss allowed (see **Schedule K-1**)	(j) Section 179 expense deduction from **Form 4562**	(k) Nonpassive income from **Schedule K-1**
A					
B					
C					
D					

29a	Totals	
b	Totals	
30	Add columns (h) and (k) of line 29a.	**30**
31	Add columns (g), (i), and (j) of line 29b.	**31** ( )
32	**Total partnership and S corporation income or (loss).** Combine lines 30 and 31	**32**

Part III   **Income or Loss From Estates and Trusts**

33	(a) Name	(b) Employer identification number
A		
B		

	Passive Income and Loss		Nonpassive Income and Loss	
	(c) Passive deduction or loss allowed (attach **Form 8582** if required)	(d) Passive income from **Schedule K-1**	(e) Deduction or loss from **Schedule K-1**	(f) Other income from **Schedule K-1**
A				
B				

34a	Totals	
b	Totals	
35	Add columns (d) and (f) of line 34a	**35**
36	Add columns (c) and (e) of line 34b	**36** ( )
37	**Total estate and trust income or (loss).** Combine lines 35 and 36	**37**

Part IV   **Income or Loss From Real Estate Mortgage Investment Conduits (REMICs)—Residual Holder**

38	(a) Name	(b) Employer identification number	(c) Excess inclusion from **Schedules Q**, line 2c (see instructions)	(d) Taxable income (net loss) from **Schedules Q**, line 1b	(e) Income from **Schedules Q**, line 3b

39	Combine columns (d) and (e) only. Enter the result here and include in the total on line 41 below	**39**

Part V   **Summary**

40	Net farm rental income or (loss) from **Form 4835**. Also, complete line 42 below	**40**
41	**Total income or (loss).** Combine lines 26, 32, 37, 39, and 40. Enter the result here and on Schedule 1 (Form 1040), line 5 ▶	**41**
42	**Reconciliation of farming and fishing income.** Enter your **gross** farming and fishing income reported on Form 4835, line 7; Schedule K-1 (Form 1065), box 14, code B; Schedule K-1 (Form 1120-S), box 17, code AD; and Schedule K-1 (Form 1041), box 14, code F. See instructions . .	**42**
43	**Reconciliation for real estate professionals.** If you were a real estate professional (see instructions), enter the net income or (loss) you reported anywhere on Form 1040, Form 1040-SR, or Form 1040-NR from all rental real estate activities in which you materially participated under the passive activity loss rules	**43**

Schedule E (Form 1040) 2021

purposes, and (2) you hire an independent contractor to perform services for your activity and pay that person by cash or check more than $600 during the year—for example, you hire a repairperson, rental agent, or gardener. You don't need to report payments by credit card or PayPal or any other similar electronic payment services.

You don't have to file any 1099 forms if your rental activity is an investment, not a business for tax purposes. (See Chapter 2.) (See Chapter 13 for a detailed discussion of the rules for filing IRS Form 1099-NEC.)

These questions are the IRS's attempt to encourage landlords and others who file Schedule E to file all required 1099s and are part of the IRS's ongoing effort to prevent businesses from failing to report all their income.

Property Description (Line 1)

In Line 1, list your rental property's street address, city or town, state, and ZIP code. In the next box, provide the applicable number code showing the type of property.

Dual Use Properties (Line 2)

Line 2 has to do with rentals that you also used for personal purposes during the year. For example, you rented your main home, vacation home, or other property part time during the year and lived in it part of the time. These short-term rentals are often made through Airbnb or another online rental platform. Short-term rentals are covered in detail in *Every Airbnb Host's Tax Guide*, by Stephen Fishman (Nolo).

Qualified Joint Venture (Line 2)

If you and your spouse want your rental activity to be characterized as a qualified joint venture (or it is already a QJV), place an x in the QJV column. (See Chapter 1 for a detailed discussion of qualified joint venture status for rentals owned by spouses.)

Rental Income (Line 3)

Enter your total annual rental income for each property in Line 3. This amount will primarily consist of the rent your tenants pay you. But it could also include:

- laundry income
- fees you charge tenants for paying rent late
- garage or other parking charges
- interest you earn on tenant security deposits
- security deposits you retain to pay for repairs, unpaid rent, or other expenses
- the value of services tenants provide in lieu of rent, or
- payments tenants make to you for repairs or other expenses. (See Chapter 4.)

A security deposit you receive from a tenant is not rental income if you plan to return it when the tenancy ends. But, if you keep all or part of a security deposit when a tenant leaves, the amount you keep is rental income. Any interest you earn on your tenants' security deposits is also rental income, unless you're required to repay it to your tenants when they move out. Some cities have this requirement under their rent control laws.

Interest you earn on your rental checking account, if any, is not rental income. It is personal interest. Don't include it in your rental income on Schedule E.

Royalties Received (Line 4)

Leave this blank unless you have royalty income—for example, income from copyrights or patents you inherited or purchased, or mineral leases. If you are a self-employed writer, inventor, artist, and so on, you report your royalty income and expenses on Schedule C, *Profit or Loss From Business (Sole Proprietorship)*.

Expenses (Lines 5–20)

You list your expenses for each property in the Expenses section, Lines 5–19. Note that if you rent your property part time, or rent only a room or rooms instead of the entire property, you'll need to prorate many of your expenses. Your expenses must be broken down into categories; Schedule E lists the following expense categories:

- **Advertising.** This category includes signs, classified ads, and other advertising expenses to rent your property.
- **Auto and travel.** This category includes both local and long-distance travel expenses. (See Chapters 11 and 12.) If you have both types of expenses, you must add them together.
- **Cleaning and maintenance.** This category includes janitorial services, gardening, and cleaning of carpets, drapes, and rugs. Do not include repairs here—repairs are done to fix property after it's broken; maintenance keeps your property in good working order so it won't break down.
- **Commissions.** This category will apply if you hire a rental agency or property management company to help you with your rentals. Such agencies and companies are typically paid a commission— that is, a percentage of the rent they collect (for example, 5% or 10%). Some property managers deduct their commissions from the rent they collect before they send it to the property owner. In this event, be sure to list the total amount of rent charged in the rental income line, not the amount the property manager sends you after deducting the commission.

- **Insurance.** This category includes any type of insurance for your rental activity, except for private mortgage insurance and title insurance (see Chapter 15).
- **Legal and other professional fees.** This category includes tax advice and preparing tax forms for your rental activity. Some legal fees incurred for buying property aren't deductible; they are added to the property's basis and depreciated. (See Chapter 5.)
- **Management fees.** Rental agencies and property management companies charge these fees.
- **Mortgage interest paid to banks.** If you have a mortgage on your rental property, list the amount of interest you paid during the year to banks or other financial institutions. If you paid $600 or more in interest on a mortgage during the year, the financial institution should send you a Form 1098 or similar statement by February showing the total interest received from you. Points, including loan origination fees, charged only for the use of money must be deducted over the life of the loan. (See Chapter 8.) Include the amount you can deduct this year in your mortgage interest total.
- **Other interest.** This is interest you paid to a lender other than a bank or another financial institution—for example, interest on a credit card you use for rental expenses, or interest you pay to the seller of rental property you purchased with creative financing. Also, if you and at least one other person (other than your spouse if you file a joint return) were liable for and paid interest on a mortgage, and the other person received Form 1098, report your share of the deductible interest on this line. Attach a statement to your return showing the name and address of the person who received Form 1098. In the left margin next to the "Other interest" line, write "See attached."
- **Repairs.** Repairs keep your property in good working order. They do not add significant value to your property or extend its life. Do not include the cost of improvements in this line; they must be depreciated over several years. (See Chapter 4.)

- **Supplies.** This category includes office supplies and supplies you use for repairs and maintenance—for example, paint and brushes, or fertilizer. It does not include materials you purchase to undertake improvements—for example, it would not include the cost of the shingles used to install a new roof on your rental property. You must depreciate these materials. (See Chapter 5.)

- **Taxes.** This category includes employment taxes you pay if you have employees—for example, a resident manager.

- **Utilities.** This category includes charges for water, garbage pickup, gas, and electricity you pay for your rental property. You may also deduct the cost of telephone calls for your rental activities—for example, calls to your renter. However, the base rate (including taxes and other charges) for local telephone service for the first telephone line into your residence is a personal expense that you can't deduct. Don't include utilities for a home office here.

- **Depreciation.** You list your total depreciation deduction for each property in the depreciation line and then include the total for all properties in the right-hand column. You must also complete and attach Form 4562, *Depreciation and Amortization (Including Information on Listed Property)*, if you are claiming:
  - regular or bonus depreciation on property first placed in service during the year
  - regular or bonus depreciation on listed property including a vehicle, regardless of the date it was placed in service, or
  - a Section 179 expense deduction or amortization of costs that began during the year.

  You should complete depreciation worksheets for each of your properties, but you don't have to attach them to your return. (See Chapter 5 for a detailed discussion of depreciation.)

- **Other expenses.** The Schedule E categories probably include most of your expenses, but you might have others that are not listed—for example:
  - de minimis safe harbor expenses (Chapter 4)
  - small taxpayer safe harbor expenses (Chapter 4)

- routine maintenance safe harbor expenses (Chapter 4)
- home office expenses (Chapter 10)
- gifts (Chapter 15)
- homeowners' association dues for rental condominiums and planned-unit developments
- start-up expenses (Chapter 9)
- wages and salaries for employees
- education expenses (Chapter 15)
- dues and subscriptions (Chapter 15)
- inspection fees, changing locks, bank charges on business accounts, apartment association dues
- casualty losses (Chapter 14), and
- equipment rental.

If you have expenses for these or other items, list them by category in the "Other" line. You create your own categories here.

You add up all your expenses for each property and put the total on Line 20.

Rental Summary (Lines 21–26)

You use this portion of Schedule E to show the amount of income you earned or loss you incurred from your rental activity, and the deductible portion of any loss:

- **Line 21.** You complete this line only if you have rental losses all or part of which are not deductible because of the at-risk rules. If this is the case, you need to complete IRS Form 6198, *At-Risk Limitations*, and attach it to your return. Few landlords are subject to the at-risk limitations. (See Chapter 16 for a detailed discussion of the at-risk rules.)
- **Line 22.** If you have a net loss for the year, the amount you can deduct may be limited by the passive activity loss rules. Most small landlords can deduct all or part of their losses by using the $25,000 offset exception to the passive activity rules. If you are

able to deduct all your losses by using the offset, you don't need to file Form 8582, *Passive Activity Loss Limitations*. If you can't deduct all your losses by using the offset, you'll have to complete Form 8582 to figure the amount of loss you can deduct, if any. Enter the deductible amount of your loss, if any, on Line 22. (See Chapter 16 for a detailed discussion of the passive loss rules.) If your activity is subject to the vacation home tax rules, you won't need to file Form 8582, but you won't be able to deduct any of your losses.

- **Line 23a.** List the total of all income you reported on Line 3 for all your rental properties.
- **Line 23b.** Put a zero here unless you earned income from royalty properties such as patents or copyrights in works you didn't create yourself.
- **Line 23c.** List the total of all amounts you reported on Line 12 for all your rental properties.
- **Line 23d.** List the total of all the depreciation you reported on Line 18 for all your properties.
- **Line 23e.** List the total of all expenses you reported on Line 20 for all your rental properties.
- **Line 24 (Income).** Add any positive amounts shown on Line 21. Do not include any losses.
- **Line 25 (Losses).** Add royalty losses from Line 21 (if any) and rental losses from Line 22. Most landlords have no royalty losses.
- **Line 26 (Total income or loss).** Combine Lines 24 and 25. If there are no other entries on Schedule E, this amount is transferred to Schedule 1, line 5 of Form 1040. Otherwise, it is combined with other amounts on Line 41, Page 2, Schedule E.
- **Line 43 (Reconciliation for real estate professionals).** If you're exempt from the passive activity loss rules because you are a real estate professional and materially participated in the rental activity (see Chapter 16), enter here the total profit or loss from all real estate rental activities.

The Net Investment Income Tax

f your rentals earn a profit, you became subject to the net investment income tax ("NIIT" for short; also called the "Medicare contribution tax"). Enacted to help fund the Affordable Care Act, this tax impacts many higher-income landlords. However, some lucky landlords are able to avoid it completely, no matter how high their incomes.

How the NIIT Works

To put it mildly, the NIIT tax is complicated. Here is an overview of how it works.

What Is the NIIT?

The NIIT is a separate 3.8% income tax on unearned income—that is, income other than from a job or business in which you actively participate. Those subject to it—primarily higher-income taxpayers, including some landlords—must pay it in addition to their regular income taxes. The tax is included on Form 1040. You report the amount you're required to pay by completing IRS Form 8960, *Net Investment Income Tax—Individuals, Estates, and Trusts*, and attaching it to your return.

The NIIT is not a tax on real estate transactions, so you don't have to calculate it or pay it when you buy or sell property. However, any gain you realize when you sell rental property might be subject to the tax— but it won't be due until you pay your income taxes for the year.

The tax is not due until April 15, when you file your tax return. However, you might need to include NIIT in your estimated taxes you file during the year, or be subject to a penalty.

Who Is Subject to the NIIT?

The NIIT is designed to affect higher-income taxpayers, leaving out many landlords. You are subject to the NIIT only if the following are true:
- Your adjusted gross income (AGI) exceeds an annual threshold amount.
- You have net investment income.

Rental Property Owned Through a Pass-Through Entity

If you own real estate rentals through a pass-through entity, such as a multi-member limited liability company, a partnership, or an S corporation, the NIIT rules still apply to you at the individual level. Your share of the profits from the entity will pass through to your individual tax return and must be included with your other net investment income for purposes of the NIIT.

Income Thresholds

You'll be subject to the NIIT only if your AGI for the year exceeds $200,000 if you're single, or $250,000 if you're married filing jointly (the threshold is $125,000 for married couples filing separately). If you add up all of your income from every source, and the total is less than the applicable $200,000/$250,000 threshold, you will not be subject to this tax.

Only a small minority of taxpayers have this much income—about the top 5%. However, even if you ordinarily have less income than the applicable threshold, you might become subject to the NIIT in any year in which you sell rental property (or other investment property) for a substantial gain. Such gain will increase your AGI and could raise it over the threshold.

Moreover, these thresholds are not adjusted for inflation. So, over time, more and more people have become subject to the NIIT.

Net Investment Income

Even if your AGI exceeds the $200,000/$250,000 threshold, you'll be subject to the NIIT only if you have "net investment income." Indeed, you could earn millions of dollars and if none of it is net investment income you won't have to pay the tax.

Net investment income consists of:
- net rental income (rents minus expenses)
- income from investments, including interest, dividends, and annuities

- income from any business in which you don't materially participate (aren't active in running), including real estate limited partnerships and other real estate investment businesses, and
- net capital gains (gains less capital losses) you earn upon the sale of property that is not part of an active business, including rental property, stocks and bonds, and mutual funds.

Net investment income does not include:

- income from a business in which you materially participate (actively run), any self-employment income, or wages you earn from employment (this exception does not apply to rental activities, even if you materially participate in them; the only exception is if you're a real estate professional; see below)
- tax-exempt income such as income from tax-exempt bonds, the amount of profit excluded from tax when you sell your principal residence ($250,000 for singles, $500,000 for married couples filing jointly), or income earned from renting your home for no more than 14 days during the year
- withdrawals from retirement plans such as traditional or Roth IRAs, 401(k)s, or payouts from traditional defined-benefit pension plans, or
- life insurance proceeds, veterans benefits, Social Security benefits, alimony, or unemployment benefits.

What Is AGI?

Your AGI is not the same as your taxable income. It is the number on the bottom of your IRS Form 1040. It consists of your income from almost all sources, including wages, interest income, dividend income, income from certain retirement accounts, capital gains, alimony received, rental income, royalty income, and unemployment compensation, reduced by certain "above-the-line" deductions such as IRA contributions and one-half of self-employment taxes. If you have any foreign earned income, you must include it in your AGI as well. (I.R.C. § 1411(a)(1)(B).) If you qualify for the pass-through tax deduction (see Chapter 7), it does not reduce your AGI, and thus will not help you avoid the NIIT.

Amount of the Tax

The NIIT is a flat 3.8% tax. However, it is not imposed on your total AGI or investment income. Instead, it is assessed only on the portion of your income determined by a formula. The tax must paid on the *lesser* of (1) the taxpayer's net investment income, or (2) the amount that the taxpayer's adjusted gross income (AGI) exceeds the applicable threshold: $200,000 for single taxpayers, and $250,000 for married filing jointly.

> EXAMPLE: Burton, a single taxpayer, has a job that pays him $300,000 in wages. He also earned $50,000 in net investment income during the year. His AGI is $350,000. Burton must pay the 3.8% NIIT on the lesser of (1) his $50,000 of net investment income, or (2) the amount his $350,000 AGI exceeds the $200,000 threshold for single taxpayers—$150,000. Because $50,000 is less than $150,000, he must pay the 3.8% tax on $50,000. His NIIT for the year is $1,900 (3.8% × $50,000 = $1,900).

You only have to pay the NIIT on income over the $200,000/ $250,000 threshold. So, for those at the lower end of the AGI threshold, the NIIT is fairly small. For example, a single taxpayer with a $201,000 AGI, including $50,000 in rental income, would only pay the 3.8% tax on $1,000, for a $38 tax.

Your net rental income is included in your net investment income, and thus makes you subject to the NIIT if your AGI is over the applicable threshold. Your net rental income consists of your gross (total) rents minus all deductible expenses you incur in operating your rental property. Your deductible expenses for these purposes will generally be the same as shown on your Schedule E (see Chapter 18). If you qualify for the new pass-through tax deduction (see Chapter 7), it doesn't reduce your rental income, so it won't help you avoid the NIIT. If you have a net loss from your rental activities, you can use it to reduce your AGI subject to the passive loss rules discussed in Chapter 16. This makes the rental property deductions covered in the rest of this book more valuable than ever.

> **EXAMPLE:** Ludmilla, a single taxpayer, earns $200,000 in gross rents and has $100,000 in expenses, ending up with $100,000 in net rental income that must be included in her AGI. She also has $250,000 in employee income. Her AGI is $350,000—$150,000 over the $200,000 NIIT threshold. She must pay the 3.8% NIIT on the lesser of $150,000 or $100,000. Because $100,000 is less, she owes $3,800 in NIIT for the year that she must pay along with her regular income taxes.

If you sell your rental property for a gain, the amount must be included in your net investment income for that year. This can make you subject to the NIIT, even if your AGI is ordinarily less than the $200,000/$250,000 threshold.

> **EXAMPLE:** Luther and Lucinda are married taxpayers, whose AGI each year is ordinarily about $100,000, including $20,000 in rental income. So, they ordinarily aren't subject to the NIIT. But this year they decide to sell one of their rental properties and earn a $200,000 profit. Their AGI for the year is now $300,000 or $50,000 over the threshold. $50,000 is less than $300,000, so they must pay the 3.8% NIIT on $50,000, resulting in a $1,900 tax in addition to regular capital gains tax they owe on their capital gain.

Real Estate Professional Exemption From the NIIT

What if you earn all or most of your income from real estate rentals? Will the NIIT vastly increase your income taxes? Maybe not. Many people who earn their living from landlording are exempt from the tax because they'll qualify for a special exemption from the tax for real estate professionals. If you qualify for this exemption, you need not include your rental income or gains in your net investment income, no matter how large. You must satisfy the following three tests to be eligible for this exemption:

- You must be a real estate professional.
- You must materially participate in the rental activity.
- Your rental activity must qualify as a business for tax purposes.

Real Estate Professional

The rules for qualifying as a real estate professional are discussed in detail in Chapter 16. The same rules apply for purposes of the NIIT. To qualify, you (or your spouse if you file jointly) must spend (1) over 50% of your work time in a real estate business or businesses, and (2) over 750 hours working in real estate businesses during the year. As a rule, people with full-time jobs outside of real estate cannot qualify.

Material Participation in Rental Activity

In addition to being a real estate professional, you must materially participate in each rental activity to qualify for this exemption. "Material participation" is discussed in detail in Chapter 16. There are various methods to establish material participation. The two most common are working over 500 hours at the activity during the year, or working 100 hours and more than anyone else.

If you have more than one rental property, unless you group your rentals together for these purposes, you'll have to materially participate in each individual rental. For example, if you have ten rentals, you'd have to materially participate in each of the ten, which would likely prove impossible. Fortunately, you are allowed to group your rental activities together for these purposes. This way, you can combine the time you spend working on each rental property to satisfy the material participation tests. You must file an election with the IRS to group your rental activities. This is discussed in detail in Chapter 16.

Ordinarily, you are only allowed to group your activities one time, and are then stuck with it. However, the IRS gives real estate professionals who have previously grouped their activities a "fresh start." They are permitted to redo their groupings starting with the first year that they have sufficient income to be subject to the NIIT ($250,000 AGI for marrieds, $200,000 for singles) and have net investment income. The regrouping applies to the tax year in which it is made and all subsequent tax years. (IRS Reg. § 1.469-11(b)(3)(iv).)

Rental Activity as a Business

Finally, your rental activity must qualify as a business for tax purposes. The IRS NIIT regulations establish a safe harbor rule for when a rental estate activity conducted by a real estate professional is a business: So long as a real estate professional devotes more than 500 hours per year to the rental activity, it will automatically qualify as a business for these purposes and the rental income will not be subject to the NIIT. Alternatively, if a real estate pro has participated in rental real estate activities for more than 500 hours per year in five of the last ten tax years, the rental activity will qualify as a business. (IRS Reg. § 1.1411-4(g)(7).)

As discussed above, if you have more than one rental property, you are allowed to group your rental activities together for these purposes. This way, you can combine the time you spend working on each rental property to satisfy the material participation and 500-hour tests.

The 500-hour rule is a safe harbor, not a minimum requirement. So, you don't absolutely have to work a minimum of 501 hours per year at your rental activity for it to qualify as a business. You can work fewer hours and still qualify as a business. But, in the event of an IRS audit, whether you qualify will require a judgment call by the IRS after looking at all the circumstances involved. However, the preamble to the new regulations provides that ownership of even a single rental unit can qualify as a business. But, again, this depends on the circumstances— for example, the type of property, number of units, and the day-to-day involvement of the owner or its agent.

> **CAUTION**
>
> **Landlords who earn profits from their rental activities will want to qualify as real estate professionals.** Before 2014, when the NIIT went into effect, landlords with profit-making rentals didn't use to care whether they qualified as real estate professionals. It didn't matter because this classification only benefited landlords who had losses they wanted to deduct from their non-rental income. This is no longer the case. Qualifying as real estate professionals benefits landlords who earn profits because they won't have to pay the NIIT

on them. So, landlords need to pay attention to whether they qualify as real estate professionals and how they'll prove it. The key to proving it and avoiding the IRS's wrath is keeping accurate records of how many hours you (and your spouse) work at your real estate activities during the year. (See Chapter 17 for more guidance on record keeping.)

Planning to Avoid the NIIT

Obviously, the way to avoid the NIIT is to keep your AGI for the year below the $200,000/$250,000 threshold or have no net investment income. There are many ways to do this:

- Increase rental losses you can deduct from your rental income.
- Avoid a large single-year gain when you sell rental property by using installment agreements, which spread your payment over many years.
- Avoid a large single-year gain when you sell rental property by using a like-kind exchange that can defer tax on your gain indefinitely.
- Don't sell your rental property—when you die your heirs can inherit it tax free.
- Convert as much income as possible to tax-exempt income that doesn't increase your AGI or net investment income—for example, take as many tax-free employee fringe benefits from your employer as you can instead of salary.
- Take stock options in place of some of your salary—when you exercise an ISO, you don't have income for NIIT or income tax purposes (however, you do have income for alternative minimum tax purposes).
- Increase above-the-line deductions on your Form 1040—for example, make tax-deductible contributions to your 401(k), traditional IRA, or other qualified retirement plan; if you're over 72 years of age, donate an IRA of up to $100,000 to charity.
- Harvest capital losses to deduct from your gains.

Index

 **NOLO**

More from Nolo

Nolo.com offers a large library of legal solutions and forms, created by Nolo's in-house legal editors. These reliable documents can be prepared in minutes.

Create a Document Online

Incorporation. Incorporate your business in any state.

LLC Formation. Gain asset protection and pass-through tax status in any state.

Will. Nolo has helped people make over 2 million wills. Is it time to make or revise yours?

Living Trust (avoid probate). Plan now to save your family the cost, delays, and hassle of probate.

Download Useful Legal Forms

Nolo.com has hundreds of top quality legal forms available for download:

- bill of sale
- promissory note
- nondisclosure agreement
- LLC operating agreement
- corporate minutes
- commercial lease and sublease
- motor vehicle bill of sale
- consignment agreement
- and many more.

www.nolo.com

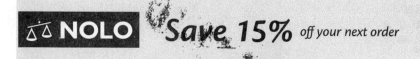